May '56

Laughter AND THE SENSE OF HUMOR

Books by Dr. Edmund Bergler:

Kinsey's Myth of Female Sexuality
(*in collaboration with* W. S. Kroger)

The Revolt of the Middle-Aged Man

Fashion and the Unconscious

The Superego

Money and Emotional Conflicts

Neurotic Counterfeit-Sex

The Writer and Psychoanalysis

The Basic Neurosis

Conflict in Marriage

Divorce Won't Help Neurotics

The Battle of the Conscience

Unhappy Marriage and Divorce

Psychic Impotence in Men

Talleyrand-Napoleon-Stendhal-Grabbe

Frigidity in Women
(*in collaboration with* E. Hitschmann)

Laughter AND THE SENSE OF HUMOR

By EDMUND BERGLER, M.D.

Men will confess to treason, murder, arson, false teeth or a wig. How many of them will own up to a lack of humor?

Frank Moore Colby

Wisdom lies in taking everything good-humouredly, and with a grain of salt.

George Santayana

Things are seldom what they seem,
Skim milk masquerades as cream.

W. S. Gilbert

INTERCONTINENTAL MEDICAL BOOK CORPORATION

New York, 1956

Library of Congress Card No. 56-7937

Printed and Bound in U. S. A.

ACKNOWLEDGMENTS

The author expresses his thanks to the publishers and copyright owners for permission to quote from the following:

The Goncourt Journals, by Edmond and Jules de Goncourt. Copyright 1937 by Doubleday & Company, Inc.

The Summing Up, by W. Somerset Maugham. Copyright 1938 by W. Somerset Maugham. Portions reprinted by permission of Doubleday & Company, Inc.

Animal Drive and the Learning Process, by Edwin B. Holt. Copyright 1931 by Henry Holt and Company.

The Sense of Humor, by Max Eastman. Copyright 1922 by Charles Scribner's Sons.

Enjoyment of Laughter, by Max Eastman. Copyright 1936 by Max Eastman. Portions reprinted by permission of Simon and Schuster, Inc.

Butterfield 8, by John O'Hara. Copyright 1935 by John O'Hara. Portions reprinted by permission of Random House, Inc.

American Humor, by Constance Rourke. Copyright 1931 by Harcourt, Brace and Company.

Humor: Its Theory and Technique, by Stephen Leacock. Copyright 1935 by Dodd, Mead & Company, Inc. Portions reprinted by permission of Dodd, Mead & Company.

The Secret of Laughter, by A. M. Ludovici. Copyright 1933 by The Viking Press.

The Collected Writings of Ambrose Bierce. Copyright 1946 by The Citadel Press.

The Story of the Confederacy, by Robert S. Henry. Copyright 1931, 1936; used by special permission of the publishers, the Bobbs-Merrill Company, Inc.

The Madwoman of Chaillot, by Jean Giraudoux. English adaptation by Maurice Valency. Copyright 1947 by Maurice Valency, published by Random House. Portions reprinted by special permission of the copyright owner.

Native American Humor, by J. R. Aswell. Copyright 1949 by Harper & Brothers.

The World of Li'l Abner, by Al Capp. Copyright 1953 by Ballantine Books, Inc. Portions reprinted by special permission of Capp Enterprises.

A Non-Deductible Friend, by Art Buchwald. Copyright 1953, The New York Herald Tribune.

Who Was Joe Miller? by Robert O. Foote. Published in Esquire, January 1942. Copyright 1941 by Esquire, Inc. Portions reprinted by their permission and permission of the author.

Nightfighter Over New York, by Phil Gustafson. Copyright 1952 by The Saturday Evening Post. Portions reprinted by their permission and permission of the author.

Contents

Foreword

THE IRONY of all investigations on laughter, wit, the comic, the sense of humor, lies in a contradiction which—so far—has not even been stated. On the one hand, we have the fact that to all *practical* intents and purposes laughter is concentrated, split-second *euphoria*. To all *scientific* intents and purposes, on the other hand, laughter consists of concentrated and interminable *dysphoria*. No two investigators of the subject fully agree in their findings, and the best that can be said for the results obtained by all but one of them is a paraphrase of Chekhov's summary on love: "Up to now but one incontrovertible truth has been said—it is a great mystery."

Josh Billings tried to solve the problem by sticking to "anatomical" facts: "Anatomically considered, laughing is the sensation of feeling good all over, and showing it principally in one spot." Scientific pedants will claim that this definition has at least three drawbacks. It does not explain *why* one feels "good all over"; it is limited to specific types of laughter (what about bitter laughter?); it fails to mention that laughter is an exclusive possession of homo sapiens. Dissenting opinions on this last point have been recorded by some investigators; Darwin believed he had observed face-laughter in apes, and others credit dogs with tail-laughter. Max Eastman, for example, declared: "Dogs laugh, but they laugh with their tails . . . What puts man in a higher state of evolution is that he has got his laugh on the right end."

In short, the study of the literature on laughter (and outstanding theories will be presented in the body of this book, despite their overwhelming dullness) seems to confirm Benjamin Stolberg's definition of an expert: "An expert is a person who avoids the small errors as he sweeps on to the grand fallacy." Not that these investigators always succeed in avoiding "the small errors," but there is no point in being too captious. These multiple theories have another quality in common; they all illustrate Samuel Johnson's dictum on professionals: "No man forgets his original trade; the rights of nations and of kings sink into a question of grammar, if grammarians discuss them." In the hands of nearly all the theoreticians who have dealt with laughter, what is comical and what is "funny" dries up and withers into a state of "fun-deficiency," to coin a phrase. One wonders whether this wasn't exactly their "original trade."

Josh Billings' theory of laughter continues, after the quotation given above: "Laughter is just as natural to come to the surface as a rat is to come out of his hole when he wants to." Here is the opening gambit for attacking the problem. When does the "rat" come to the surface, and what spur to human risibility is equivalent to the hunger that drives the rat from its hole?

When do we laugh? Bewildered and disappointed by the plethora of contradictory theories offered by the experts, let us consult the scientifically untouched laughers themselves. The usual *popular* explanations are no more illuminating; they offer redundancies and circumlocution instead of theoretical contradiction. The question itself is greeted with surprise—why question the "self-evident?"—and then lamely answered: "We laugh when something is funny." If one objects that the reply leaves a few points unaccounted for (such as the inevitable dissenters who complain, after a joke is told, "I don't think that's funny"), the omission is patched up with, "The fellow who doesn't laugh at the jokes I consider funny just has no sense of humor." According to the popular theory, one laughs when and because something is funny, and something is funny because and when one laughs.

Obviously, people don't know why they are impelled to laughter on certain occasions, and the rationalizations they offer are not too bright. It is surprising that their rationalizations should be weak; understandable that they should be ignorant of the reasons for their laughter. Out of inner necessity, people are unaware that laughter possesses a complicated unconscious substructure: the unconscious, to be unconscious, must be completely hidden. No bargaining is possible on that score. The term, "unconscious," has but one meaning: exclusion of conscious knowledge.

The language of the typical scientific theories on laughter is more careful, more complex, more highbrow than that of the popular explanation. None the less, typical scientific theory on laughter also works on the level of rationalizations. And all of these theories, including the contemporary ones, are dwarfed to insignificance by Freud's famous theory on wit, published half a century ago in *The Wit and Its Relation to the Unconscious.*

Fifty years ago, psychoanalysis was a young science; since then it has accumulated an ever-increasing body of clinical observations. Time and again these empirical facts have produced reformulations of earlier tentative theoretical assumptions. Freud himself repeatedly adjusted his theories to accord with newly uncovered facts. Unfortunately, so healthy a procedure has not been applied to the theory of laughter; this has remained static since 1905. Whatever the objections leveled against psychoanalysis, it cannot be accused of being a static science. Freud had nothing but contempt for the shibboleth of dogmatism and conservatism in a science in its developmental stage.

The major step forward towards understanding the psychology of laughter in wit was taken when Freud shifted the scene from outward appearances to the forum internum of his psycho-oeconomic theory of "saving of inhibition cathexis," which is transformed into laughter. According to Freud, unconscious material is held in repression by specific amounts of psychic energy; when the other fellow hits at this material by telling a joke, the psychic energy diverted to the task of holding the material in repression becomes superfluous for a second, and is transformed into laughter. That fact alone secures a lasting place in science to Freud's early discovery of *one* of the inner mechanisms in laughter. But two factors which were unknown, or not seen as pertinent at the time, are missing from Freud's theory on wit and laughter. First, Freud had not yet, at the time he put forward this theory, divided the unconscious personality into the triad: superego, id, unconscious ego; the metapsychological viewpoint,[1] therefore, was still to be enounced by the creator of psychoanalysis. Second, and this is of equal importance, laughter was not studied clinically; the theory was deduced from casual observation of the attitudes of people who laugh. This was quite reasonable, of course, but analysis has since then learned to adduce the principle that psychopathology teaches us a great deal about so-called normal reactions. Thus, the psychology of people suffering from the lack of a "sense of humor" can profitably be studied in clinical analysis and used as supporting evidence. People with *neurotic* "fun-deficiency" (there are no people who do not possess the potential ability to laugh), people who bore or are bored, are sources of important clues to the psychology of healthy laughter. I am adducing this material. Moreover, a series of instances are analyzed in which it was possible to study production of a witticism and perception of the comic *in statu nascendi* during the analytic procedure.

The present volume attempts to bring the analytic theory on laughter and wit up to date. In it are suggested some modifications of the theory. This book proposes to show that laughter is a *necessary and healthy INTERNAL debunking process* and therefore a *fear-reducing process*, and that it is not directed at *external* powers, as more than fourscore investigators have claimed for centuries, but at *internal* powers. The fact that wit is a *method of attacking one sector of the inner conscience* (*ego ideal*) was first pointed out two decades ago[2] by myself in collaboration with Dr. Ludwig Jekels, the most distinguished of Freud's Old Guard.

[1] Later, in his study on *Humor* (*Gesammelte Schriften* XI, 1927), Freud applied metapsychology to one aspect of laughter, unfortunately with little success, in my opinion. (For further elaboration see Chapter Seven, p. 201ff.)

[2] "Transference and Love," *Imago*, Vienna, XX, 5–31; 1934. (The exact statement is on p. 14.) First presented as lecture before the Vienna Psychoanalytic Society, Nov. 9, 1933. The study was translated in the *Psychoanalytic Quarterly*, 8, 325–350; 1949. Later elaborated on in "A Clinical Contribution to the Psychogenesis of Humor," the *Psychoanalytic Review*, 24, 34–53; 1937; "Anxiety, 'Feet of Clay,' and Comedy," the *American Imago*, 6, 97–109; 1949; "The Dislike for Satire at Length," the *Psychiatric Quarterly Supplement*, 26, 190–201; 1952; *The Superego*, Grune & Stratton, New York, 1952, pp. 134ff.

The child is constantly confronted with "stern reality." Educators lay down and enforce moral precepts; the child, from his vistas of infantile megalomania, can only view these as frustrating and maddening impositions. Moreover, since the infant cannot understand either the motives or the purposes behind the educator's rules, they are considered senseless—and malicious, to boot. The child does not, at first, see his parents and their educational substitutes in all their weakness and unavoidable human frailties. On the contrary, they are for the child a sort of moral obelisk, fashioned of marble which cannot erode. To make matters worse, the child projects a great proportion of his own inexpressible aggression on to these very same authorities of the nursery. These two factors contribute to the unconscious creation of a parental image much more severe, more uncompromising, than the true one. And the child's unconscious identification is with precisely this distorted image, to which he adds his own megalomania. It is thus that he builds up his unconscious "ego ideal" (Freud), the first cornerstone of the superego.

The ego ideal represents Department I of the inner conscience, or superego. Very soon after it is established it is seized upon by Department II of the superego (technically called "Daimonion"), and used as an instrument of torture. Daimonion is made up of the child's inexpressible and hence rebounding aggression; its methods and effects are but "torture for torture's sake." Its modus operandi is simple and devastating. By constantly confronting the frightened ego with the image of its self-created ego ideal, the monotonous question is posed: "Have you lived up to your own precepts?" Since these "precepts," stemming from distorted external models, mingled with the child's megalomania and resulting in high-pitched expectations of future success, are unachievable, the answer is unfailingly, "No." Failure is expressed in consciously perceived (though secondarily rationalized) dissatisfaction, depression, guilt.

The human child is caught in his own net. Unable to live up to his own ego ideal, he has either to accept constant guilt, or sugar-coat this guilt by transforming it into an *unconscious* pleasure. And *the only pleasure one can extract from displeasure is to make displeasure into pleasure.* That ingenious solution leads directly to *psychic masochism*, the *pleasure-in-displeasure pattern.*

But the inner jailer is not bluffed by the trick for long; the poor prisoner is reproached for this hidden pleasure, too. As a result, a *secondary* defense[3] must be instituted to "prove" that the ego does not enjoy psychic maso-

[3] This corresponds to the *clinical* picture in psychic masochism. The *genetic* picture had been described, though little utilized, by Freud. The clinical picture, comprising the triad of the "mechanism of orality," and its interconnection with the oral phase, was worked out by the author. For elaboration, see *The Basic Neurosis* (Grune & Stratton, New York, 1949).

chism, that it is but a victim of the external world's malice, and that, contrary to the accusation, it is highly "aggressive." Subsequently, spurious aggression—"*pseudo-aggression*"—becomes the guiding pattern. The consequence is a steady succession of attempts to find a flaw in the otherwise air-tight armor of the tormentor. This is accomplished by proving that the authorities are not perfect either: every time the *child in the adult* can show up an adult, he can inwardly point out, "Look what these big people *really* are!" This accounts for the familiar eagerness with which all people greet rumors or proofs of hypocrisy, inconsistency, or baseness in the "great," and for the constant inner necessity to debunk the "great" by ridiculing them.

It is precisely at this point that laughter in the *adult* sense enters the picture. By proving that every *externally* encountered "hero" is at bottom just another Tom, Dick or Harry, the *internal* "heroes" are cut down to size as well. The unending battle with too-lofty internal models reduces, *for a short moment which is exactly identical with the duration of laughter*, the human being's fears and dilemmas. Laughter is an internal necessity of such importance that the *debunking alibi called laughter* is even hoarded for use in the next attack of the inner jailer, thus serving as a stockpile of alibis.

It should not be necessary to mention that all these interconnections take place *unconsciously*. The key to the meaning of laughter is so top-secret that even intelligent people have no more to say about these "involuntary and convulsive movements" (William Hazlitt) than that they laugh "because it is funny."

The unconscious ego sustains its very existence by producing its defensive weapons—wit, the comic, irony—in reply to the constant avalanche of reproaches emanating from unconscious conscience. By proving, through wit and the comic in general, that "the great isn't so great," that there is a seamy side to everything and flaws in everybody, the *child in the adult* uses the tactic of *anticipatory attack* to gain a respite and a breathing spell. By using the "sympathy joke" to out-distance the other fellow's suffering and "grim humor" to out-distance one's own masochism, the *child in the adult* tries to disprove inner conscience's indictment of that very same psychic masochistic allure. And the use of anticipatory self-irony is an attempt on the part of the *child in the adult* to forestall the other fellow's ridicule of him, which would again push him into the passive-masochistic corner and provide the inner Frankenstein with new torture material.

Thus, all forms of wit, humor and the comic are *directed at one specific inner danger: the accusation by inner conscience that one is a lover of the pleasure-in-displeasure pattern—psychic masochism.* The orphaned ego's answer is specious aggression. Marshall Foch's pseudo-heroic dictum applies: "My center is giving way; my right is pushed back; excellent, I'll attack." Internally, this strategy amounts to no more than whistling in the dark, frequently in anticipation and for hoarding purposes.

Laughter is a debunking process—*plus*. This "plus" consists of two parts. First, the frightened *child in the adult* goes one step beyond simple defense and offers the ogre of inner conscience a *substitute victim, artificially created*. The plea here is: "I'm not the masochistic one—the other fellow is! If you are thirsty for blood, drink his!" The internal technique in all witty, comic and humorous productions improves on the banal strategy of the schoolboy who must show his poor report card at home: production of the card is simultaneous with the announcement that his pal Johnny got a bad report, too. In its less primitive version, this very tactic calls for forgetting one's own report card and laughing one's head off over Johnny's, notwithstanding the fact that it may not be Johnny's report card at all, but one's own, cunningly slipped into Johnny's books, and with the name erased.

The enormous literature on the topic of laughter has bogged down completely on one question: does one laugh *at* or *with* the other person? The investigators have never doubted that those laughed "at" or "with" are real people. The whole problem is a sham because of this crucial point, for people are neither laughed at or with, but merely *used as unconscious alibis or as the raw material for the creation of artificial victims to be presented as substitutes to one's inner conscience*. So essential is the substitute victim that he is synthetically produced when not conveniently found at hand. Moreover, the problem of laughter *at* or laughter *with* simply confuses different types of humorous and witty production. In wit one laughs *at* the substitute victim; in sympathy jokes one *out-distances* the pitiful situation of the substitute victim, and seemingly laughs *with* the hostage, saving pity.

Doggedly working away at the problem of "laughing at or with," investigators have overlooked the salient point: why should human foolishness or suffering be laughable at all? Why not disregard both and save "energy?" If the human being is as overflowing with aggression as is commonly claimed, why not be callous? The contradiction can be solved, for the human being is neither brimming with aggression nor overflowing with sympathy for the other fellow's unhappiness. Humanity's motto is still Boswell's, "My favorite subject—Myself,"[4] and this "Myself" is filled with the unconscious ego's masochistic elaboration of reproaches of inner conscience. This troube must be alleviated, and it is. By using the triad of pseudo-aggression, out-distancing, and creation of a scorned or deprecated artificial victim to be offered as hostage, the trick is done in laughter.

The creation of the "artificial victim" serves another purpose, and this function is the second part of the "plus" in the inner debunking process. As described above, the hostage is sacrificed to the principle, "The gods are athirst," but at the same time (and this is not a contradiction according to

[4] Letter to Temple, June 26, 1763.

infantile metalogic!) the hostage is unconsciously perceived as projection of one's own ego ideal, which represents a part of the superego. By humiliating the latter, the illusion is fostered that the inner torturer is *too weak to be dangerous.*

Laughter is not an inborn instinct and therefore the term, "sense of humor," is a misnomer. Laughter has a highly complex, individual, though typical, "case history," intimately connected with infantile fears, which are perpetuated in the fantastic severity of the inner conscience, the superego. Thus, this volume is a continuation of ideas presented in my previous books on the inner conscience, *The Battle of the Conscience* (1948) and *The Superego* (1952). I subscribe once more to the idea that the superego is the decisive part of the personality and that any attempt to understand human motivations must be out of focus unless the superego *and* the all-important defense mechanism, psychic masochism based on oral regresson—created by the unconscious ego to escape the superego's tyranny—are put in the center.

Nobody but the author is to blame for the demerits of the theory presented; the kudos awarded for the merits of a theory are not likely to accrue in our times and hence can be disregarded. A wit once claimed that the heresies of one generation are the common sense of the next. Although the wit credits progress (especially in science) with too rapid a pace, there is no conclusive proof, so far, that progress in thinking is impossible. Here, too, laughter has its place: "Progress is nothing but the victory of laughter over dogma" (Benjamin DeCasseres).

Strangely enough, nobody has remarked on the fact that laughter is not only the most personal but also the *only* incorruptible human trait. Men can be bought and their allegiances swayed; men can be drugged (even without money or promises) through the use of slogans, lies, prejudices, and what not. Laughter can be officially pointed in the wrong direction or misused for unsavory purposes. But no dictator in the world can successfully interdict personal laughter. Even people who are submissive on the surface rescue their corrupted self-esteem with inner laughter at their tormenters. Perhaps a pessimist would claim that laughter cannot be completely corrupted and prostituted because it is not under *conscious* control.

The attributes, "personal" and "incorruptible," as applied to laughter, can be explained by studying the genesis and infantile precursors of this "emotion that hath no name" (Thomas Hobbes). Laughter wasn't born yesterday, and you can't put anything over on involuntary laughter.

EDMUND BERGLER

New York City and Dummerston Center, Vermont
April, 1953–December, 1955.

1. Ephemeral Theories—Eternal Laughter

One inch of joy surmounts of grief a span,
Because to laugh is proper to man.
François Rabelais

BOOKS ON THE THEORY of laughter traditionally begin with a humble apology to the reader for "murdering laughter." A modern author, Max Eastman, starts his *Enjoyment of Laughter*[1] with:

> I must warn you, reader, that it is not the purpose of this book to make you laugh. As you know, nothing kills the laugh quicker than to explain a joke. I intend to explain all jokes, and the proper and logical outcome will be, not only that you will not laugh now, but that you will never laugh again. So prepare for the descending gloom.

Nothing so tragic is in store for the readers of this book. It is certified not to do away with the reader's ability to enjoy laughter—in the future. As to the present, readers of books on the theory of wit and laughter seldom buy these books to be informed; the typical reader views and values these works as anthologies of humor. This has happened, alas, even to Freud's monumental book on wit. Apart from the proper development of theory, therefore, the essential task is to make sure that the witticisms used as examples are relatively novel. Unfortunately, the novelty of a joke or a wisecrack cannot be guaranteed nowadays. Today's readers are just too well informed. Most of them belong to the last of the four great categories into which all listeners to jokes are divided: they never laugh at all because they have heard the joke before, and can tell you a better one. This automatically assures their superiority over Category #3, members of which laugh three times: when you tell a joke, when you explain it, and when they finally get it. Category #2 is composed of more modest people who laugh only twice: when you tell a joke and when you explain it—they will never understand it. Finally, those in Category #1 laugh only once: when the joke is told. These exclusive gentlemen do not allow you to explain the joke, and they would never understand it anyway.

This division into four categories is age-old. The purpose of the division is reassurance: the reader is thus assured that he belongs in Category #4, and nothing will happen to his ability to laugh. I have never heard of a gynecologist who lost his interest in women merely through the hazards of his profession; his gynecological scrutiny of patients in his office and his interest in a specific woman in his home remain on different psychic levels.

[1] Simon and Schuster, New York, 1936.

One danger does exist, however. There are people who behave like the passenger who sits silently in his place in a train, but every half minute makes a disgusted grimace and a derogatory gesture with his hand. Another passenger questions him about his peculiar behavior, and he explains: "It's nothing; I'm bored, so I'm telling myself jokes—but I know them all."

Following is a representative sampling of already available theories on laughter. The samplings number a mere eighty.[2] I do not wish to interfere with the countless Ph.D. theses of the future which will deal solely with their enumeration. Why damage future generations of autonomous thinkers in desperate search of a topic? Moreover, I consider that *most* of the theories presented by my precursors in the field are of dubious value. Of course, this opinion is counterbalanced by my belief that my own theory is the only correct one. This, too, is stated in complete modesty, and for the sole purpose of sticking to tradition.[3] Traditionally, every promoter of a theory has nothing but ironic contempt for the workers who have preceded him, even when (and this happens seldom enough) he admits that one or the other of these workers (preferably a dead one) had "some unclear inkling of the truth," as witness the fact that this "unclear inkling" tangentially approaches his own theory. All this is tradition; besides, it is unavoidable. The only promise I can make, therefore, is to avoid superciliousness, although superciliousness, too, is part of the unwritten tradition.

In presenting the various theories on laughter, I have tried to sum each up in a concise headline. It has been my experience that theories are easier to retain in the memory if thought of in terms of content rather than in terms of author or promoter. As far as possible, the sequence is chronological. For impatient readers who cannot wait to "come to the jokes," the few theories which should *not* be skipped are starred. These starred theories are essential for the understanding of the subsequent text.

* *The "lack of self-knowledge" theory* was put forward by Plato, whose opinion on laughter is the most ancient of the theories on laughter to have come down to us. In *Philebus*, Plato claims that the ridiculous is based on ignorance of "know thyself."

According to Plato, this ignorance of self is ridiculous only in the weak;

[2] J. C. Gregory says, in *The Nature of Laughter* (1924): "Since a full survey of theories on laughter would be tedious *if not impossible*, a representative of the old must be chosen to contrast with a representative of the new" (p. 15). There are but four compilations of these theories: Eastman's, Piddington's, Greig's and Kimmins'. None is complete; none goes beyond the 1930's. All of them are serious and scholarly, though the first two are marred by constant polemics designed to put the specific author's specific point across. Greig's compilation is objective, but it ends with 1922. The Kimmins compilation is too skimpy. I have tried to be as accurate as possible, but I do not claim that my compilation is either complete or unimpeachable.

[3] Since irony is notoriously misunderstood, this *is* irony.

in the strong, it is hateful. Plato construes a pleasure-pain theory, although he uses the terms in a different connotation. Having previously defined lack of self-knowledge as a misfortune, he reasons as follows: laughter is a pleasure, thus, to laugh at the conceit of our friends is to gloat over their misfortune. Such gloating implies malice, which is painful. Otherwise, Plato compares the appreciation of the ludicrous to the relief which comes from scratching an itch. Of importance is the fact that recognition of the aggressive connotation of laughter dates back twenty-three hundred years. (Plato lived from 427–348 B.C.)

* *The theory of the "not too tragic defect"* stems from Aristotle (384–322 B.C.) who stated in *Poetics*: "The ludicrous is merely a subdivision of the ugly. It may be defined as a defect or ugliness which is not painful or destructive. Thus, for example, the comic mask is ugly and distorted, but does not cause pain." In effect, Aristotle subscribes to Plato's assumption that malice is essential to laughter. However, he enlarges the scope of the investigation by distinguishing between comedy and irony directed at individuals. He also introduces the matter of aesthetics in laughter, declaring that the malicious element, though indispensable to laughter, is aesthetically undesirable. In *Nicomachean Ethics*, Aristotle writes:

> Now those who go into excess in making fun appear to be buffoons and vulgar, sticking to their joke at all hazards, and aiming rather at raising a laugh than at saying what is seemly and avoiding pain to their butt. But those who would not say anything funny themselves, and who are annoyed at those who do, seem to be savage and austere. But those whose joking is in good taste are called witty . . .

All this adds up to appreciation of laughter, with an added note of caution: the precious gift is not to be misused. (Aristotle even hints at legal restriction.) In his *Rhetorica*, however, the philosopher subscribes to the opinion of Gorgas, who advocated that one "kill the opponents' earnestness with jesting and their jesting with earnestness."

The two nihilistic theories of laughter put forward by the ancient Romans, Cicero and Quintillian, have in common the doubt that anyone has sufficiently explained laughter. Neither adds anything of importance to the body of ancient theory. Both echo the "baseness and deformity" theme of the Aristotelian text. Cicero stresses that the defeat of expectation causes laughter, and sums up: "For it is by deceiving expectation, by satirizing the character of others, by making merry of our own, by comparing a thing with the worse, by pretending, by talking seeming nonsense, and by reproving follies, that laughter is stimulated." Confirming Cicero, Quintillian adds that laughter arises from surprise or defeated expectation, and from twisting another's words to express a meaning he did not intend. In short, both Cicero and Quintillian are purely descriptive; their psychological contribution is a shrug of a toga-draped shoulder.

The five Italian Renaissance theories of laughter which J. Y. T. Greig dug up (Trissino, Maggi, Munzio, Minturno, Scaliger) remind one of the participant in a discussion who finally gets the floor and begins his remarks with the announcement: "I *also* have nothing to say." Trissino is moralistic: the comic poet must present base actions in order to condemn them, for laughter arises from the pleasure in the low. Maggi echoes Cicero's "surprise" theory. Munzio regrets that comedy is not sufficiently successful in correcting manners through laughter. Minturno defends laughter, whereas Scaliger devotes his attention to problems of form; a comic poem, in his definition, is "made of intrigues, in popular style and with a happy ending."

The theory of "correction of human follies" follows after a gap of centuries. Neither the Romans nor the writers of the Renaissance made substantial contributions to the *theory* of laughter. The next idea of significance grew out of Ben Jonson's (1572–1637) essentially moralistic definition of comedy as some kind of pedagogic instrument, designed to correct faults rather than to provoke laughter. (The theoreticians on laughter in the sixteenth and seventeenth centuries concentrated mainly on comedy.) According to Jonson, comedy has therapeutic functions; it can be compared with such methods of physical therapy as purging and bleeding. The idea was not exactly new; "Ridendo castiga mores" is age-old, and Munzio's rather more limited application of the same point is described above. Nevertheless, it became the vogue as Jonson's theory, and remained so until it was successfully contradicted by John Dryden (1631–1700). Dryden's quite reasonable objection was to the effect that *the purpose of comedy is to delight*, and he expressly recognized "malicious pleasure" as one of the ingredients in laughter.

* *The "sudden glory" theory* of Thomas Hobbes (1588–1679) represents the first psychological theory on laughter ever put forward. In *On Human Nature, IX* (1650), Hobbes claims that there exists a "passion that hath no name," manifesting itself in laugher which is "always joy." He disputes the theory that laughter is mere appreciation of wit: "Men laugh at mischances and indecencies wherein there lies no wit nor jest at all." Whatever may be the mysterious ingredient which arouses laughter, it must contain something new and unexpected. Then follows Hobbes's famous sentence: "Laughter is nothing but the sudden glory arising from some sudden conception of some eminence in ourselves; by comparison with the infirmity of others, or with our own formerly."

One could object that this, in part, stresses a banality: that there must be some *inner* reason in the laugher to account for laughter. Nevertheless, it was only after some two thousand years of recorded theories on laughter that this point emerged. One could also say that the aggressive element in laughter was clarified by Plato and Aristotle, and that Hobbes's description of "sudden glory" is therefore nothing but a rehash. However, the presence of the aggressive element in laughter is violently denied in more modern theories on laughter (to be summarized later in this chapter); this makes Hobbes's description of the existence of an inner, aggressive, satisfaction—expressed by him as the "conception of some eminence in ourselves"—important.

One could also point out that the definition of laughter as "passion that hath no name" in no way explains the verbal mechanisms which either evoke or smother laughter. Obviously, a witticism stands or falls on its formulation, for if the formulation is faulty, the witty saying deteriorates into a statement of fact, true or distorted. And a final question might be put: Why does the "sudden glory" manifest itself exactly in laughter, and not in another form of expression? Minor quibbles could also be adduced. Still, it was "new" and thought-provoking for Hobbes to have located the gravitational center of the laugh within the laugher himself, although this in itself did not and does not solve the over-all problem.

A physio-psychological blend is presented in René Descartes' (1596–1650) theory of laughter. The French philosopher's physiological deduction is a museum piece by now; the more incidental remarks about laughter are still of some pertinence, however. In his *Traité des Passions* (1649), Descartes describes laughter as a sign of joy. But joy, per se, does not produce laughter unless two specific conditions are adhered to: the amount of joy must not be too great, and the joy must be mixed with other elements, such as surprise, hostility, admiration. His remarks concerning the type of laughter which occasionally accompanies indignation are of interest. Descartes considers this type of laughter to be a fake; if natural, it denotes a triumph over a person who tried but failed to inflict an injury upon an object of the laugher's affection or sympathy.

Descartes also makes some comments on derision, representing it as joy combined with hostility. Most remarkable is his explanation of the malicious joy exhibited by people with bodily defects: their derision is based on the wish to see other people "disgracié," as they feel themselves to be. They maliciously cheer every "evil" which befalls another, for in their opinion "the other" deserves it.

With some stretching of the point, one could say that Descartes found in this procedure some hint of the role of the inner conscience; when the deformed person feels that other people "deserve" a misfortune similar to his own, he can only have convinced his conscience, by his suffering, that retaliatory justice is in order. This explains the absence of any guilt feelings from his gloating.

It is possible that Descartes merely modified ideas expressed a century earlier by the French royal physician, L. Joubert, in *Traité de Ris* (1579).

Joubert's theory is also physio-psychological; his idea is that laughter is based on happiness mixed with pain. The physiological section is totally outdated.

* *The "separation theory"* of the English philosopher John Locke (1632–1704) applies only tangentially. An attempt is made in *An Essay Concerning Human Understanding* to draw a distinction between wit and judgment:

> For wit lying most in the assemblage of ideas, and putting those together with quickness and variety, wherein can be found any resemblance or congruity, thereby to make up pleasant pictures and agreeable visions in the fancy; judgment, on the contrary, lies quite on the other side, in separating carefully, one from another, ideas wherein can be found the least difference, thereby to avoid being misled by similitude, and by affinity to take one thing for another.

Neatly presented, with complete avoidance of the real problem: what allows for the half-suspension of judgment in wit? Locke had, by the way, some vague inkling of unconscious factors, as can be seen in his statement: "The thoughts that come often unsought, and, as it were, drop into the mind, are commonly the most valuable of any we have, and therefore should be secured, because they seldom return again."

Incidentally, William Hazlitt attacked Locke for having "borrowed" from Hobbes, offering the following quotations as proof of his contention:

LOCKE

If in having our ideas in the memory ready to hand consists quickness of parts, in this of having them unconfused, and being able nicely to distinguish one thing from another, where there is but the least difference, consists in a great measure the exactness of judgment and clearness of reason, which is to be observed in one man above another. And hence, perhaps, may be given some reason of that common observation, that men who have a great deal of wit and prompt memories, have not always the clearest judgment or deepest reason. For wit lying mostly in the assemblage of ideas, and putting them together with quickness and variety, wherein can be found any resemblance or congruity, thereby to make up pleasant pictures and agreeable visions in the fancy; judgment, on the contrary, lies quite on the other side, in separating carefully one from another, ideas wherein can be found the least difference, thereby to avoid

HOBBES

This difference of quickness in imagining is caused by the difference of men's passion, that love and dislike some one thing, some another, and therefore some men's thoughts run one way, some another, and are held to and observe differently the things that pass through their imagination. And whereas in this succession of thoughts there is nothing to observe in the things they think on, but either in what they be like one another, or in what they be unlike, those that observe their similitudes, in case they be such as are but rarely observed by others, are said to have a good wit, by which is meant on this occasion a good fancy. But they that observe their differences and dissimilitudes, which is called distinguishing and discerning and judging between thing and thing; in case such discerning be not easy, are said to have a good judgment; and particularly in matter of conversation and business, wherein times, places, and persons are to being misled by similitude, and by affinity to take on thing for another.

Essay, Vol. 1

be discerned, this virtue is called discretion. The former, that is, fancy, without the help of judgment, is not commended for a virtue; but the latter, which is judgment or discretion, is commended for itself, without the help of fancy.

Leviathan

An appendix to the "separation theory" of Locke was provided by Joseph Addison (1672–1719), who made many remarks pertaining to the theory of laughter in various issues of *The Spectator*. In these, Addision approves of both Hobbes's and Locke's theories, but adds a proviso to Locke's, maintaining that the unexpected juxtaposition and resemblance of ideas must produce delight and surprise in order to constitute wit. He also points out that opposition as well as resemblance in juxtaposed ideas often produces laughter. A moralistic note frequently enters his discussions; for example: "I shall endeavor to enliven morality with wit, and to temper wit with morality"; and "In a word, a man should not live as though there were no God in the world; nor, at the same time, as if there were no men in it." On the other hand, he also said: "We are growing serious, and, let me tell you, that's a very step to becoming dull."

The "insolence theory." From Aristotle's "Wit is educated insolence" to the aphorism of La Rochefoucauld (1612–1680), "Wit enables us to act rudely with impunity," runs a straight line of misunderstanding. Not every witticism is insolence, not every insolence is wit. The real question—what distinguishes a boor from a wit?—is not even touched.

The "division theory" separating derision from laughter is implied in the *Ethics* of Baruch Spinoza (1632–1677). Spinoza writes: "I recognize a great difference between derision . . . and laughter and jest. For laughter or jest are a kind of joy, therefore are, if not excessive, good." The moralistic viewpoint obscures the fact that derision produces laughter, too.

* *The "nascent cry" theory of laughter* was first stated by David Hartley (1705–1757) in *Observation of Men*, in 1749. The theory is important because it represents the first scientific elucidation of the connection between fear or unhappiness and laughter. To quote Hartley:

> Young children do not laugh aloud for some months. The first occasion of doing this seems to be a surprise which brings on a *momentary fear first*, and then a momentary joy in consequence of the *removal of that fear*,[4] agreeably to what may be

---

[4] This observation, made two hundred years ago, has been confirmed time and again by both non-analytic and analytic observers. An example of the former is Max Eastman, whose pertinent theory is quoted on page 197f.; an example of the latter is E. Jacobson, who wrote in "The Child's Laughter," *Psychoan. Study of the Child*, 2,

> observed of the pleasures that follow the removal of pain. This may appear probable, inasmuch as laughter is a nascent cry, stopped of a sudden; also because if the same surprise, which makes young children laugh, be a very little increased, they will cry.

The laughter reaction is much influenced by imitation—"children learn to laugh, as they learn to talk and walk."

The "nascent cry" theory was later echoed by Pierre-Augustine Beaumarchais, who said, "I laugh at everything, for fear of being obliged to weep," and by Friedrich Nietzsche, who declared, "Man alone suffers so excruciatingly in the world that he was compelled to invent laughter."

Hartley has another "first" to his credit; he was the pioneer in scientifically observing and recording the development of laughter in children. The only observer to antedate him was Pliny, and Pliny merely stated that the first laugh of the child takes place forty days after birth.

The "midwife" and "reason" theories of laughter play on the words "justness of thought" and "reason," respectively. The "midwife theory" was proclaimed by Alexander Pope (1688–1744) in a letter to the dramatist William Wycherly on December 26, 1704: "Wit may be defined as justness of thought and a facility of expression, or (in a midwives' phrase) a perfect conception with an easy delivery." The "reason" theory is deposited in *Épitre à Voltaire*, by Marie-Joseph Blaise Chenier, brother of André Chenier (1762–1794): "What is wit? Reason expressed artfully."

The theories are of dubious value. A just statement combined with facility of expression does not make a witticism; elegant phrasing and elegant style, per se, do not make people laugh, or render reason palatable to people who dislike the dish. Moreover, artful expression in itself does not give birth to a witticism, even with the help of a good midwife. Only the opposite is true: every witticism *includes* a specific technique of "artful expression." Neither theory concerns itself with explaining this "artful expression." And as for "reason," there are many witticisms which do not even purport to represent reason. The conspicuous pleasure we all derive from nonsense attests to that.

The "occult resemblance" theory has the once-redoubtable authority of Samuel Johnson (1709–1784) behind it: "Wit may be considered a combination of dissimilar images, or discovery of occult resemblances in things apparently alike." (The similarity to Locke and Addison is obvious.) Mme. de Stael subsequently came to the same conclusion: "Wit consists in discerning the resemblance between things that differ, and the difference between things that are alike."

39–60; 1946: "When intense, especially rhythmical stimulation of the whole or a part of the motor system produces a sudden or surprising fast enjoyable experience which, though first suggesting danger, arouses pleasant anticipation of relief, laughter comes about as final intensely pleasurable motor release."

Neither of these authorities realized that they were confusing the technique with the content of some witticisms. It is true that "occult resemblances and dissimilarities" are included in some examples of wit; however, this fact has no direct connection with laughter. One can discover these interconnections and wonder at them, one can become conscious of hidden passageways between pigeonholes and register the fact that the separations are faulty—and all this without laughter. The theory thus fails to explain the essential: laughter.

The "unification theory" of the Scottish poet James Beattie (1735–1803) is mentioned here not because it contributes to our understanding, but because it indicates the extent of the adverse criticism provoked by Hobbes's inclusion of aggression and "superiority" in his theory of laughter. Beattie objects to Hobbes on two grounds. First, laughers are not necessarily proud, nor are serious people humble. Second, "The theory of Mr. Hobbes would hardly have deserved notice if Addison had not spoken of it with approbation" (*Essays*). This feeble argument—since when is achievement followed by immediate appreciation?—is supported by an even feebler theory:

> Laughter arises from the view of two or more inconsistent, unsuitable or incongruous parts or circumstances, considered as united in one complex object or assemblage, or as acquiring a sort of mutual relation from the *peculiar manner* in which the mind takes notice of them.

This description overlooks a point which is unfortunately the heart of the matter: what does the "peculiar manner" consist of?

* *The "nothing theory"* can claim the philosopher Immanuel Kant (1724–1804) as its originator. In his *Critique of Pure Reason* (1781) Kant states: "Laughter is an affection arising from the sudden transformation of a strained expectation into nothing." The "nothing" theory consists only of holes, which are not filled with explanations of wit and laughter. Many a "strained expectation" which fails to materialize leads to a letdown and not to laughter. If this were not so, there would be no disappointments in life.

The only important contribution that Kant made was the idea of "transformation," although his observations of the material used in this process are incorrect. Kant is so insistent on his eventual "nothing" that in discussing the ludicrous he expressly stresses that the strained expectation "does not transform itself into the positive opposite of an expected object—for then there would still be something, which might even be a cause of grief—but it must be transformed into nothing."

The double-feature theory of "wise and foolish" laughter views laughter as either a proof of wisdom or of foolishness, depending on what is laughed at. The chain of contradictions comprises, for example: "The loud laugh that spoke the vacant mind" (Oliver Goldsmith); "Laughter is the hiccup of a fool" (John Ray); "Laughter is the mind sneezing" (Wyndham Lewis). Some of these adherents to the double-feature theory go so far as to claim that *all* laughter is foolish; reserved for the wise is only—the smile. In a letter to his son written on October 19, 1748, Lord Chesterfield decreed:

> Loud laughter is the mirth of the mob, who are only pleased with silly things; for true wit or good sense never excited a laugh since the creation of the world. A man of parts and fashion is therefore only seen to smile, but never heard to laugh.[5]

This exclusion of the intelligentsia from the prerogative of laughter neither corresponds to observable facts nor explains what distinguishes the "silly things" laughed at from the wise ones smiled at. One should also mention the fact that the formula fails to cast light on the knotty problem of why "good sense" should provoke laughter in the first place. Probing behind the verbiage, one finds that Lord Chesterfield is aware of no more than that different people laugh at different things, and the levels of their senses of humor differ. His fiat on the "bad form" of the laugh and the "good form" of the smile does nothing, of course, to illuminate the mechanism of laughter.[6]

* *The "split-second before adaptation" theory of laughter* was promoted by William Hazlitt (1778–1830), who stated, in the Introductory Lecture of his essays on *The English Comic Writers* (1819):

> Tears may be considered as the natural and involuntary resource of the mind overcome by some sudden and violent emotion, before it has had time to reconcile its feelings to the change of circumstances: while laughter may be defined to be the same sort of convulsive and involuntary movement, occasioned by mere surprise or contrast (in the absence of any more serious emotion), before it has time to reconcile its belief to contradictory appearance.

In short, Hazlitt appears to view laughter as the split-second before adaptation: "The essence of the laughable then is the incongruous, the disconnecting one idea from the other, or the jostling of one feeling against another."

Hazlitt fully acknowledges the aggressive content of some types of laughter: "We laugh at a damned author, in spite of our teeth, and though he may be our friend. 'There is something in the misfortune of our best

[5] Lord Chesterfield failed to mention his source: "A fool lifteth up his voice with laughter, but a wise man doth scarce smile a little" (*Ecclesiastes*, XXI, 20).

[6] A more modern version of this principle is reported in Eastman's *Enjoyment of Laughter*. The *New Yorker* brand of humor, he says, is "almost a demure, a self-containing, kind of humor. . . . New Yorkers . . . are so given over to the ideal of 'playing down' jokes . . . that they would almost feel pained if they saw somebody laugh out loud while reading their magazine."

friends that pleases us'." There is nothing especially new or original in Hazlitt's deduction, save for two points.

The first of these is his use of experiences with children (a starting point Hartley utilized before him). This constitutes "clinical observation," an unusual contribution to have made to the study of laughter in 1819. Hazlitt wrote, for example:

> If we hold a mask before our face, and approach a child with this disguise on, it will at first, from the oddity and incongruity of the appearance, be inclined to laugh; if we go nearer it, steadily, and without saying a word, it will begin to be alarmed, and half inclined to cry; if we suddenly take off the mask, it will recover from its fears, and burst out a-laughing; but if, instead of presenting the old well-known countenance, we have concealed a satyr's head or some frightful caricature behind the first mask, the suddenness of the change will not in this case be a source of merriment to it, but will convert its surprise into an agony of consternation, and will make it scream for help, even though it may be convinced that the whole is a trick at bottom.

Hazlitt leaves the beaten track of theories on laughter, again, when he attempts to discourse on laughter at the forbidden. Although he cannot explain this adequately, his observations are of interest. "All the attractions of a subject that can only be glanced at indirectly, that is a sort of forbidden ground to imagination, except under severe restrictions, which are constantly broken through . . ." are sources of laughter, he declares.

Hazlitt also claims that the "shrewd separation or disentangling of ideas that seem the same . . . is wit just as much as the bringing together those that appear at first sight totally different." The reminiscent ring of this statement contrasts oddly with his polemic against Locke for having "borrowed" Hobbes's ideas (see p. 6).

It is easy to spot the lacunae in Hazlitt's over-all theory,[7] but this does not in any way lessen his merit as a precursor of later discoveries.

The "sudden contrast" theory of laughter has many adherents; the most notable of these (though not its originator) is Arthur Schopenhauer (1788–1860) who, in *The World as Will and Idea* (1819), states: "The cause of laughter in every case is simply the sudden perception of the incongruity between a concept and the real objects which have been thought through in some relation, and laughter itself is just the expression of this incongruity." Once more, the idea of incongruity, but no explanation of why perception of the sudden contrast should not produce surprise without laughter. Surprise does not always produce laughter; what, then, is the distinction?

[7] In one of her lectures, Anna Freud described a little boy who had been afraid of lions for a long time, but suddenly began to find this symbolic representation of his Oedipal fears rather "ridiculous and pitiful."

The "sin-theory" of laughter is rooted in some deep distrust of all laughter; its theological orientation permits it to dispense with the obligation of explaining laughter as a psychological phenomenon, and to concentrate instead on laughter as an antechamber to, or indication of, sinfulness. St. John Chrysostom (ca. 345–407) claimed: "Laughter does not seem to be a sin, but it leads to sin." Robert G. Ingersoll said mockingly: "Laughing has always been considered by theologians as a crime." A. M. Ludovici, who in 1933 wrote an angry book about laughter[8] (see the "showing teeth" theory, p. 27f.) claims that "there is not a joke in the whole of the New Testament and even the laughter of the Bible is nearly always an expression of scorn and not of mirth (exceptions: Psalms CXXVI, 2 and Job VII, 21) and no saint, prophet or apostle is ever spoken of as laughing" (Introduction to the Secret of Laughter, p. 10). Ludovici adduces Letter XI of Blaise Pascal's (1623–1662) *Lettres à un Provincial*, where Pascal contends that saints may and do laugh at human errors, supporting his argument with quotations from Augustine, Jerome and Tertullian. Pascal says:

> Je m'assure, mes pères, que ces examples sacrés suffisent pour faire entendre que ce n'est pas une conduite contraire à celle des saints, de rire des erreurs et des égarements des hommes [I am certain, my fathers, that these holy examples suffice to make it clear that it is not unsaintly conduct to laugh at the errors and strayings of men].

On the other hand, G. K. Chesterton took great pains to prove that Christ had a sense of humor; in *Orthodoxy* he contradicted the conventional biographers, maintaining that if Christ is not reported to have laughed, it is because he deliberately hid his mirth from men, covering it "constantly by abrupt silence or impetuous isolation." This argument is cited by Ludovici, who is scornful of "the most exalted of modern Anglo-Saxon virtues—a sense of humor." Ironically, Ludovici adds: "Evidently the Bishop of Tasmania (the Right Rev. J. E. Mercer, D.D.), as a modern Anglo-Saxon, felt the same impulse as Chesterton; for in an article in The Hibbert Journal (Vol. 9, No. 34, January, 1911), after painstakingly purging laughter of all malice, pride and malevolence, he tries to prove that God Himself has a sense of humor." Ludovici concludes: "How much more reverent and more indicative of a profound understanding of laughter is Lammenais' protest: 'Who could ever imagine Christ laughing?'"

The "perfection-imperfection" theory was stated by Moses Mendelssohn (1729–1786) in *Philosophische Schriften*, (Vol. II). He does not consider laughter a sign of pleasure, but a manifestation based "as well as crying, on a contrast between perfection and imperfection." This contrast must be light, however; in Mendelssohn's words:

> Every lack of harmony between means and ends, cause and effect, between thought,

[8] *The Secret of Laughter*, Viking Press, 1933.

and manner of their expression, above all, every contrast of the great, venerable pompous and significant, with the valueless, contemptible and little, whose consequences put us in no embarrassment, is laughable.

The poet G. E. Lessing (1729–1781) improved on Mendelssohn's theory in *Laokoon* by adding that this contrast between perfection and imperfection must not be too sharp, and that the opposites must be of such a nature as to admit of blending with each other.

A trio of philosophical authorities substituting for a theory on wit was submitted by Poinsinet de Sivry in his "Traité des Causes Physiques et Morales du Rire" (1778). This relic of the eighteenth century was disinterred by Greig.

De Sivry's authorities were Destouches, Fontanelle, and Montesquieu, all equally well-known in that day. In the course of their imaginary discussion, Destouches claims that laughter has its origin in a "reasoned joy"; Fontanelle maintains that "the principle of laughter is folly"; Montesquieu adopts Hobbes's view and calls laughter the expression of pride. As for de Sivry himself, his introduction contains this definition:

Comedy, that unfailing source of useful pleasure, diverts us with its teaching, and teaches us by presenting a picture of faults and vices, Laughter is its true attribute, and it is through laughter that comedy proceeds to its respectable aim of *correcting man while amusing him.*

The "moral contrast" theory was originated by Johann Wolfgang von Goethe (1749–1832); he defines laughter as "a moral contrast which is brought into unity for the mind in a harmless fashion."

The "bull-wit theory" of laughter was aphoristically stated by the Reverend Sydney Smith (1771–1845) in a review of Richard Edgeworth's "Essay on the Irish Bull" (*Edinburgh Review*, 1803). The bull and the witticism are opposites, according to Smith; the bull suddenly discovers an apparent congruity in a real incongruity of ideas, whereas a witticism is the discovery of a real congruity (or similarity) in an apparent incongruity or dissimilarity. The essence of wit is sudden surprise. Much thought, or much passion, impair if they do not destroy the "tendencies which wit has the tendency to excite." And finally, the less obvious the relation established by wit, the higher is the gratification the witticism affords.

The nine "esthetic dead-end" theories of laughter came from the German aesthetic school of the nineteenth century. With the exception of one of their number, Theodor Lipps, none of them contributed anything of value. (Max Eastman has collected these theories with a diligence worthy of a better cause.) They all take as their point of departure the deductions of Jean Paul Richter (1763–1825) as published in *Die Vorschule der Aesthetik* in 1804 under the pseudonym "Jean Paul." Humor, to Richter, represents not only art but ethics, and a philosophy of life. We laugh at the petty and inimical, he declares, contrasting it with the ideal of infinite sublimity. All things being petty, the tendency of laughter is to promote sympathy for mankind. When we laugh at other people's stupidity, we are lending them our own insight.

Interestingly enough, Richter assumes the existence of some kind of autonomy in jest: "The jest has no purpose other than its own being—the poetic bloom of its nettle does not sting, and one can scarcely feel the blow of its flowering switch full of leaves." He therefore opposes Hobbes's theory. Richter's own definition of humor as the fruit of a comparison between the petty and the sublime has a more realistic appendix, dealing with wit, "the disguised priest who marries all couples."

Christian W. Weisse put forward the "*elevation theory*" in his *System der Aesthetik* (1830). Humor, he claims, is not an enemy of art, but an enricher; it raises up the ugly and abominable. According to this author, the "comic is highness elevated, or beauty reconstructed out of her absolute negation."

K. W. F. Solger presented the "*theory of restfulness*" in *Vorlesungen ueber Aesthetik* (1829). Since the basic "idea" is ubiquitous, it has the quality of restfulness, he declares, concluding: "Even in our temporal being we live ever in the beautiful." Why the beautiful part of the mixture should produce laughter is not clarified by the author.

A. W. Bohtz, like Richter and Vischer, pondered over the problem of two contradictions in *Ueber das Komische und die Komoedia* (1844). According to this aesthetician, the artist's work consists of affirming the affirmative part of the mixture. Laughter still remains unexplained in this "*double affirmation theory*."

* Theodor Vischer modified Hegel's theory of laughter in his *Aesthetik* (1846). Vischer goes one step beyond Richter by postulating that contrast is not enough; a contradiction between the two ideas is essential. He enlarges on Richter's description of wit as "the disguised priest who marries all couples" by stating that wit prefers to marry those whose relations do not approve of the match. Otherwise, Vischer is Hegelian—the two themes brought together in wit must be actively antagonistic in order to entwine in a Hegelian synthesis.

H. Lotze propagated the "*for-each-otherness theory*" in *Geschichte der Aesthetik in Deutschland* (1868): "Only in this happy contemplation of the indestructability of the universal for-each-otherness of things can I find the charm of the absolute comic."

J. Bahnsen argued against Lotze's theory of the benevolent universe in *Das Tragische Als Weltgesetz* (1877). Bahnsen's "*tragic contradiction theory*" claims that "tragic contradiction is the universal law; what humor does is an uplifting job—the contradiction is lifted to the intellectual sphere where aesthetic freedom of contemplation reigns and where it can be enjoyed in spite of itself."

* K. Fischer (*Ueber den Witz*, 1889) subscribes to the theory that "*wit is playful judgment*." Beginning with a complicated deduction on the nature of aesthetic freedom, he goes on to conclude that wit grows out of aesthetic freedom, and "wit is nothing but a free play of ideas."

* Theodore Lipps, writing in *Beitrage zur Aesthetik* ("Komik und Humor," 1898), formulated an "*expectation theory*," claiming that wit is the subjective side of the comic; "in general we classify as wit every conscious and clever evocation of the comic, whether the comic lies in the viewpoint or in the situation." Lipps traces pleasure in the comic back to expectation, thus assuming—to a certain degree—unconscious processes. He accepts Herbert Spencer's theory (see p. 16), and Spencer's assumption of "descending incongruity"—an incongruity of which we become conscious when our attention passes from the great to the small. He offers as an example a row of small houses standing near a great palace, imitating the palace in miniature, one tiny house imitating a whole series of palaces. The comic effect, he explains, is attained by the contrast; the feelings are prepared for the perception of the great, and the difference between the imagined demand and the actual demand on them gives rise to the feeling of gaiety.

The "meeting of extremes" theory was promoted by Leigh Hunt (1784–1859) in *Table Talk* (1851): "Wit is the clash and reconcilement of incongruities, the meeting of extremes round the corner." Reconciling two extremes does not spell wit, even if the dubious process of appeasement (which, like crime, does not pay) takes place "round the corner." Hunt's idea is merely a reformulation of theories made familiar by earlier authors, and is equally unilluminating. But he did create a good term for laughter; he calls it "happy convulsions."

The "I'm ashamed of my ancestors" theory of laughter can be found in the *Essays* of George Eliot (1819–1880), in her article on "German Wit, Heinrich Heine" (pp. 82–83): "Strange as the genealogy may seem, the original parentage of that wonderful and delicious mixture of fun, fancy, philosophy and feeling, which constitutes modern humour, was probably the cruel mockery of a savage at the writhing of a suffering enemy—such is the tendency of things toward the better and more beautiful."

The "sympathy theory" takes as its polemical point of departure the passage in *Ecclesiastes VII*, 6: "As the crackling of thorns under a pot, so is the laughter of a fool," countering with Thomas Carlyle's: "Laughter means sympathy; good laughter is *not* the crackling of thorns under the pot." Voltaire made a similar statement long before Carlyle: "In laughter there is always a kind of joyousness that is incompatible with contempt or indignation" (*L'Enfant Prodigue*). Once more one asks why sympathy should produce precisely laughter. The more logical reaction would be a helping hand. It is true that certain jokes are based on sympathy (Freud's "saving of expenditure of pity"); these humorous productions comprise but a small percentage of all humor and require a separate explanation (see Chapter Five).

* *The "overflow of nervous energy" theory,* highly renowned in the last century, was the work of Herbert Spencer (1820–1903). The theory was first published in *Macmillan's Magazine,* in March, 1860. It is physiologically-neurologically oriented. Nervous energy, active within any part of the nervous system, must escape through one of three channels: first, channels leading to other nerves not directly connected with the motor apparatus; second, motor nerves leading to muscular activity; third, efferent nerves (leading from the central nervous organ outward) leading to the viscera. The deduction is thus based on the "overflow" principle: if any one of the three means of escape is blocked, the open route or routes must carry a greater amount of energy than normally carried, while, if any one of the three routes is found adequate for the escape of the nervous energy present, the other routes will not be used.

In laughter, Spencer declares, the nervous energy escapes via habitual channels: the speech apparatus and the respiratory mechanism. If these channels do not suffice to carry off the amount of energy present, the entire body is convulsed.

Spencer accepts the concept of incongruity as a basis for the ludicrous, but insists that the incongruity must be "descending"; if there is "ascending" incongruity, only the reaction of wonder appears. In Spencer's definition, therefore, the ludicrous must present a situation in which we are keyed up for something great, and are confronted with something small.

The facial involvement in laughter is also explained by this theory: the "habitual channels" for the escape of energy in laughter end in the mouth and the nose, "the mouth first becoming active because the muscles are small and easily moved."

The "primeval fall from grace" theory of laughter comes from the author of *Fleurs du Mal.* According to Charles Baudelaire (1821–1867), "le sage . . . n'a jamais ri." Only *after* loss of innocence does laughter occur, because laughter arises from the feeling of superiority over our fellow men. Laughter itself is contradictory; it is characterized both by "grandeur infinie" and "misère infinie." Baudelaire's conclusion, as stated in "De L'Essence du Rire" (1869), reads: "C'est du choc perpetuel de ces deux infinies que se dégage à rire [The constant collision of these two infinites produces laughter]."

* *Charles Darwin's "we don't know" theory* is the most cautious of them all, past and present. Darwin (1809–1882) claimed, in *The Expression of*

the Emotions in Man and Animals (1872), that we cannot understand why the sounds expressive of pleasure take the particular reiterated form of laughter, but we can readily see that they should be as different as possible from those screams which express distress. The facts are in accord with this logic, Darwin finds, for expressions of distress take the form of cries in which the expirations are prolonged and continuous and the inspirations short and interrupted, while pleasure is expressed by sound in the production of which short and broken expirations together with prolonged inspirations are used.

In the animal kingdom, Darwin reports, "vocal and instrumental sounds are employed either as a call or as a charm by one sex for the other; they are also employed as the means for a joyful meeting between parents and their offspring, and between the attached members of the same social community."

Darwin calls the smile "the first stage in the development of the laugh." He accepts Spencer's theory, and cites the case of soldiers "who after strong excitement from exposure to extreme danger were particularly apt to burst into loud laughter at the smallest joke." He states further that the reaction of laughter is widespread in all races as an expression of satisfaction, although it is sometimes supplanted by mimicry; some primitive peoples express pleasure by actions suggestive of eating, or of the satisfaction of hunger. But when laughter expresses an emotion other than joy or happiness, it is used in a secondary and "forced manner" in order to conceal other emotions: anger, shame, shyness, derision, contempt.

The theory of "two contradictory propositions" was expounded by Léon Dumont (1837–1876) in *Des Causes du Rire.* He finds that the laughter-provoking situation arises when one is confronted with a duality: a single proposition must then be simultaneously affirmed and denied. The ludicrous object then presents itself as both possessing and not possessing a given attribute. The spectator's pleasure is derived from the intellectual activity involved in realizing the contradiction between the two propositions.

Dumont's theory was promptly attacked by Charles Leveque in his study, *Le Rire* (Revue de Deux Mondes, 1863). Objecting that it is impossible to affirm and negate at the same time, Leveque advanced his own deduction, the "*theory of duality.*" Though laughter may occur *when both* affirmation and denial are called for, the laughter represents *either* acceptance or negation, as in laughter at a dwarf who stoops to go through a doorway. The laughter still regards him as a dwarf even though he has behaved like a giant. (Compare Pascal's statement: "Nothing produces laughter more [readily] than a surprising disproportion between that which one expects and that which one sees.")

Leveque therefore stipulates his own duality: appreciation of a contradiction and an affective response to it. As postulated, the sequence of events is cognitive appreciation, followed by affective response. He puts the accent on intellectual activity, and invokes the manes of Aristotle by quoting, "Se sentir agir librement, forcement, est un plaisir."

* *The "degradation theory"* was introduced by Alexander Bain (1818–1903). In his book, *The Emotions and the Will* (1888), Bain states that one of the causes of laughter is triumph over an enemy; the general setting for laughter, in his opinion, is the fact that after "a fit of activity, when our work is done, we need to let off steam, and this is done by spasmodic outbursts of laughter." Laughter is thus intimately related to the pleasure following victory.

Bain distinguishes two elements in laughter: a feeling of superiority, and a sudden release from constraint. He claims that the degradation of the enemy, an essential in the ludicrous, is attenuated in humor, for humor must possess an air of the "genial and loving"; here the element of degradation is "as it were, oiled." He defines comedy as the light treatment of topics or objects which (or who) are mean and low but had previously been dignified. Basically, he accepts Spencer's theory.

The "liberty-theory" of A. Penjon is closely related to the Aristotelian echo in the Leveque statement quoted above. Penjon regards liberty (which he considers essentially pleasurable) as *the* cause of laughter ("Le Rire et La Libertè," *Revue Philosophique*, 1893). His theory bears an interesting resemblance to K. Fischer's deduction on wit as the outgrowth of aesthetic freedom (see p. 15).

Penjon describes our life as hedged in by constant restraints; the revolt against these produces the joy expressed in laughter. Thus, killing the tyrants around us (unfortunately he does not specify whether they are inner or outer tyrants) is the basis of laughter. Unfortunately, too, Penjon does not pursue the idea; he drops it for a series of banal comments like the following: Laughter is produced whenever the normal course of events is suddenly interrupted without arousing an intense emotion. After these banalities, however, comes another revealing insight, though this one is naively expressed. Children, he declares, laugh more readily than adults because adults have become inured to "laws of nature" and are not so easily struck by the bizarre, the novel, or the uncanny. Finally, Penjon suggests that laughter may be traced to the pleasure of satisfied hunger, "since this is the most universal source of satisfaction among men."

Penjon was also the first, I believe, to record the observation (since then generally acknowledged): "S'il est une chose au monde dont on se soucie peu, c'est de savoir en riant pourquoi on rit [If there is one thing in the world which we hardly trouble ourselves about, it is knowing—while we are laughing—why we are laughing]."

Eastman dug up a quotation from Lord Shaftesbury's (1671–1713) essay, "The Freedom of Wit," published in 1711, which anticipates Penjon, though it refers to external factors:

> The natural free spirits of ingenious man, if imprisoned or controlled, will find out other ways of motion to relieve themselves in their constraint; and whether it be in burlesque, mimicry, or buffoonery, they will be glad at any rate to vent themselves, and be revenged on their constrainers . . . 'Tis the persecuting spirit has raised the bantering one.

One also sees connections with Bain's "degradation theory"; moreover with Charles Renouvier's (1815–1903) *theory of "deliverance from the constraint of rationality,"* described in *La Nouvelle Monadologie* (1899):

> One sometimes sees, on the face of the person who laughs, uncertitude and astonishment. He seems for a moment to make an effort at attention, in order to find a reasonable meaning in the thought that is offered to him. This being impossible and recognizing that the unreason is voluntary, he feels that it is not the moment to make sense, and releases himself. This release of the reason translates itself physiologically by laughing. The reasonable animal, the same as the risible animal . . . in playing the fool, escapes for a time from the constraints of the rational faculty, and experiences a joy of deliverance in going outside of its normal laws and producing nonsense.

John Dewey seems to have endorsed this theory in 1894 in his "Theory of Emotion," where he defined laughter as "a sudden relaxation of strain." According to the philosopher, it marks "the attainment of unity" after a period of expectancy and suspense.

The "Hobbes plus" theory of Harold Hoeffding (*Outlines of Psychology*, 1891) accepts the Hobbesian position, but triumphantly points out that Hobbes left one angle unaccounted for. In Hoeffding's opinion, Hobbes' "one-sidedness consists in not inquiring whether the sense of power which breaks out in laughter does not sustain essential changes and acquire a different character, according to the nature of the specific occasion." Thus, pure superiority may be colored by sympathy; in the latter case humor arises.

Otherwise, Hoeffding's deduction is a blend of many theories: Hobbes plus Penjon plus injection of the "instinct of self-preservation" into laughter. Blend or not, the sum total of the deduction amounts to very little; as in so many other of the attempts at explanation previously mentioned, the basic question is circled but never approached, and we still do not know why the specific reason ("liberty" or "self-preservation" or "superiority" or what not) produces the specificity of the reaction—laughter. One cannot but suspect that many authors have been so eager to find a theory which would distinguish them from their precursors that their success in turning up a difference blotted out all interest in the main question, why laughter is produced.

The "fountain of sound sense" theory of George Meredith (1828–1909) impresses one as a return to the seventeenth-century controversies on the meaning of comedy rather than as a modern theory of laughter. The conclusion that comedy is a fountain of sound sense is neither illuminating nor new, but his statement that the comic spirit requires only "situation" and no "accessories" is of interest:

> Comedy is a game played to throw reflections upon social life, and it deals with human nature in the drawing-room of civilized men and women, where we have no dust of the struggling outer world, no mire, no violent crashes, to make the correctness of the representation convincing. Credulity is not wooed through the impressionable senses; nor have we recourse to the small circular glow of the watchmaker's eye to raise in bright relief minutest grains of evidence for the routing of incredulity. The comic spirit conceives a definite situation for a number of characters, and rejects all accessories in the exclusive pursuit of them and their speech. For being a spirit, he hunts the spirit in men; vision and ardor constitute his merit; he has not a thought of persuading you to believe in him. Follow and you will see. But there is a question of the value of a run at his heels.

The "oscillation theory" of laughter was formulated by Ewald Hicker (*Physiologie und Psychologie des Lachens*, 1873), and reads: "Comic feeling consists of a rapid oscillation between pleasure and pain." The theory is a more modern version of Joubert's outdated physiological assumptions (see p. 5f.).

E. Kraepelin's *"unexpected intellectual contrast" theory* assumes that in a conflict of feelings one feeling—that of pleasure—wins out (*Zur Psychologie des Komischen*, 1886).

W. Wundt (1832–1920) *elaborated* on and *combined the "oscillation" and "contrast" theories* mentioned above. His conclusion, in his famous work, *Grundzuege der Physiologischen Psychologie*, reads:

> In the comic the separate ideas which enter into a totality of perception or of thoughts are partly harmonious and partly contradictory either to each other or to the manner in which they are united. Thus arises an oscillation of feelings, in which, however, the positive side, the pleasure, not only prevails, but gains the mastery in a particularly strong way, because it is, as all feelings are, increased by immediate contrast.

The theory of "lack of fundamentality in contradictions" in laughter, suggested by Camille Melinard ("Pourquoi Rit-On," *Revue De Deux Mondes*, 1895), stressed the contention that ludicrous perceptions leading to laughter presuppose not only appreciation of a contradiction, but simultaneously and especially the realization that this contradiction is *not* fundamental.

Melinard adduces the example of a man who forces open an unlocked door: first, we appreciate the contradiction between the open door and the waste of effort; second, we realize that the man's error is based on his subjective conviction that the door is really locked, and therefore we remind ourselves that we would have done the same thing in similar circumstances. The ludicrous thus presupposes a situation which is absurd when viewed from Vista No. 1, but perfectly natural when seen from Vista No. 2. In general, Melinard believes that when one is confronted with the new or the absurd, the attempt to classify the situation within a familiar category leads to the pleasure of rediscovering rationality.

* *The "minimal-touch" theory* was presented by Stanley Hall and Arthur Allin in "The Psychology of Tickling, Laughing and the Comic" (*American Journal of Psychology*, Vol. IX, 1896). Tickling, which is considered the prototype of laughable situations (children, for example, often refer to the ticklish zones as "funny places"), is taken as the point of departure. In primitive organisms the sense of touch is the beginning and end of sensation; the senses of smell, sight, hearing, which all develop later, are but "anticipatory touch." Even later minimal touch impressions represent the oldest stratum of psychic life. This accounts for our sensitivity to tickling, itching and other tactile impressions. Then we read:

> The substitution of joy for fear in overcoming of childish fears is one distinct element in the very manifold causes of laughter, because it again widens the range of the soul's activity instead of contracting it as does pain.

Thus, laughter is considered an expression of a primitive state of mind; it implies a cruel quality, excited by misfortune or by the unconventional or exceptional. A sense of superiority (Hobbes) is always included in ridicule.

Going on to an explanation of wit, the authors assume that "wit is shock reduced to almost its faintest terms, and is related to it somewhat as the tickle sensations of minimal contact are related to the more definite forms of touch." Two factors are essential, suddenness and lightness:

> Culture and practice consist largely in inhibiting irrelevant reactions. By anticipatory suppression of these, the attention foresees its way and economizes energy. Wit, however, because it touches the soul in an unexpected zone, evokes a clotted mass of reflex movements of the mind, perhaps not unlike a first experience before the will has suppressed needless reactions. The intermittence of inhibition for the mental area thus unexpectedly invaded is thus analogous to partial psychic decapitation.

* *The "mechanization" theory* of Henri Bergson (1859–1941), developed in *Le Rire* (1901) has been in vogue for a long time. The formula: "the ludicrous is something mechanical encrusted on the living", has become a

slogan. The theory is so important that it will be dealt with in a separate chapter (see Chapter Seven).

The "play-mood" theory of laughter, suggested by James Sully (*An Essay on Laughter*, 1902), assumes that the enjoyment of the laughable is rooted in a sudden arousing of the play-mood, and involves that refusal to take the situation seriously which is the characteristic feature of play. Far-reaching conclusions are deduced from this idea that reality can be viewed as a game. One searches in vain, however, for a passage explaining how this "play-mood" is achieved, or where it comes from. The objection that children take their play seriously more often than not, is not touched on.

The "goodness of the environment" theory of laughter has as its optimistic author Horace M. Kallen (1882–). Writing in The *American Journal of Psychology*, Vol. XXII, 1909, ("The Aesthetic Principle in Comedy"), Kallen declares that laughter has a function similar to the appreciation of beauty, namely, "the directly felt goodness of the environment." How and why, by what means and whose grace this benevolent look at the world is accomplished is not stated, aside from the following reference to the earliest laugh: "the well-fed, replete, resting child repeating in its contentment the pleasurable movements of sucking." If our equilibrium is disturbed and subsequently restored, the restoration is marked by laughter, Kallen states. Laughter, he believes, is a satisfactory adjustment to disharmony; at bottom it is the "frustrated menace of things"which causes laughter.

* *The "anti-annoyance" theory* of William McDougall (1871–1938) was originally stated in aphoristic form in *Nature* in 1903, and later enlarged in "The Psychology of Laughter and Comedy." Its basis is the denial that laughter is an expression of pleasure. McDougall claims that laughter-provoking situations are all unpleasant, and would be actively annoying if they were not laughed at. This is in contradiction to the scores of theories which see laughter as a proof of joy. The entire misunderstanding began, McDougall declares, when the smile and the laugh were identified; they should be differentiated, since only the smile is a sign of pleasure.

Posing the question, "What does laughter do for us?', McDougall enumerates laughter's physiological advantages, such as stimulating respiration and circulation, heightening the blood pressure, increasing the flow of blood to the brain. As for the psychological advantages, laughter produces euphoria by interrupting every train of thought and every sustained activity, physical and mental. According to the author, laughter arises in situations which would otherwise be unpleasant; the ludicrous consisting of those minor misfortunes of our fellow men which would excite sympathetic pain in us if we did not laugh. Laughter is Nature's antidote for the sympathetic tendencies.

In later years, McDougall accepted a biological theory of laughter: "There is some special differentiation of instincts which finds expression in playful activity." This differentiation came about in this manner: In order to develop into a social being, it became necessary for man to foster and strengthen his sympathetic tendencies; these, however, would render him "liable to suffer a thousand pains and depressions upon a thousand cases of mishap to his fellows. [As countermeasure] Nature endowed Man with the tendency to laugh on contemplation of these minor mishaps to his fellow-men, and so made of such mishaps occasions of actual benefit to the beholder."

The "rationalization-theory" of laughter is a rather shamefaced attempt on the part of E. F. Carritt ("A Theory of the Ludicrous," *Hibbert Journal*, Vol. XXI, 1923) to justify the moral right to laughter. He defines the comic as the ugly; the pleasure one derives from the comic is attributed to the pleasure of expressing or feeling dissatisfaction. What, then, distinguishes laughter from any other form of disapproval? And why is this dissatisfaction expressed specifically in laughter?

The "gymnastic exercise" theory of laughter (G. W. Crile, *Man and Adaptive Mechanism*, 1916) sees in laughter a stimulation to motor activity of "some kind." Laughter results when the stimulated motor activity is for some reason interrupted or checked. Thus, the value of laughter as an adaptive mechanism is that of a "gymnastic exercise" which "clarifies the body," just as the original motor activity would have done if it had not been interrupted.

The "two-types-of-laughter" theory of George Dumas (*Traité de Psychologie*, 1923) is based on the question:

> What is the origin of the excitation which manifests itself in laughter? One cannot answer this question without first making a distinction, too often ignored, between the laugh which expresses the general excitation of pleasure and the laugh which expresses the pleasure of the comic.

Dumas stresses two childhood situations conductive to laughter: sudden relaxation of restraint and sudden appearance of some pleasing presentation. Otherwise, he accepts the theories of Spencer, and Bergson, Darwin and Sully.

* *The "instinctive enjoyment" theory* of laughter was promoted by Max Eastman (1883–). His formula reads: "Unpleasant experiences *playfully* enjoyed" (*Enjoyment of Laughter*). The theory assumes a biological substratum, and leaves the transformation-mechanism untouched: "The mechanism of comic laughter may never be explained."

Eastman's book contains highly critical polemics on the theories of Hobbes, Bergson, Freud. His own theory is built on the Kantean and Aristotelian assumptions, combined in a novel blend. His wrath is aroused by any statement which claims that laughter contains derisive and aggressive elements. In an earlier book, *The Sense of Humor*, (Scribner's, 1922), he goes so far as to assume that the unsympathetic or ungracious elements in laughter are but pollutions of it, and not inherent in it. He accuses many authors of "confusing laughter with the act of scoffing" (p. 16).

Eastman's theory has a commonsense appeal which is fascinating as well as fashionable; because of its interesting attacks on Freud and its relative novelty, it will be discussed at length in a separate chapter (Chapter Seven).

The theory of "interrupted love reaction" as the laughter-provoking agent was presented by J. Y. T. Greig in *The Psychology of Laughter and Comedy* (1923). In a rather unclear manner, Greig offers a melange of Sully's, Freud's, Havelock Ellis' and Spencer's assumptions on laughter. His investigations begin with observations made on infants, and arrive at the conclusion that the prerequisite for laughter is the presence of a second person. Following Havelock Ellis, he considers tickling a stimulation related to an erogenous zone. He uses the word "love" in an all-inclusive sense, so that it becomes the equivalent of an emotional relation in all its derivatives. The earliest emotional experiences are the touch experiences of sucking. He accepts Freud's assumption of the genesis of the smile as the reaction of the satiated nursling.

To explain the development of laughter, Greig adduces Havelock Ellis' assumptions on the relation of the respiratory excitement to tumescence and detumescence, and also Herbert Spencer's "overflow" theory. He concludes from these assumptions that laughter arises when a love reaction is momentarily interrupted. Thus, laughter in either child or adult is at bottom an expression of displeasure. Tickling is again brought into the picture to explain the paradox, since (as stated) tickling involves an "intermittent tactual stimulation of an erogenous zone." The intermittence is produced by the fact that the love-reactions stimulated by touch are repeatedly interrupted by fear and pain:

> When behavior containing love with it is interrupted, energy is mobilized against the interruption; when the interruption is suddenly removed, or weakened, some of this energy becomes surplus and escapes in the laugh.

Greig's statements seem to indicate his belief that laughter tends to appear when the transition between two parts of ambivalence occurs; one is led to this interpretation by his explanation of hate reactions, as in laughter at the obscene: man's general reaction to woman is ambivalent, and when this reaction is interrupted in any way, laughter is the result.

The "relief-theory" of laughter was presented by J. C. Gregory in *The Nature of Laughter* (1924). The laughter of children, Gregory states, originally includes cruelty, and becomes "humanized" only gradually. (See

La Fontaine's statement: "Children are without pity;" from *Fables*, 1617.) Though laughter may take many forms, all these aspects have one common denominator: relief. The primitive form is the "sheer unsophisticated laughter of pure relief," observable in children free from a condition of tension. (This opinion owes much to Spencer.) Playful tickling arouses laughter because here a reaction acquired for the originally serious purpose of evading a threatened attack is used in a play situation, thus relaxing tension. In general, Gregory does not consider laughter a direct expression of pleasure, but an expression of pleasure incidental to a feeling of relief, or a feeling of deliverance.

"Relief," as Gregory interprets it, is so all-inclusive that even laughter based on freed repressions is subsumed under this sweeping heading. There are times when his book even gives the impression that he is trying to rewrite Freud—on the conscious level.

The "perception of unreality" theory of laughter of Herbert Barry ("The Role of Individual Differences in the Sense of Humor," *Journal of Genetic Psychology*, Vol. 35, 1928) is introduced by the recital of deductions arrived at by observing two test objects. It concludes:

> Topics which are capable of evoking a humorous reaction in an individual seem to be frequently loaded for that individual with an unpleasant emotional affect. . . . It seems probable that the humor is due to a change of affective tone of the original perception from unpleasant to neutral and pleasant.

The change is attributed by Barry to a perception of the unreality of the unpleasantness when it is presented in the form of a humorous story.

The "extension theory" of laughter was suggested by C. W. Kimmins (*The Springs of Laughter*, 1928). Although this theory makes no new contribution, it does cast light on phenomena already described by adding to the body of observations on children and to the body of statistical data. Kimmins echoes nearly verbatim Dumas' theory of two kinds of laughter.

> The laughter of young children can be clearly shown to be of two kinds, the laughter of pleasure in the well-being of the child, especially at the completion of any experiment successfully performed; and the laughter of amusement at comical incidents.

More important are his statistical data:

> The misfortunes of others as a cause of laughter rise to a high proportion at the age of seven and afterwards gradually decline: With children of seven years of age, about 25% of the boys' stories, and 16% of the girls' are of this nature. At eight years of age there is a decrease to about 18 and 10% respectively. At nine and ten years there is further very considerable reduction, and beyond the age of ten the proportion is negligible.

All this adds up to quite an optimistic view of adult malice.

The "relax in safety" theory of laughter, originated by Donald Hayworth ("The social origin and function of laughter," *Psychological Review*, Vol. XXXV, 1928), denies that laughter is the cause of joy or joy the cause of laughter. Laughter is simply "a vocal sign to other members of the group that they may relax in safety." Hayworth gets into hot water when trying to fit the laughter aroused by intense misfortune into this definition, and admits the flaw in his theory.

A sister-theory, promoted five years earlier by H. C. McComas (*Psychological Review*, Vol. XXX, 1923) views laughter, in addition, as some kind of "information"; it is a means of communicating joy.

The "theory of pure sociology" in laughter outlined by E. Dupreel in his "Problème Sociologisme du Rire" (*Revue Philosophique*, 1928) is so exclusively sociologically oriented that the author classifies the theories of Bergson and Sully as "half-sociological." Dupreel asserts that there are two kinds of laughter. The first is the laughter of companionship (the prototype for this being the substitution of laughter for cries of woe and distress when the infant, "deserted" by his mother for a moment, sees her reappear, and the later manifestation being pleasure at the solidarity of a group). The second is the laugh of exclusion (when this is based on race bias, one could call it a "restricted area" laugh). The latter corresponds to derision of the excluded. These variations are attached to Dupreel's general approval of Bergson's view of "mechanization" as the cause of laughter.

The "good-old-times" theory of laughter stems from a good humorist, Stephen Leacock (1869–1944). In *Humor, Its Theory and Technique* (1935) he writes:

> Our laughter originated then, it would seem, long before our speech as a sort of natural physical expression, or outburst, of one's feeling suddenly victorious. It was a primitive shout of triumph. The savage who cracked his enemy over the head with a tomahawk and shouted, "Ha, ha," was the first humorist . . . It seems a far cry to this primitive humor, and yet it is surprising how easily we slip back into it. It had never been quite civilized out of us. Even if we no longer find the triumph of active destruction a "funny" sensation, we can certainly get fun out of the imagination of it. Compare, for example, Bret Harte's famous account of the breaking up of the scientific society organized at the Stanislaus Mining Camp—how, in the middle of a paleontological discussion:
>
> Then Abner Dean of Angel's raised a point of order when
> A chunk of old red sandstone took him in the abdomen,
> And he smiled a kind of sickly smile, and curled up on the floor,
> And the subsequent proceedings interested him no more.
>
> . . . The Romans liked to see a chariot and its occupants smashed in the circus; we prefer to see a clown fall off a trapeze . . . The original humor was expressed by actions, not by words. It was, and is, represented by progressive gradations, as victory, cruelty, teasing, horseplay, hazing, practical jokes and April Fool . . .

Humor in its highest meaning and its furthest reach is that which does not depend on verbal incongruities, or on tricks of sight and hearing. It finds its basis in the *incongruity of life itself.* The contrast between the fretting cares and the petty sorrows of the day and the long mystery of the tomorrow. Here laughter and tears become one, and humor becomes the contemplation and interpretation of our life. (pp. 8–15, my italics)

The "two contradictory social situations" theory of laughter, elaborated on by Ralph Piddington (*The Psychology of Laughter*, 1933) reduces laughter to a social problem, and thus follows in the footsteps of Dupreel and Bergson, though remaining independent of either. The theory does, however, show some similarity to the ideas put forward by Dumont. According to Piddington:

The ludicrous essentially involves two contradictory social evaluations and it follows that the laughter which it arouses is essentially a socially conditioned reaction. Elementary laughter might be said to express an attitude of complete satisfaction with things as they are. This reaction, by a process of social conditioning, comes to be aroused by the ludicrous, which we have seen to involve a socially disturbing situation . . . By laughing we adopt an attitude which from our infancy has expressed an attitude of complete satisfaction with things as they are; by adopting this attitude we inhibit any tendency to change in our social system of social evaluations . . . Laughter at the ludicrous, then, arises fundamentally from the multiplicity of social evaluations and the possibility of conflict between them. . .

In its complete one-sidedness, Piddington's theory over-emphasizes and over-extends the secondary uses to which laughter can be put. The static-conservative element in his deduction is amazing as is the meager advantage derived from his phenomenal knowledge of the literature. However, Piddington's appendix to *The Psychology of Laughter*, a critical compilation, covering nearly the entire literature on the topic, is a first-class piece of scholarly work.[9]

* *The "show-teeth" theory of laughter*, originated by A. M. Ludovici (*The Secret of Laughter*, 1933) is a melange of Hobbes revived, Adler resuscitated, and violent emotions traceable to no particular author. It starts with this amazing statement: "I am going to suggest that there is something sinister in laughter." After a prolonged polemic against the social

[9] Such experiences are not unusual. When, for example, a witty man writes a joke book or a dictionary of quotations, the results are not necessarily witty by any means. Finding some humorists' wit very taking, I have bought their books or anthologies, only to be disappointed by finding them the most boring compilations of banalities ever put between covers. Thus, Woodrow Wilson was not quite right when he stated: "I would not trust a saturnine man, but I would trust a wit." Two laudable exceptions should be mentioned: *Dictionary of Humorous Quotations* by Evan Esar (Doubleday, 1949) and *Little Book of Aphorisms* by F. B. Wilcox (Scribner's, 1947). Both are first-rate compilations.

requirement of laughter, the author introduces the term "to show teeth" as a synonym for "to laugh," and explains that it denotes "superior adaptation."

"Superior adaptation" is borrowed, as Ludovici states, from one Dr. Wrench; "show teeth" is derived from Darwin's statement that in laughter "the upper teeth are commonly exposed." From the combination, Ludovici concludes:

> Animals show teeth only when they wish to warn a fellow, a foe, a man, of pursuing certain tactics too far . . . "Here are my weapons; if you come any nearer, if you pursue these hostile tactics, or carry even the present ragging too far, I shall use them on you!". . . To display teeth, therefore, is to make a claim of superior adaptation. (p. 70)

The eulogy of Hobbes is combined with Adlerianism to justify the suggestion that laughter may be "neurotic compensation":

> . . . there seems to be the danger that laughter is becoming no more than one of the many anodynes with which modern men are rocking themselves into a state of drowsy insensibility.[10] (p. 115)

The two Charlie Chaplin theories on laughter are reported by Max Eastman in *The Sense of Humor* and the *Enjoyment of Laughter*. The theories are many years apart, since the first book appeared in 1922 and the second in 1936. In Eastman's first interview with Chaplin, the comedian reduces laughter to a "shock" which brings home to people "the sanity of a situation which they think is insane." Chaplin exemplifies with a scene from one of his screen comedies in which he slaps a woman for having given him a contemptuous look. What he does is really right, says Chaplin, and though the spectator refuses to admit it, he does laugh, because the action is right. In short, laughter grows out of "making people conscious of life."

The second, later, statement is in a different vein. In it, Chaplin agrees with Eastman that humor is playful pain. According to Chaplin, the spectator at one of his comedies often feels sympathetic to him, despite his laughter. "The minute a thing is over-tragic it is funny."

[10] The amount of polemical heat generated by theorists on laughter fighting among themselves can be gauged from the fact that Ludovici attacks Eastman's theory in terms like these: "Mr. Eastman . . . whose one anxiety is to purge laughter of every trace of unpleasantness . . . In fact, so anxious is he about this one object, that he does not mind in the least how confused and incoherent his arguments become." (p. 65.) Eastman retaliates by calling Ludovici's theory "fantastic." His wrath is especially provoked by Aldous Huxley's endorsement of Ludovici: "A first rate piece of work—the completely satisfying hypothesis." Eastman's reply: "That Aldous Huxley permits himself to be quoted on Mr. Ludovici's jacket to the effect that his is 'the best hypothesis' must be put down as one more evidence of the irresponsibility of the literary mind."

It is interesting that a man who intuitively knew[11] only too well how to make people laugh, and showed real genius in applying this knowledge, should have so limited an opinion on the reasons for laughter. The first statement refers to external reality exclusively; it makes out of laughter a purely social problem where, at best, social hypocrisies are debunked. This presupposes a topsy-turvy world in which the originality of the comedian, revealing the "insanity" of social customs, evokes laughter in his audience. The second statement refers to over-compensation of pity and the saving of pity; it echoes McDougall's theory that laughter has the exclusive purpose of immunizing against pain.

The two statements are hardly illuminating, aside from their illustration of the fact that it is a far cry from intuitive knowledge of a phenomenon to the ability to understand or describe it. What Chaplin overlooks is an element of profound importance: In creating pitiful and helpless human beings in his wonderful screen sketches and comedies, he offers himself as a living example of the extent to which the inner masochism in the spectator could reach—provided he were the figure depicted. The spectator laughs an "*out-distancing laughter*."

The "will-to-laugh" theory, stated aphoristically and with pseudo-humor by Edward Frank Allen in the Introduction to *The World's Best Jokes* by Lewis Copeland (1941), simply claims that the joke as a general phenomenon, and almost all individual jokes as well, originated in the dark dawn of human history when mankind first developed the will to laugh. No doubt the caveman, he declares, inquired, "Who was the lady I seen you with last night?" and was assured "That was no lady; that was my wife." The joke, still evoking laughter after untold centuries, persists both in its original text and in paraphrases; a well-known paraphrase sets the scene under water, with two sharks as protagonists. In this version, the query runs: "Who was that lady I seen you with this morning?" and the answer is: "That was no lady; that was my breakfast."

Well, the "will-to-laugh" explains nothing, not even where this "will" came from.

The "roar-of-triumph in an ancient jungle duel" theory of laughter, repeated in not so new wrappings by Albert Rapp (*The Origins of Wit and Humor*, 1951) assumes that human laughter originally grew out of aggression, and only aggression. This can be compared with Leacock's previously quoted statement. It is also reminiscent of George Eliot's "I'm ashamed of my ancestors" theory (see p. 15), or the statement by J. C. Gregory (see p. 24f.): "As laughter emerges with man from the mists of antiquity it seems to hold a dagger in its hand."

[11] This ability seems to have been lost by Chaplin as time progressed; his last creation, *Limelight*, is pitifully non-comical.

In addition to these echoes, Rapp makes use of a watered-down version of the Freudian mechanism of repression (confusing it with suppression) in order to explain some witticisms. As compensation, he meticulously refers to Freud as *Mr.* Freud. He does not hesitate, in spite of his borrowing from Freud, to stigmatize Freud's theory on wit as "confused and contradictory." His attempt to clarify the distinctions between wit, humor and the comic is limited to criticism of that triad as a "hopelessly absurd classification" of Continental origin; humor, to him, always means "ridicule plus love."

The book is unduly and unnecessarily popularized and sometimes devastatingly naive; nevertheless it contains two points which can boast of tangential merit. Disinterring a once over-quoted query from Sir Thomas Browne's *Urn-Burial*—"What songs the Sirens sang, or what name Achilles assumed when he hid himself among the women, although puzzling questions, are not beyond all conjecture"—is one point; the other is his attempt at a breakdown of one hundred current unprintable jokes. His findings, as far as the latter project is concerned, are: 60 sexy jokes, 12 jokes about denuding the female, 10 scatological jokes, 8 penis reference jokes, 10 unclassifiable.

* * *

The extensive literature on laughter conveys the impression that the main differences among non-analytic authors center around these strategic points:

1. They cannot agree on whether laughter is of a pleasurable nature or not (see Plato, Descartes, et al. versus McDougall).

2. They cannot agree on whether laughter is an inborn instinct or an individually acquired ability (see Eastman and McDougall versus nearly all other authors).

3. They cannot agree on whether or not laughter contains aggressive components (see the phalanx Plato-Hobbes-Bergson-Ludovici et al. versus Voltaire-Eastman).

4. They cannot agree on whether laughter contains moralistic notions of betterment or appears spontaneously (see divergence between the theories of Ben Jonson and those of Dryden, etc.).

5. They cannot agree on terminology: wit, the comic, grim humor, self-derision, humor are constantly confused.

6. They cannot agree on whether a theory on laughter must explain (in addition to the causes of laughter) the "transformation of energy," or whether it is permissible to delegate this question to posterity and future research (Spencer-Freud versus many authors, notably Eastman).

7. They cannot agree on whether the utilization of laughter for social purposes is secondary or primary (the latter theory is promoted by Bergson, Dupreel and Piddington).

8. They cannot agree on whether laughter is a purely aesthetic problem (Jean Paul Richter, Theodor Lipps, K. Fischer, Th. Vischer, et al.) or a psychological one.

9. They cannot agree on whether laughter is an exclusively human attribute (nearly all authors versus Darwin, Eastman).

10. They cannot agree on the reasons and the mechanisms which produce laughter, and therefore they produce innumerable theories which by and large magnify one aspect of the problem, mistakenly taking it for the essential.

11. They cannot agree on the mood which precedes a belly laugh: Bergson declares that all emotion must be absent, Greig that laughter essentially involves emotion, Eastman that "you must be in a playful mood," etc.

12. Last but not least, they cannot agree on whether the unconscious plays any role in laughter at all (Freud versus nearly all authors).

* * *

Freud's theory on wit, first published in 1905, is an outgrowth of and sequel to his studies of dreams. Freud was struck by the similarity between "dream-work" and "wit-work." His investigations on wit, which followed, introduced a new element into the literature on the subject; whereas writers on aesthetics had previously dealt with wit as a subdivision of the comic, Freud reversed the process, claiming autonomy for wit. Freud states repeatedly, in developing his theory, that he feels on firm ground only in his investigations of wit; his conclusions on the comic are much more tentative.

Freud begins by investigating the different techniques which are applied in wit:[12]

a. *Condensation with substitutive formation in "mixed words";* example, Heine's words, put into the mouth of one of his pitiful characters: "Rothschild treated me just like an equal, quite *famillionaire.*"

b. *Condensation with modification and substitution;* example, "I was driving with him tête-à-*bête.*"

c. *Wit formed by word division;* example, a red-headed and uncouth young man, claiming to be a relative of Jean Jacques Rousseau, was characterized by the hostess at a party as "homme roux et sot, mais pas un Rousseau."

d. *Manifold application of the same material;* example: a baptized Jew made an anti-Semitic remark and was told: "I am familiar with your *ante*-Semitism, but your *anti*-Semitism is new to me." Or: Traduttore—Traditore; Amantes—Amentes.

e. *Double meaning and play on words (allusion);* example: "This satire would not have been so biting had the author of it had more to bite." (Heine.) Or (from Horatio Winslow's *A Tale of Two American Generations*): Gold mine—gold spoon—gold cure (for alcoholism). Or a physician's statement about a female patient: "I do not like her looks," and the husband's rejoinder: "I have not liked her looks for a long time."

f. *Ambiguity;* example: Heine's dictum about a complaisant lady, "She could pass nothing except her water." (The German word "abschlagen" means both "refuse" and "pass water.")

[12] "Wit and Its Relation to the Unconscious," *Gesammelte Schriften* IX. Internationaler Psychoanalytischer Verlag, Vienna 1925.

Freud remarks on the peculiar tendency to economy and condensation in wit, adducing Hamlet's words;

. . . the funeral baked meats
Did coldly furnish forth the marriage tables.

Continuing the breakdown of techniques, we come to

g. *Puns;* example: "The play was so poor that the first act had to be re-written." To which the punster replied: "And now it is re-rotten."

h. *Displacement;* example: Two people of rather primitive habits meet near a public bath. "Have you taken a bath?" asks one. "How is that?" replies the other, "Is one missing?"

i./j. *Nonsense and absurdity as technical means.* A witticism often presents an outer face of nonsense; further scrutiny proves that "sense lurks in such witty nonsense, and that this sense in nonsense transforms nonsense into wit." Example: "Never to be born would be best for mortal man."—"But," added the sages of a humorous publication, "hardly one man in a hundred thousand has this luck."

It is never clearly stated, but one gathers the impression that Freud accepts only "nonsense which makes sense" as humorous production. In other passages of *Wit*, Freud seems to assume that for the child the pleasure in nonsense is derived from the absence of the restrictions of the subsequently imposed reality principle.

k. *Sophistic faulty thinking*, a technique which differs from displacement or absurdity. Example: A gentleman entered a shop and ordered a fancy cake, which, however, he soon returned, asking for liqueur instead. He drank the liqueur and started to leave. The shopkeeper stopped him. "What do you want of me?" asked the customer. "Please pay for the liqueur," asked the shopkeeper. "But I gave you the fancy cake in exchange."—"Yes, but you haven't paid for that, either."—"Well, neither have I eaten it."

l. *Automatic errors of thought.* A person who reacts the same way to a succession of similar situations will continue in the identical vein on the next occasion, even when the reaction is inappropriate and contrary to his intentions.

m. *Unification*, which is analogous to condensation by compression into similar words. Example: "The French poet J. B. Rousseau wrote an ode to posterity (à la posterité). Voltaire, thinking that the poor quality of the poem in no way justified reaching posterity, wittily remarked, 'This poem will not reach its destination.' " Unification is the technique of repartee.

n. *Representation through the opposite*, substituting a "yes" for the "no" which rightly belongs there. Example: "While Duke Karl of Wuertenberg was riding horseback, he met a dyer working at his trade. 'Can you color my white horse blue?'—'Yes, Sire, if the animal can stand the boiling.' "

o. *Outdoing-wit.* "Here 'yes' which would be proper in the reduction, is replaced by 'no,' which, owing to its context, is equivalent to a still stronger 'yes.' " The same emphasis results when the case is reversed, and the contradiction takes the place of an exaggerated confirmation. Example: Lessing's epigram, "The good

Galatea! 'Tis said that she dyes her hair black, yet it was black when she bought it." There are connections with irony.

p. *Indirect expression with allusion.* Examples: "The girl barely twelve *modes* old" (Lichtenberg; the witticism replaces the calendar yardstick with the fashion-yardstick). Or the story of the two sharp business men who exhibit their own portraits hung side by side, until a visitor asks: "And where is the Savior?" (Allusion to the two thieves crucified with Christ.) Or "every fathom a queen," substituting for the Shakespearian standard of inches in "every inch a king" the six-foot standard of the fathom, in order to suit the voluminousness of the lady referred to.

q. *Omission.* Omission represents condensation without substitutive formation. Example: "When X (a satiric and bellicose writer, repeatedly the target of physical attacks by his opponents) hears this, he will receive another box on the ear." Omitted is: "then he will write such a caustic article that . . ."

r. *Representation through trifles and minutiae.* Example: The physician in attendance at the confinement of a nouveau riche's wife disregards her cries of distress while they are elegantly expressed in French, but rushes in when she starts to use the more familiar vernacular.

s. *Comparison.* This technique is frequently combined with the absurd, anal or obscene. Examples: "Until at last the buttons tore from the pants of my patience" (Heine). Or: "It is a pity that one cannot see the learned bowels of the writers in order to find out what they have eaten" (Lichtenberg). Or (Lichtenberg again): "Every person has also his moral backside which he does not show except under the stress of necessity and which he covers as long as possible with the pants of good breeding."

t. *Peculiar attributions.* Example: Lichtenberg's remark on certain odes, "They are in poetry what Jacob Boehm's immortal writings are in prose—they are a kind of picnic in which the author supplies the words and the reader the meaning."

After reviewing the twenty techniques of wit, Freud subdivides wit into two groups: *harmless wit* and *tendency wit.* The latter gives access to two otherwise repressed tendencies—the lewd and the hostile.

Freud states that the technical means of wit technique (condensation, displacement, indirect expression, etc.) are the sine qua non for the production of wit. This is his Axiom No. 1; his second axiom is that the character of wit depends on the mode of expression, and has *the purpose of evoking pleasure in the listener.* In general, wit works on the principle of economizing psychic energy; its purpose is to produce pleasure. Adducing repressed tendencies (aggression, sexual precursors connected with the element of the forbidden), Freud demonstrates that the pleasure in wit corresponds to the extent of the *economy of psychic expenditure* thus achieved. Repressed material is freed (for in listening to a joke, the responsibility is shifted to the narrator); the psychic energy required for repressing the objectionable is released and transformed into explosive laughter.

When psychic energy is in this way diverted from its use in the cathexis of some paths, and freely discharged, Freud explains, the pleasure attendant upon the witticism has been virtually presented to the listener. A considerable expenditure of psychic energy would have been required for the creation of the witticism spontaneously; an equal expenditure would have been needed to equalize the force of suppression or repression of the inhibition. The extent of the listener's pleasure matches the extent of his economy of psychic energy. The cathexis used in the inhibition has been neutralized and made superfluous because the forbidden idea came from the outside and was merely overheard; it can therefore be discharged through laughter. The listener devotes to his laughter the amount of psychic energy which was freed by the suspension of inhibition cathexis. In other words, he laughs away exactly that amount of psychic energy.

The example of tendency wit shows that "forepleasure" corresponds to the "alluring premium"—"with the aid of a small sum of pleasure a very large and almost inaccessible amount is obtained."

The "formula for wit-work" reads: "A fore-conscious thought is left for a moment to unconscious elaboration and the results are forthwith grasped by the conscious perception."

It is interesting that Freud's text in *Wit* should contain a precise description of the importance of aggression,[13] an acknowledgment not pursued further by Freud in the two decades which followed. It is probable that Adler's naive stressing of conscious aggression, at that time one of his points of departure from psychoanalysis, contributed to Freud's too protracted concentration on libido exclusively. Only in the latter part of the nineteen-twenties did Freud revert to the importance of aggression; he then worked out its unconscious tributaries and made it into an equal partner of libido in the id.

Freud views the *comic* as topographically different from the witty; the location of the comic production is the *preconscious*, not the unconscious. Freud deduces this from the absence of typical wit-devices (condensation, displacement, unification, faulty thinking, and so on). The comic is unlike the witty in its social behavior; the comic requires only *two persons*—the one who finds the comical, and the one in whom it is found—while in wit the third person is indispensable for the pleasure-bearing process.[14] Moreover, one *makes* a witticism, but merely *finds* something comical. The comic is found first of all in persons; only later, by a process of shifting is it seen in objects, situations, events. The comic often serves wit as a facade to replace fore-pleasure.

The subdivision of the comic that is most closely allied to wit is the

[13] The details will be elaborated on in subdivisions of Chapter Four dealing with cynical, obscene and aggressive witticism.

[14] The most important contribution of Theodor Reik was the proof that the third person is necessary to diminish the sense of guilt in the narrator.

naive. The naive cannot be simulated or manufactured; the naive originates when one puts oneself completely outside of inhibition, denying its existence for oneself. What conditions the function of the naive is the listener's concession that the inhibition does not exist in this case; without this concession the reaction would be indignant rejection of "such impudence."

The naive is mostly found in children and uneducated adults. Freud illustrates the naive by a theatrical performance put on by some children. In their drama, a husband leaves home to look for treasure and remains away for years. When he returns with a big bag of money, his wife brags: "Nor have I been idle in the meanwhile," and exhibits the results of her industry—twelve dolls, representing twelve children. . . . The question, says Freud, is simply whether we assume the producer of the naivete intended to make a witticism, or whether we concede that he wished to draw an earnest conclusion, one which he held in good faith but which was faulty because he was ignorant of the real interconnections. In all cases of production of the naive, the listener or spectator imagines himself in the actual psychic state of the producer, and tries to understand that state by comparing it with his own. *This putting ourselves into the psychic state of the producing person and comparing it with our own results is an economy of expenditure* which we discharge through laughter.

Freud suspects that this process of putting oneself into the psychic process of the producing person (resulting in economy of psychic expenditure)—a process which is completely foreign to wit—is paradigmatic for the comic in general. Whereas *wit* has "*a kernel of word-pleasure and nonsense-pleasure and a shell of removal-and-release pleasure*," the pleasure in the *comic* seems to derive from the *difference in expenditure which is the result of our effort to understand the other person.*

The comic, Freud claims, appears primarily as an *unintentional* discovery in the social relations of human beings. It is found in movements, shapes, actions, characteristic traits of persons, and (later on) in their mental qualities. Even animals and inanimate objects can be personified and become comical. However, the comic is not inextricable from the person in whom it is found; if the condition under which an individual becomes comical can be ascertained, the "comic situation" is discovered. A person can then be made comical ("a figure of fun") by thrusting him into a situation in which the conditions essential to the comic are bound up with his actions. A person can be turned into a "figure of fun" in order to make him appear contemptible, or to deprive him of his claims to dignity and authority. These hostile or aggressive tendencies use several means to achieve this end: shift to *comic situations*, *imitations*, *disguise*, *unmasking*, *caricature*, *parody*, *travesty*, *etc.*

The comic originates from a wide-spread source. Freud approaches this aspect of the problem by asking why we laugh at the actions of clowns; their grimaces and antics appear immoderate and inappropriate to us, and thus we are really laughing at the sight of an excessive expenditure of energy. There is a parallel outside the sphere of the artificially comic, when the condition, while not contrived, is favorable; we do not find the child comical even if he jumps and fidgets, "but it is comical to see a little boy or girl follow with his tongue the movements of his pen-holder when he is trying to master the art of writing; we see in these additional motions a superfluous expenditure of energy which under similar conditions we save." The same applies to exaggerated or hyper-expressive motions of adults. (Freud is obviously thinking of gesticulation.) Freud then adduces the example of the motions made by the bowler after he has released the ball; he follows the ball's course as though he were still able to control it.

The next step in the deduction is a physiological argument. The impulse to echo with movements of one's own body arises when one perceives another's motion; the subsequent substitution for this impulse is the idea of the echo, through memory traces of the expenditure of energy necessary for similar motions. Hence, we are conscious of the surplus in the first impulse; if the other person fails to make the substitution, his extravagance of expenditure appears comical when compared with our theoretical economy of expenditure.

"Ideational mimicry" is based on this principle. People who are given to mimicry are apt to raise their hands high when referring to a mountain, to lower their hands to the ground when referring to a dwarf, etc. If they do not make use of gross motor movements, the equivalent commentary on their words is supplied by the placing of the voice, twitches of the eyebrows, and so on. In any case, the ideational mimicry presupposes two tendencies: that of automatic (though inhibited) imitative motility, and that of putting oneself in the place of the person observed. In observers of such immoderate motion, the surplus is inhibited in statu nascendi, and stands free for further use, or discharge in laughter.

Comparing this "discharge of the surplus" at the sight of movement so immoderate that it becomes comical, with the comical nonsense stammered by a candidate at an oral examination, Freud deduces that the unconscious processes in these two situations are exact opposites. The candidate is economizing in expenditure at a time when the listener considers full expenditure indispensable, "for nonsense and foolishness are nothing but inferior functions . . . In the first case I laugh because he makes it too difficult for himself, and in the latter case because he makes it too easy for himself." As to the comic effect, it is obviously only a question of the difference between the expenditure involved in the two cathexes—the one of empathy, and the other of the ego—and not of the direction in which this difference inclines.

Freud thus arrives at the conclusion that the origin of pleasure in the comic lies in a comparison between the other person and one's own self, with respect to the difference between the *empathy expenditure* and *one's own expenditure*. The "feeling of superiority" does not enter at all; comic seems always to refer to the person experiencing the comic. (Freud appears to regard the other person merely as a catalyst.) In what Freud calls the "comic situation" this is even clearer. We laugh, he declares, when we admit to ourselves that the antics we are viewing would have been our antics in the identical situation. The element of the comic here derives from the relationship of the individual to the frequently all-too-powerful outer world. This powerful outer force is represented by the conventions and requirements decreed by society, and even by the individual's bodily needs. A typical example of the latter symbolism is the situation of a person engaged in an activity which fully occupies his mind, who is "suddenly disturbed by pain or an excremental need."

"Comic of expectation" arises as a special case of ideational mimicry, to which is added a real investment in expected expenditure. "If I am expected to catch a ball thrown at me, I put my body in states of tension in order to enable me to withstand the collision with the ball, and the superfluous motions which I make if the ball turns out to be light make me look comical to the spectators. I allow myself to be misled by the expectation to exert an immoderate expenditure of motion."

Caricature is the comic intentionally produced. Freud adduces the fact that the feeling of superiority does not appear in the spectator who is viewing self-caricature for humorous purposes, "and this furnishes a good new proof that the comic is independent in principle of the feeling of superiority." There are two typical techniques in caricature: degradation by inordinate emphasis on one feature, or manipulation of a comic situation. The latter is accomplished when a person of "dignity," regardless of his personal qualities, is put into a situation which proves his dependence on external circumstances.

In the practical joke, this transformation is real indeed, as when a dignified person is deliberately tripped and made to look clumsy and flustered. The transformation can also be effected by making a merely credulous person appear stupid because he innocently takes the nonsense told him at face value; it can be simulated by means of a speech or a play. The comic situation is an aid in aggression, as is the comic in general; the element of aggression serves to make the comic pleasure independent of the realities of the comic situation (which may, objectively, be pitiful). Because of this, there is no real defense against the danger of being turned into "a figure of fun."

Imitation is another technique of the comic, although its theory is more difficult to explain. Freud takes issue with Bergson on this point (see p. 193f.) because of Bergson's failure to touch on the problem of economized expenditure. According to Freud, caricature, parody, travesty and unmasking are all directed against objects who command authority, and are popularly believed (on a greater or lesser scale) to be exalted in some sense. The procedures mentioned above tend to degrade. In this connection Freud quotes Alexander Bain's *The Emotions and The Will*: "The occasion of the ludicrous is the degradation of some person of interest possessing dignity, in circumstances that excite no other strong emotions." The "exalted" is equivalent to "the great": psychic greatness, like somatic greatness, is always connected with increased expenditure, which is reduced by the comic effect.

The process of unmasking works by calling attention to human frailties in general, but most particularly by revealing the dependence of the mental functions upon physical needs. Freud exemplifies with the joke (already mentioned) about the new-rich lady in labor whose physician disregards her cries of "Ah, mon Dieu!" but knows she means business when she starts screaming, "A-a-a-ai-e-e-e-e-E-E-E." Frequently wit and the comic are united in such circumstances.

Freud comes to the conclusion that the child "lacks all feeling for the comic . . . This sentence seems to say no more than that this comic feeling, like many others, first makes its appearance in the course of psychic development . . . It is easy to see that it cannot be otherwise, if our conception is correct, that the comic feeling results from a difference of expenditure produced in the effort to understand the other."

Freud assumes that "certain pleasure motives of the child seem to be lost for us grown-ups, but as a substitute for these we perceive under the same conditions the 'comic' feeling." The child laughs "out of pure pleasure"; his motives are clear and assignable. If, for instance, someone slips on the street and falls, the adult will laugh because the impression—though he does not know why—is comical. In the same situation, the child laughs because of a feeling of superiority or out of joy over someone else's calamity. In effect, the child is saying, "You fell, but I didn't." Freud conceives of the comic as a means of regaining "the lost infantile laughter." It could be put this way: "I always laugh at a difference between my expenditure and someone else's *when I discover the child in the other person.*" Freud's formula reads, therefore; "He does it this way; I do it differently; he does it just as I did when I was a child." The comparison between the ego of the grown-up and the ego of the child results in laughter.

Freud's final conclusion is that there should be some revision of Bergson's tentative theory that the comic has some connection with childish pleasure and play. "It is enough," Freud declares, "if it touches the childish nature in general, *perhaps even childish pain.*" (Italics are mine.)

Humor is the only subdivision of the sense of humor in general in which Freud undertook to explain both the psycho-oeconomical and the metapsychological factors. (The former was dealt with in *Wit*, 1905; the latter in a short study entitled "Humor," in 1928.) In my opinion, his interpretation of the psycho-oeconomical factor is indisputable, his metapsychological deduction very dubious (see Chapter Seven, pp. 201f.).

The difficulties begin with so apparently simple a matter as terminology. The term, "humor," as Freud uses it in German, is by no means the equivalent of the English counterpart. Freud's term refers to a series of *painful* emotions transformed in a manner that produces pleasure. Two phenomena, therefore, must be explained:

a. What enables the afflicted individual to achieve this transformation?
b. What enables the listener and spectator to view this transformation as pleasurable and enjoy it?

In 1905 Freud answered the second question only. The spectator's pleasure is made possible by the *economy of expenditure of affect.* Instead of feeling pity, for example, at the miserable lot of the victim, the observer saves cathexis when he realizes that the victim himself is not taking the situation too tragically. Examples are "humor of the gallows and grim humor." If the condemned man, on his way to the gallows, says, "This week is beginning well," the prerequisites as stipulated by Freud are all present.

Humor is the "most self-sufficient of the comic forms"; all its processes can be exercised in a single person. Its localization is the foreconscious.

The forms of humor vary according to the nature of the emotion which is economized on; an unconscious saving on the expenditure of sympathy, anger, pain, compassion, etc. will result in humor. Freud draws attention to the fact that some of Mark Twain's stories are based on this type of psychic production. He adduces several Mark Twain plots: one is the story of how his brother, working for a road construction company, was caught in a premature explosion and blown high in the air, landing far from the place where he was working. At this point, Freud notes, the reader's reaction is sympathy and concern, but the story-teller cuts this reaction short with an unexpected twist: the brother lost half a day's pay for being absent from the place where he worked.

Another Mark Twain story, of the same type, is again about his brother. The brother once dug a hole, furnished it with a bed, a lamp and a table, covered it with a large piece of sailcloth which had a hole in the middle, and took up residence in this underground home. That night a cow fell through the roof on to the table and extinguished the lamp. The brother helped to hoist the cow to the surface, cleaned up the damage and rearranged his home. The next night, again, the cow fell through the roof. And again the night after, and then every succeeding night. At this juncture the story is comical because of the repetition, Freud comments, but the humorous reaction becomes unrestrained when Twain relates that on the forty-sixth night his brother finally remarked that this was beginning to become monotonous. The reader, Freud explains, "had long expected to hear how the brother would express his anger over this chronic misfortune. The slight humor which we draw from our own life we usually produce at the expense of anger instead of irritating ourselves."

After stating that humor is "one of the highest psychic functions, enjoying the special favor of thinkers," Freud attempts some kind of explanation of the first, still unanswered question: What enables the victim to transform pain into humorous production?

If this displacement is to be solved, it should be considered as a defense process, psychically related to the flight reflex, which has as its purpose the task of guarding against pain originating in inner sources. The defense process is a species of automatic adjustment, therefore, which in itself tends to become harmful unless controlled by conscious thinking. Humor is one of many defense functions, and the loftiest of them. Unlike repression, it does not smother the painful idea, but finds a means of withdrawing the energy from the painful emotion, and "through discharge changes the same into pleasure." It may be, Freud declares, that the connection with the infantile provides humor with the apparatus for this change. For in childhood we are all profoundly pained by circumstances which as adults, looking back, we find laughable. A humorist laughs at his *present* pain, his displacement, announcing that he is "too big to have these causes affect me painfully,"[15] testifies to the evaluation of his ego, achieved through comparison of his present ego with his infantile ego. "This conception is to some extent confirmed by the role which falls to the infantile in the neurotic processes of repression."

Obviously, Freud was not quite satisfied with this deduction, since he took up the problem again in 1928, in the study entitled "Humor." Attempting to clarify the *metapsychological* aspect of humor, he begins by dividing it into two types: humor directed against oneself, and humor commenting on the behavior of others. He finds the basis of humor in a hypercathexis of the superego; although otherwise a stern master, in humor the inner conscience seems to play a consoling role, pointing out to the frightened ego: "Look, this is the world which seems so menacing. It's

[15] Adlai Stevenson's quotation from Lincoln, in his speech conceding the 1952 election to President Eisenhower, aptly illustrated the point as well as the process of displacement itself: "I feel like the little boy who stubbed his toe in the dark; I'm too big to cry and it hurts too much to laugh."

child's play, just worth joking about!" Apparently, Freud recognized that this statement in some ways contradicted his previous assumptions concerning the superego, for he added that there was still much to learn about the structure of the superego.

Freud concludes his book on *Wit* with these sentences:

> We have concluded that the pleasure of wit originates from an *economy* (saving) *of expenditure in inhibition*, pleasure in the comic from an *economy of expenditure in thought*, and that of humor from an *economy of expenditure in feeling*. All three modes of activity of our psychic apparatus derive pleasure from saving psychic expenditure. All three methods have one point in common: they represent ways of bringing back from the psychic activity a pleasure which has been lost in the development of this very activity. For the euphoria which we are thus trying to attain is nothing but the state of bygone times in which we were accustomed to accomplish our psychic work with a minimum expenditure. It is the state of our childhood, in which we did not know the comic, were incapable of wit, and did not need humor to make us happy. (*Gesammelte Schriften*, IX, p. 269)

Wit and Its Relation to the Unconscious is a difficult book; the American editions, translated by the eminent Dr. A. A. Brill, pioneer of analysis in this country, are easier reading than the original, because of Dr. Brill's introduction of subdivisions into the chapters. He also substituted American equivalents for many untranslatable witticisms. But Freud's book by no means deserves the epitheta disornantia bestowed upon it by Max Eastman, who declared: "Freud has chosen a method of exposition which would leave his reader in a state of refined doubt and madness" (*The Sense of Humor*, p. 190). Whatever the method of presentation chosen by Freud, the book is rich with fine observation, and represents a first-rate example of *fruitful* scientific research. It illuminated, for the first time, a defensive sector of that dark continent, the unconscious.[16]

[16] The analytic literature on all types of humorous production is numerous and especially unenlightening; it is mostly of a confirming nature. This is particularly notable in the vain attempts to reconcile the superego's cruelty with its allegedly benevolent role in humor. The very few valuable analytic studies on wit, the comic, and humor will be mentioned later in the course of the discussion of these topics.

2. The Three Triads of the Individual Pre-History of Laughter

Don't be afraid; I won't eat you.
Common saying in nearly all languages.

IN RE-READING Freud's book on wit fifty years after its original publication, one is struck by two impressions: admiration for the basic principle expounded—the freeing of counter-cathexis and its transformation into laughter—*and* surprise at the long way psychoanalysis has traveled since the first years of the century. How uncomplicated is the description of the psychic mechanism of wit in *Wit and Its Relation to the Unconscious*! A reservoir of repressed wishes, a force holding down that forbidden material, an externally provided alibi which for a split second renders the internal "army of occupation" superfluous—with these three instrumentalities, the whole problem of wit is expounded.

Still unknown, still undiscovered by Freud in 1905 were the interplay of the three psychic provinces: id, superego, unconscious ego; the assumption that there is a duality of instincts, Eros and Thanatos, that they fuse and defuse in clinically visible libidinous and aggressive tendencies; the existence of pre-Oedipality; the whole gamut of inner defense mechanisms, including psychic masochism.

One other vital factor was to remain unknown for a longer period of time—the matter of the power exercised over the total personality by the superego. Having an understandable predilection and a sentimental attachment for his first great discovery, that of the existence of repressed libidinous wishes within the dynamic unconscious, Freud never undertook the task of clearly elaborating on the superego's fantastic power. Early in his researches he clarified the existence of a benevolent ego ideal; subsequently he introduced the term "superego," and gave it a connotation of stern, even malevolent opposition to the ego; he repeatedly though reluctantly spoke of the superego's irrationality and cruelty. But never did Freud precisely and unequivocally stipulate and describe the connection between ego ideal and superego. The result has been a truly over-dimensional confusion among his disciples with respect to the unconscious conscience. The majority of analysts still believe that the superego is some kind of inner mentor, a friendly guide whose sword is drawn only if Oedipal wishes are at stake. It is difficult to understand how this can be reconciled with such of Freud's statements as the following:

> The superego seems to have made a one-sided selection, to have chosen only the harshness and severity of the parents, their preventive and punitive function,

while their loving care is not taken up and continued by it. (New Introductory Lectures on Psychoanalysis, pp. 89–90.)

Or this quotation from *Civilization and its Discontents*:

What methods does culture use to inhibit counteracting aggression, to neutralize the latter, or even to exclude it? . . . This can be studied in the development of the individual. What is done in order to render his lust for aggression harmless? The method is very strange, and at the same time very obvious, although we did not guess it. *The aggression becomes introjected, internalized*; finally it is returned to its place of origin, hence *directed against the individual's own ego*. There it is absorbed by one particular sector of the ego, the superego, which is counterposed to the other parts of the ego. Now, *"conscience" exhibits towards the ego that identical severe readiness to aggression which the ego would have liked to expend on an outside individual*. We call this tension between the severe superego and the subjected ego "feeling of guilt"; it manifests itself in the need for punishment. (p. 100, *Gesammelte Schriften*, XII, 1930, my italics)

Observations pointing in this direction are not frequently met with in the body of Freud's work, but they cannot be dismissed.

Twenty-three years ago, Dr. Ludwig Jekels and I presented a joint study in the Vienna Psychoanalytic Society; this study was an attempt to correlate Freud's newer findings with the previously outlined and still unclarified structure of the superego.[1] The following year we applied these precepts to the theory of dreams, in a paper read before the XIII International Psychoanalytical Convention in Lucerne.[2] The ideas contained in these two papers were enlarged and partly modified years later, and presented in my books, *The Battle of the Conscience* (1948) and *The Superego* (1952).

Since the decision in a scientific controversy is not the result of a majority vote pro or con, it is impossible to determine to what degree a scientific idea is accepted—or if it is accepted at all. Fortunately for the freedom of scientific research, such problems are not licensed for investigation by a chorus of "ayes." But it does not require particularly shrewd observation to realize that in the case in question there is neither wide popularity nor deep penetration.

A brief account of my personal viewpoint, therefore, is necessary here.

In my opinion, the unconscious conscience is an internal dictator, all-powerful and all-pervasive, dedicated to *torture for torture's sake*. It is not to be confused with conscious conscience, that compendium of cultural restrictions communicated to the child by the educators and accepted by him via identification. Both conscious and unconscious conscience, it is

[1] Published under the title "Transference and Love," *Imago*, XX, 5–32; 1934; American translation in the *Psychoanalytic Quarterly*, 8, 325–350; 1949.

[2] Published under the title "Instinct Dualism in Dreams," *Imago*, XX, 383–392, 1934; American translation in the *Psychoanalytic Quarterly*, 9, 394–414; 1940.

true, are possessed of the power to veto, but these vetoes are radically different in both direction and purpose.

The superego is an inner monster created and enthroned by the child himself. Its beginnings can be traced to the long period of motoric helplessness in infancy, when the child's aggression—quantitatively identical, at least potentially, to that of an adult—cannot find satisfactory outlets and is therefore channeled in the wrong direction, against himself. There is no possible cultural solution for this problem, contrary to the currently popular notion that "avoiding all frustration" could prevent the child's latent aggression from erupting. The child's frustration is complex and not simple; he is resenting both a libidinous and a megalomaniacal offense, and there is no way of eliminating megalomaniacal frustration. In the child's misconception of reality, he is the center of the universe, autarchic and supreme; the very fact that other people exist is a blow at this cherished fantasy and must produce fury and aggression.

The child's aggression, backfiring against himself because his only available outlets—crying, vomiting, spitting—are pitifully insufficient, accumulates within him, and this store of self-directed aggression is a vital factor in his first fumbling attempts to cope with external difficulties.

At approximately the age of two the child develops an ingenious device for the purpose of maintaining all possible vestiges of the most cherished of infantile fantasies—that of his alleged omnipotence. The child identifies with the restrictions laid down by his parents, and thus substitutes an *internal* taboo for the long list of *external* taboos he has been subjected to. The end result remains the same—restriction; the difference is the direction of the restriction and the elimination of the offense to his megalomania. The child's identification with authority reinforces whatever is left of his old illusion of omnipotence and, by eliminating punishment, eliminates further attacks (from that particular sector) on this valued illusion.

The composition of the ego ideal, therefore, consists of the child's original, indestructible megalomania, (subsequently watered down to "narcissism" and self-love), plus an internalized body of parental prohibitions. The megalomaniacal element is quantitatively greater than the element of internalized taboos; the combination, though not homogeneous, holds firm even under stress.

It should be remembered that the ego ideal is not a direct copy of the parents, but an introjected picture of the parents "as the child perceives them." (This point has been admirably worked out by our English colleagues.) The child's image of his parents is a reality picture amended and intensified by the addition of his own projected aggression. Moreover, the ego ideal is not merely an introjected image of the educators, but is also a depository of the child's own narcissim. The effect of the latter sector is largely protective, but since it contains the child's braggadoccio—that highly vocal reflection of the child's original megalomania pertaining to future plans—it eventually becomes a rich source of unconscious self-torture, for one of the preferred preliminaries to unconscious self-punishment is contrasting the adult's actual achievement with the expectations of eminence so well advertised in childhood.

The second constituent of the superego is called Daimonion, a term borrowed from Socrates. Daimonion is the unconscious adversary within the human psyche, a force which attempts to bar the way to happiness, success, enjoyment of life, and which has as its purpose unhappiness, despair, and even self-destruction. Ironically enough, the ego ideal becomes an instrument in Daimonion's campaign of torture. Constantly and monotonously, Daimonion asks: "Have you achieved all the ambitions you promised yourself as a child?" The almost inevitable negative reply is the preamble to guilt.

As far as the ego is concerned, therefore, the creation of the ego ideal is a failure. The purpose of the ego ideal was to protect the ego from humiliation and loss of self-esteem; the result of the tactic was to provide the inner adversary with a supremely effective weapon.

There was one vital flaw in the child's otherwise brilliant idea. The tactic was designed to solve an external conflict; it made no provision for the equally serious, though unsuspected, internal problem. The external conflict was successfully neutralized; the tragic fact that success on one front intensified the difficulty of fighting on another could not have been foreseen —or helped. Nor can any subsequent tactic change the internal structure thus set up. Once the inner departments have been established, they cannot be altered or sealed off; the struggle must continue, throughout life, on the battlegrounds marked out in childhood.

Inner torture therefore persists; the individual's ego is granted no cessation of pain or humiliation. Since it is impossible to modify or withdraw the grandiose picture of the future painted in infancy, this once-confident promise of grandeur becomes the basis for Daimonion's daily torture. "You promised yourself you would be the greatest engineer in the world—and now look at yourself, you third-rater!" runs the unconscious taunt. The discrepancy between the glory prophesied and the mediocrity achieved is the measure of the severity of the punishment meted out by Daimonion.

Excuses are no more acceptable than attempts at modification of the original text. Realistic factors—economic, cultural or technical—carry no weight; they are rejected as arguments and punishment is imposed. And punishment it is, for Daimonion has the power to enforce its own laws.

The superego's constant barrage of reproaches is countered by the unconscious ego; it attempts to fight back with one or another defense mechanism. All these defense mechanisms are constructed on the principle of "accepting the guilt for the lesser crime," and submitting to punishment for the crime admitted. The term, "lesser crime," should not be confused with the "lesser crime" of the conscious moral or legal code, for the moral codes of the external and internal lawbooks are far from identical. Infractions or even illegalities which are "greater crimes" according to the conscious code can be used as *unconscious* alibis or defenses when the ego is accused of a crime which would be consciously classed as "lesser."

Among these inner defenses, one stands out: psychic masochism. The genetic picture of psychic masochism originates when the infant's libidinous wish is not instantly fulfilled, and the ensuing double frustration—libidinous and megalomaniacal—results in inexpressible fury. As we have seen in the description of the origin of the superego, fury which cannot be directed outward boomerangs, and is directed inward, against the individual himself. At an early age, aggression is channeled inward because of motoric helplessness; as the child grows older motor helplessness disappears, but in its stead comes a moral barrier which is, in its own sector, as effective in preventing the discharge of aggression outwards. This barrier is the triad of retribution which parents use to enforce educational restrictions—the triad of punishment, moral reproach and guilt.

Faced with this triad of retribution, children conform to a greater or lesser extent; as stated earlier, they identify with the parental prohibitions and thus retain some vestiges of the delusion of omnipotence. They also bask in the newly-bestowed accolade of "good boy" or "good girl." But this conformation cannot be complete, and there are children whose "identification" leaves large areas of rebellion and disobedience wholly untouched. There are no pleasurable accolades in the lives of these children, no "proofs" of omnipotence; there is only punishment, reproach, and guilt. But the human psyche cannot exist without "happiness" and pleasure, and therefore the child solves this difficult problem by libidinizing guilt and punishment. Psychic masochism is the technique of transforming consciously felt displeasure—namely, punishment—stemming from the internal torture machine, the superego, into unconscious pleasure.

Psychic masochism is the *unconscious* approval of—and desire for—rejection, humiliation and defeat. It nullifies punishment by transforming pain into satisfaction. The psychic masochist will provoke disappointment and refusal by his behavior, or by his misuse of an external situation (unconsciously identifying the outer world with the "refusing" pre-Oedipal mother). Since psychic masochism is the *crime of crimes* in the unconscious legal code, and the superego immediately vetoes this unconscious pleasure, the psychic masochist will promptly provide an alibi in the form of a lesser crime—pseudo-aggression. He will retaliate vigorously for the wrong done him; consciously he will be both unaware of the fact that the injustice was self-engineered, and convinced that his indignation is righteous and his action is in self-defense. But it is unconscious, not conscious self-defense that is his real purpose, for his pseudo-aggression is the only effective denial available to him when he is accused of psychic masochism by his superego. The final scene in this clinical picture of the psychic masochist is a bath of self-pity—"This can happen only to poor little me"—accompanied, again, by unconscious masochistic pleasure.[3]

I believe that the superego is *the* key to the theory and therapy of neurosis. This sentence is also the subtitle of my book, *The Superego*. It is impossible to reproduce in a few words the ideas set forth in the 370 pages of this study. I was once asked to provide a "short and sweet" formula to explain my opinion concerning the superego; my answer was: "Imagine a monster inside you, blaming *you*, and *you* exclusively, for everything that happens; imagine yourself completely at the mercy of this Frankenstein who dictates penance in the form of guilt, depression and dissatisfaction. Now you have an approximate idea of what the superego is like." I amplified by relating an incident amusing only at first glance, which hits the heart of the matter. A woman patient, a masochistic neurotic, was on the analytic couch when a short circuit extinguished the light fixture which was hung on the ceiling slightly to her left. She jumped up, very much disturbed, and in a frightened-apologetic tone exclaimed: "But I didn't do anything!" Without going into an analysis of this complicated joke, its connection with the transference, and so on, one can take it as a model of the superego's technique: if a stone falls from the roof of a building in China, the ego of a neurotic in New York is accused of complicity.

* * *

One must view the first one and a half years of the child's life as filled with inner fright and inner megalomania. At the beginning, the "danger" of the outer world is neutralized by ignoring its existence. In the long run, however, scotomization is not enough, and a peculiar "septet of baby fears" is built up. In analyzing the inner fears of adult neurotics, we are confronted with this prehistoric gargoyle: the infantile view of the mother as a witch who is capable of starving, devouring, poisoning, choking, chopping to pieces, draining or castrating him.

These fears have little or no connection with reality factors; in my opinion they are the outgrowth of the child's continuing struggle to maintain his infantile illusion of autarchy and to nullify reality's constant inroads upon that illusion. The struggle is marked by a series of concessions and reformu-

[3] For differentiation of genetic and clinical pictures in psychic masochism, see Foreword, footnote to p. ix.

lations; the first of these is the acknowledgement that "something outside of myself" does actually exist, but this "something" is seen as merely an instrument of the child's magical power. In a later concession, the infant further narrows his sphere of magical influence by moralistically dividing the world into the "good," which comes from himself, and the "bad," which comes from mother. This division into "good" and "bad" lays the foundation for the view of the mother as a threatening witch which characterizes the pre-Oedipal phase. A still later concession to reality, the long-deferred partial realization that the mother is loving and kind, marks the end of this phase of development.

The septet of baby fears is of sufficient importance in the unconscious life of the adult neurotic to warrant detailed discussion.

The fear of starvation arises from offenses to megalomania, which consist of enforced waits—perhaps of even a few seconds—for breast or bottle. Any waiting period is viewed as an insult by the infant; since moderation is unknown in megalomania, the accusation is starvation instead of tardiness.

The fear of being devoured has been clarified by the English school of psychoanalysis as a projection of the child's own aggressive designs upon the nipple or bottle. Instead of "I want to bite," the formulation becomes: "Mother wants to devour me."

The fear of being poisoned is a tacit acknowledgement that the fear of starvation is unfounded; the child shifts from his wholly untenable complaint to one which seems to him convincing: "Mother does feed me, but the food is poisonous and harmful."

The fear of being choked is a fantasy of being choked by the mother's breast or body. It does *not* have a reality basis, though this may seem plausible because of the disproportion between the mother's body and the child's. Neither do these fears grow out of the mother's or the nurse's clumsiness or abruptness in putting nipple or bottle into the baby's mouth.

The fear of being chopped to pieces originates in the baby's bewilderment and fear when confronted with the routines of washing and cleaning. The baby perceives these harmless manipulations as a procrustean bed fantasy. Again we see a fear for which a reality basis may seem plausible; again the fantasy of evil is imputed to the mother by the child *without* a reality basis.

The fear of being drained grows out of the infant's "helplessness" when he is seized by "propelling forces" in the elimination of urine and feces. The child feels that he is being "drained" by some mysterious force. Megalomaniacal and aggressive ideas connected with both products are his secondary retaliation.

The fear of castration is the climax of this septet of terrors. It carries over into the Oedipal phase, and is most clearly visible during this period. It is marked by further concessions to reality in the form of more or less rational disguises.

Countermeasures of course exist; the most effective of these is mother's love. Assuming, however, that the mother's love is lavishly bestowed, there still remains a crucial question: How is one to convince the immature bundle of fears that mother's intentions are loving?

We have reason to doubt the dictum that "every child understands mother's love." The child does come to understand it, but only after a way has been found to counteract the dreary septet of baby fears. Interestingly enough, *the mother's smile and the mother's laughter are among the most effective of reassurances and countermeasures.* Here is the paradoxical formula: *The meaning of the mother's smile, to the infant or baby, is "Don't be afraid, I won't eat you."*

To explain this paradox, we have to go back to the genesis of the child's smile. We have seen that a series of investigators have agreed that the source of the nursing baby's smile is his feeling of satisfaction when replete with milk. To recapitulate, here are some significant statements from a number of observers:

1. Erasmus Darwin (1731–1802), writing in *Zoonomia* (1794–6), clearly stated that the sphincter muscles of the mouth relax after the fatigue of sucking; this relaxation is visibly embodied in an infant's smile. Strangely enough, this common sense explanation of the genesis of the smile has been ignored by generations of scientists who followed the elder Darwin, even though they, in their turn, searched assiduously for "common sense" precepts which would clarify the problem. Even if they had not passed over Darwin's brilliant explanation, however, their progress from that point would have been negligible, since they have rejected the unconscious and its fears altogether. In the meantime, the popular interpretation of the infant's smile continues to be the succinct comment: "Gas."

2. W. Preyer, *Die Seele des Kindes* (Leipzig, 1884): This observer believes that the infant's smile is frequently misunderstood; the mere facial expression when smiling denotes little if the perception of the feeling of satisfaction is not added. In the first days of life neither the repletion of feeding nor the warmth of the bath produce a smile in the infant; they evoke only an expression of satisfaction. Should this expression of satisfaction be called a smile, however, then the infant smiles from the tenth day onward, even in his sleep. Preyer is inclined to believe that an inborn ability is involved.

3. Charles Darwin (see p. 17f.) noted that certain primitive peoples express pleasure by actions suggestive of eating.

4. A. Penjon (see p. 18) made the general suggestion that laughter could be traced to the pleasure of satisfied hunger.

5. Freud, in *Three Contributions to the Theory of Sex*, written in 1905, declared: "He who sees a satiated child sink back from the mother's breast and fall asleep with reddened cheek and blissful smile will have to admit that this picture remains as typical of the expression of sexual satisfaction in later life."

And in *Wit*, Freud asserts that the twists and contortions of the mouth that accompany laughter repeat the mouth-movements made by the nursing infant when, replete with milk, he relinquishes the breast. In the nursing infant, these motions are eloquently expressive of his determination to take no more milk. The smile may perhaps be traced back to this primal sense of pleasurable satiety. Subsequently, the smile remains the basic phenomenon of laughter, retaining its connection with pleasure, although the pleasure now is that of discharge.

6. Horace M. Kallen explains the earliest laugh as "the well-fed, replete, resting child repeating in its contentment the pleasurable movement of suckling." (See his theory of "goodness of the environment," p. 22.)

7. Erwin B. Holt, in *Animal Drive and the Learning Process* (Henry Holt, 1931), stated: "But if, when among its random movements, the child has got its own lips into the smiling position, the mother will *then* smile back to it (assuming that the child sees her), the child will soon learn to smile back at her. Since most mothers do return the infant's random 'smile,' most infants learn truly to smile."—After the word "position," Holt inserts this footnote: "Which I suspect to be the position of rest after nursing. See also Freud (*Three Contributions to the Theory of Sex*) and W. Preyer (*Die Seele des Kindes*, pp. 217–218); but Prof. H. M. Kallen is convinced, from observations of his own, that some factor other than mere rest is involved in this posture of the lips. For the child, of course, this posture has not as yet the significance of a smile."[4]

Personally, I agree with Erasmus Darwin and Freud: *the smile of the infant and baby is originally a facial expression resulting from the relaxation of the muscles employed in sucking. This facial expression follows the satis-*

[4] Professor Weston LaBarre refers to Holt critically in "The Cultural Basis of Emotions and Gestures" (published in *Personal Character and Cultural Milieu*, edited by G. Douglas, Syracuse University Press, 1949). Characterizing Holt as a "behaviorist," he concedes that Holt's tracing of the ontogenesis of the smile back to the relaxation of the baby's facial muscles when replete with milk may well be the case, *if* the smile is in fact a physiological expression of pleasure which subsequently becomes a part of a network of complex conditioned reflexes. But even if Holt is correct, Professor LaBarre continues, this cannot be the whole story, for the effect of colic in the child is sometimes a grimace which appears to be a smile of pleasure. Much the same *ad hoc* quality renders doubtful such explanations as the one which claims the smile to be phylogenetically a snarl. Another of Professor LaBarre's statements is apposite; he points out that physiologically conditioned and purely cultural responses, in varying mixtures, combine to create "the language of gesture" all over the world, and that it is often difficult to trace the influence of either response.

faction of hunger, and of the libidinous pleasure experienced in sucking—both pertaining to the infant's personal experience. Later this very same facial expression, when seen on the adult's face, is interpreted by the child to mean what it meant in his own experience, "I am not hungry, I will not eat you up." The identical phrase is a common cliche of facetious reassurance to a frightened person: "Don't be afraid, I won't eat you!"

By projecting his *own* experience, therefore, the infant and baby comes to understand that the smile is a "*No danger*" signal. This line of unconscious reasoning comes to the surface in the actions of some rather naive adults (and many children), who, in a fit of laughter, stroke their own (full) bellies.

In speaking of the generally poor results of permissive education, Anna Freud once pointed out that the child cannot be convinced by words alone; the child accepts as approval only the adult's *active* participation in the allegedly forbidden occupation. In the case of masturbation, for example, an attitude of verbal permissiveness means nothing, since "participation" is impossible.[5] The smile, which telegraphs the message, "I'm satiated, and therefore will not devour you," is quite another matter. Here "participation" is active and overt, and the result is genuine reassurance.

In dissecting the infant's smile, therefore, one finds a triad of elements: *the relaxation of oral muscles after sucking; the baby's own satiety experienced while producing this facial expression; the baby's interpretation of the mother's smile as a signal of "no danger"*—the mother will not devour him. The connotations of this triad explain why the transition from laughter to tears is so easily accomplished in infants, babies and very young children. At the beginning the reassurance is only tentative, and underlying terror derived from the ominous septet of baby fears is still great.

In general, investigators have overlooked, underestimated or misunderstood the role this triad plays in the complicated process by which the baby learns by experience that the exaggerated fears and projections of infancy and babyhood in *no* way correspond with objective facts.[6]

The indefinite line of demarcation between the baby's smile and the baby's tears (fear) has been noted by many observers. Hartley's and Hazlitt's statements to this effect seem to have priority; they date from 1749 and 1819 respectively. (See pp. 7 and 10.) Subsequent observers have confirmed this impression of the uncertain borderline between laughter and fear in small children. For example:

C. W. Kimmins, in *The Springs of Laughter:* "In learning to walk, the

[5] For further elaboration, see my contribution to the Symposium, *Theory of Therapeutic Results*, held at the XIV International Psychoanalytic Convention in Marienbad, August, 1936, (published in *Int. Journal of Psycho-Analysis*, London, 1937).

[6] Though starting from a different premise, Hall and Allin (see p. 21) mention "the substitution of joy for fear in overcoming childish fears."

child appears to delight in mishaps, such as sitting down with a thud during an interval of standing, as it gives rise to uproarious merriment . . . The 'jack-in-the-box' with its element of surprise, sometimes at the beginning with a slight sense of *fear*—so soon dissipated—is the starting point for a whole series of mirth-provoking games." (Author's italics.)

R. W. Washburn, in *A Study of the Smiling and Laughing of Infants in the First Year of Life* (Genetic Psychology Monographs, No. VI), conducted the well-known experiment of the "fifteen Yale babies." The experiment proved that the babies' mothers could tickle them into laughter fifteen times as often *as any stranger could.* If these babies did not react with a smile, they reacted with a direct opposite: "*withdrawing, whining, fussing or crying.*"

* * *

The original triad of elements which make up the baby's smile—the relaxation of oral muscles after sucking, the baby's own satiety, the perception of the mother's smile as a "no danger" signal—does not remain static. Comparatively early, there is a transition into another triad of facts, frequently observed and not less frequently misunderstood.

Kimmins correctly observed that children show signs of "uproarious merriment" at their own mishaps when learning to walk. To generalize this reaction, however, is to exaggerate it; such falls result in solemn bewilderment or tears as often as they do in laughter. Nevertheless, though laughter may be less frequently encountered on such occasions than Kimmins claimed, the phenomenon exists and needs to be explained. The explanation can be deduced from the attributes of infantile megalomania.

To recapitulate: the child begins life with an unvarying dual burden: his *subjective* illusion of autarchy and his *objective* passivity and complete dependence. From the very beginning of his life, objective and unyielding facts battle with his subjective fantasy, and he is forced into semi-recognition of facts, re-interpretations of reality as he perceives it, and successive reformulations of his fantasy. Thus, his original belief that nothing exists "outside of himself" is amended to become the conviction that everything "good" is self-produced, and everything "bad" a product of the outer world. Thus, the earliest of the septet of baby fears, which have no relation whatever to reality factors, are supplanted in later stages by more "sophisticated" fears in which certain objective facts are acknowledged. (It has already been noted that the fear of poisoning includes the tacit acknowledgment that the mother does feed the child, and is therefore a reformulation of the earlier fear of starvation.) In still later stages, the original fears of infancy are again reformulated: starvation is modified into refusal of love, kindness, or attention; the fear of being choked becomes a fear of confined places, etc.

Remote as the connection may sometimes appear, all these reformulations represent a slow and unwilling retreat from the infantile illusion of autarchy. Nor need the connection be remote, even in the adult neurotic; for example, the role played by infantile megalomania is immediately evident in the actions of the psychic masochist. When, in the first act of the psychic masochist's habitual drama, he *provokes* a crisis in which he will be unjustly treated, he is echoing the childhood reformulation with which he once rescued vestiges of his illusion of autarchy. His childhood provocation was proof of autarchy and a denial of passivity, and he derived pleasure from punishment because he had "*made them*" punish him, and again proved his all-power.

Precisely the same reformulation is used by the child who laughs at his own painful tumble. Mental sleight of hand can twist even a mishap into an intention: "I fell because I wanted to." The use of megalomania to sugar-coat a defeat is not at all unusual in adults; it is very common in children.

The megalomaniacal sweetening of defeat is not all. In the child, the "laughter of well-being" means that he does not accept external defeat, and that he is reassured by the familiar. In other words, such laughter indicates the absence of fear. The Yale experiment, which established that babies are more amenable to tickling by their mothers than by "strangers," is therefore quite consistent with theoretical deductions. This attitude, in which the familiar is recognized with a smile, remains paradigmatic throughout life. The language has a term for it: the "smile of recognition." Why a smile? If the smile is one of the earliest of the child's reassurances, the familiar (as long as it is not the familiarity of hatred or disgust) simply means that there is *no danger, and hence no fear*.

The reformulated second triad which now constitutes the smile therefore involves: infantile megalomania plus the reassurance provided by the familiar, plus a more generalized diminution of fear.

The child who is no longer an infant gradually begins to find that certain objects or events are "funny" (comical). The child's private code of the comic is not identical with that of the adult.

Careful observation of the child's laughter at the comic reveals that he now sees as "funny" what was originally frightening; he has now demoted the terrifying object or phenomenon to the status of the ludicrous.[7] This

[7] E. Kris, in *Psychoanalytic Explorations of Art* (Int. Universities Press, 1952), expressed his suspicion that the conclusion of Hobbes's famous sentence "infirmity in others, or our own formerly," is "more akin to Freud than any other psychologist"; he also assumes that in the comic "a fear signal, however faint, may take its place" (p. 209). Kris concludes: "When we laugh at the fool we never forget that in his comic fancy dress, with bladder and cap, he still carries crown and scepter, symbols of Kingship" (p. 213).

sequence of events—demotion of the "frightening" to the "funny"—is part and parcel of the developmental procedure of elaborating on one's fears and, at least consciously, overcoming them.

Two other elements are included in this procedure. One is the resort to *pseudo-aggressive attacks on the main upbringer*; the other is the scornful dismissal of him as "*stupid*" because he is not familiar with all the child's secrets.

The latter element can be directly observed in the analytic transference. A graphic example of this was provided by a female patient, a 38-year old physician. At the high point of her repetition of a violent "injustice conflict" with her mother, which had been shifted to the analyst, she came laughing to an appointment. When asked what had amused her so much, she explained that the analyst seemed stupid to her because he did not know what she had just been thinking in the elevator . . .

The child's discovery of the comic marks his third reformulation, and a new triad of fear-diminishing elements is put into operation.

Here are the three triads controlling the fear-smiles-laughter sequence which follow one another in quick succession during the first one and a half years of life:

TRIAD NO. I (Direct reassurance)	Baby's oral muscles relax after feeding	Feeling of satiation (pseudosmile)	Mother smiles; meaning perceived by infant: "She is not hungry and will not devour me."
TRIAD NO. II (Megalomania)	Megalomania negating defeats	Reassurance of the familiar ("smile of recognition")	Generalized diminution of fear
TRIAD NO. III (Demotion or indirect reassurance)	Beginning of demotion of the dangerous to the "comical" and "funny"; laughter at the "ludicrous"	Pseudoaggressive actions attacking rules made by main upbringers, and practical jokes	Demotion of upbringer as "stupid" because he is ignorant of the child's "secrets"

All three triads of the individual pre-history of laughter have one common denominator: diminution of fear. *Hence children laugh more and more easily than adults do; they have more fears to counteract!* Initially, *the sequence assuages irrational infantile terror-like fears;* reformulated, it *utilizes infantile megalomania to scotomize defeats;* again and finally amended, it is *colored by increasing quantities of defensive aggression.* The basic reason for the appearance of defensive aggression is the fact that every offense to infantile megalomania produces fury; the fury is either inexpressible or insufficiently expressible to afford complete relief. The unexpressed residue is subsumed in *comical and malicious laughter*. But in the meantime the unconscious conscience has become an inner reality. As a result, more and more of the aggression which was originally directed outwards is diverted for use against the internal "enemy"—inner conscience.

The genetic picture also explains the confusion which haunts many authors when the attempt to explain the absence of any link or evident relationship between the laughter of "pure pleasure" in children and the laughter of derision in adults. The former is simply the outward evidence of self-reassurance against infantile fears; the latter is the offensive weapon subsequently developed.

Scientific observers have also been bewildered by the multitude of meanings, ranging from benevolence to malevolence, which are all expressed by a smile or a laugh. The two extremes—reassurance and malice—are explainable in the light of the beginning and end of the infantile precursors of laughter: its development, the increasing reassurance shown in Triad No. II, the increasing malice in Triad No. III.

One difficulty, however, remains: psychic masochism. The next chapter will deal with this problem.

3. Laughter in the Adult Sense: Internal Antidote Against Fear of One's Own Psychic Masochism

Wit is a serious matter.
Ambrose Bierce

LAUGHTER IN THE *adult* sense appears when the human being reaches that crossroads where exaggerated external fears are transformed into exaggerated internal fears; in other words, at the time when the inner Frankenstein, the superego, is triumphantly and permanently enthroned. One of the important mechanisms which the unconscious ego uses as a defense against the constant barrage of cruelty emanating from the superego is reinforcement of the pleasure-in-displeasure pattern: psychic masochism. As already stated, this ingenious feat of mental legerdemain changes externally perceived punishment into internally perceived pleasure. Unfortunately for the ego, the superego sees the trick, and extends its veto to include this newly devised inner pleasure. Resisting the new menace and the new accusation, the unconscious ego emphasizes the more superficial alibi: pseudo-aggression. This in turn arouses, within one of the sectors of the personality, either a *constant readiness for the production of witty or comical remarks and actions*, or else an appreciation of them, since *in these productions the internal precepts of authority are constantly attacked and ridiculed.* "Forced" wit (and forced laughter), brought into play at any time, on any occasion, anywhere and regardless of penalty, denotes exaggerated inner defenses against exaggerated inner fears; with this goes a pronounced tendency to "hoard" the alibi for future use. One is reminded of Aristotle's observation that "melancholy men are most witty"; the observation becomes accurate and revealing when the scientific term, "depressed," is substituted for the popular misnomer, "melancholy."

Laughter in the adult sense is not confined to adults; it is seen in children as young as three or four. At this age, the inner conscience is fully established. This explains the young child's predilection for cruel jokes (see Kimmins, Chapter One, p. 25).[1]

Since most laughter-provoking productions have an aggressive connotation, a good many observers have concluded that the human being possesses so inexhaustible a storehouse of aggression that it is bound to overflow

[1] Kimmins' statement that children's interest in reading or listening to aggressive stories becomes "negligible" after about the age of ten is partly an exaggeration; to the extent that there is some decrease in the attractiveness of the aggressive story, the decrease is due to stronger repression of the primitive-cruel. In any case, adults are less "cultured" than Kimmins' ten-year-olds.

constantly. Most of the theories based on Hobbes's assumptions implicitly take this position. I cannot subscribe to this thesis. I believe that the *stasis in the typical personality is not unplaceable inner aggression, but unplaceable inner masochism.*

The difference between real and pseudo-aggression is summarized in the following table:[2]

NORMAL AGGRESSION	NEUROTIC AGGRESSION (Pseudo-Aggression)
1. Used only in self-defense.	1. Used indiscriminately when an infantile pattern is repeated with an innocent bystander.
2. Object of aggression is a "real" enemy.	2. Object of aggression is a "fantasied" or artificially created enemy.
3. No accompanying unconscious feeling of guilt	3. Feeling of guilt always present.
4. Dosis: Amount of aggression discharged corresponds to provocation.	4. Dosis: Slightest provocation—greatest aggression.
5. Aggression always used to harm enemy.	5. Pseudo-aggression often used to provoke "masochistic pleasure" expected from enemy's retaliation, or to refute inner conscience's accusation of masochistic passivity.
6. Timing: Ability to wait until enemy is vulnerable.	6. Timing: Inability to wait, since pseudo-aggression is used as defense mechanism against inner reproach of psychic masochism.
7. Not easily provoked.	7. Easily provoked.
8. Element of infantile game absent; no combination with masochistic and defensively "sadistic" feelings; the only feeling is that a necessary though disagreeable job had to be performed.	8. Element of infantile game present, combined with masochistic and *defensively* "sadistic" excitement, usually repressed.
9. Success expected.	9. Defeat unconsciously expected.

The differentiation between *real* and *pseudo*-aggression seems to me of paramount importance for the understanding of human behavior. Confusing the one with the other leads to tragic errors in psychopathology. In my opinion, *every* person emerges from the infantile stage with *some* remnants of masochistic tendencies. To ward these off, use is made of neurotic pseudo-aggression, a defense designed to placate the inner conscience. The ever-ready alibi is pseudo-aggression. The defendant's formula is simple: "How can I be accused of masochism? See how aggressive I am!"

Investigators have always been puzzled by the fact that a joke loses its

[2] First published in *Quarterly Review of Psychiatry and Neurology*, 1, 1; 1946.

point—even when the "plot" is scrupulously preserved—as soon as it is stripped of the mechanisms of allusion, condensation, displacement, substitution, hint, psychic shift, exaggeration. To exemplify: Ambrose Bierce defined a kiss as "a word invented by poets to rhyme with bliss; it is supposed to signify, in a general way, some kind of rite or ceremony appertaining to a good understanding; but the manner of its performance is unknown to this lexicographer" (*The Devil's Dictionary*).

When the condensation is eliminated and the story "rephrased"—"I hate kissing; it was invented by hypocrites and welcomed by sentimentalists; in short, I don't want to hear anything about it"—the joke evaporates, leaving at best a bitter taste for the poor misanthrope.

Every joke has as its prerequisite the inclusion of a half-riddle to be solved by the listener. Without this touch of allusion, condensation, shift, substitution or displacement (as Freud originally pointed out), there can be only statements of fact, true or false. It is these unconscious mechanisms, visible in seemingly formal aesthetic disguises, which account for that peculiarity, the witticism.

In short, a joke can be evolved only through the use of the half-riddle technique. A joke is primarily a statement containing lacunae which must be filled in by the listener. The psychic work of completing the statement correctly enough to "see the point" is, interestingly enough, taken as proof of the listener's "activity."

It is my opinion that *pseudo-aggression alone is released in the response to wit.*[3] This opinion is based upon ten clinical facts. The first is the half-riddle technique of every joke.

Second, the half-riddle technique of every witticism has an additional connotation: the child in the listener *is taken into the half-confidence of adults.* A joke activates the situation, consciously long forgotten, in which questions were asked and replies postponed or refused. ("You will find out when you are grown up.") In the case of a witticism or a humorous anecdote, the narrator supplies the answer, only thinly veiled, to the listener. This veil is penetrated, and the joke understood. But the child in the listener interprets the subtlety as meaning that he still needs to outsmart the adult, for the forbidden remains half-forbidden.

Third, the ease with which he assembles and draws on the mass of miscellaneous information required to understand a joke proves to the child in the adult that he has "*mastered*" *all* (*sexual*) *riddles—actively*. Simply because it is a commonplace, and therefore nothing to brag about, this need for an extensive body of information is frequently overlooked. If we summarize the background of knowledge, conscious and unconscious, needed in order to grasp the point of Bierce's joke about so familiar a phenomenon as a kiss, we realize that a more typical joke requires a surprising amount

[3] The germ of points I to VI is to be found in *The Superego*.

of information in a variety of fields, as well as familiarity with the twists and turns of human behavior. The caption under a cartoon about golf, for example, must be meaningless to a person unaware of the rules of the game, its social elaborations, and the innumerable joke stereotypes which have grown up around the game and become inextricably associated with it.

Fourth, the person listening to the joke *behaves as if the above-mentioned activities—solution of the half-riddle, acceptance into the half-confidence of adults, information-please mastery of "forbidden" knowledge—were performed in the face of the educators' prohibition.* These educators are enshrined in the unconscious conscience. Paradoxical as this may sound, *the explosive laughter that greets a joke is thus directed at the inner conscience. The joke*—every joke—*is on the superego*, which thus becomes a figure of fun "in its own house." In effect, this laughter is the defensive triumph of the psychic masochistic part of the personality, through the use of pseudo-aggressive props. In "Transference and Love" (1933), Jekels and I stated specifically that wit is one of the techniques used by the ego to attack the superego.[4]

Fifth, the child in the adult puts a brave face on the situation and listens with apparent self-possession to the "forbidden" joke, but he is in reality trembling at his own daring. The very fact that he is the listener is a pseudo-aggressive alibi; he participates in the "forbidden" action on the one hand, but at the same time denies responsibility for the action, shifting the blame to the teller of the joke. His alibi runs: "I didn't do anything; I just listened. *He* did it." In his original formulation, Freud clarified this element of shifted responsibility.

Sixth, observation of circumstances lending themselves to the production of jokes proves conclusively that not real but pseudo-aggression is involved in witticisms. In general, two situations predominate: one, when the individual is unconsciously accused by the inner conscience of being afraid; two, when he is accused, again by the inner conscience, of tolerating a consciously painful state of affairs for the sake of masochistic pleasure. Confronted with the reproach of passivity, the inner lawyer (the unconscious ego) mobilizes would-be aggression as alibi. The result takes two

[4] This statement was later indirectly taken up by L. Eidelberg ("A Contribution to the Study of Wit," the *Psychoan. Review*, 32, 1; 1945), to subsume a scopophiliac sideshow. Also utilizing the voyeuristic-exhibitionistic exchange mechanism (according to which both parts of scopophilia can be used as defense) as postulated by Eidelberg and myself in our joint study on depersonalization ("The Mechanism of Depersonalization", *Int. Zeitschr. fuer Psychoan.*, 1935), the deduction reads something like this: In listening to a joke, the child in the listener plays the voyeur; via identification with the narrator, voyeurism is transformed into exhibitionism; since this change takes place under pressure of the superego, deception of the latter is a prerequisite. Otherwise, Eidelberg holds that real aggression is displayed in wit, a point which I dispute—the pseudo-aggression, covering more deeply repressed psychic masochism, seems to me of prime importance for understanding the psychology of wit.

forms: "*jokes out of fear*," or "*jokes out of ennui*." In the first case, the lawyer's brief reads, "My client is not passively frightened, but actively above the situation." In the second case it reads, "My client is not passive-masochistic, but fed up with the situation, and even bored with it." In either circumstance, the inner lawyer's objective is to prove that a joker, or a bored person, is *active*.

Poets have instinctively sensed this interconnection, although consciously they could not have known either cause or effect. The fear-joke is neatly summed up in Lessing's "Not all are free who ridicule their chains," while the fed-up type is hinted at in Nietzsche's previously quoted dictum, "Man alone suffers so excruciatingly in the world that he was compelled to invent laughter."

Seventh, the tendency to hold back the breath (while listening, grasping at and then actually seeing the "point" of the joke) before releasing the explosion of a laugh hints at an unconscious perception of danger. It is as if the riddle *had* to be solved, "or else," [5] or as if the situation involved some inexplicable adult malice. In more mature people, a premonitory smile substitutes for this "examination fright."

The *unconscious fright–conscious surprise* sequence in every witticism reproduces in an attenuated fashion the child's fear of what mother (father, teacher) will "come up with next." *Gradual indoctrination of the child with ever-enlarged background knowledge produces more than a "smartening-up" process; the fact that knowledge is perpetually being "thrown at him" arouses in the child the feeling of being PASSIVELY OVERWHELMED.* In wit, the element of unexpectedness which all investigators declare to be an indispensable prerequisite is changed from direct, infantile, *unmastered* fear to *mastered* surprise. Hence, the masochistic remnant of fear is preserved, and at the same time the fear is emotionally mastered—in understanding the witticism. One can state that the adult surprise element is the masochistic dosis refracta of the original infantile fear. The question seems to be: "What will those impossible adults come up with next?" It is the frightening unpredictability of adults, viewed from the vistas of the child, that is now made harmless (not frightening) and even pleasurable.

Eighth, every witticism is at bottom a strategic *out-distancing operation.* The butt of the joke is an *artificially created masochistic victim—a projected*

[5] It is possible that this inner perception accounts for statements in our literature (Reik, Grotjahn) connecting wit and attenuated shock. Reik believes that the first reaction when listening to a witticism is that of fear; this "thought fright" is promoted through the unconscious allure which the "Triebdurchbruch" in the witticism brings nearer. As a result of warding off the unconscious wish, the repression-inhibition is increased; this, since it is superfluous, is discharged. The transformation of fear into pleasure is thus accomplished. Reik's idea is ingenious; however, he omits the masochistic and pseudo-aggressive defense; Reik places the emphasis on id-wishes, not on superego reproaches.

image of the listener himself. The tables are also turned via the unconscious repetition compulsion[6]—the active repetition of passive experiences in order to restore a lesion in narcissism. The cruelty of the joke corresponds to the *imagined* cruelty of the educators, a judgment later enshrined in the superego. The victim of the joke, successfully externalized, is triumphantly exhibited: "He is masochistic; I'm not." *Out-distancing one's own psychic masochism seems to be the essence of every laughing matter.*

Perhaps even the division of jokes into "good" and "poor" has its affective basis at this point. The more efficient a joke is in enabling the listener to out-distance his own psychic masochism, the more highly he will rate it—unconsciously, although his conscious rationalizations will naturally not include this detail. Just as "beauty is pleasure regarded as the quality of a thing" (George Santayana), wit is an internal alibi, secondarily perceived as coming from the outside.

Ninth and tenth, *jokes "out of fear"* and *jokes "out of ennui"* have one common denominator: they are both *alibis* offered to the inner conscience. Having heard that the best defense is attack, the frightened child in the adult attacks.

Most people assume, without pondering over the question, that "a gay mood" engenders jokes; they do not suspect that jokes are manufactured for use as defensive weapons in an unconscious battle with an inner adversary. Nor do they suspect that a minimum of fifty percent of the psychic energy of every human being is spent in presenting alibis and defenses to the accusing ogre of inner conscience.

There is a more accurate explanation of mutual appreciation of witticisms. Freud pointed out that when people laugh at the same jokes they are proving the inner proximity of identical inner conflicts. The development from crude jokes of the slapstick variety to "psychological" jokes marks the development from simpler to more complicated defenses.

Jokes "out of fear" are sometimes intuitively understood by severe masochists. Heinrich Heine wrote about them:[7]

> In jenen Naechten hat Langeweil' ergriffen
> Mich oft, auch Furcht—nur Narren fuerchten nichts—

[6] Freud's concept of the unconscious repetition compulsion, theoretically postulated in *Beyond the Pleasure Principle* (*Ges. Schriften*, VI, 1920) was never *clinically* applied by its originator. Actually, it has great clinical importance in resolving the breast complex, in the He-Man psychology, and even in understanding the psychological superstructure of the sex act. For literature and elaboration, see *Neurotic Counterfeit-Sex*, Grune and Stratton, New York, 1951.

[7] It is impossible to understand how Heine was able to express his intuitive perception except by studying the poet's masochistic regression. For further elaboration, see *The Writer and Psychoanalysis* (second, enlarged edition, Brunner's Psychiatric Books, New York, 1954).

Sie zu verscheuchen hab' ich dann gepfiffen
Die frechen Reime eines Spottgedichts.[8]
(*Romanzero, II*, *Lamentationen*, "Enfant perdu")

A physician who later achieved renown as a pathologist reported that he lived through the "strongest fear of his life" when applying for the position of assistant in a pathological institute at a foreign medical school. The cause of his fear was the reputation of the chief pathologist, a man of intimidating personality as well as a recognized authority in his field. This man was notorious for the sarcastic criticism which he freely bestowed on his subordinates; to enlarge his opportunities for criticism, he would subject his staff to frequent extracurricular examinations. The young physician, who later became my patient, was told to perform a complete autopsy, according to specific rules established by the professor. The vigilant eye of the professor followed every move, but all went well until the bladder had to be removed from the body for inspection. The young physician's technique was too forceful; the bladder burst, spattering everyone around the table with the dead man's urine. The professor, faithful to his motto—"Anger will not do, irony is the only thing"—was at the point of opening his mouth to express his derogatory opinion of the young man's ability, but the culprit forestalled him by stating, "Well, at least my mishap achieved one result—it proved that dead men can urinate." The professor laughed and said, "That's exactly what I was about to say." And to take revenge on the "wise guy," the professor added, "Perhaps you should apply for a job as a mind reader; as pathologist you are not so good."

Without going into the complicated network of what the young physician unconsciously projected upon the professor, what dissecting unconsciously meant for him, and whether the "mishap" could have been avoided, the fact remains that the young man was in a state of severe fright. The superego reproach usually evoked by misfortune, "This can happen only to you, you passive weakling," was personified in the malice of the professor, who was in the habit of ascribing *typical* mistakes to the individual and exclusive incompetence of his various assistants. Moreover, there was good reason for the assumption that the young man provoked the incident in order to be verbally castigated (castrated) by the "big shot." In any case, the witticism he produced was defensive in character.

A well-known writer told me an anecdote from his journalistic past. He had been assigned by his editor to report an electrocution. The condemned murderer sat in the electric chair watching the executioner as he fumbled among the wires and electrodes, and remarked, "What's the matter with you, are *you* nervous?"

[8] In these nights, boredom gripped me, and so did fear—only fools fear nothing; to counteract fear I whistled the impudent stanzas of a satiric verse.

The situation preceding the production of a joke need not be either objectively menacing or objectively crucial. When it is not, *inner* fear—unconsciously and *not* consciously perceived—substitutes for the external danger.

In the type of joke which grows out of "alleged ennui," the groundwork is laid by an endlessly protracted crisis of pain or humiliation, which is seized on by the inner conscience for the purpose of torture. The defense is a denial: "The crisis is not giving me masochistic pleasure. On the contrary, it bores me, and I even joke about it."

From the early days of his marriage a certain man, now aged, had endured his wife's liaison with her lover; the triangle persisted despite all his efforts to break it up. An ironic friend asked him, "How is X. (the lover) getting along?" He replied, "I haven't seen him for a long time; I am trying to get in contact with him through the newspapers."—"How?"—"Well, I check the obituary column every day to see if he died."

That great satirist, Heine, was paralyzed during the last decade of his life; he suffered from a disease which has never been clearly identified, but was probably tabes, a late sequel of syphilis. When someone asked him how he endured his suffering, he answered that God had sent this visitation to him only to prove that He is a better satirist than Heine himself . . .[9]

One particular impediment to the clarification and discovery of genetic reasons is almost universally evident in the literature on laughter. This is the desire to find a monistic formula to cover *all* forms of laughter, despite the "protean nature" (Gregory) of this emotion. Since there are so many aspects of the smile and the laugh, and so many meanings for each manifestation, how can they all be assembled under the all-embracing roof of a single formula? As one result of this dilemma, the obstreperous forms of laughter that did not fit into the chosen formula were either entirely disregarded (thus providing the next investigator with excellent excuses for poking holes in the earlier theory by pointing out the missing facet), or declared to be pollutions or aberrations of true laughter, and again disregarded. On the other hand, when the investigator declined this seemingly easy way out of his dilemma, and revised his formula instead of his enumeration of the types of laughter, the formula became so generalized that it lost all meaning.

Amazing contortions of logic can be found in the works of authors who disregard the unconscious. Instead of seeing that they are on the wrong path, they plod on bravely if heavily, negating the importance of the unconscious by declaring it an extravaganza, or (if more up-to-date) by

[9] Not all people are capable of producing jokes; those who cannot are fascinated by, and repeat, jokes of the specific variety which pertains to their specific inner conflict.

awarding it a wary and noncommittal mention in what is in effect a footnote, though politely included in the text. Gregory's attempt to subsume repression-laughter under his "relief" theory, hauling it in as "a special case," is paradigmatic for this type of reluctant compromise.

Now, the confusion surrounding the "protean" nature of laughter arises from one simple fact: the subdivisions of emotions are *manifold*, the mode of expression *uniform*. Gregory mentions these forms of laughter: " . . . laughters of triumph, of scorn and contempt, of superiority, of self-congratulation, of play, of greeting, and of amusement, which includes pure comic perception of the ludicrous and humour with sympathy" (*The Nature of Laughter*, p. 7). He might have continued, by pointing out that there are literally dozens of types of smiles and laughter. Taking the smile as our example, here is a partial list, a mere fifty varieties:

> Friendly-benevolent, ironic, sarcastic, meaningless, empty, bitter, gloating, self-pitying, cruel, hypocritical, shy, embarrassed, enigmatic, confused, sheepish, sexy, charming, alluring, promising, triumphant, defensive, "stupid," frozen, joyous, reminiscent, pretending, cynical, amused, tragic, paradoxical, forced, involuntary, sophisticated, knowing, regretful, shamefaced, surprised, hysterical, pitying, encouraging, coquettish, convulsive, homeric, dry, "nervous," reassuring, inviting, motherly, "bitchy," wry.

Two factors, when known and applied, will clear up this confusion. First, it must be realized that both the smile and the laugh possess a *specific* meaning in the context of the individual's early personal history. The identical gesture which expresses that specific meaning is generalized in later life to include other emotions. In just this way, one encounters an enormous variety of neurotic pictures based on penis-neurosis: one penis, used for hundreds of neurotic meanings. (This subject is elaborated in my book, *Neurotic Counterfeit-Sex*.)

The second factor is the cultural element. Professor Weston LaBarre has treated this question at some length in "The Cultural Basis of Emotions and Gestures." His main thesis is that the basis for familiar meaningful gestures is rarely if ever instinctual. A forward and backward rocking of the skull to indicate "yes" and a side-to-side rotation to indicate "no" have been so thoroughly accepted as "natural" and instinctive gestures that at least one psychologist (and Professor LaBarre makes it clear in a footnote that he is referring to E. B. Holt's statements on page 111 of *Animal Drive and the Learning Process*, New York, 1931, and in personal conversations) has tried to explain this presumably universal sign-language by tracing it back to motions used by the infant in feeding. The "yes" gesture, in the light of this explanation, descends from the infant's motions when in search of the breast, and the "no" gesture from its motions when avoiding or rejecting the breast. This is an ingenious explanation, Professor LaBarre comments, but it cannot be conclusive because these "yes" and "no" signs are by no means as widespread, even among the races of man, as is mammalian behavior biologically.

Even if the search for alternatives is limited to the Orient, many can be found. The Ainus of northern Japan, for example, are ignorant of the head noddings familiar to the West. For "no," the right hand is usually passed from right to left and back in front of the chest; for "yes," both hands come up to the chest in a graceful movement and then are waved downwards with the palms upwards. (As authority for this statement, Professor LaBarre cites *Alone With the Hairy Ainu* by A. H. S. Landor, London, 1893, pp. 6, 233–234.)

As for the smile, Professor LaBarre tells of a conversation he had with a great anthropologist, the late Edward Sapir. Professor LaBarre asked whether "other tribes" cried and laughed as we do; in response, Sapir laughed, but immediately grasped the crux of the question: in which of these universal phenomena are people alike everywhere, and in which are they different?

Smiling, according to Professor LaBarre, is very much like any other culture trait, and the incidence of laughter is in some ways a "geographical variable." In the Southwest Pacific, for example, there are areas where "Papuan hilarity" will be encountered, and other distinct areas where "Dobuan, Melanesian dourness" is characteristic. Geoffrey Gorer is quoted as stating, in *Africa Dances* (New York, 1935, p. 10), that the Negro uses laughter to express surprise, wonder, embarrassment and even discomfiture. The Negro's laughter should not be automatically considered a sign that he is amused; more often than not, this is not its meaning. It is a mistake to assume that symbols, because they are similar, have identical meanings.

Time and again in the works of many of the authors quoted in Chapter One, stress is laid on "incongruity" and "absurdity" as foundations for laughter. The observations are accurate, the explanations are faulty. The incongruous per se does not provoke laughter; laughter results from it because the incongruity is unconsciously seized upon by the child in the adult as proof positive of the *faultiness of the adult logic which had been forcibly imposed on the child.* We do not, therefore, laugh at the incongruous, but at the triumph over the educator. The immediate and unconscious reason for laughter is *this "proof" of the fallibility of those who promoted the thesis of the "congruous"; only in a secondary shift is this inner pleasure externalized and rationalized.*

This explains, also, why all purely sociological theories on laughter must necessarily be far out "in the left outfield." Not clarification, but fog, must be the result of a failure to differentiate between inner and outer reality.

At the same time, all purely biological theories which explain laughter as an explosion emanating from the "natural well-being of the child" are built on an utterly untenable premise, for it is the massive fears and the offenses against megalomania in very early childhood which are the basic material of laughter, and not the child's contemporary well-being.

The best summary of my opinions on this topic that I know was presented by a patient, a famous humorist, who told me in analysis: "According to you, there are two items that are 'musts' on the psychic menu—the 'masochistic stew,' to stew in and nibble on, and the 'pseudo-aggressive cocktail,' to counteract the effects of the stew. Misuse of reality serves the first, wit the second, purpose." A witty if malicious explanation, but at least on the periphery of the facts as I see them.

4. Wit: The Intellectual High Point of All Adult Laughing Matter

Laughter is the cipher-key wherewith we decipher the whole man.
Thomas Carlyle

WIT IS LAUGHTER with the accent on intellectualism. It is, as people believe, the final layer—and the least primitive layer—in the composite structure known as "the sense of humor." Nevertheless, its origin is humble. Its ancestor is the dramatized, primitive, practical joke, and the highest and lowest forms of humor reveal their relationship by a common characteristic: the core of each is dramatized action, direct in the practical joke, verbalized and shifted to the intellectual sphere in wit.

In its subdivisions, wit comprises the witticism, the witty story, the witty aphorism,[1] and the witty short poem.

It was Freud who said, "It is easy to laugh, but difficult to explain why one laughs." Fortunately for the amusement industry, people are grateful for the opportunity to laugh and do not stop to question their reasons.

I remember the incident which brought to my attention how much is still unclarified in the field of laughter. A few years ago, I had a pleasant and satisfying conference with a publisher on a Saturday morning. As we left his office for lunch, the elevator man greeted him and said, "*I hope you have a pleasant weekend.*"—"*No,*" replied the publisher, "*I have different plans.*" Though his expression was as grim as his words, my reaction was a prolonged belly laugh, and throughout our otherwise pleasant luncheon I was distracted and annoyed by my inability to find an explanation for either his reaction or my own.

Our business conversation continued, but behind the scenes I was busy trying to explain my own reaction to myself. I asked, first, what repressed material had been heaved up to the surface. Aggression against the holy institution of weekend "fun"? The idea was immediately rejected; no connection could be established with the "Sunday-neurosis" (Ferenczi) common to so many people; moreover, I genuinely look forward to my weekends, for it is then that I indulge in my favorite hobby: writing.

[1] An aphorism is a short, concise statement embodying an astute observation on some facet of human behavior; it may, or may not be witty. E.g., La Rochefoucauld's "If one judges love by its effects, it resembles hate more than affection," or Elbert Hubbard's "Genius is the ability to act rightly without precedent—the power to do the right thing for the first time." These are brilliant aphorisms, but not witticisms. But Napoleon's statement, "The only victory over love is flight," is an aphorism *and* a witticism, simply because it applies a layer of allusion and condensation *over* the aphoristic meaning.

Next, I asked myself whether I had laughed because I was gloating over the publisher's spoiled weekend. This, too, was excluded. We were on casually friendly terms with each other; I felt no special anger where he was concerned, and I was quite conscious of the minor irritations which had arisen. In general, we both benefited from our pleasant relationship.

I then attempted free associations. Nothing came of this, either. My only association was the recollection of what I had said to the publisher when my laughter subsided: "Your excellent joke reminds me of my favorite Shaw story. At the opening of *Man and Superman* in London, everybody cheered except a man in the first row. This man hissed, and you know that in Europe hissing in the theatre expresses the utmost contempt. Shaw turned to him and said, 'I quite agree with you, but what are we two against this multitude?' " This association only complicated an already complicated situation. Shaw's witticism was a reductio ad absurdum of the boor; in a spurious split-second identification, Shaw simply said: "The multitude wants witty trash, hence I'm giving it to them; don't believe for a moment that I'm personally taken in by my own sub-standard wares."

Having rejected this "explanation," too, I examined the possibility that my laughter might not have pertained to the witticism at all. Perhaps it was an example of "economy of emotional expenditure," saving me from the sympathy due to the publisher for his expectation of a dreary weekend. This "economy" was in effect suggested by the publisher's witticism, which was "wit directed against oneself." My laughter was thus for, and not against, the narrator.

I finally came to the convenient conclusion that the problem could not be solved unless I went more thoroughly into what I knew about the publisher. I was vaguely conscious that this conclusion was a trick—a joke that has been greeted with uproarious laughter must be explained via the listener's unconscious, and not solely in terms of the narrator's—but I pushed this objection aside. My purpose now was to "explain" why the publisher had produced the witticism in the first place. I knew that the gossips had him tagged as a man with an inheritance-complex;[2] he wooed his aging wealthy mother although she made his life a veritable torture chamber. I assumed that he would have to spend the weekend with her, and thus his witticism really meant: "My *mother* has different plans for me." This explained the grim and accusing facial expression. His actual formulation: "*I* have different plans," amounted to a narcissistic safeguard: "If I weren't willing to play the old bitch's game, nobody could force me." Basically, I concluded, the witticism pertained to a warded-off reproach of his inner conscience, the accusation being—psychic masochism.

[2] For further elaboration, see *Money and Emotional Conflicts*, Doubleday, 1951, Chapter I.

My feeling of satisfaction at having found a solution disappeared when I realized that I had solved his part of the problem, but not mine. "Remember," I told myself ironically, "you started to 'explain' your own laughter. How about that?"

Since I had known all these details of the publisher's private trouble before I laughed, a search for some similarity in my own life seemed indicated. I found nothing to fit the picture. I had never suffered from an inheritance complex—I had never had the opportunity. I could not even brag, as Louis Bromfield once did, "I inherited nothing by my family." I had again reached a dead end.

Some time later I realized that there was one specific situation in my life that could fill the bill. I have always been proud of being a "self-made man." My parents did not wish me to study medicine; when I began my studies, World War I had just ended, and neither the general condition of the country (Austria) nor my father's financial circumstances warranted so ambitious and costly a five-year-plan as a medical course. Actually, my parents strongly urged me to leave school and take a job in a bank. I rejected their suggestion, left home, and supported myself (a very unusual move in Vienna) throughout my entire medical course. Working in the daytime and studying at night was not exactly fun for a youngster, but still I went through with my plan.

Obviously, the publisher's witticism had unconsciously revived my memories of this long forgotten era. My belly laugh was not directed at the publisher, nor was it an expression of sympathy for him. *It was a triumph over my own inner conscience* (partially represented in the internalized parental images): "See what happens when you run after superficial advantages! This man is my age and he still suffers from dependence on his mother, and his mother's whims. *I* overcame this problem more than thirty years ago—and came out on top."

In reconstructing what happened internally before I laughed, I have to assume that my Daimonion must have seized the opportunity of saying, ironically, "Here, but for the grace of God, go you." With characteristic tactlessness, Daimonion must also have alluded to the masochistic allure of following unpalatable parental advice, and have reminded me of my bitter curses during the years when I was an over-worked slave to my medical ambition, thus equating my medical apprenticeship with the publisher's masochism ("The house of masochism has many rooms.") All these superego attacks were finally countered by the triumphant ego defense: "*I* made it!"

The majority of jokes are not so complicated.[3] But if one attempts to

[3] Obviously, the approach to the real meaning of this joke was so disagreeable that one monkey-wrench after another was thrown in my path—by myself. The Shaw retort, which had nothing to do with the publisher's wise-crack, is a case in

explain the dynamism of the joke, it is found that *all* jokes are deeply rooted in the unconscious, and become clear only if treated with a good dose of knowledge of unconscious motivations. Here is an example, a witticism produced by the same humorist who so neatly summarized my opinions on wit as a menu featuring "masochistic stew" and a "pseudo-aggressive cocktail." We had been discussing wit, and the man asked, with a deadpan expression:

"Was Freud hard up around 1905, when he wrote his book on wit?"

"Quite possible," I answered. "The early years of analysis were lean years."

"I thought so. The man was obsessed with *saving—saving* of expenditure of inhibition in wit, *saving* of expenditure of thought in the comic; *saving* of expenditure of sympathy in humor. Well, that's a whole battery of savings accounts."

The joke hinges on the double application of the word "saving"; obviously, saving of psychic energy is not identical with saving money. The purpose of the joke was to "deflate" Freud; the humorist hated Freud's theory, because it "explained away" the ever-ready repartee that was his pride. He thought of his talent for repartee as a "God-given gift"; dissecting it psychologically was viewed as sacrilege, or at the very least as denigration. As he once put it, he lived with all analytic theories in a state of "suspended animosity."

This witticism about Freud was not produced at random; it came at the *specific* time when the humorist achieved partial understanding of his own truly fantastic self-damaging tendencies. The witty-malicious remark was produced—as a *defense*—at exactly the high point of this "crisis." If Freud's theory can be explained in terms of economics, the inner defense claims, its scientific value must be nil; if Freud himself was so influenced by economic factors that they penetrated into his so-called "science," how can a pupil of Freud's justify *his* thesis that his patient's economic troubles are masochistically induced? (This was one of the important points dealt with in the man's analysis at that time.) The patient's demolition bomb did not hit at Freud but at his own inner conscience, for his superego had gradually taken over the analytic interpretations for use as torture material, and insistently pointed out how the patient himself had turned his life into a series of intricate and elaborate projects of self-torture. (His dreams were hardly-disguised ' lectures on masochism" as he called them.)

It is exactly from such examples as the above, observed in statu nascendi,

point. On the other hand, the very appearance of the Shaw retort shows that unconsciously I had grasped the meaning of the wise-crack. Otherwise, why should I have recalled an incident in which a man was put on the spot and rescued himself with aggression? It is clear that we unconsciously grasp the meaning of a joke well before conscious perception of that meaning takes place.

that my conclusion was derived: the aggression manifested in witticism does not pertain to real but to compensatory aggression, and the target is one's own accusing superego.

Clearly, it is a dangerous business to claim that the driving power of wit constitutes an alibi against unconscious masochism. If you offer proof that a wit is "aggressive," the listener is flattered; if you offer convincing proof that he is driven by psychic masochism, covered by a thin layer of pseudo-aggression, he is angered—who wants to be a masochist, anyway? All psychic masochists, as a witty female acquaintance declared, belong to the "Who—me?" Club.

A pertinent example presented itself during my recent summer vacation. It concerns a writer, in analysis with me because of writer's block.[4] He sent me a clipping from the New York *Times' Sunday Magazine* for June 29th, a short feature entitled "Limits of Tolerance—A Listing of Some Activities Which Recently Led Husbands and Wives to the Divorce Courts." In this humorous compilation, twenty-one rather unusual grounds for divorce were listed, all of them taken from actual court records. My patient underlined the following items:

> A divorce was granted a Newark, N. J. woman whose husband struck her in the face with one of the eels she had refused to cook for him and then had put the wriggling thing down her back.
>
> A statuesque St. Louis matron sued for divorce because her four-foot husband stood on a chair and punched her in the eye.
>
> In Vancouver, B.C., a divorce was won by a woman whose husband tore a piece out of the middle of their marriage license and ate it.
>
> A judge in Corpus Christi, Tex., granted a woman a divorce because her husband turned off his hearing aid whenever she began to speak to him.

The patient's triumphant comment, written in large red letters in the margin, was: "Prove that in these four cases the action was masochistic and not aggressive!"

My answer was not too consoling:

> Dear Mr. X.:
>
> I am afraid that you will have to eat your own words once more, and I hope with

---

[4] This particular writer was the first to use the term "block-buster" in referring to my book, *The Writer and Psychoanalysis,* which substantiated with clinical proofs my contention that writer's block can be analytically removed. To show how quickly witticisms travel, even when they are "clean" and deal with a subject limited in its appeal: Two weeks after this writer, in New York, called my book a "block-buster," the *Hollywood Reporter* carried the following "news item": "It's the truth s'help us: There's a psychiatrist in the East whose big specialty is working on playwrights who can't sit down to write the last act. When the scriveners are blocked they go to see 'Bergler, the Block Buster' " (April 12, 1951).

more effect than the husband who ate parts of his own marriage license. You remember how sceptical you originally were about the curability of writer's block; you remember that you ironically called me a "block-buster"? Well, according to your own statements, you have started to write again; you have already presented your astonished publisher (who had written off the advances he had paid you over a period of years for your undelivered novel) with half the book—and this after a few short months of analysis. What remains now is your "theoretical" scepticism, since you have had a practical demonstration proving that "not everything in analysis is a fake."—To revert to your four heroes of divorce, I have bad news for you: they all acted masochistically. You are unduly impressed by surface appearances; the gauge for deciding whether an act is pseudo-aggressive or genuinely aggressive is not whether or not there has been hitting. Both types hit, but the means of attack is different. One type attacks effectively, and *without* self-damage; the other ineffectively and *with* self-damage. Obviously, the penalties these four gentlemen paid were out of proportion to the satisfaction derived from their attacks. Obviously, too, since their wives sued for divorce, these husbands had no intention of doing so themselves; the usual collusive divorce, instigated by the husband but legally brought by the wife, does not make use of such scandals as grounds. Whether financial, social or masochistic reasons were involved is not made clear by these abbreviated reports. The means resorted to by your heroes were ineffectual because they were uncultured, and subject to heavy social penalties. For example, the husband who ate his "I do," recorded on the marriage license. Did "eating his words" automatically achieve annulment of his marriage, or did he have to pay alimony anyway? And isn't it likely that the husband who had to stand on a chair so that he could reach his wife's eye with a punch was pushed into a corner when his statuesque spouse recovered from the blow? As for the other two, neither eels nor hearing aids are weapons of any particular effectiveness in coping with the thousand little and big miseries every infuriated wife can inflict on her husband. Last but not least: why did these four people choose wives whom they later considered shrews? Why were they not forewarned by the unconscious—or, as you would prefer to say, by their "instincts"?

How frequently we have discussed this very subject—the fact that your "woman troubles" are unconsciously self-chosen, self-created, self-perpetuated! And isn't this precisely the reason for your amusement at your four divorce heroes, who aren't heroes at all but whining masochists whose only ability is to hit—*when the end effect* of the blow is that their wives pay them back, with usurious interest added?

* * *

Superficially, both the producer of a witticism and the listener enjoy freed aggression. If one is not familiar with the intimate troubles of the individual or is unaware of the particular superego reproach he is inwardly defending himself against, the elation which accompanies wit seems to prove that the human being is a storehouse of aggression, which he unloads on every possible and impossible occasion when he can do so with impunity. A witticism—even a bad one—provides such protection. This superficial impression is correct, but the explanation is wrong. The superficial aggression is but camouflage—unconscious, to be sure. Freud's original assumption that witticism affords the opportunity of saving inhibition cathexis is thus accurate within its limitations. It should be amplified with the addition of one more layer: what is freed is basically the cathexis of the defense, not of the repressed wish.

"*Like most other people, I often feel mean, and act accordingly,*" Mark Twain confessed in *Sketches New and Old*. Why do we laugh? The observation Twain makes is common enough; still it is a joke, or becomes a joke with the addition of the last three words, which unexpectedly provide candor when hypocrisy is taken for granted. Hypocrisy in public utterances is almost a convention; as Emerson said, "Nothing astonishes men so much as common sense and plain dealing." Hearing the first half of Mark Twain's sentence, the listener automatically supplies the conventional conclusion: "I often feel mean, and *suppress the impulse*." In this form, the sentence corresponds to what might be called the "working level" of the listener's repressions and half-suppressions. But when "meanness" is frankly and publicly admitted, the counter-cathexis holding down the repressed aggression is freed, and in accordance with Freud's deduction, transformed into laughter. Thus the joke seemingly pertains to repressed aggression, momentarily freed in a situation in which guilt can be shifted to the satirist who expresses the aggression.

Still other ramifications exist, however. There are differences in kind as well as degree in the hilarity which greets Twain's witticism. The person who quoted it to me was a man in analysis because of his fantastic subservience to his wife. She left him in spite of this, complaining that he was "wishy-washy." The divorce threw him into a depression. In analysis, he never reported his masochistic actions as such; to him they were objective accounts of his wife's ingratitude, greed and shrewishness. This epitome of psychic masochism laughed uproariously at Twain's joke. He had quoted it in connection with his report of an incident which had made him "see red for the first time" in his marriage. He and his wife had a rather peculiar financial arrangement. At the beginning of the month he would sign a number of blank checks; as expenses arose, she would fill in the checks and cash them or tender them as payments. "One day, I happened to examine the bank statement, and the cancelled checks for the month. I was disturbed about the amounts my darling wife had spent senselessly." The next sentence was the Mark Twain quotation, accompanied by a belly-laugh from the patient.

The admission of aggression inherent in this joke covered exactly the amount of psychic masochism which was this man's *real* "crime."

A joke can be considered "poor" by the vast majority of people, and yet be thought "wonderful" by a specific individual who is afflicted with the precise psychic situation attacked in the joke. A patient who suffered from pronounced psychic masochism had constant conflicts with his wife centering about her "governess-like tone." It was pointed out to him in analysis that he himself had unconsciously chosen a shrew for a wife, but he rejected this explanation. The official reasons for these marital conflicts were trifling. Often they had to do with the patient's food habits; he disliked vegetables, while his wife was a vitamin-devotee. One day this otherwise depressed man came to his appointment laughing his head off. He had come across the following lines in reading Byron's *Don Juan:*

Man is a carnivorous production,
And must have meals, at least one meal a day;
He cannot live, like woodcocks, upon suction,
But, like the shark and tiger, must have prey;
Although his anatomical construction
Bears vegetables, in a grumbling way,
Your laboring people think beyond all question,
Beef, veal and mutton better for digestion.

When asked why he rated these mildly amusing lines so highly, the patient became cautious, and "passed the buck," saying, "You tell me."

"I suspect that your defense against passivity is bolstered by considering yourself akin to the shark and the tiger," I said.

The man looked blank; he had assumed that his laughter was prompted by the ironic dismissal of vegetables as food.

Specific mishaps are always greeted with laughter; this is infantilism finding expression. A certain New Yorker cartoon, now well over two decades old, is a case in point. This is the Peter Arno drawing of a fat and middle-aged lady reaching the climax of her rendition of a song. Only her accompanist has as yet realized that her dress is splitting dangerously at the seams. A cultured person should, theoretically, overlook such mishaps, but he just doesn't. The cartoon provokes uproarious laughter.

Manhattan Tales, a motion picture released some years ago, consisted of a series of episodes showing a tail coat in the process of "coming down in the world." In one scene, a poor musican borrows the coat to conduct the first public performance of his symphony. The coat tears and people start to laugh. A famous conductor, seated prominently in the loge, takes off his own tail coat, thus counteracting the infantile laughter.

Does all this prove that people are "cruel"? I don't think so. Laughter originates in infancy, when it attaches itself to infantile things. Laughter at silly mishaps is really the laughter of revenge—the revenge of a child who scoffs at adult rules, and suddenly sees them shown up and debunked. What seems to be infantile is just infantile-directed. From the viewpoint of the child, there is good sense in this debunking process.

* * *

If one attempts to break up the general heading, "witticism," into subdivisions, one finds that all types of witticism have one common denominator. Regardless of the butt of the joke, the real aim is always *deflation for the sake of diminishing inner fears.* In its final expression, the witticism may be highly intricate, but it will still preserve its original unconscious basis: *the half-frightened child proving to himself that there is no reason to be either frightened or overawed. To counteract his own fear, the frightened child seeks contradictions, absurdities, "stupidity"—in the adult.* This is not the whole story, of course, because the battle of contradictions and unmaskings is internalized as well, and the unconscious adversary is the inner conscience, the representative of the adult world.

With this reservation, a few typical subdivisions can be cited.

Witticisms Directed at Authority, Venerated Institutions, Cherished Beliefs and Accepted Customs

Injustice collectors of whatever level, from the primitive to the sophisticated, all possess an inexhaustible store of witticisms of this type. The "idea" behind all these attacks is very simple. If you can prove that the "authority" is ridiculous, you will be killing two birds with one invective: you will be proving that you are "aggressive" and that your fears are unreal. The psychic masochism behind all this is gratuitously overlooked.

To take a typical example, here is an anonymous witticism attacking the venerated—or at least venerable—institution of monogamy. "Bigamy is having one wife too many. Monogamy is the same." The witticism is built on the double use of the phrase "too many," applied first in the legal sense, and then subjectively to express the feelings of the husband who has been "hooked." The irony is not directed at the law, nor at the institution of monogamy; the official target is *woman* and the unofficial one's own masochism.

Witticisms on this particular subject make wonderful reading—for men, especially masochistically subjected husbands.

> The legend that marriage is a lottery nearly ruined the lottery business. (Anon.)
>
> Love is the star men look up to as they walk along, and marriage is the coal-hole they fall into. (Anon.)
>
> Woman would be more charming if one could fall into her arms without falling into her hands. (Remy de Gourmont, also attributed to Ambrose Bierce)
>
> Even in civilized mankind, faint traces of a monogamistic method can sometimes be traced. (Bertrand Russell)
>
> I plucked a lemon in the garden of love. (Old song)
>
> When a man has once loved a woman, he will do anything for her except to love her. (Oscar Wilde)
>
> Love is a conflict between reflexes and reflections. (Magnus Hirschfeld)
>
> More things belong to marriage than four bare legs in a bed. (John Heywood)
>
> The reason why so few marriages are happy is because young ladies spend their time in making nets, not in making cages. (Jonathan Swift)

Venus, a beautiful, good-natured lady, was the goddess of love; Juno, a terrible shrew, the goddess of marriage; and they were always mortal enemies. (Jonathan Swift)

Marriage by its best title is monopoly, and not of the least insidious sort. (Charles Lamb)

Every man, as the saying is, can tame a shrew but he that hath her. (Robert Burton)

She was almost too hospitable—she kept open bed. (Aldous Huxley)

The one charm of marriage is that it makes a life of deception necessary for both parties. (Oscar Wilde)

Marriage is an exchange of bad humor during the day, and of bad odors during the night. (French proverb)

Marriage is fever in reverse; it starts with heat and ends with cold. (Anon.)

Think you, if Laura had been Petrarch's wife, He would have written sonnets all his life? (Lord Byron)

It does not much signify whom one marries, as one is sure to find next morning that it is someone else. (Samuel Rogers)

He is dreadfully married. He's the most married man I ever saw in my life. (Artemus Ward)

It's an experiment frequently tried. (W. S. Gilbert)

There may be good, but there are no pleasant marriages. (La Rochefoucauld)

Marriage—the state or condition of a community of a master, a mistress, and two slaves, making, in all, two. (Ambrose Bierce)

The trouble with wedlock is, there's not enough wed and too much lock. (Christopher Morley)

I never married, and I wish my father never had. (Anon.)

Advice to persons about to marry—"Don't!" (*Punch*)

They stood before the altar and supplied the fire themselves with which their fat was fried. (Ambrose Bierce)

The only solid and lasting peace between a man and his wife is doubtless a separation. (Lord Chesterfield)

She'd fight a rattlesnake and give it the first two bites. (Harry Leon Wilson)

The female of the species is more deadly than the male. (Rudyard Kipling)

If we take matrimony at its lowest, we regard it as a sort of friendship recognized by the police. (R. L. Stevenson)

She is intolerable, but this is her only fault. (Talleyrand)

In order to avoid being called a flirt, she always yielded easily. (Talleyrand)

A husband is what is left after the nerve has been extracted. (Helen Rowland)

Love, the quest; marriage, the conquest; divorce, the inquest. (H. Rowland)

Marriage—a souvenir of love. (H. Rowland)

Matrimony is a bargain, and somebody has to get the worst of the bargain. (H. Rowland)

The hardest task of a girl's life is to prove to a man that his intentions are serious. (H. Rowland)

When a man makes a woman his wife, it's the highest compliment he can pay her, and it's usually the last. (H. Rowland)

As long as a woman can look ten years younger than her daughter, she is perfectly satisfied. (Oscar Wilde)

The Bible says that the last thing God made was woman; He must have made her on a Saturday night—it shows fatigue. (A. Dumas fils)

I wish Adam had died with all his ribs in his body. (Dion Boucicault)

A woman can forgive a man all the harm he does her, but she can never forgive the sacrifice he makes on her account. (Somerset Maugham)

The chain of wedlock is so heavy that it takes two to carry it, sometimes three. (A. Dumas père)

Marriage is a ghastly public confession of a strictly private intention. (Ian Hay)

Adultery: democracy applied to love. (H. L. Mencken)

Time and tide wait for no man, but time always stands still for a woman of thirty. (Robert Frost)

The worst thing you can possibly do to a woman is to deprive her of a grievance. (Beverly Nichols)

A capacity for self-pity is one of the last things any woman surrenders. (Irvin Cobb)

My notion of a wife of 40 is that a man should be able to change her, like a bank-note, for two 20's. (Douglas Jerrold)

The music of a marriage procession always reminds me of the music of soldiers marching to battle. (Heinrich Heine)

Marriage is perhaps the most popular subject for witticism, but this does not mean that other insititutions and customs are neglected. Ammunition is even expended on such minor and harmless customs as Thanksgiving Day, a day, according to H. L. Mencken, "devoted by persons with inflammatory rheumatism to thanking a loving Father that it is not hydrophobia." The cover here, since it is so unimportant, is more than usually transparent; it is immediately obvious that Mencken's target is the doctrine of unvarying sweetness and light. The witticisms tend to be less forced and more pungent when they are aimed at big game:

On business and work in general:

Business? That's simple—it's other people's money. (Alexandre Dumas)

Only horses work, and they turn their backs on it. (American hobo proverb)

Work is the curse of the drinking classes. (Jerome K. Jerome)

On governments:

The government is mainly an expensive organization to regulate evildoers and tax those who behave; government does little for fairly respectable people except to annoy them. (Edgar W. Howe)

Gentleman talk of government by the people, for the people, etc. There never was such government; that was one of Abe Lincoln's jokes. (Edgar W. Howe)

He had his desk moved into the men's room of the War Department because that was the only place in the building where anyone knew what he was doing. (Popular international joke)

Democracy becomes a government of bullies tempered by editors. (Ralph Waldo Emerson)

On that sacrosanct stereotype, love for babies:

Here we have a baby. It is composed of a bald head and a pair of lungs. (Eugene Field)

A soiled baby, with a neglected nose, cannot be conscientiously regarded as a thing of beauty. (Mark Twain)

Adam and Eve had many advantages, but the principal one was that they escaped teething. (Mark Twain)

On that emblem of respectability, the family tree:

A great many prominent family trees were started by grafting. (Anon.)

Debunking Ironies, in the Form of "Jokes of Wisdom"

In his brilliant novel, *Nobody's Fool,* Charles Yale Harrison says: "Every failure who can't make the grade likes to think that success and prostitution are identical. It's a convenient and consoling thing to believe when you're not in the chips. It sustains that cringing, whimpering ego that all failures have."

Or, also from the same source:

The Earl of Chatham was wrong when he said that where the law ends tyranny begins. Where the law ends public relations begins.

Sometimes the cruelest thing you can wish for an enemy is that his wildest dreams of avarice come true, because then his last defense is shot to hell and he can no longer blame it on not getting the breaks or not having the right connections.

The stopgap became a way of living, which is how it is with stopgaps.

These debunking ironies can also be called "jokes of wisdom." There is more to it than the acknowledgment, "How true!" What distinguishes them from simple statements of fact is the "wit work" they all contain, as described by Freud. The simplest test is reformulation of the irony; the wit then evaporates, while the fact per se remains. To take an example: "It is better to give than to lend, and it costs about the same" (Sir Philip Gibbs). Had Gibbs said, "It has been my experience that borrowers seldom repay their debts; consequently to bestow a gift and to lend money are virtually synonymous," he would have been recording a minor and unenlightening fact. His actual words, of course, add up to far more. Beginning with a pseudo-pious moral precept, the sentence ends on a note of practicality; the unexpectedness of the contrast, plus the injection of a few drops of contempt for all "gimmes," contributes to the transformation of the remark into a witticism. The wit is based on contempt for chronic borrowers, and on the ironic deflation of the lender's illusion that he will be repaid (or at least repaid with gratitude).

"Good advice is one of those injuries which a good man ought, if possible, to forgive, but at all events to forget at once" (Horace Smith). Reformulated, this becomes, "Never ask or accept advice"; obviously as far removed from the original in meaning as it is in syntax. In his witticism, Smith hits at a series of human frailties: the universal tendency to offer advice despite the universal inability to make it sound ("An expert is an ordinary man away from home giving advice," declared an anonymous jokester); the fact that when people ask for advice they really want confirmation; the observation that the adviser, under the disguise of a helping hand, is mostly satisfying his own defensive tendencies, and should therefore be grateful for the opportunity of placing them (reduced to absurdity, this tendency may be so strong that an "injury" results). Finally, the witticism reverses the popular and accepted sequence in which it is assumed that the adviser does the advice-seeker a favor. On the contrary, Smith's irony declares, the advice-seeker should cash in on the good turn he did the adviser.

Witticisms Directed at That Catch-All Criminal, "Human Nature"

Wits whose stock in trade is making fun of people "as they really are" quite conveniently overlook a patent contradiction: if people are "made that way," they obviously cannot be held responsible for their "faults." Conversely, if the fault really lies with an individual's personal malice, how can either biology or "human nature" be blamed?

The wit cannot afford to take the contradiction into account, since this form of witticism provides the frightened child within him with a double alibi which he badly needs. When he hits at biology, he means his parents; when he hits simultaneously at a specific trait, he is again hitting at his parents. In this way he flanks his target, attacking from two directions at the same time, but he can do so only by disregarding elementary logic.

For example:

Man is Nature's sole mistake. (W. S. Gilbert)

Man is the only animal that blushes. Or needs to. (Mark Twain)

The earth has a skin, and that skin has diseases. One of those diseases is called man. (Friedrich Nietzsche, *Thus Spake Zarathustra*, XL)

On ingratitude:

If you pick up a starving dog and make him prosperous, he will not bite you. This is the principal difference between a dog and a man. (Mark Twain)

Every time I bestow a vacant office I make a hundred discontented persons and one ingrate. (Louis XIV)

Don't lose faith in humanity: think of all the people in the U. S. who have never played you a single nasty trick. (Elbert Hubbard)

On gambling:

The gambling known as business looks with austere disfavor upon the business known as gambling. (Ambrose Bierce)

Gambling—a mode of transferring property without producing any intermediate good. (Samuel Johnson)

I hope I come out even today: I need the money. (Old gambling joke)

On possessions:

No man can be a conservative until he has something to lose. (James P. Warburg)

When a man says money can do everything, that settles it; he hasn't any. (Edgar W. Howe)

On honesty:

Watch the butcher when he weighs the roast. Otherwise you'll buy his hand. (Dorothy Disney)

Whatever is not nailed down is mine. Whatever I can pry loose is not nailed down. (Collis P. Huntington)

Men are able to trust one another, knowing the exact degree of dishonesty they are entitled to expect. (Stephen Leacock)

On intrusion:

The real problem of your leisure is to keep other people from using it. (Oscar Wilde)

On elevation:

In politics, merit is rewarded by the possessor being raised, like a target, to a position to be fired at. (C. N. Bovee)

When they come downstairs from their ivory towers, idealists are apt to walk straight into the gutter. (Logan Pearsall Smith)

On cowardice:

Coward: One who in a perilous emergency thinks with his legs. (Ambrose Bierce)

On loneliness:

We boast that we are never lonely only because we are too vain to admit that we find ourselves poor company. (La Rochefoucauld)

On resignation:

The mass of men lead lives of quiet desperation. What is called resignation is confirmed desperation. (H. W. Thoreau)

On malice:

Every other enjoyment malice may destroy; every other panegyric envy may withhold; but no human power can deprive the boaster of his own encomiums. (Samuel Johnson)

The belief in a supernatural source of evil is not necessary; men alone are quite capable of every wickedness. (Joseph Conrad)

On fear:

The measure of a man's real character is what he would do if he knew he would never be found out. (Thomas B. Macaulay)

On admiration:

Admiration is a very short-lived passion, that immediately decays upon growing familiar with its object. (Joseph Addison)

On lies:

Advertisements contain the only truth to be relied on in a newspaper. (Thomas Jefferson)

Half the world knows not how the other lies. (George Herbert)

Any fool can tell the truth, but it requires a man of some sense to know how to lie well. (Samuel Butler[5])

As universal a practice as lying is, I do not remember to have heard three good lies in all my conversation, even from those who were most celebrated in that faculty. (Jonathan Swift)

Ask me no questions, and I'll tell you no lies. (Oliver Goldsmith)

On sophism:

What is a fine lie? Simply that which is its own evidence. If a man is sufficiently unimaginative to produce evidence in support of a lie, he might as well speak the truth at once. (Oscar Wilde)

Questions are never indiscreet. Answers always are. (Oscar Wilde)

On boredom:

Men and women can endure to be ruined, to be torn from their friends, to be overwhelmed with an avalanche of misfortune, better than they can endure to be dull. (Anthony Trollope)

On artificiality:

The first duty in life is to be as artificial as possible. What the second duty is no one has yet discovered. (Oscar Wilde)

On genius:

The world has a standing pique against genius. (William Hazlitt; also attributed to Oscar Wilde)

The public is wonderfully tolerant. It forgives everything except genius. (Oscar Wilde)

Genius is the talent of the man who is dead. (E. de Goncourt)

On knowledge:

That sure is a great school. It's practical. They don't teach no goddam grammar there. (A Kansas farmer, to Nelson Antrim Crawford)

---

[5] This is the author of *The Way of All Flesh*. Quotations from the other Samuel Butler will be identified as: Samuel Butler, from *Hudibras*.

Knowledge is not happiness, and science
But an exchange of ignorance for that
Which is another kind of ignorance. (Lord Byron)

On imitation:

There is much difference between imitating a good man, and counterfeiting him. (Benjamin Franklin)

On instinct:

As the intelligence improves, the instincts decay. (J. De La Mettrie)

Benevolence is a natural instinct of the human mind; when A sees B in distress, his conscience always urges him to entreat C to help him. (Sydney Smith)

He's simply got the instinct for being unhappy highly developed. (Saki)

On complaints:

Complaints is the largest tribute Heaven receives. (Jonathan Swift)

On insult:

One insult pocketed soon produces another. (Thomas Jefferson)

Injuries accompanied with insult are never forgiven; all men on those occasions are good haters, and lay out their revenge at compound interest; they never threaten until they can strike, and smile when they cannot. (C. C. Cotton)

On experience:

The burnt child loves the fire. (Oscar Wilde)

Experience is of no ethical value; it is simply the name we give our mistakes. It demonstrates that the future will be the same as the past. (Oscar Wilde)

To most men, experience is like the stern lights of a ship, which illuminate only the tracks it has passed. (Samuel T. Coleridge)

Nobody will use other people's experience, nor have any of his own till it is too late to use it. (Nathaniel Hawthorne)

Experience inkreases our wizdum but don't reduse our phollys. (Josh Billings)

On folly:

I know of nothing in the world that is not a monument of the folly of mankind. (De Fontanelle, 1686)

There are follies as catching as infections. (La Rochefoucauld)

Every man hath a fool in one sleeve. (George Herbert)

Every man has a sane spot somewhere. (R. L. Stevenson)

On greed:

He is so mean, he won't let his little baby have more than one measle at a time. (Eugene Field)

When a fellow says, "It ain't the money but the principle of the thing," it's the money. (Frank McKinney Hubbard)

Never burn bad incense before good gods. (Chinese proverb)

Only a few things are needed to make a wise man happy, but nothing can satisfy a fool: that is why nearly all men are miserable. (George Herbert)

On morality:

We know no spectacle so ridiculous as the British public in one of its periodical fits of morality. (Thomas B. Macaulay)

Morality is the best of all devices for leading mankind by the nose. (Friedrich Nietzsche)

An Englishman thinks he is moral when he is only uncomfortable. (G. B. Shaw)

Englishmen will never be slaves; they are free to do whatever the Government and the public opinion allows them to do. (G. B. Shaw)

Morality is simply an attitude we adopt toward people whom we personally dislike. (Oscar Wilde)

A New England conscience does not prevent you from doing anything; it just spoils the pleasure. (Anonymous)

On self-deception:

With most people, doubt about one thing is simply blind belief in another. (Georg C. Lichtenberg)

On thinking:

Thinking is the most unhealthy thing in the world, and people die of it just as they die of any other disease. Fortunately, in England, at any rate, thought is not catching. (Oscar Wilde)

All thought is immoral. The very essence is destruction. If you think of anything you kill it. Nothing survives being thought of. (Oscar Wilde)

One of the worst diseases to which the human creature is liable is the disease of thinking. (John Ruskin)

He thinks by infection, catching an opinion like a cold. (John Ruskin)

Most people would die sooner than think; in fact, they do so. (Bertrand Russell)

A great many people think they are thinking when they are merely rearranging their prejudices. (William James)

On advice:

In matters of religion and matrimony I never give any advice; because I will not have anybody's torments in this world or the next laid to my charge. (Lord Chesterfield)

Only when a man is safely ensconced under six feet of earth, with several tons of granite upon his chest, is he in a position to give advice with any certainty, and then he is silent. (A. E. Newton)

Advice, the smallest current coin. (Ambrose Bierce)

I give myself sometimes admirable advice, but am incapable of taking it. (Lady Mary Wortley Montagu)

The only thing to do with good advice is to pass it on. It is never of any use to oneself. (Oscar Wilde)

On plagiarism:

Great literature must spring from an upheaval in the author's soul. If that upheaval is not present then it must come from the works of any other author which happen to be handy and easily adapted. (Robert Benchley)

But Kipling defies plagiarists to do their worst with him:

They copied all they could follow, but they couldn't copy my mind.

Other authors feel less confident:

They lard their lean books with fat of others' work. (Robert Burton)

He invades authors like a monarch, and what would be theft in other poets is only victory in him. (John Dryden, about Ben Jonson)

Plagiarists are always suspicious of being stolen from—as pickpockets are observed commonly to walk with their hands at their breeches' pockets. (S. T. Coleridge)

To disguise his stolen horse, the uneducated thief cuts off the tail; but the educated thief prefers tying on a new tail at the end of the old one, and painting them both sky blue. (Edgar Allan Poe)

What a good thing Adam had—when he said a good thing, he knew nobody had said it before. (Mark Twain)

Plagiarists, at least, have the merit of preservation. (Disraeli)

Witticisms Directed at Judgment of People

Though nobody is willing to admit it, judgment is only too frequently based on unconscious factors, secondarily rationalized. In most cases it would be more accurate to say, instead of "judgment," misjudgment, because of inner bias and inner necessity. There is little reason to mobilize one's store of wit for the sake of attacking the fact that the unconscious is unconscious. Since people know so little of the latter, misjudgment of others is used to prove how "unjust," how "irrational," that childhood enemy, the adult, was. Such witticisms are still the triumphs of the child who is always in search of a "justified" complaint.

The very thing that men think they have got the most of, they have got the least of, and that is judgment. (Josh Billings)

Every man knows that others are mistaken in their judgment of him, but not that he is mistaken in his judgment of others. (Andre Maurois)

Men do not suspect faults which they do not commit. (Samuel Johnson)

Distance is a great promoter of admiration. (Denis Diderot)

You probably wouldn't worry about what people think of you if you could know how seldom they do. (Olin Miller)

In any quarrel, that person will generally be thought in the wrong who it was foretold would quarrel. (Lord Chesterfield)

Experience is not what happens to a man. It is what a man does with what happens to him. (Aldous Huxley)

There may be infirmities in the human consciousness which make it incurably incapable of comprehending its own nature. (H. L. Mencken)

Imagination was given a man to compensate him for what he is not, and a sense of humor was provided to console him for what he is. (Anon.)

The secret of success in life is known only to those who have not succeeded. (John Churton Collins)

One can always recognize women who trust their husbands, they look so thoroughly unhappy. (Oscar Wilde)

One learns in life to keep silent and draw one's own confusions. (Cornelia Otis Skinner)

No brain is stronger than its weakest *th*ink. (Tom Massen)

The world, like an accomplished hostess, pays more attention to those whom it will soonest forget. (John Churton Collins)

The history of human opinion is scarcely anything more than the history of human errors. (Voltaire)

Man can believe the impossible, but man can never believe the improbable. (Oscar Wilde)

A duchess is never more than thirty to a bourgeois. (A French duchess)

To make a trade of laughing at a fool is the highway to become one. (Thomas Fuller)

I hear a great many of the fools are angry at me, and am glad of it, for I write at them, not to them. (William Congreve)

Fools set stools for wise folks to stumble at. (William Camdon)

Some fools have wit, but none have discretion. (La Rochefoucauld)

A fool's tongue is long enough to cut his own throat. (Thomas Fuller)

The greatest, the most dangerous and the least endurable of fools are the reasoning ones. Without being any the less foolish, they conceal from the unreflecting the disorder in their heads by the dexterity of their tongues, and are accepted as wise because they rave more coherently than their brethren in the asylum. (C. M. Wieland)

One half of the human race spends its time in laughing at the other half, and all are fools. (Japanese proverb)

Adam was human; he didn't want the apple for the apple's sake; he wanted it because it was forbidden. (Mark Twain)

Nothing so easily persuades people of little sense as that which they cannot understand. (Jean Cardinal Retz)

Every one complains of his memory, and no one complains of his judgment. (La Rochefoucauld)

When we are too young, our judgment is weak; when we are too old, ditto. (Blaise Pascal)

On account of the stupidity of some people, or (if talent be a more respectable word) on account of their talent for misconception . . . (Edgar Allan Poe)

It's no good crying over spilt milk, because all the forces of the universe were bent on spilling it. (Somerset Maugham)

I come from Indiana, the home of more first-rate second-class men than any state in the Union. (Thomas Marshall)

Every man is a damn fool at least five times every day. Wisdom consists in not exceeding the limit. (Elbert Hubbard)

Witticisms Appealing to Discarded Infantile Megalomania

In the course of childhood development, we have all had to give up parts of our inherent infantile megalomania. The percentage which is relinquished varies; those who have not renounced much are suspicious of those whose renunciation was more thorough. This internal problem is of basic importance in the psychology of the comic (see next chapter). As far as wit is concerned, a specific sub-group remains. It is characterized by a seemingly unashamed admission of one's own greatness; the greatness is of course illusory.

Canute and Mohammed are the classic prototypes of this group, though Mohammed emerges with more credit from his trial of strength with a colossus. How Canute covered his defeat by the tide has not been recorded;[6] but Mohammed's declaration, "If the mountain will not come to Mohammed, Mohammed will come to the mountain," has accumulated symbolic overtones through the centuries, and now stands as a rather jocular example of wise practicality.

Here are other pronunciamentos by people in high, low, and medium places:

Caesar supra grammaticos. (The Emperor is above grammar. Emperor Sigismund)

We are not amused. (Queen Victoria's comment upon seeing an imitation of herself by the groom-in-waiting to the Queen)

Artists, like the Greek gods, are only revealed to one another. (Oscar Wilde)

Telephone operator in publisher's office: "A man who says he is the world's greatest author is here to see you." Publisher: "Send Private Saroyan in." (Bennett Cerf in *Try and Stop Me.*)

You cannot disappoint a continent. (James McNeill Whistler, when discussing some friends' suggestion that he visit his homeland)

Whistler was once confronted with a stranger who told him that he was just his age and a local compatriot—they had both been born 68 years before in Lowell, Massachusetts, "So you are 68 years old and were born in Lowell. Well, sire, I refuse to be 68 years old or to have been born in Lowell."

I may not always be right, but I am never wrong. (A movie tycoon)

I never made a mistake in my life; at least, never one that I couldn't explain away afterwards. (R. Kipling)

Frank Sullivan wrote a laudatory review of Fred Schwed, Jr.'s hilarious book on Wall Street, *Where Are the Customer's Yachts*? Schwed then wrote him the following letter, which he is allowing me to use:

Dear Mr. Sullivan:

I read with pleasure your flattering review in the New York Herald Tribune, and I thank you gratefully.

[6] The popular legend of Canute as obstinacy personified is contradicted by some authorities who claim that he used this means to puncture the exaggerated adulation of his followers.

However, there was one part of your review that especially interested me, where you said that if you were J. P. Morgan, you would invite me to become a partner. You also said that you had no reason to believe that you were not Mr. Morgan.

What I would like you to do is to examine yourself thoroughly and determine, once and for all, if you are Morgan or only Sullivan. Frankly, things have not been going too well with me financially so I would be definitely interested in becoming a Morgan partner if it is possible. Of course if it turns out that you do not have a big black mustache, all my dream castles come tumbling down.

In return for your trouble, I agree that if it ever turns out that I am Mrs. Ogden Reid, publisher of the Herald Tribune, I will make you chief editorial writer at a generous salary.

Sincerely, etc.

Mr. Schwed informs me that Sullivan replied to this with an equally formal letter. "It said that I should not bother to become Mrs. Reid—that all he wanted me to do was to put Pennsylvania Railroad stock back at 40 from its then price of 12."

Around 1910, an anti-Semitic deputy to the Parliament of Imperial Austria, Carl Lueger, who had formerly been Mayor of Vienna, delivered a harassing speech against an adversary. The adversary was attacked for being a Jew. A heckler interrupted the speech, calling out that the adversary was *not* a Jew. Lueger answered: "*I* determine who is or is not a Jew."

When I want to read a book, I write one. (Disraeli)

Aesop's fly, sitting on the axle of the chariot, has been much laughed at for exclaiming, "What dust I do raise!" (Thomas Carlyle)

Father expected a good deal of God. He didn't actually accuse God of inefficiency, but when he prayed his tone was lucid and angry, like that of a dissatisfied guest in a carelessly managed hotel. (Clarence Day)

Some movie stars wear their sunglasses even in church; they're afraid God might recognize them and ask for autographs. (Fred Allen)

The way Bernard Shaw believes in himself is very refreshing in these atheistic days when so many people believe in no God at all. (I. Zangwill)

Few people think more than two or three times a year; I have made an international reputation for myself by thinking once or twice a week. (G. B. Shaw)

He admits that there are two sides to every question—his own and the wrong side. (Channing Pollock)

We are both great men, but I have succeeded better in keeping it a profound secret than he has. (Edgar Wilson Nye)

To love oneself is the beginning of a lifelong romance. (Oscar Wilde)

One of my chief regrets during my years in the theatre is that I couldn't sit in the audience and watch me. (John Barrymore)

I often quote myself; it adds spice to my conversation. (G. B. Shaw)

To his dog, every man is Napoleon; hence the constant popularity of dogs. (Aldous Huxley)

"The more articulate, the less said," is an old Chinese proverb which I just made up myself. (Don Herold)

We reproach people for talking about themselves; but it is the subject they treat best. (Anatole France)

Talk to a man about himself, and he will listen for hours. (Disraeli)

I've given up reading books; I find it takes my mind off myself. (Oscar Levant)

Witticisms Directed at Misjudgment of Oneself and Other People

When Jonathan Swift, whose writings have been described as satires of "savage indignation," said of himself in *Polite Conversation*: "I hate nobody; I am in charity with the world"; when Samuel Johnson, the Great Cham and great bully of his time, opined: "I look upon myself as a good-humoured fellow" (an opinion to which even the admiring Boswell dissented)—one laughs at the enormity of the misjudgment, and recalls Nietzsche's dictum: "The most common sort of lie is that by which a man deceives himself; the deception of others is a relatively rare offense." The "lie," of course, is not a lie in the conscious meaning of the word.

The same interpretation applies to Oscar Wilde's definition: "Conscience and cowardice are really the same things; conscience is the trade name of the firm." This from Wilde, whose conscience-directed unconscious self-destructive tendencies brought him jail, exile and poverty!

On the other hand, many people justify and approve self-deception:

I lie, therefore I persist. The art of survival is the art of lying to oneself heroically, continuously, creatively. The senses lie to the mind, the mind lies to the senses. The truth-seeker is a liar; he is hunting for happiness, not truth. (Benjamin De Casseres)

Goethe abhorred "knowing oneself":

Man is a darkened being; he knows not whence he comes, nor whither he goes, he knows little of the world and least of himself. I know not myself, and God forbid that I should! (From Goethe's *Conversations With Eckermann*)

Eulogies have a niche to themselves. In a statement to the press after Mark Twain's death, President William Howard Taft said: "He never wrote a line that a father could not read to a daughter." This statement has the air of solemn approval suitable for eulogies, but it is merely laughable to anyone who knows of Twain's ribald productions, or who has learned, as one of his biographers said, that his wife "not only edited his work but edited him." Taft should at least have said "published" instead of "wrote."

There is a wealth of other examples, pro and con self-deception:

Man cannot make a worm; yet he will make gods by the dozen. (Michel de Montaigne)

Satire is a sort of glass wherein beholders do generally discover everybody's face but their own, which is the chief reason for that kind of reception it meets with in the world. (Jonathan Swift)

On me, when dunces are satiric,
I take it for a panagyric. (Jonathan Swift)

Self-esteem = $\frac{\text{Success}}{\text{Pretensions}}$ (William James; definition contained in *Psychology, Briefer Course*, Chapter XII)

Strange that a Man who has wit enough to write a Satire should have folly enough to publish it. (Benjamin Franklin)

Every absurdity has a champion to defend it. (Oliver Goldsmith)

Culture is what your butcher would have if he were a surgeon. (Mary Pettibone Poole)

To observations which ourselves we make, We grow more partial for th'observer's sake. (Alexander Pope)

Many a man fails as an original thinker simply because his memory is too good. (Friedrich Nietzsche)

A man finds he has been wrong at every preceding stage of his career, only to deduce the astonishing conclusion that he is at last entirely right. (Robert Louis Stevenson)

I much prefer a compliment, insincere or not, to sincere criticism. (Plautus)

Adversity introduces a man to himself. (Anon.)

Men occasionally stumble over the truth, but most of them pick themselves up as is nothing had happened. (Winston Churchill)

In this world, truth can wait; she's used to it. (Douglas Jerrold)

Minds are like parachutes: they only function when open. (Lord Dewar)

Witticisms Consisting of Making a Reproach into a Virtue

This type of witticism is closely allied to repartee (see Chapter Six). Its purposes, both conscious and unconscious, are immediately apparent—and identical as well.

Lying, the telling of beautiful untrue things, is the proper aim of art. (Oscar Wilde)

Yes, I am a Jew, and when the ancestors of the right honorable gentleman were brutal savages in an unknown island, mine were priests in the temple of Solomon. (Benjamin Disraeli, replying to an anti-Semitic remark by Daniel O'Connell)

My father was a tailor; my mother was a housemaid. Except for these, I have no notable ancestors. (A. E Coppard)

I came upstairs into the world, for I was born in a cellar. (William Congreve)

A memorable example of this form of wit turned up some years ago. As is well-known, when a business firm makes an exaggerated claim for the efficacy of its product, the Federal Trade Commission has the right to issue a summons calling upon the firm to appear before the Commission in order to prove its claims. This summons is called a "citation." One firm, having received its summons, promptly stated in its ads: "Cited by the Federal Trade Commission."

The well-known, and perhaps not apocryphal, story about Fritz Kreisler falls into this category. Kreisler was invited to play at a private musicale before a gathering of society people. He requested a fee of $1000. The hostess reluctantly agreed, specifying, "But remember, you are only an entertainer, and cannot mingle with my guests." Kreisler replied, "In that case, my fee will be $500."

Witticisms Directed at Pretending Not to Mind Whereas One Minds Very Much

These witticisms represent a veiled attack on the educators who implanted "higher values" in the child. By recourse to the primitive-"essential," the educators are satirized by the child in the adult, and the alleged hypocrisies of the educators are revealed:

The discovery of a new dish does more for the happiness of mankind than the discovery of a star. (Brillat-Savarin)

Some people have a foolish way of not minding, or pretending not to mind, what they eat. For my part; I mind my belly very studiously and very carefully; for I look upon it that he who does not mind his belly will hardly mind anything else. (Samuel Johnson)

A man seldom thinks with more earnestness of anything than he does of his dinner. (Samuel Johnson)

All human history attests
That happiness for man—the hungry sinner!
Since Eve ate apples, much depends on dinner. (Lord Byron)

He was an ingenious man that first found out eating and drinking. (Jonathan Swift)

There is no love sincerer than the love of food. (G. B. Shaw)

Indigestion is charged by God with enforcing morality on the stomach. (Victor Hugo)

All men will naturally commit fornication, as all men will naturally steal. (Samuel Johnson)

Every great man now has his disciples, and it is always Judas who writes the biography. (Oscar Wilde)

It is with epigrams as with inventions in general: the best are just those which annoy us because we did not think of them ourselves. (Georg C. Lichtenberg)

The official language of the State of Illinois shall be known hereafter as the American language, and not as the English language. (Act of the Legislature of Illinois, Ch. 127, Sec. 178, 1923)

The thought that a great many people must be in a worse position than ourselves does not, indeed, put a roof over our heads, but provides a good enough shelter during a passing shower. (Georg C. Lichtenberg)

Jokes About Exhibitionism of Thoughts

This type of witticism is directed at loquacity and mental exhibitionism of scholars. The target of attack is the teacher who claims that scientists' work is the pursuit of the elusive goddess of truth—for the sake of truth.

Knowledge is not knowledge until someone else knows that one knows. (Lucullus)

Knowledge is, in most of those who cultivate it, a species of money, which is valued greatly, but only adds to our well-being in proportion as it is communicated, and is only good in commerce. Take from the wise the pleasure of being listened to, and knowledge would be nothing to them. (Jean Jacques Rousseau)

"Fishing for Contradiction" Witticisms

Once more, the child in the adult is attacking the hypocrisy of adults. Elbert Hubbard's aphorism is paradigmatic: "All the world loves a lover, but not while the love-making is going on." The scene is set for sentimentality by borrowing Emerson's familiar phrase; the second half of Hubbard's aphorism destroys the sentimental effect of the first, and reveals the hypocrisy behind it.

A modest man is usually admired—if people ever hear of him. (Edgar W. Howe)

A sharp tongue is the only edged tool that grows keener with constant use. (Washington Irving)

It is difficult to get a man to understand something when his salary depends upon his not understanding it. (Upton Sinclair)

I once knew a fellow who spoke a dialect with an accent. (Irvin Cobb)

We may convince others by our arguments, but we can only persuade them by their own. (Joseph Joubert)

A cow is a very good animal in the field, but we turn her out of the garden. (Samuel Johnson)

The roulette table pays nobody except him who keeps it. Nevertheless a passion for gaming is common, though a passion for keeping roulette tables is unknown. (G. B. Shaw)

A bank is a place where they lend you an umbrella in fair weather and ask for it back again when it begins to rain. (Anon.)

Everybody wants to live long, though nobody wants to be old. (La Rochefoucauld)

A vagabond, when rich, is called a tourist. (Paul Richard)

When the rich assemble to concern themselves with the business of the poor, it is called charity. When the poor assemble to concern themselves with the business of the rich it is called anarchy. (Paul Richard)

If one plays good music people don't listen; and if one plays bad music, people don't talk. (Oscar Wilde)

Witticisms Based on Sophisms

The purpose here is to reduce logic to absurdity; at the same time the parents who instilled logic and respect for logic in the child are ridiculed.

In K. Immerman's version of the legends of Baron Muenchhausen, the legendary liar proves that "sweet milk is but a product of the degeneration of the only natural state—sour." Muenchhausen is telling of his adventures among the Apapurincasiquinitischchiquisaqua, an apocryphal tribe of South American Indians, and he fortifies the point mentioned above by arguing that apples and plums are sour to begin with, and turn sweet only after the "treacherous sun" takes away their virginity.

One of Abraham Lincoln's stories fits into this category: "He reminds me of the man who murdered both his parents, and then, when sentence was about to be pronounced, pleaded for mercy on the grounds that he was an orphan."

A stingy millionaire (some authorities would call this a redundancy) invited all his acquaintances to an elaborate dinner to celebrate his daughter's marriage. The fittings of the table were magnificent, but the menu consisted of—water. Everyone was enraged until the millionaire explained: "I wanted to serve you the best, and went out to buy fish. 'Are they any good?' I asked the owner of the fish-market. 'Good? The best in the world. They taste like sugar.' I realized that sugar is better than fish. 'Is the sugar any good?' I asked the grocer. 'Good? My sugar tastes like honey.' I went to buy honey. 'Is the honey any good?' I asked the honey-dealer. 'Good? The honey is as clear as oil.' I didn't like the answer, 'as oil,' only the best is good enough for my guests. I went to buy oil. 'Is the oil any good?' I asked the oil-dealer. 'Good? My oil is clear as water.' So I served you the best there is—water."

Two poor cousins, otherwise enemies, visited their wealthy uncle together. The stingy uncle offered them plenty of watery tea and two pieces of pastry, one slightly larger than the other. After a good deal of hesitation and many polite suggestions of "After you, my dear cousin," one cousin reached out and helped himself to the larger piece. The second cousin was furious. "You boor! How could you be so impolite as to grab the bigger piece?"—"Well, what would you have done in my place?"—"Taken the smaller piece, of course!"—"Then what are you complaining about? You got the smaller piece anyhow!"

And in more epigrammatic form:

Thou hast committed Fornication, but that was in another country, and besides, the wench is dead. (Christopher Marlowe)

The stones that critics hurl with harsh intent
A man may use to build his monument. (Arthur Guiterman)

Truth is an imaginary line dividing error into two parts. (Elbert Hubbard)

Witticisms Using Faulty Reasoning to Reduce Reasoning to Absurdity

These witticisms use a complicated disguise. Purportedly attacking "stupidity," they actually attack the forcibly instilled logic of the educators, later enshrined in the severe superego. This joke is typical:

A man in a restaurant, looking over his bill, discovers that the waitress has made an error to her own disadvantage. According to her private arithmetic, seven plus seven adds up to eleven. He draws her attention to the error, but the waitress is not grateful; instead, she becomes impatient with him, and tells him: "I can prove that seven and seven make eleven. My husband and I are both married for the second time. We each had four children in our previous marriages, and we have three children in this marriage. So we each have seven children, but both together we have eleven. Please pay your bill, and leave me alone."

A man made a nuisance of himself to his liquor dealer by constantly asking why salt should be so cheap when whiskey is so dear. One day the dealer lost his patience, smiled benevolently, and enlightened the customer: "I finally figured out the answer to your question. Once upon a time, a group of liquor consumers were plagued with the identical problem which is bothering you. They decided to send a deputation to Lot, the Biblical drinker. But the deputation made a mistake, and ended up at the grave of Lot's wife instead of Lot. They told their tale, and asked for help, but unfortunately Lot's wife's influence in Heaven extends only to her own department. And so salt remained inexpensive."

Three wise men of Gotham
Went to sea in a bowl,
And if the bowl had been stronger
My tale had been longer. (Old English rhyme)

Eve was the unluckiest woman alive; she could not throw up to Adam the better men she might have married. (Anon.)

Witticisms Taking as Target the Wrong Reasons for Otherwise Approved Moral Attitudes

These jokes are a cross between those attacking hypocrisy and those attacking impeachable reasons for applying otherwise unimpeachable moral precepts. Macaulay's remark, in his *History of England*, Vol. I, is typical: "The Puritans hated bear-baiting, not because it gave pain to the bear, but because it gave pleasure to the spectators."

The Puritans were an easy target for this type of witticism. Here is another example:

To Banbury came I, O profane one!
Where I saw a Puritan once
Hanging his cat on Monday
For killing a mouse on Sunday. (Richard Brathwaite)

Witticisms Directed at Exaggerated Moral Obligations

In unmasking and debunking exaggerated moral obligations, the child in the adult once more attacks the educators who tried to instil hyper-respect for these obligations in him.

The good end happily, the bad unhappily. That is what fiction means. (Oscar Wilde)

The wages of sin is death, and the wages of virtue is death also. (Anon.)

Duty is what one expects from others. (Oscar Wilde)

A friend is one who knows your faults, yet loves you in spite of your virtues. (Anon.)

It is easier to fight for one's principles than to live up to them. (Alfred Adler)

The peculiarity of prudery is to multiply sentinels in proportion as the fortress is less threatened. (Victor Hugo)

I like work. It fascinates me. I can sit and look at it for hours. I love to keep it by me; the idea of getting rid of it nearly breaks my heart. (Jerome K. Jerome)

Some would have children. Those who have them moan
Or wish them gone. (Francis Bacon)

Compromise makes a good umbrella, but a poor roof. (James Russell Lowell)

Confession may be good for the soul, but it doesn't get one much reputation for sense. (Anon.)

The worm of conscience keeps the same hours as the owl. (Johann Wolfgang Schiller)

Listen to conscience, and you will have nothing to eat. (Chinese proverb)

There is no one who does not exaggerate. (R. W. Emerson)

Exaggeration is a truth which lost its temper. (Kahlil Gibran)

If you can't be good, be sanitary. (American soldiers' saying in France in World War I)

"There is," said Candide, "a great amount of evil in the world"—"What does it matter," said the dervish, "whether it is good or evil? When His Highness sends a ship to Egypt does he worry about the comfort or discomfort of the rats aboard?" (Voltaire)

If those who are the enemies of innocent amusement had the direction of the world, they would take away the spring, and youth, the former from the year, the latter from human life. (Honoré de Balzac)

Amusement is the happiness of those who cannot think. (Alexander Pope)

The true artist will let his wife starve, his children go barefoot, his mother drudge for his living at seventy, sooner than work at anything but art. (G. B. Shaw)

The great artists of the world were never Puritans, and seldom even ordinarily respected. (H. L. Mencken)

Let us have wine and women, mirth and laughter,
Sermons and soda-water the day after. (Byron)

Witticisms Directed at Hypocrisy

Witticisms debunking alleged hypocrisy are the classical example of the inner battle directed at enshrined educators; the purpose is "to cut them down to size." The motto is always the same: "They voted dry and lived wet." Having established the contradication (real or spurious), the child in the adult is on firmer ground in his attempts to counteract the reproaches of conscience.

Hypocrisy, per se, is a complicated phenomenon. It is an unconscious technique used in the battle of the conscience. It is a simulated surrender to the inner dictator; it perpetuates the temporary situation, in childhood, when a rigid and severe educator (or one whom the child believes to be rigid and severe) emphasizes the importance of lip-service conformity with his commands, and is not concerned with their inner acceptance. The conflict, dating from that period, is internalized and made permanent in the hypocrite's smiling pseudo-submission. This fake submission is a caricature of the now internalized educator.

If you give him time, man often succeeds in living up to his hypocrisies. (Anonymous, quoted by J. A. Spender)

Hypocrisy at the fashionable end of town is very different from hypocrisy in the City. The snobbish hypocrite endeavors to appear more vicious than he really is, the other kind of hypocrite more virtuous. (James Addison)

I hope you have not been leading a double life, pretending to be wicked, and being really good all the time. That would be hypocrisy. (Oscar Wilde)

Foolish to judge, for we are sinners all. (William Shakespeare)

There are three things that are not to be credited: a woman when she weeps, a merchant when he swears, nor a drunkard when he prays. (Barnaby Rich)

The general principle upon which the newer morality differs from the traditional morality of Puritanism is that: We believe that instinct should be trained rather than thwarted. (Bertrand Russell)

A man who drinks only water is highly suspect to me. He has some secret vice to hide. (Baudelaire)

Being a woman is a terribly difficult trade, since it consists principally of dealing with men. (Joseph Conrad)

Reading the epitaphs, our only salvation lies in resurrecting the dead and burying the living. (Paul Eldridge)

There is no man so good, who, were he to submit all his thoughts and actions to the laws, would not deserve hanging ten times in his life. (Michel de Montaigne)

Old men are fond of giving good advice, to console themselves for being no longer in the position to give bad examples. (La Rochefoucauld)

Without some dissimulation no business can be carried out at all. (Lord Chesterfield)

It is not true that suffering ennobles the character; happiness does that sometimes, but suffering, for the most part, makes men petty and vindictive. (Somerset Maugham)

A wealthy man was building a house. A bystander watched him at the site, supervising the excavation for the foundation. The bystander said, "Good luck to you!"—"Nothing good about my luck so far—I take my money and put it into the earth," was the reply.—"Don't worry," was the reassuring answer. "With God's help you will soon get to your money."

While on a train trip, two friends were held up by a band of masked bandits. "Your money or your life!" they were told. As they were about to comply, one friend turned to the other and said, "I owe you $1000. Take the money and let me have the satisfaction of being a man without debts!"

Witticisms Directed at Specialized Professions

Every profession is ridiculed in wit. Modern specialization has been a fruitful and satisfying source of witticisms, though similar attacks were by no means unknown in the good old days when one storekeeper was butcher, watchmaker, and repairer of umbrellas. "Jack of all trades, master of none" is a witticism, not a formula. Attacks on specialists arise from an unconscious offense against infantile megalomania: specialization means undisputed, though circumscribed, power.

On the lawyer:

One who protects us against robbery by taking away the temptation. (H. L. Mencken)

One skilled in circumvention of the law. (Ambrose Bierce)

On physicians:

He has been a doctor a year now and has had two patients—no, three, I think—yes, it was three; I attended their funerals. (Mark Twain)

Anatomists see no beautiful woman in all their lives, but only a ghastly sack of bones with Latin names to them, and a network of nerves and muscles and organs inflamed by disease. (Mark Twain)

A lie is useful only as a medicine to man. The use of such medicines should be confined to physicians. (Plato)

A physician is only a consoler of the mind. (Petronius)

He's the best physician that knows the worthlessness of most medicines. (Benjamin Franklin)

I observe the physician with the same diligence as he the disease. (John Donne)

Every physician, almost, hath his favorite disease. (Henry Fielding)

The most dangerous physicians are those who, being born actors, imitate born physicians with perfect imposture. (Friedrich Nietzsche)

A physician who demands no fee is worth none. (The Talmud)

Strive to preserve your health; and in this you will the better succeed in proportion as you keep clear of the physicians, for their drugs are a kind of alchemy concerning which there are no fewer books than there are medicines. (Leonardo da Vinci)

Doctors think a lot of patients cured who have simply left in disgust. (Don Herold)

"Ever had appendicitis?"
"I was operated on—whether it was appendicitis or professional curiosity I never found out."

Doctor to Coroner: "Do you wish a death certificate for the body?"
Coroner: "Just state that you treated him."

"Some time ago," recollected a pompous doctor, "when I started my practice, I used to make entries for non-existent patients in my book, just as Osler did with his entry for his first patient, 'Removed speck in cornea, 50¢.' I used to sit in my office like patience on a monument."
"And now," was the rejoinder, "you have monuments on all your patients."

A famous surgeon is making his hospital round followed by a train of young physicians. Stopping at the bedside of a man whom he had declared to be inoperable, he states laconically, "Casus perditus (hopeless case)." His entourage respectfully registers the verdict and notes with relief that the patient does not understand Latin. A few weeks later, the very same patient, who has in the meantime recovered with Nature's inexplicable help, meets the great surgeon on the street. He thanks the surgeon for his help, and adds, "It is really marvellous what progress medicine has made. You just said two words—'Casus perditus'—and pronto, I recovered."

Irvin S. Cobb describes the tribulations of a patient in his satire, *Speaking of Operations.* The first physician tells the patient he needs an operation, which will have to be performed by someone else, for he is merely a diagnostician. An expert diagnostician, the patient agrees; how did he know, without being told, that the patient had only fifteen dollars with him? The patient asks the diagnostician about surgeons, and is told that a certain surgeon specializes in eye, ear, nose and throat operations only. The modern practitioner, the patient concludes, obeys certain strict laws which the patient knows nothing about. The patient is "divided up" and "partitioned": the torso for one surgeon, the legs to another, and so on.

On osteopaths:

One who argues that all human ills are caused by the pressure of hard bone upon soft tissue. The proof of his theory is to be found in the heads of those who believe it. (H. L. Mencken)

On advertising specialists:

Advertising agency: 85% confusion and 15% commission. (Fred Allen)

On politicians:

Politician: an animal who can sit on the fence and yet keep both ears on the ground. (Anon.)

A straw vote only shows which way the hot air blows. (O. Henry)

Party is madness of many for the gain of few. (Alexander Pope)

Politics are now nothing more than a means of rising in the world. (Samuel Johnson)

In politics there is no honor. (Disraeli)

An honest politician is one who, when he is bought, will stay bought. (Simon Cameron, 1799–1889, party boss of Pennsylvania)

On actors:

A character actor is one who cannot act and therefore makes an elaborate study of disguises and stage tricks by which acting can be grotesquely simulated. (G. B. Shaw)

On the stage he was natural, simple, affecting; 'Twas only that when he was off he was acting. (Oliver Goldsmith, of David Garrick)

On geneologists:

One who traces back your family as far as your money will go. (Anon.)

On philosophers:

Philosophy—unintelligible answers to insoluble problems. (Henry Adams)

If a man proves too clearly and convincingly to himself . . . that a tiger is an optical illusion— well, he will find out that he is wrong. The tiger will himself intervene in the discussion in a manner which will be in every sense conclusive. (G. K. Chesterton)

Philosophers there are who try to make themselves believe that this life is happy, but they believe it only while they are saying it, and never yet produced conviction in a single mind. (Samuel Johnson)

Can a donkey be tragic? Is it tragedy to perish under a load one can neither bear nor throw off? This is the case of the philosopher. (Friedrich Nietzsche)

A metaphysician is a man who goes into a dark cellar at midnight without a light looking for a black cat that is not there. (Bowen Colwood)

He who regards another's wife as his mother, another's goods as clods of earth, and all mankind as himself, is a philosopher. (Tertullian)

There is no statement so absurd that no philosopher will make it. (Cicero)

Philosophers quarreled with one another like drunken men in dark rooms who hate peace without knowing why they fight, or seeing how to take aim. (Sydney Smith)

No living creature is subject to the privilege of absurdity, but man only. And of men, those are of all most subject to it that profess philosophy. (Thomas Hobbes)

"We two have much to think of," said the louse to the head of the philosopher. (German saying)

On professors:

O passionate Heloise,
I, too, have lived under the ban,
With seven hundred professors,
And not a single man. (J. E. Spingarn)

On historians:

Very few things happen at the right time, and the rest does not happen at all; the consciencious historian will correct these defects. (Ascribed to Herodotus)

History books which contain no lies are extremely dull. (Anatole France)

History is something that never happened, described by a man who wasn't there. (Anon.)

My dear Smollett (author of *History of England*) disgraces his talent by writing those stupid romances commonly called history. (Lady Mary Wortley Montagu)

If an historian were to relate truthfully all the crimes, weaknesses and disorders of mankind, his readers would take his work for satire rather than history. (Pierre Bayle)

Histories are a kind of distilled newspapers. (Thomas Carlyle)

History is a fairy tale whose end is death. (J. A. Cramb)

On critics:

Insects sting, not in malice, but because they want to live. It is the same with critics; they desire our blood, not our pain. (Friedrich Nietzsche)

Critics! appalled I venture the name,
Those cut-throat bandits on the path of fame. (Robert Burns)

Critics in general are venomous serpents that delight in *hissing*. (W. R. Daniel)

For critics, I care the five hundredth thousandth part of the tythe of a half-farthing. (Charles Lamb)

Pay no attention to what the critics say; there has never been set up a statue in honor of a critic. (Jan Sibelius)

The absence of humility in critics is something wonderful. (Arthur Helps)

A critic: a man who writes about things he doesn't like. (Anon.)

A critic is a legless man who teaches running. (Channing Pollock)

Critics are like brushers of noblemen's clothes. (Henry Wolton)

The title of ultra-crepidarian has been given to those critics who find fault with small and insignificant details. (William Hazlitt)

A fly, sir, may sting a stately horse, and make him wince, but one is but an insect and the other still a horse. (Samuel Johnson)

Nature fits all her children with something to do; He who would write and can't, can surely review. (J. R. Lowell)

Criticism strips the tree of both caterpillars and blossoms. (Jean Paul Richter)

Criticism itself is much criticized, which logically establishes its title. (W. C. Brownell)

Authors are judged by strange, capricious rules,
The great ones are thought mad, the small ones fools. (Alexander Pope)

The greatest misfortune of a man of letters is not being the object of his confreres' jealousy, the victim of a cabal, the despised of the men in power, but of being judged by fools. (Voltaire)

I can live for two months on a good compliment. I like criticism, but it must be my way. (Mark Twain)

A brilliant epigram is a solemn platitude gone to a masquerade ball. (R. L. Stevenson)

On journalists:

In centuries before ours the public nailed the ears of journalists to the pump. In this century journalists have nailed their own ears to the keyhole. (Oscar Wilde)

The difference between literature and journalism is that journalism is unreadable, and literature not read. (Oscar Wilde)

Modern journalism justifies its own existence by the great Darwinian principle of the survival of the vulgarest. (Oscar Wilde)

Translated from journalese into plain English. (Anon.)

Journalists have always been our most old-fashioned class, being too busy with the news of the day to lay aside the mental habits of fifty years before. (Frank Moore Colby)

On writers:

Poets have a license to lie. (Pliny)

All poets are mad. (Robert Burton)

Astronomers, painters and poets may lie by authority. (Sir John Harrington)

Whenever a poet praises the verses of another poet you may be sure that they are stupid and of no real value. (J. de la Bruyere)

Poets, like whores, are only hated by each other. (William Wycherly)

There is a pleasure in poetic pains
Which only poets know. (William Cowper)

Poets, being liars by profession, ought to have good memories. (Jonathan Swift)

He that lives with the muses shall die in the straw. (Thomas Fuller)

It is not necessary for a writer to be crazy, but it is useful. (Anon.)

The reason why so few good books are written is that so few people who can write know anything. (Walter Bagehot)

Witticisms Based on Misunderstandings of Human Motivations

A. E. Coppard's delightful story, "Alas, Poor Bollington," is an elaboration and enlargement of this type of witticism. Coppard describes Bollington as an "unassertive" man, so "mild and modest he cut no figure at all." He had been married, and he had irritated his wife in many ways, among them, by not objecting to her philandering. When he, in his turn, "paid some attention" to a lady they had met in Belfast, the marital quarrels became more violent, and in a fit of strongmindedness Bollington left his wife. Thereafter he was consumed with remorse for his crime. He could not forget his crime—or his wife; after some years of self-imposed exile in America, he returned to London and finally found his wife again. To his surprise and delight, she greeted him with kisses. To his pleas for forgiveness, she repeatedly said, "I have nothing to forgive." She was being perfectly truthful, for she had walked out of their hotel immediately after his departure, never suspecting that he did not mean to return, and *she* had never returned. When she learned that he, not she, had done the running away, she told him indignantly, "Now I *never* want to see your face again!"

The aphorists do not neglect this theme:

Women are never disarmed by compliments; men always are. (Oscar Wilde)

It is often more necessary to conceal contempt than resentment, for the former being never forgiven, but the latter sometimes forgot. Wrongs are often forgiven; contempt never. (Lord Chesterfield)

Witticisms Praising the Trifle Leading to Great Events

This form of wit is a favorite with some people. It stems from the disparity between the child's and the adult's evaluation of a particular mishap or offense to megalomania suffered by the child. Minutiae are thus magnified.

The approach of the average adult toward details is replete with contradictions. He admires people who, like the great detectives and diagnosticians, are capable of drawing far-reaching conclusions from little details. At the same time he satirizes the detail-hunter of the Sherlock Holmes variety and believes such nonsense possibly only in fiction. To complicate matters, he is irritated with people who are incapable of seeing a situation in its complex entirety and considers the person who concentrates on a few unimportant details to be below his own level of intelligence.

The adult never stops to clarify his attitude toward details. Hence, one finds in the same person admiration, rejection, anger, complaint—all centered around the use or misuse of details.

Could one pin down an intelligent adult and force him to clarify his attitude, he would, after thinking it over, very likely say something like this: It is important to be able to see a situation as a whole, overlooking hundreds of details and concentrating on essentials and general trends. Most people do exactly the opposite: they observe only unimportant details and thus arrive at erroneous conclusions. On the other hand, details may be indicative of the situation as a whole: the problem is obviously to distinguish between unimportant trimmings and significant details.

A patient of mine was laughed at by her rather sophisticated friends when, asked for her impressions after attending a performance of *Hamlet*, she observed: "The actor who played Hamlet's part must have been left-handed: he was holding the skull in his left hand during the churchyard scene."

She then went on to point out that in a well-known thriller the whole problem of who committed the murder hinged on the discovery that because of the type of wound inflicted the guilty person must be left-handed. In the big trial scene, the lawyer asked to borrow the watch of the witness, then threw it back to him. Instinctively, the guilty suspect caught the expensive watch with his left hand. My patient complained that the same people who had laughed at her comment on the play, admired the cleverness of the mystery's denouement. The difference is clear-cut: in the first case, her friends expected a psychological analysis of Hamlet's indecision and got instead a rather pointless observation of an irrelevant detail. In the murder story, the detail of left-handedness was a decisive clue.

In general, it can be stated that, more often then not, for reasons unknown to them, intelligent people mistrust details. The reason for this can be traced back to the child's reaction to disappointment. We know that the child is apt to draw far-reaching and general conclusions from small incidents; a child of three or four, if he is confronted with either a specific disappointment or a particularized reproach, reacts with a *general* feeling of hatred. He cannot make the fine distinction of which the adult is capable, and remember that he "likes" the educator in general but "dislikes" his behavior in this particular instance. The child's reaction, though transitory, is immediate and generalized.

This hatred and rejection is promptly followed by a feeling of guilt, since these negative tendencies are directed at mother, father or their representatives. Consequently, the child is torn between the generalized feeling of hatred and the superego's reproach, "Mother is good to you in general; you should love her even if she disappointed you this time." The child's aggression, mobilized through the mother's offense against his omnipotence, wants to assert itself *despite* that feeling of guilt. In order to prove its case, therefore, the ego must *magnify and deepen the importance of the specific disappointing detail.* Since the detail is thus used as defense against a superego reproach, it is magnified out of all proportion. The child clings to his specific disappointment, showing it obstinately and using the formula: "You can say what you want; that small disappointment was *real.*" In this way the detail becomes the basis and pattern of every affective experience.

While a cadet at West Point, Whistler took an oral examination in chemistry during which he defined silicon as a gas. This answer ended his career at the Academy. In later years, Whistler commented: "If silicon were a gas, I would be a major general."

A wealthy upstart attempted to purchase Whistler's studio in toto; he wanted "the whole shooting match," meaning works in progress as well as finished pictures, furnishings, etc. Whistler asked for five million dollars; when the prospective purchaser gasped, the artist explained, "My posthumous prices."

Even where the sense is perfectly clear, a sentence may be deprived of half its force —its spirit—its point—by improper punctuation. For the want of merely a comma, it often occurs that an axiom appears a paradox, or that a sarcasm is converted into a sermonoid. (Edgar Allan Poe)

If Columbus had not sailed westward with the obstinacy of a maniac, he would not have encountered some pieces of wood, worked by the hand of man, twenty-four hours before he came to San Salvador, and that ridiculous circumstance would not have given courage to his crew, and he would have had to swallow his shame, return to Europe, and count himself lucky to get there. (Hector Berlioz)

Cromwell was about to ravage all Christendom; the royal family was lost, and his own forever powerful, had it not been for a grain of sand that got into his ureter. (Blaise Pascal)

Amoebas at the start
Were not complex;
They tore themselves apart
And started sex. (Arthur Guiterman)

But words are things, and a small drop of ink,
Falling like dew upon a thought, produces
That which makes thousands, perhaps millions, think.
(Lord Byron)

Political Witticisms

The purely contemporary political joke or "crack" is a kick constructed *ad hoc;* most of the time its ammunition is a detail of the passing political scene, and becomes a dud as soon as the scene itself loses its importance. Purely political jokes are devastating only when new. William Hazlitt, by no means a negligible judge of wit in general, overlooked this factor in stating that

> . . . Mr. Sheridan's description of Mr. Addington's administration as the fag-end of Mr. Pitt's, who had remained so long on the treasury bench that . . . 'he left the sitting part of the man behind him,' is as fine an example of metaphorical wit as any on record. ("On Wit and Humor")

This joke stood up only as long as it was protected by a more or less contemporary flavor.

There are political jokes, however, which should really be classed as "name-dropping jokes"; the essential witticism has nothing to do with politics, but gains added zest by being ascribed to persons of prominence and achievement. An example is the devastating retort once supposed to have been made by William Pitt to Robert Walpole, Earl of Oxford, and a century later credited to Disraeli as his reply to Gladstone:

> "Sir, you will either die upon the gallows or of some unspeakable disease!"
> "That depends on whether I embrace your principles or your mistress."

If medical science had not advanced, or such forms of invective had not gone out of fashion, the retort would surely have been brought up to date again.

Some political jokes represent an entire epoch; these stand up very well:

God bless the King—I mean the Faith's Defender;
God bless (no harm in blessing) the Pretender!
But who Pretender is, or who is King,
God bless us all!—That's quite another thing. (J. Byrom)

Ireland never was contented.
Say you so? You are demented.
Ireland was contented when
All could use the sword and pen,
And when Tara rose so high
That her turrets split the sky,
And about her courts were seen
Liveried angels robed in green,
Wearing, by St Patrick's bounty,
Emeralds big as half the county. (Walter Savage Landor)

Here lies our Sovereign Lord the King,
Whose word no man relies on,

Who never said a foolish thing,
Nor ever did a wise one. (Earl of Rochester, "Epitaph on Charles II")

Some of the following witticisms have still to prove themselves; some are already "established":

If you can't lick 'em, join 'em. (Anon.)

A liberal may be likened to a wench who is constantly being seduced and who prays that the result, please God, will not prove permanent. (Charles Yale Harrison)

He was a visionary, a radical liberal whose political sympathies ranged from right center to the extreme left; in short, he was an ideological Marco Polo. (Charles Yale Harrison)

A conservative is a man who will not look at the new moon, out of respect for that "ancient institution," the old one. (Douglas Jerrold)

A conservative is a statesman who is enamored of existing evils, as distinguished from the liberal, who wishes to replace them with others. (Ambrose Bierce)

Interestingly enough, some essentially silly political utterances of the past, originally meant to be serious pronunciamentos, accumulate a retrospective wit simply because they are thoroughly and uncompromisingly wrong. For example:

They (Americans) are a race of convicts, and ought to be thankful for everything we allow them short of hanging. (Samuel Johnson, March 21, 1775)

I am willing to love all mankind, except an American. (Samuel Johnson, April 15, 1778)

An American is an Anglo-Saxon relapsed into semi-barbarism. (Bayard Taylor, 1859)

God looks after drunks, children, and Americans. (Bismarck, in ascribing this nation's greatness and ingenuity to luck)

In part, the sour grapes attitude belongs in this category, provided it applies to politics. The letter which George III wrote to the Earl of Shelburne on Nov. 10, 1782, after the American colonies were irrevocably lost, is today merely humorous:

I cannot conclude without mentioning how sensibly I feel the dismemberment of America from this empire, and that I should be miserable indeed if I did not feel that no blame on that account can be laid at my door, and did I not also know that knavery seems to be so much the striking feature of its inhabitants that it may not in the end be an evil that they will become aliens to this kingdom.

Witticism of "Cutting Down to Proper Size"

Once more, the child is fighting the unbearable (to the child!) conceit of adults, now projected outward.

The Fitzpatricks are so ancient that the best Irish antiquaries affirm that they reckoned many generations before the first man was created. (Horace Walpole, 1783)

There is no great genius without a touch of madness. (Seneca)

Genius is one per cent inspiration and ninety-nine per cent perspiration. (Thomas A. Edison)

He is so good that he is good for nothing. (Italian proverb)

He was in Logick a great Critick,
Profoundly skill'd in Analytick.
He could distinguish, and divide
A Hair 'twixt South and South-West side. (Samuel Butler, *Hudibras*)

O fortune, fortune, thou art a bitch! (John Vanbrugh)

The bitch-goddess, success. (William James)

If you do big things they print your face, and if you do little things they only print your thumbs. (Arthur Baer)

Rousseau knows he is talking nonsense, and laughs at the world for staring at him. (Samuel Johnson)

We need new friends; some of us are cannibals who have eaten their old friends up; others must have ever-renewed audiences before whom to re-enact an ideal version of their lives. (Logan Pearsall Smith)

There are more elaborate jokes on the same topic:

The conversation turns to wagering habits; Jim, a gambler, is finally acknowledged to have made the prize wager. When Jim saw a suicide jump into the Hudson, he bet Jack that the man would drown, and Jim and Jack watched, fascinated, as the suicide struggled. A policeman was just ready to jump in and rescue the drowning man when Jim stopped him: "It's unfair to interfere with our bet." Jim was arrested, brought before a judge, sentenced to a severe dressing-down and a substantial fine—but he won his bet.

A famous writer was in analysis with me at the time when Hemingway published his *Across the River and Into the Trees*. My patient's view of the book, which he discussed at some length during his appointments, was that it was the epitome of disguised writing block; to support his argument, he pointed out the change in the once-brilliant novelist's style. He was especially angered by a review in the New York *Times* Book Review in which John O'Hara declared Hemingway to be the greatest writer since Shakespeare. Some time later, O'Hara answered a questionnaire-interview in the New York *Herald Tribune;* in this interview he divulged the fact that he reads no novels except those sent him for review; his favorite literary pastime, he declared, is studying the successive editions of *Who's Who*. Whereupon my patient sarcastically remarked: "There you have the explanation of O'Hara's linking Shakespeare and Hemingway. An anthology of selections from Shakespeare must have been the last book he read in high-school before he got hold of *Across the River and Into the Trees*."

In *Le Rire*, Bergson mentions a French farce in which a citizen of Monaco (the miniature state which mostly consists of the gambling casino at Monte Carlo) is decorated by his sovereign. Shortly afterward he appears at a party wearing, not one medal, but three dozen. He explains that he went to the roulette table with his medal, put it on a certain number, won, and received thirty-five times his original stake.

The core of this joke is deflation of the decoration awarded by the sovereign. The honored man dismisses his medal as a mere gold piece, to be tossed on the roulette table like any other coin. Superficially, the joke is directed at the ruler of Monaco: "Why play monarch when all you reign over is the roulette table? Why be hypocritical, instead of calling a chip a chip?" In a larger context, the irony pertains to all rulers whose wealth—and therefore power—is drawn from questionable sources, and who, without this wealth, would not be considered worthy of distributing these metal insignia of honor, called medals.

In *Effrontes*, Biboyer says of a forty-year-old bride whose bouquet is made of the conventional orange-blossoms: "Oranges would suit her better." The joke is directed at the virginal-juvenile pretensions of the bride.

In Gogol's *The Inspector-General*, a minor Czarist employee is told: "For an official of your rank, you steal too much." Aside from its attack on corruption and venality, the effectiveness of the witticism grows out of its automatic assumption that every government employee steals, and the only difference is in the magnitude of the spoils. At the same time, the rigid protocol of rank in a bureaucracy is satirized; bureaucrats, those sticklers for form, have even worked out an unwritten code in which honor regulates dishonesty, and profits increase according to rank.

Don Marquis sums up this entire wit-tendency:

> . . . too many creatures both insects and humans estimate their own value by the amount of minor irritation they are able to cause to greater personalities than themselves.

Skeptical Wit

The blindness of pessimism pervades this type of wit; it it directed at unwarranted self-confidence and, in a larger sense, at any reliance on or trust in what is generally accepted as truth. Thus, H. L. Mencken defined self-respect as the "secure feeling that no one, as yet, is suspicious."

> A fellow who is always declaring he's no fool, usually has his suspicions. (Wilson Mizner)
>
> I'm not interested in facts, I want the truth. (Talleyrand)
>
> Hope is itself a species of happiness, and perhaps, the chief happiness which this world affords. (Samuel Johnson)
>
> Life is a hospital in which every patient is possessed by the desire of changing his bed. One would prefer to suffer near the fire, and another is certain that he would get well if he were by the window. (Charles Baudelaire)

Life is not a spectacle or a feast, it is a predicament. (George Santayana)

Opportunities always look bigger going than coming. (Anon.)

You must have rules in poetry, if it is only for the pleasure of breaking them, just as you must have women dressed if it is only for the pleasure of imagining them as Venuses. (George Moore)

Doubt everything at least once—even down to the proposition, "twice two are four." (Georg C. Lichtenberg)

A cigarette is the perfect type of pleasure; it is exquisite and leaves one unsatisfied. (Oscar Wilde)

It is a fact that there are numbers of people who read merely that they need not think. (Georg C. Lichtenberg)

The book had the effect which good books usually have: it made the fools greater fools, the intelligent more intelligent, and left the remaining thousands as they were. (Georg C. Lichtenberg)

Nothing recedes like success. (Anonymous; a variation on Alexandre Dumas, "Nothing succeeds like success.")

God may forgive you your sins, but your nervous system won't. (Alfred Korzybski)

Don't ever prophesy: for if you prophesy wrong, nobody will forget it; and if you prophesy right, nobody will remember it. (Josh Billings)

Wisdom is divided into two parts: a) having a great deal to say, and b) not saying it. (Anon.)

A wise man will live as much within his wit as his income. (Lord Chesterfield)

Never be as funny as you can be. (Anon.)

The Eleventh Commandment: Mind your own business. (Anon.)

Why should not conscience have vacation
As well as other courts o' th' nation? (Samuel Butler, *Hudibras*)

It is wonderful that 5,000 years have now elapsed since the creation of the world, and still it is undecided whether or not there has ever been an instance of the spirit of any person appearing after death. All argument is against it, but all belief is for it. (Samuel Johnson)

And this is the sum of lasting love,
Scratch a lover, and find a foe. (Dorothy Parker)

These are the things I am never without,
Love, curiosity, laughter and doubt. (Dorothy Parker)

Don't tell me of fact, I never believe facts; you know Canning said nothing was so fallacious as facts, except figures. (Sydney Smith)

Witticisms Directed at Small Differences

This type of joke derives its driving power from the "theory of details" (see p. 101). At the same time, the child in the adult satirizes the "big interconnections" enforced in childhood. How frequently parents and teachers reproach the child with "You don't understand what it is all about!" The necessary educational process of forcing the child to take the over-all picture into account is reversed in these witticisms, and minutiae are stressed.

The arithmetic teacher in a Ghetto school asks a boy in first grade: "I owe your father $100; I paid back $50; how much do I still owe him?"—"Teacher, have you got a receipt for $50?"—"What difference does it make? Well, I don't have a receipt; how much do I still owe him?"—"$100." "Idiot! You don't know how to count."—"I know how to count, teacher, but you don't know my father."

Two acquaintances meet. The first asks: "Is there anything to the rumor that your clerk ran away with your cash *and* your daughter?"—"Yes, it's true, but it's not as bad as it sounds; I'll get it all back. He sent me one installment already."—"You mean he sent back some of the stolen money?"—"No, but he's already returned my daughter."

Two friends meet on the street; one mentions a front-page story which has shocked him—the death of a millionaire. He reads the story to his friend and cries bitterly. "I didn't know this millionaire was a relative of yours," the friend says. "No, he wasn't," sobs the weeper, "that's why I'm crying."

President Grant was besieged with malcontents complaining about his Secretary of State; their charges included the accusation that he didn't even believe in the Bible. "Why should he?" replied Grant. "He didn't write it."

We have really everything in common with America nowadays, except, of course, the language. (Oscar Wilde)

There is a great difference between believing a thing and not being able to believe the contary. I often come to believe in things without being able to prove them, and to disbelieve in others without being able to disprove them. (Georg C. Lichtenberg)

No court has ever attempted to define fraud. (Mr. Justice Lindley, judgment Allard vs. Skinner, 1887).

As nations improve, so do their gods. (Georg C. Lichtenberg)

To say that a man is *vain* means that he is pleased with the effect that he produces on other people. A *conceited* man's satisfied with the effect he produces on himself. (Max Beerbohm)

A mother takes twenty years to make a man of her boy, and another woman makes a fool of him in twenty minutes. (Robert Frost)

Witticisms of Outsmarting and Getting Oneself Out of A Tight Spot

Nolens volens, people admire the "smartness" of the braggart or the smart aleck type of desperado who, when caught with his pants down, manages to put them up again with a diversionary movement. One forgets the pants and remembers only the diversion. The response to the diversion is not evoked by the ingenuity of the trick, but rather by the recollection of one's own defeats; by identifying with the braggart, the authority of the adult is—post facto—ridiculed.

An American tourist in Paris, middle-aged and obese, heard fabulous tales of a certain reducing establishment that guaranteed results. Consulting the management of the establishment, he was told that they offered two types of treatment, one for $50 and the other for $100. Thrifty and suspicious by nature, he decided on the less expensive treatment. After a routine of baths, massages, etc., he was ushered into an enormous, dimly lighted, seemingly empty room. Suddenly a few lights flashed on, illuminating a corner of the room, where stood a beautiful woman, completely nude except for a placard saying, "If you can catch me, you can have me." The girl happened to be an Olympic running champion, but the tourist did not know that; he started to chase her. Two hours later, he was as far from catching her as ever, but he had lost four pounds. The next day he was back again. If this was what they offered for $50, he though, what could he get for $100? The same procedure was repeated, but when the lights flashed up in the otherwise empty room they revealed a huge Senegal Negro wearing a placard which said: "If I catch you, I shall have you." This time the customer lost eight pounds.

An industrialist was bragging about his "unlimited capacity for work"; he enumerated his activities for the day. "Why, you work twenty-five hours a day!" was the comment.—"It practically comes to that."—"But the day has only twenty-four hours."—"I always borrow an hour from the next day."

A traveling salesman got into a row in Ithaca; he was beaten up. When he returned to New York, his friends teased him about the incident. "Is it true that they boxed your ears in the town of Ithaca?"—"Ithaca!" excalimed the salesman, contemptuously. "Do you call that a town?"

A peddler is canvassing the patrons of a restaurant; he is making a nuisance of himself, but nothing deters him, and he approaches one annoyed group of diners again and again. "I'll teach him a lesson," the smart aleck of the party announces. He calls the peddler over and asks to see a pair of suspenders. He specifies that he wants the best; "price is no object." An obviously inferior article is handed to him. "How much?" he asks.—"One dollar."—Without bargaining, and even without hesitating, the diner passes over a dollar bill and takes possession of the suspenders. The peddler stands there; his expression is doubtful and disturbed. "He thinks the bill is counterfeit," suggests a member of the group. "That's not what's worrying him," the purchaser replies, "he's eating his heart out because he didn't ask for two dollars."

A Schnorrer (a Jewish beggar with a pseudo-religious standing in the community) invites himself to dinner at the home of a wealthy and stingy man. There is brandy on the table; since brandy is so expensive, the wealthy man merely uses a few drops to moisten a crust of bread; he then eats the bread. The "guest" imitates the host, but with a difference; he uses big chunks of soft bread instead of crusts, and he soaks the bread thoroughly instead of limiting himself to a few drops. The outraged millionaire does not dare to object directly; instead, he swallows his fury and says with cunning, "I don't understand why God and Moses had to perform such a great miracle when the Jews fled from Egypt. Every Jew could have taken a piece of soft bread, dipped it into the Red Sea, and dried it up in no time." The Schnorrer solemnly ponders the idea. "That's true," he acknowledges, "but you forget one thing. When the Jews crossed the Red Sea it was Passover, and they were forbidden to eat bread; with hard matzos[7] your idea wouldn't have worked."

A well-known newspaper editor had a handwriting so illegible that only one typesetter could read it. One day the editor was sick at home; he sent his editorial to the office by messenger. Unfortunately, the one typesetter who could decipher the manuscript was ill at home too. The sub-editor desperately searched for a solution, and finally found one. He reasoned that pharmacists were used to the illegible prescriptions written by physicians; a pharmacist could surely take the editor's scrawl

---

[7] "Matzos" are crisp, hard crackers of unleavened dough.

in his stride. He sent the editorial to the nearest pharmacist; he got back a bottle of medicine.

A politician met with considerable embarrassment because of his inability to remember the names of people who had been introduced to him; this failing imperiled his political career. His press agent found a remedy: he advised the politician to ask these people whether they spelled their names with an "e" or an "i." The trick worked wonderfully, until the day the politician was introduced to a lady named "Hill." He lost the next election.

For several weeks, a boy of seven spent all his allowance on the movies; he saw the same movie again and again, following the film from one theatre to the next. His uncle asked him why this particular picture fascinated him. "You know, uncle," the smart boy replied, "there is a good-looking girl in this picture; she wants to take a swim in a lake and starts to undress. Just then a train passes by right in front of her, and you can't see anything. Some day that train's sure to be late."

Darling: the popular form of address used in speaking to a person of the opposite sex whose name you cannot at the moment recall. (O. Herford)

There is a subdivision in this category, covering those people who believe that where other people failed they will not fail, because they will improve on the technique originally used. Since the result, technique or not, is foreseeable, they make themselves into public laughing stocks. According to newspaper reports, the Canadian fur industry recently made a deal with the Russians; the deal called for an exchange of breeding stock of Canadian minks and Russian sables. The animals arrived from Russia, and they were excellent specimens; unfortunately the males had all been castrated.

Self-Derogatory Witticisms

A writer inhibited in his productivity (suffering from writer's block) came into analysis with me because of this symptom of his neurosis. When I asked him how he supported himself, he replied, "I am writing for the comic strips—the second lowest of all forms of writing."—"And what is the lowest?" I asked.—"Writing dirty words in toilets." This preventive irony is a specific form of the over-all technique of masochism; it enables the masochist to stay one step ahead of the adversary's inevitable attack.

Here are some examples:

I am Wrath. I had neither father nor mother; I leap'd out of a lion's mouth when I was scarce half an hour old; and ever since I have run up and down the world with this case of rapiers, wounding myself when I had nobody to fight withal. (Christopher Marlowe)

A million million spermatozoa,
All of them alive;
Out of their cataclysm but one poor Noah
Dare hope to survive.
And among that billion minus one

Might have chanced to be
—Shakespeare, another Newton, a new Donne—
But the One was Me. (Aldous Huxley)

The classic that the world has lost,
The little Book I never wrote. (Robert W. Service)

All generalizations are dangerous, even this one. (A. Dumas, *fils*)

Nobody can describe a fact to the life, without much patient self-inspection. (Frank Moore Colby)

It is true, I never assisted the sun materially in his rising; but, doubt not, it was of the last importance to be present . . . For many years I was self-appointed inspector of snow-storms and rain-storms, and did my duty faithfully. (H. W. Thoreau)

My idea of an agreeable person is a person who agrees with me. (Disraeli)

The Jewish joke is a specific sub-group of this form of witticism. This joke is characterized by the peculiar fact that its originators are Jews themselves. Freud believed that the uniqueness of this type of joke comes from the Jewish tendency to be ironic at the expense of "Jewish peculiarities . . . I do not know whether one often finds people that make merry so unreservedly over their own shortcomings. . . . "

Another element should be mentioned. Certainly a good dose of psychic masochism must be required before one can elevate one's "shortcomings" to the position where they become the sole topic of one's jokes and witticisms. From the one point of view, it is both brave and unusual to "know one's own shortcomings." Nevertheless, this specific form of irony does not develop without the masochistic admixture. It is interesting that people who have little contact with Jews cannot "understand" Jewish jokes. What they fail to understand is the direction of aggression inward, instead of outward.[8]

The Jewish joke is so out of the ordinary that it has produced three curious consequences. First, as Freud has already observed, non-indigenous Jewish jokes—those made up by non-Jews about Jews—are "nearly all brutal buffooneries in which the wit is supplied by the fact that the Jew appears as a comic figure to the stranger." The really good Jewish joke is thus Jewish in origin, which is completely a-typical, for as a rule good jokes about specific people are created by their enemies, not friends.

The second consequence is that even friendly observers tend to be confused about the meaning of the Jewish joke. Louis Untermeyer, for example, declares in *A Treasury of Laughter* that the Jewish joke is "essentially

[8] An interesting controversy took place between E. Hitschmann and Theodor Reik. In 1929, Reik claimed that the self-irony of the Jewish joke is akin to the self-accusations of melancholia; Hitschmann contradicted this viewpoint in 1930 (*Imago* and *Psychoanalytische Bewegung*, respectively).

logical. It is often so painstakingly logical that it reduces reason to absurdity. Argument becomes an art that is both hair-splitting and side-splitting." Exactly the opposite is true; the purpose of the Jewish joke is reducing reason to absurdity.

Third, the Jewish joke (lifted from the Jewish milieu) is *the* most plagiarized joke of them all. There is no more telling testimony to the universal quality of human reactions than the fact that jokes created in the seclusion of European ghettoes can, with slight modifications, apply to modern Western civilization. Many of the jokes about Baron Rothschild are told about Western millionaires. Jewish jokes dealing with the impudent "Schnorrer" are told about ungrateful applicants for help all over the world. And jokes about the rabbi, the most authoritative figure in the Jewish ghetto world, are easily tailored to fit semi-religious, religious, or purely secular authorities wherever they exist. Moreover, the sceptical cynicism so often manifested in the Jewish joke is universal in all cultures.

In short, the Jewish joke is not distinguished from all others by its contents, but by its creators. I do not believe that Jews are more masochistic than any other people; I believe, however, that certain external situations are more favorable or less favorable to the external expression of this tendency. The seclusion, poverty, absence of opportunity and bitterness of life in the ghetto certainly favored psychic masochism; so did the persecution and bias encountered outside the ghetto. On the other hand, the very same circumstances made for a high degree of resiliency—a prerequisite for the ability to "take it" and a quality essential for survival when the conditions of life are difficult, if not impossible.

The butt in many Jewish jokes is the rabbi: the authority who stands for strict adherence to old customs. To make the jokes clear, a few terms should be translated and a few dietary laws described: *trefe* means ritually unclean; *kosher* means ritually clean; *milchig* means milk food (milk, butter, cheese, etc.); *fleishig* means meat food. Milk food may be eaten before meat food but not with or after it, while neutral foods such as fruits and vegetables may be eaten with either. Neutral foods become milk or meat, however, if they come in contact with one or the other. The taboo on mixing meat with milk foods extends even to dishes and silver; in devout Jewish households, two complete sets of cooking utensils and dishes are maintained.

A women came to the rabbi in a state of great excitement. "My boy's hat fell into the chicken soup; do I have to throw away the soup?"—"That depends; what was on the hat?"—"On the hat? Who knows! A boy plays on the street; maybe his hat falls on the dirt."—"Dirt," says the rabbi, "that's kosher. What else?"—"What else? Who knows! A little boy's hat—maybe a louse or a flea."—"Louse? That's kosher. What else?"—"What else? The boy has scabies; maybe a little of that was on the hat."—Scabies? Kosher. What else?"—"Maybe, when he was eating a piece of bread and butter, a little smear of butter got on the hat."—The rabbi is electrified. "Butter! That's milchig! Throw away the soup!"

A Jew was denounced to his rabbi; he had committed the terrible sin of eating a chicken cooked with butter. The rabbi gave him a severe dressing-down, calling him "Apykouros, Goy, Mamser" (unbeliever, Gentile, bastard). The culprit took the lecture meekly enough, but when it was over he asked, quietly, "Rabbi, what am I?"—"What do you mean, what are you? I told you already—a traitor to Israel!"—Yes, rabbi, I heard; but what else am I?"—"This isn't enough for you? You scum of the earth, you . . . "—"Yes, rabbi, I know all that. But what I don't know is, am I fleishig or milchig?"

A Jew brings a problem to the rabbi. "Rabbi, I have a hen and a cock. If I try to slaughter the cock, the hen squawks and complains; if I try to slaughter the hen, the cock makes a rumpus. What am I to do?" The rabbi asks for a few days to consult the Talmud; when the man returns he has made his decision. "According to the law, you have to kill the hen."—"But rabbi, the cock will cry."—"Let him cry."

In another subdivision of Jewish jokes, the theme is self-irony.

A certain Jew was fascinated by a passage in a psalm which read, "God protects the stupid." By testing this passage, he reasoned, he could find out whether he himself was stupid or clever. His test was to jump from the second floor window. He jumped, breaking one hand and one foot. He cried out for help, and neighbors rushed to him. "What did you do?" they asked. "Do? Oh, my God, am I clever!"

Other jokes apotheosize pessimism:

An old Jew is dying. His sons listen as he tells them the sorrowful story of his life—toil, misery, no luck. He concludes, "I would laugh if things are no better in the other world."

On his deathbed, a witty Jew asks for a rotten plum. His weeping wife asks why he wants a *rotten* plum. "That's simple. In the other world, one is beaten with rods for every sin, and every sin is announced. When I hear the words, 'rotten plum,' I will know that my punishment is near its end."

The variety of objects of attack is infinite; Freud dealt with the jokes on marriage-brokers and Schnorrers. One other type should be mentioned: some of these jokes contain an amazing degree of intuitive insight:

A man brings this problem to his rabbi: he must take a trip and he is uneasy about leaving his business in the charge of his clerk. The rabbi asks the business man to go back to his store and watch his clerk dealing with a customer. The man does so; he hears the clerk put a price of $5 on a piece of merchandise. The customer offers $2; the clerk replies: "My boss would never agree to that." He reports this incident to the rabbi, and the rabbi tells him: "You cannot leave; come back in two weeks and report again." At the end of two weeks, the clerk is saying to customers, "We cannot give it to you for that price."—"That is still no good," the rabbi declares. "Come back in a month." When the businessman returns for the third time, the clerk is saying, "*I* cannot sell the merchandise for such a price."—"Now you can leave," says the rabbi.

The whole problem of unconscious identification is included in the witticism.

"One-Way-Street" Witticisms

This is a subdivision of skeptical wit; it utilizes the fact that some statements cannot retain their original meaning when reversed:

Though the people support the government, the government should not support the people. (Grover Cleveland)

The witticism is built on the double meaning of "support."

Any party which takes credit for the rain must not be surprised if its opponents blame it for the drought. (Dwight W. Morrow)

As soon as the children are good the mothers are scared, and think they are going to die. (Ralph Waldo Emerson)

There are two times in a man's life when he should not speculate: when he can't afford it, and when he can. (Mark Twain)

Logical consequences are the scarecrows of fools and the beacons of wise men. (Thomas H. Huxley)

When a man wants to murder a tiger he calls it sport; when a tiger wants to murder him he calls it ferocity. (G. B. Shaw)

It is the customary fate of a new truth to begin as heresy and to end as superstition. (Thomas H. Huxley)

A robbery was committed in the house of a wealthy man, but the burglar took only things of minor value. Diamonds and other precious objects were left undisturbed. The police finally caught the burglar, and when he was tried, the judge asked, "How did it happen that you took the trifles and left the real valuables untouched?" "Please, judge, I heard enough from my wife about that; do you have to start on that too?"

A drunk was riding on a cross-country bus from New York to Chicago. Every few minutes he would go up to the driver and ask him the distance between New York and Chicago; the driver would politely tell him. After the question had been asked and answered half a dozen times, the drunk began asking the distance between Chicago and New York. With this, the driver lost his politeness. "Are you kidding?' he howled. "The distance between Chicago and New York is the same as the distance between New York and Chicago!"—"I wouldn't be so sure," said the drunk cunningly. "It's only a week from Christmas to New Year, but it's a hell of a lot more from New Year to Christmas!"

Witticisms Using Sex as Target: Obscene jokes

Freud explained, in *Wit*, that obscenity is primarily directed toward the woman as an attempt to seduce her by the purposeful accentuation of sexual facts and relationships through the medium of conversation. When a man enjoys recounting or listening to obscenities in male company the original situation, which because of social impediments cannot be realized, is portrayed. In the original situation, sexual talk is directed toward a person by whom the talker is sexually excited and who through hearing the smutty stories becomes aware of his sexual intentions, so that she too may become sexually aroused in consequence. If he succeeds in bringing about a sense of shame or embarrassment, his object of exciting her has been attained. He who laughs at an obscene story laughs as though he were an onlooker at a sexual aggression. These "sexualities" are closely related to excretion in its total extent.

The obscene anecdote is like undressing the person of the opposite sex toward whom it is directed. Through the verbalization of the obscene expressions, obscenity forces the affected person into mental exhibition of the organ concerned, or of its function, and indicates to her that the aggressor portrays it to himself by this device. There is no doubt that the pleasure derived from seeing the sexual exposed is the prime motive of obscenity.

The active and the passive exhibitionistic libido (exhibitionism and voyeurism) also plays a role in the sexual act itself. However, when the more or less immediate approachability of the woman cannot be counted on, sexually stimulating conversation in the form of obscene stories may serve the same purpose. Since in such a situation sexual aggression in its progress toward the sexual act is delayed, it dwells on the development of excitement, and derives gratification from the indications of the woman's excitement. In this manner the aggression alters the character in the same way as any libidinal impulse which finds itself confronted with an obstacle. The inflexibility of the woman, which to be sure presents the prospect of a possible yielding later, is a further prerequisite for the development of obscenity, there being no taking account, indeed, of the presence of the woman. Little by little, instead of the woman, the third person becomes the occasion for the obscene story, and it is this metamorphosis which allies the latter with wit. One can describe the proceeding thus: First the libidinal impulse unfolds; as soon as it finds gratification from the woman impeded, a hostile tendency toward her arises and sets up an alliance with the originally unwelcome third person. Through the obscene talk of the first person, the woman is exposed to the third person, who now as listener has been bribed by the effortless gratification of his own libido.

These were Freud's views in 1905, reproduced nearly verbatim. The additional literature on obscene words (Ferenczi, Jones, Hitschmann, Nelken, Reitler) is an extension of Freud's original deduction.

In continuation of Freud's statements, I pointed out in *The Basic Neurosis*[9] that predilection for the use of obscene words in general must be traced back to the oral phase. The child "gives" words to the mother as a proof of love. As a consequence of alleged disappointment with the mother,

[9] This is a summary of my paper "Obscene Words," the *Psychoanalytic Quarterly*, 5, 226–248; 1936.

these "gifts" may be withdrawn, and a period of obstinate silence ("oral obstipation") may set in during childhood. As a tertiary development, giving is re-established at a phallic level with negative manifestations. These negative manifestations may take the form of obscene words, which are in reality pseudo-aggressive expressions of abuse and disparagement. None the less, there is an element of the once experienced pleasure in giving words concealed within this active utterance of obscenities.

These words also derive a pleasure-giving quality from the economy of inhibition and expenditure inherent in them. Normally, too, obscene words play a variable role among healthy people as an act of forepleasure.

In general, people make no distinction between anti-sex jokes and smutty stories. This failure to acknowledge a very real difference arises from the conventional puritanical attitude towards sex as a whole, an attitude in itself ridiculed by the anonymous witticism: "The Puritan always thinks below the belt."

Actually, witticisms using sex as target are anti-sex utterances, ("A sweetheart is a bottle of wine; a wife is a wine bottle," wrote Baudelaire) while the contrary is true of smutty and obscene stories: the purpose of these is sexual stimulation.

The well-known appraisal of the sex act, "The position is ridiculous, the pleasure momentary, the expense damnable," is certainly an anti-sex statement; the effect of wit is involuntary, and arises from the speaker's betrayal of the fact that he finds in sex no more than a problem of posture and expense.

The same applies to a patient who claimed that fellatio is the only reasonable sex activity: "It is the only position which allows one to read one's newspaper undisturbed."

It is interesting that Somerset Maugham should assert that the anti-sex attitude in Shaw's comedies accounts for their wide popularity and great success:

> Bernard Shaw owes his originality to an idiosyncrasy, not of course peculiar to himself, that had never before found expression on the stage. The English, whatever they were in the Elizabethan era, are not an amorous race. Love with them is more sentimental than passionate. They are of course sufficiently sexual for the purpose of reproducing their species, but they cannot control the instinctive feeling that the sex act is disgusting. They are more inclined to look upon love as affection or benevolence than as passion. They regard with approval its sublimations which dons describe in scholarly books, and with repulsion or with riducule its frank expression . . . It was a welcome relief to come upon a dramatist for whom love was a tiresome, secondary business, a quick gratification of a momentary impulse whose consequences were generally awkward . . . It corresponded to the deep-seated puritanism of the Anglo-Saxon race. (*The Summing-Up*, in *The Maugham Reader*, Doubleday, 1950; pp. 568–569)

Obscene stories, on the other hand, are verbal aphrodisiacs:

> Mme. de Stael, the famous busybody and intriguante of the Directoire period, was regarded with suspicion by Napoleon, but this did not deter her from appearing in his private rooms on one occasion in order to obtain an immediate audience with the "first consul."—"Impossible, madame," answered his adjutant, "the first consul is taking a bath."—"Never mind," replied Mme. de Stael, "genius is sexless."

Mme. de Stael collected "important" people as lovers, an avocation for which she was well suited. She had social background (she was the daughter of a secretary of finance under the ancient regime), wealth and wit. She was successful with such people as Talleyrand, although she failed in her aspiration to become Napoleon's Egeria. Napoleon both resisted and disliked her from the start; a few years later he even banned her from Paris. In the witticism quoted above, one can see Mme. de Stael's desire for revenge at work; the remark implies devaluation of Napoleon's sexual powers, and contains the innuendo, "I'm not curious; there is nothing to see." The joke is on Napoleon, and it is a good one, judging from the reaction of his contemporaries; the witticism was much quoted and applauded. At the same time, there was never any question of Napoleon's mechanical potency; he had given too many proofs of that. But jokes about potency rarely if ever fail to score, simply because every man or woman has a direct or indirect personal tale of occasional fiascos to tell.

This joke gains further interest because it equates purely mechanical potency with impotence; the problem is elaborated on in my book, *Neurotic Counterfeit-Sex*. We have, by the way, a shrewd witness to Napoleon's attitude toward sex proper[10] in Stendhal, who wrote a little-known book about the Emperor, *Memorabilia on Napoleon*. Stendhal suspected that the Emperor was shy with women:

> He was afraid of their jokes. This man, otherwise not affected by fear, took revenge on women in his days of power by expressing his disdain for them in uncouth words; he would not have spoken thus were his feelings genuine. Before his elevation, he wrote to a friend, Rey, referring to a passion which engulfed his brother Lucien: "Women are filthy sticks; one cannot touch them without dirtying oneself." . . . If Napoleon hated women, he did so because he was in the highest degree afraid of the ridicule in which they could potentially involve him. . . At a dinner, being also in the company of Mme. de Stael (whom it would have been easy for him to conquer), he shouted at her words to the effect that he liked only women who were solely occupied with their children . . . He wanted to possess all the women of his court, and, as the rumor goes, actually possessed them, through the intervention of his valet, Constant . . . One of these women, who recently married, said on the second day of her stay in the Tuileries to another woman, "My God, I don't know what the emperor wants of me; I received an invitation to appear in his private

[10] For an analysis of Napoleon's relations with women, see my essay in my book *Talleyrand-Napoleon-Stendhal-Grabbe*, Int. Psychoan. Verlag, 1935.

suite at eight p.m.!" . . . The next day, the ladies of the court asked her whether she had seen the emperor. She blushed, and explained: When she arrived, the emperor was sitting at a small table, fully dressed, even to his sabre. He was signing decrees. Without interrupting his work, the emperor asked her to lie down on the bed. Shortly afterwards, himself carrying the candlestick, he escorted her out of the room, and then went back to his desk to continue reading, correcting, and signing decrees. The essentials of the affair took no more than three minutes. Frequently, his mameluke was present behind a paravant . . . Napoleon had sixteen encounters of this sort with Mlle. Georges; on one occasion, he handed her a handful of bills, twenty-six, to be exact . . . Sometimes he would ask these ladies only to drop their clothes, and would then send them away without interrupting his work . . . This behavior exasperated Parisian women. To send them away after three minutes, to continue to sign his decrees, sometimes not even taking off his sabre—this seemed abominable to them. It meant that he was making women swallow his contempt, in little morsels.[11]

Mme. de Stael once announced to her friends that she intended to publish her memoirs. Some women were incredulous: "Do you really intend to give a full-sized portrait?"—"Well, it will be more like a picture *above* the waist."

The allusion to her many lovers is obvious; no less obvious is the attempt at concealment. Where is the joke? I believe the witticism is at the expense of feminine ambiguity, based on the popular belief that women are "liars." In a more superficial layer, the sexual connotation serves as palimpsest.

Literary examples, curiously enough, only multiply the complications of the problem of obscene witticism. Of course, there are books which clearly speculate on the exploitation of sex. Others use sex as a sounding board, upon which they can test their concept of life as it is. Books of this type are not classed as "dirty," even by the puritanical-minded; it is conceded—in literature and art, if not in life,—that sex is a part of reality. (The differing attitudes towards nudes in sculpture and painting on the one hand, and nudity on the beach on the other hand, come to mind immediately.) In any case, there are instances in which an obscene witticism does not impress one as obscene.

In John O'Hara's *Butterfield 8*,[12] a promiscuous girl wakes up, feeling guilty, in the apartment of the man who had picked her up the night bebefore. She meditates:

For one thing, you get up and get dressed. On this Sunday morning she did something she often did, which gave her a little pleasure. The drawstrings of the pyjamas she was wearing had come undone in the night, and she opened the pyjamas and laughed. She said to herself, "I wonder where he is." She got out of bed, holding the pyjamas to her, and she was unsteady and her body was pretty drunk, but she walked all over the apartment and could not find him. (p. 12)

---

[11] Author's translation.

[12] Harcourt, Brace, New York, 1935.

Puns

The pun is a play on words and sounds. It may be mere word-play, in which case the result is no more than half-comical; it can be word-play combined with the technique of wit; in this case the result is usually memorable as well as witty. There is a wide gulf between the primitive and refined varieties:[13]

1. Success—is to get what you want; happiness— to want what you get.
2. "When the judge handed down the decision forcing you to pay up your back alimony, how did you feel?"—"Chagrined."—"And how did your loving ex-wife feel?"—"She grinned."

Pun No. 1 is "high-class"; it contains, behind its mask of word-similarity, deep and bitter wisdom: What good is success if you cannot enjoy it? On the other hand, how typical it is to envy "naive" people who seem contented with what they have! The pun makes fun of your own everlasting search for happiness—and everlasting failure to find it. It hits at the core of self-delusion in each of your successive aims.

Pun No. 2 is "primitive"; in a word-sound similarity, it merely expresses the expected dissimilarity of opposing feelings.

Many excellent witticism are disguised as puns:

Some cause happiness wherever they go; others, whenever they go. (Anon.)

An optimist sees an opportunity in every calamity; a pessimist sees a calamity in every opportunity. (Anon.)

She was a good cook as cooks go, and as cooks go she went. (Saki)

I must get out of these wet clothes and into a dry martini. (A. Woolcott)

If " you can't make a man think as you do, make him do as you think. (Anon.)

What is mind? No matter. What is matter? Never mind. (Thomas Hewitt Key, in *Punch*, XXIX)

A gigolo is a *fee*-male. (Isaac Goldberg).

The finest pseudo-pun, or word-play witticism, known to me is Charles Yale Harrison's: "Why hasn't someone written a book entitled *The Phallacy of Marriage*?" By merely changing the appearance of the word, "fallacy," a most unexpected thought is produced: what is all this nonsensical talk about the fallacy, worthlessness, hopelessness of marriage? It all skirts the real problem—that of impotence and frigidity; complaints on this score are conveniently shifted to indictments of the institution of marriage.

There is a difference between seeing the irony of a situation, and occasionally summing it up with a pun, and *compulsively* meeting every situa-

[13] "A pun is the lowest form of humor—when you don't think of it first." (Oscar Levant)

tion with a pun. There are numerous jokes about the inveterate punster:

The King was tired of his clown, a perpetual punster. He issued an ultimatum: "Unless you produce a good pun at once, you will be hanged."—"Challenge accepted," retored the punster. "Name a subject."—"Myself. The King."—"The King is not a subject."—"Still, you ridicule my big belly, and make jokes at my expense."—"Sire, everybody pokes fun at somebody else's expanse."—"Enough!" cried the King. "Hang the scoundrel!"—But when the noose was around the jester's neck, the King said, "Your life will be spared if, as soon as the noose is removed, you promise never to make another pun."—"I promise," said the punster. "No noose is good news."—They hanged him.

The inveterate punster, although he no longer runs the risk of being hanged, is still a nuisance; the helpless listener feels that he has been made the victim of a cheap trick, and resents it. The psychology of this type of punster, as I have reconstructed it in a series of analyses, is at bottom that of a frightened, masochistic child, trying to extricate himself from the coils of reality by alleged aggressive smartness. In a study on that topic entitled "The Psychopathology of the 'Wise Guy' "[14] I called the "wise-guy" attitude an essential for frightened people who could not stand uncertainty. The habitual punster and "wise-guy" is not above the situation and therefore able to joke about it; the situation is perpetually looming over and threatening to overwhelm the "wise guy." He must prove to himself that he is not afraid, and this proof must be confirmed by others, which accounts for his pronounced exhibitionism. His whistling in the dark takes the form of wit.

This inner process is of course unconscious. The wise guy's superego is a cruel taskmaster; in any new situation the reproach of masochistically tinged passivity is sure to be leveled, and must then be countered with an "aggressive" joke. But even that technique embodies an attempt to placate: "I'm just joking, don't take me seriously." He asks for leniency by putting himself on a level with a witty child.

Puns and Plays on Words Using Metaphors and Incorrect Comparisons as Vehicle

An example of metaphoric witticism:

Don Armando in *Love's Labours Lost* (V.I. 94–7) becomes Don Posterior after saying, "Sir, it is the King's most sweet pleasure to congratulate the Princess at her pavilion in the posterior of this day, which the rude multitude call the afternoon."

An example of witticism via grandiloquent comparison:

Correspondences are like small clothes before the invention of suspenders: It is impossible to keep them up. (Sydney Smith)

[14] *Samiksa*, Calcutta, 3, 26–29; 1949.

The first example is grist for the mill of the "watcher of metaphors"; these people are experts in showing up mixed metaphors,—a simple way of proving the other fellow ridiculous. Example No. 2 is via the visual imperative, a half-exhibitionistic scene.

Cynical Witticisms

Freud links cynical jokes with aggression. There is more to it; the problem of cynicism is complicated. I believe it contains the following elements:

In the cynic's own estimation he is the only person who really "knows the score"; everyone else is taken in by the spurious values of accepted institutions, creeds, mores and morals. He alone knows that everything is worthless.[15]

This pose covers a frightened child whose inner problem is masochistically tinged ambivalence. He unconsciously harbors two contradictory feelings for the same person at the same time. In this unconscious conflict with his superego, he seeks for allies who will strengthen his defense. He enlists them on his side by openly expressing irreverent and even heretical opinions which appeal to the hidden ambivalence of the listener. His unconscious invitation to his audience reads: "Don't be a coward! Have the guts to admit that you agree with me!"

The cynic is then content, for he has *consciously* proved to himself that he is aggressive, active, brave—and a wit besides. But this conscious reassurance is merely a double inner defense. He is too busy organizing his defense to realize that he recognizes no positive values, and sees no affirmative human qualities. Nor does he realize that he is not a free agent, but an instrument of his inner battle with conscience. Still less does he realize that his environment rejects him; his conviction that he is the sole bearer of the banner of truth bars him from objective judgment. Finally, he is unmoved by the disadvantage—which he unconsciously perceives and uses for masochistic purposes—of never being taken seriously.

People who have no weaknesses are terrible; there is no way of taking advantage of them. (Anatole France)

Many a crown of wisdom is but the golden chamberpot of success, worn with pompous dignity. (Paul Eldridge)

Success covers a multitude of blunders. (G. B. Shaw)

All the historical books which contain no lies are extremely tedious. (Anatole France)

An idea isn't responsible for the people who believe in it. (Don Marquis)

Christmas is over and Business is Business. (F. P. Adams)

Mr. Max Beerbohm attempted to analyze the jokes at which the mob laughs. He

---

[15] "A cynic is a man who, when he smells flowers, looks around for the coffin." (Mencken)

divided them into three sections: jokes about bodily humiliation, jokes about things alien, such as foreigners, and jokes about bad cheese. (G. K. Chesterton)

Give me six lines written by the most honorable of men, and I will find an excuse to hang him. (Cardinal Richelieu)

"There is no middle course between the throne and the scaffold," declared Charles X. "Your Majesty forgets the post-chaise," retorted Talleyrand.

Dry Humor

Dry humor is a specific form of laconic understatement mixed with self-irony. Inwardly, the aggression is directed against the upbringers: "See what they have made of me!" It is summed up nicely in the tale about the Yankee farmer who declared, after a decade on a stony New England farm, "I'm holding my own. I didn't have nothing when I came here, and I ain't got nothing now."

A man hired out to a miserly farmer. After a few years of tolerating his stingy treatment, he decided to show his annoyance. At supper, he skillfully caught a fly and dropped it into his porridge, expecting the farmer to protest at the waste of good food. The farmer began the expected lecture: "There is a fly in your porridge," he said. "Don't worry, she can't drown," said the hired hand. "You trying to tell me you didn't get enough milk?" asked the farmer. "Milk? There's plenty of milk—for all this porridge."

Calvin Coolidge, who was noted for his taciturnity, is the hero of this anecdote. A lady told him she had bet she could make him say three words. "You lose," was Coolidge's answer.

Once Coolidge gave the press an "interview"; one after another, reporters asked if he had anything to say about the world situation, prohibition, his coming message to Congress, etc., and one question after another was answered, "No." As the reporters were dismissed, Coolidge warned them: "Don't quote me."

"The only time you realize you have a reputation is when you're not living up to it," said José Iturbi.

Winston Churchill's pleasant witticism, dating from a period when he held no political position, belongs in this category:

I am a man without an office, without a seat, without a party, and without an appendix.

Nonsense Witticisms, With and Without Sense

There exists a controversy of long standing: can pure and unadulterated nonsense be funny, or must there be sense using pseudo-nonsense as camouflage? (For elaboration, see Chapter Eight.) In any case, nonsense jokes are directed at educators who tried to instill "sense" into their children. Reducing sense to nonsense seems to be a favorite pastime of the child in the adult.

A suburbanite hired a gardener; the man was to start work at exactly eight a.m. on a Monday morning. Monday morning came and went, but the gardener did not appear, nor did he send word all week. The next Monday, at precisely eight a.m., he turned up. The suburbanite was indignant, and asked for an explanation. "You told me to come last Monday," said the gardener. "Monday, I forgot; Tuesday, I forgot; Wednesday, I knew I would be busy on Thursday; by Friday, the week was over and I didn't want to disturb you on the weekend, especially since you told me to come on Monday. That's the true story; what are you complaining about?"

Two friends watch as a young boy is escorted with much solicitude to an expensive car. "Who is the child?" one asks of the other. "That's Morgan's boy."—"So young and already a Morgan!"

Customer: "That coat doesn't fit." Owner of second-hand store: "Well, what do you expect for five bucks? An attack of epilepsy?"

This is an excellent example of "sense in nonsense." Obviously, the owner's answer is meaningless; if he had said, "What do you expect for five bucks, a Fifth Avenue custom tailor's creation?" he would have ironically reduced the bargain-hunter to absurdity. Instead, he uses as a comparison something which a), cannot be bought, b), would not be bought—the dread disease, epilepsy. This pseudo-nonsense is what makes the joke excellent instead of commonplace. It is a *hyper-* reduction to absurdity: there are worse things in life than a badly-fitted, second-hand coat. Also included in the joke is the basic philosophy of all humans: we live on the small margin of profit derived from contemplating our more unfortunate neighbors.

Witticisms of "Bidding Up"

These witticisms use a specific technique in order to reduce the opponent to absurdity. Instead of an outright contradiction, they feint with a seeming confirmation, but the confirmation so over-extends the original statement that it collapses of its own weight. The paradigm of these witticisms is the child's ironic pseudo-acceptance of many educational precepts.

A society snob bragged to his Jewish dinner-partner: "One of my ancestors signed the Declaration of Independence."—"That's interesting; one of mine signed the Ten Commandments."

Two newcomers to New York are exclaiming at the amazing tempo of American life. One of them marvels: "Yesterday I watched them building a skyscraper—in one hour they finished a 150-story building!" The other retorts: "That's nothing. I was there, too; five minutes later the tenants were in the building and the first suicide was falling from the tower; as he passed the second floor he glanced in and saw someone reading a newspaper report of his suicide."

Two insurance agents are working on the same prospect, each agent extolling the service provided by his company. "Why," says the first, "if something happened to you,—let's say, after you paid your premiums for two years you decided to commit suicide—your widow would get the check next morning."—"Our company beats that," retorts the second agent. "As soon as you jump, our agent hands you the check, and you have it before you hit the pavement."

Two city slickers, both with country backgrounds, are bragging about their home farms. "My father always used to kiss us kids goodbye when he went out on Monday to milk the cows, and he never got back before Saturday. That's how big our farm was."—"Really. My father's farm was so big that when he sent a pair of newlyweds out to milk the cows, the milk was brought back by their kid."

There is a variation on the over-bidding joke; this is the witticism in which the values are bid up so high that they collapse, but the eventual butt is the over-bidder, and not his intended victim. This happens when hyper-caution becomes detrimental. The classical example is the story of the American tourists, father and son, who are delighted by the friendliness of a British father and son who are sharing their railroad compartment during a journey from London. As they reach their destination, the British father suggests that the Americans visit them, introducing himself as the Duke of X, and his son as Lord Z. The Americans, of course, are from Missouri, and the father responds to the introduction, "This is my son, Jesus Christ."

A New Yorker is showing a visitor from Los Angeles the sights of New York; the visitor is brutally frank about admitting that he sees nothing to compare with the sights of Los Angeles. He sneers at everything he sees—the harbor, the skyline, even the traffic. As their taxi passes the corner of 34th Street and Fifth Avenue, he asks the New Yorker: "What is that tall building?" The New Yorker glances up at the Empire State and says indifferently, "I really don't know. It wasn't there this morning."

Witticisms Derived from the Relativity of Human Happiness

The principle of these witticisms is the accusation: "Someone must be responsible." Unconsciously, this "someone" represents the parents, and later the superego.

The following story is paradigmatic for this type:

An orthodox Jew consults his rabbi about a serious problem. He, his wife, and five children are all living in one room, and they are asked to take in his brother-in-law and his family, which would make a total of seventeen persons in all to occupy that one room. After consulting the Talmud, the rabbi makes his decision: regardless of the inconvenience, the man's duty is to take in the brother-in-law and his family. A few weeks later, the man consults the rabbi again. The brother-in-law's daughter has now asked for shelter; she, her husband and six children would bring the total living in that one room to twenty-five. Once more, the rabbi's decision is to take them in. Some weeks later, the man appears at the rabbi's house again; this time he is shaking with wrath. "Rabbi, this is too much! My niece now has a goat, and the goat, too, lives with us! What am I to do—throw out the whole lot of them?" The rabbi declares the problem worthy of further research in the Talmud; after two weeks of study he renders his decision: "Throw out the goat!"

The variation on this story is equally illuminating. This time, the man consults the rabbi *after* he has taken in his horde of relatives; life in the one-roomed hovel has become insupportable, what is he to do? The Talmud provides the answer: "Take the cow into the house." Incredulous but obedient, the man complies, returning two weeks later in despair—the situation, of course, is more intolerable than ever. He is told: "Now take in the goat." A week later, he again appeals for relief, and is told: "Take in the hen, the rooster, and the chicks." At the end of his rope, he comes to the rabbi the next day, and hears the welcome words: "Throw out the cow, the goat, and the chickens." In the morning he runs to the rabbi's house, glowing with gratitude: "O rabbi, thank you! So much space, so much comfort!"

John Stuart Mill said: "Unquestionably it is possible to do without happiness; it is done involuntarily by nineteen twentieths of mankind." Still, people want happiness, and at least manage to derive some pleasure from gloating at its absence from other people's lives. As a result, many statements which—strictly speaking—are not witticisms, are greeted with the laughter that would be their due if they were.

This form of wit also has some connections with "bitter laughter" (see Chapter Thirteen).

Don't part with your illusions. When they are gone you may still exist, but will have ceased to live. (Mark Twain)

The first half of life consists of the capacity to enjoy without the chance; the last half consists of the chance without the capacity. (Mark Twain)[16]

What we call "Progress" is the exchange of one nuisance for another nuisance. (Havelock Ellis)

Doubtless the pleasure is as great
Of being cheated as to cheat. (Samuel Butler, *Hudibras*)[17]

Blessed is he who expects nothing, for he shall never be disappointed. (Alexander Pope)

It is with true love as it is with ghosts; everyone talks about it, but few have seen it. (La Rochefoucauld)

If we undertake an examination of what is generally understood by happiness, as it has respect either to the understanding or the senses, we shall find all its properties and adjuncts will herd under this short definition, that it is a perpetual possession of being well deceived. (Jonathan Swift)

---

[16] This is another illustration of the fact that wit relies on technique of expression more than on idea; Twain's witticism has precisely the meaning of the sharp, but *not* witty, "If youth but knew, if age but could."

[17] Enlarged on by Swift in *Tale of A Tub*, where he sets forth the thesis that happiness in life consists of being well cheated.

Be nice to people on your way up because you'll meet them on your way down. (Wilson Mizner)

Love kills happiness; happiness kills love. (Miguel de Unamuno)

A woman filled with faith in the one she loves is the creation of a novelist's imagination. (H. de Balzac)

Perhaps they were right in putting love into books . . . Perhaps it could not live anywhere else. (William Faulkner)

In the spring I have counted 136 different kinds of weather (in New England) inside of 24 hours. (Mark Twain)

To fill the hour—that is happiness. (R. W. Emerson)

Man's real life is happy, chiefly because he is ever expecting that it soon will be so. (Edgar Allan Poe)

Most ov the happiness in this world konsists in possessing what uthers kant git. (Josh Billings)

Once in every man's life, happiness passes him by. (Old proverb)

Pleasure is the only thing to live for. Nothing ages like happiness. (Oscar Wilde)

Man is never happy, but spends his whole life in striving after something which he thinks will make him so; he seldom attains his goal, and when he does, it is only to be disappointed; he is mostly shipwrecked in the end, and comes into harbor with masts and rigging gone. (Arthur Schopenhauer)

Malchisedec was a really happy man. He was without father, without mother and without descent. He was an incarnate bachelor. He was a born orphan. (Samuel Butler)

I found the original of my hell in the world which we inhabit. (Dante)

No man is happy but by comparison. (Thomas Shadwell)

When I count up the rare minutes of real happiness in my life, I do not believe they make more than twenty-four hours in all. (Otto von Bismarck)

We are born crying, live complaining, and die disappointed. (Thomas Fuller)

Why are we so fond of life that begins with a cry and ends with a groan? (Mary, Countess of Warwick, on her death-bed, 1678)

What is the life of man? Is it not to shift from side to side—from sorrow to sorrow—to button up one cause of vexation and unbutton another? (Laurence Sterne)

A bridge of groans across a stream of tears. (P. J. Bailey)

The past and present are only our means; the future is always our end. Thus we never really live, but only hope to live. Always looking forward to being happy, it is inevitable that we should never be so. (Blaise Pascal)

Gilbert White discovered the formula for complete happiness, but he died before making the announcement, leaving it for me to do so. It is to be very busy with the unimportant. (A. E. Newton)

Satire lies about literary men while they live, and eulogy lies about them when they die. (Voltaire)

The most interesting things in life are either immoral, illegal, or too fattening. (Alexander Woollcott)

Social Witticisms

Witticisms of this type make use of social settings, differences between the mores of one group and another "foreignisms," etc. Charles de Montesquieu's pungent comment is an example: "Happiness means, for queens, fertility—but for maidens, sterility."

A nouveau riche decides to send his two boys to an exclusive boarding school. In his interview with the head master, he makes no bones about the fact that he puts the greatest value on politeness, and expects that his sons' manners will be carefully supervised. When he returns to the school for a visit, some months later, he is told that the boys' scholastic progress has been remarkable. "But they are still so crude," the father complains. "They didn't even ask me if their mother is well." The headmaster reassures the father, and he leaves. When he returns for his next visit, the boys greet him in chorus with, "Is mother *still* well?"

The country fair brings so many visitors to a small town that two strangers are forced to double up, and share one room in a hotel. They go down to the bar together, and on the way one of them drops his wallet. He does not notice his loss, but the roommate does, and restores the wallet to him. Nothing is missing, and the owner thanks him profusely. The next day it is discovered that a large sum of money is missing from the wallet. The police are notified. Suspicion of course falls on the roommate, but the owner of the wallet vouches for his honesty—had he not returned the lost wallet the night before? Nevertheless, he is searched, and the money is found on him. The owner of the wallet is flabbergasted. "I don't understand it!" he says, over and over. "What's so mysterious about it?" asks the roommate. "It's every citizen's duty to return found money, and I'm a good citizen, but stealing is another matter—that's how I make my living."

The final test of truth is ridicule . . . How loudly the barber surgeons laughed at Harvey,—and how vainly! What clown ever brought down the house like Galileo? Or Columbus? Or Jenner? Or Lincoln? Or Darwin? They are laughing at Nietzsche yet! (H. L. Mencken)

The truth that survives is simply the lie that is pleasantest to believe. (H. L. Mencken)

I wonder why murder is considered less immoral than fornication in literature. (George Moore)

All the jokes which contrast the customs of one country with those of another belong in this category:

A European visits New York. At night he puts his shoes out in the hall to be cleaned, as is customary in Europe, where the shoe-shine boy is unknown. In the morning, the maid knocks and politely returns his shoes to him, saying, "You must have forgotten your shoes outside the door."

This anecdote, a true story, is contributed by Fred Schwed, Jr.: "There used to live in this town a gifted comic artist, who like most of that ilk is a very nice fellow and also very neurotic. I had met him only once or twice before. Chancing upon him at the local post office we chatted a little.

Then I said: "Say, some of the neighbors are dropping in at our house after supper tonight. It would be nice if you and your wife (I wasn't even sure of her first name) would come in too." I then received the goddamdest reply I ever yet heard in casual conversation. "Gee," he said seriously, "we'd love to, but I don't know. My wife is having her menstrual period." For a few seconds I was stricken as dumb as though I were being throttled. Then, I am proud to say, I regained my tongue. I said, "Well, why don't you two come over anyway? All we were planning to do this evening was talk."

Mr. Schwed adds: "If you care for that one, you may have it, gratis. You can perceive why I never tried contributing it to a magazine."

Here is an old academic riddle which also makes fun of social contrasts:

What is the difference between a theory, a hypothesis, and a theoretical assumption? When the chief of the clinic makes a guess, it is called a theory; if his assistant does the same, it is called a hypothesis; if the brainwave comes from an intern, it is called an assumption.

Witticisms Directed at Everything New

"There is no adequate defense, except stupidity, against the impact of a new idea" (Percy Williams Bridgeman, *The Intelligent Individual and Society*). As a clinical observation, this witticism is surprisingly accurate—within its limitations; the inner conscience uses a failure to understand the unfamiliar as a proof of passivity, leading to fear, thus necessitating an immediate defense in the form of an "active" explanation. When the explanation is hasty and ad hoc, the chances are it will be a stupidity, or a sophism, or at the very least a betrayal of ignorance. All of these things, it goes without saying, are not direct proofs of "stupidity." Normally, people realize that new phenomena will be digested and clarified with time, and their attitude in the meanwhile is one of watchful waiting. When there is a malign inner conscience, the unfamiliar is a threat, and the surface reaction of stupidity merely covers the fear aroused by the new.

As I pointed out in *The Talent for Stupidity* (in preparation), the inner obstacles to progress in every field of endeavor are heightened when the new touches emotional strings in the uninitiated. When this occurs, the habit of avoiding thought is challenged, inherent convervatism is challenged, and a very specific emotional resistance is added. The record is dark enough when the innovation is impersonal, for instance, in the case of Leban's invention of the gas light. The French inventor died without having convinced anybody that a lamp without a wick could actually give light, and gas light was not adopted in Paris until fourteen years after his death. (The city fathers of Birmingham England, were more adventurous; they accepted the improvement in 1805, thirteen years before Paris did.) How much more tempestuous is the reaction to an innovation which affects the individual emotionally!

Freud's discovery of the dynamic unconscious is the obvious example. Freud shook the complacency of self-determination; he proved that neither Babbitt nor genius is master in his own house, but merely a puppet manipulated by an invisible puppet-master, the unconscious. Seldom in the history of any discovery have otherwise intelligent people produced such nonsensical arguments against an idea as did the early detractors of Freud, and their successors are not far behind them. The rather helpless ineptitude of most of the jokes attacking analysis is also noteworthy (see Chapter Twelve).

No grand idea was ever born in a conference, but a lot of foolish ideas have died there. (F. Scott Fitzgerald)

There are well dressed foolish ideas just as there are well dressed fools. (Nicholas Chamfort)

To die for an idea; it is unquestionably noble. But how much nobler it would be if men died for ideas that were true! (H. L. Mencken)

Witticisms Using the "Taking Literally" Technique

This type of witticism covers one of the most important techniques used in fighting the superego—"the pseudo-moral connotation of neurotic symptoms." This technique is part of the secondary defense embedded within every neurotic symptom. It consists of a mocking irony directed at the internalized images of the educators, and its raw material is the body of moral precepts communicated to the child in the course of the educational process. These precepts, which in time become part of the ego ideal, are secondarily reproduced verbatim by the unconscious ego whenever such literal repetition will distort, instead of reflect, the meaning originally intended. These precepts are thus parroted at the *wrong* time, in the *wrong* place, on the *wrong* occasion, out of context and with *wrong* intention. The outcome is that the particular precept is reduced to absurdity.

The technique of spurious conformity to the demands of the ego ideal immobilizes Daimonion, for it neutralizes Daimonion's major instrument of torture. When Daimonion can demonstrate a discrepancy between ego ideal and ego, the unconscious ego accepts the sentence of guilt. *But this finality of judgment works both ways.* When the unconscious ego can prove that it has acted in accordance with the "mutually accepted yardstick"—the precepts of the ego ideal—Daimonion is temporarily silenced. The "double immobilization trick" is one of the few aggressive retorts possible for the otherwise feeble unconscious ego. The pseudo-moral connotation is a formidable defensive weapon in the unconscious ego's struggle against Daimonion; it assists in both the creation and the maintenance of the unconscious ego's spurious secondary defense.

The strength of this defense has not so far been generally recognized;

neither has its universality. Nevertheless, the mechanism itself has frequently been mentioned by a number of authors, including myself.

Here is an illustration of lip-service conformity to the precepts enshrined in the ego ideal. A patient recalled that as a child she had been forbidden by her father to pick any of the fruit from his cherished apple-orchard. The father was a stern educator, and his word was not to be trifled with. When harvest time came, his prized fruit was still on the trees, but much of the fruit had been nibbled at—the girl had climbed the trees and nibbled at the apples as they hung from their stems. She had a perfect defense against her father's severe reprimand: "You didn't say anything about eating. All you said was—'Don't pick!' "

A puritanically educated young man had an affair with his neighbor's wife, and suffered from guilt feelings. One day he found himself thinking, "Love Thy neighbor."

Typical of this form of witticism is a certain Jewish joke dealing with a melamed, a professional student of the Talmud who is by tradition thoroughly impractical, and whose quasi-religious importance relieves him of the duty of working for a living and supporting his family. This melamed is told by his wife to go to the fair in the next town and buy a cow. She explains, painstakingly, all the earmarks of a good cow—full udders, silky coat, high shoulders, etc. The husband looks bewildered, and she goes over the list again, adding, "Never mind if one of the small points is different—just get a good cow." Lost in his thoughts, as usual, the husband plods off, and returns the next day with a bull. "Idiot, fool!" shouts the the indignant wife. "Didn't you see that the udders are missing?"—"So in one small point it is different—is this a reason to call me a fool?"

A traveling salesman, making his first trip for a certain firm, is given a formidable list of customers in cities dotted all over his territory. "Get back in two weeks," he is told, and two weeks later he returns, exhausted but triumphant. "Did you see everybody?" the boss asks. "Sure did!" he replies. "And did you do much business?"—"Business! All I had time for was to show my card and run for my train!"

Shakespeare endorses polygamy: he speaks of the merry wives of Windsor; how many wives did Mr. Windsor have? (Artemus Ward)

Witticisms Directed Against Logic and Common Sense

This is the happy hunting ground of the child in adult clothes, who has a deep inner need to show up the inconsistency of adults.

Logic's a large drawer, containing some useful instruments, and many more that are superfluous. (C. C. Colton)

Logic is nothing more than a knowledge of words. (Charles Lamb)

The application of whips, racks, gibbets, gallows, dungeons, fire and faggot in a dispute may be looked upon as popish refinements upon the old heathen logic. (Joseph Addison)

Your true logician gets, in time, to be *logicalized* and then, so far as regards himself, the universe is one word. A thing, for him, no longer exists. He deposits upon a sheet of paper a certain assemblage of syllables, and fancies that their meaning is riveted by the act of deposition. (Edgar Allan Poe)

Art is limitation, the essense of every picture is the frame. (G. K. Chesterton)

A gifted small girl has explained that pins are a great means of saving life, "by not swallowing them." (C. E. Montague)

A subdivision of these witticisms pretends to follow logic, only to reduce it to absurdity. For example, Mark Twain's: "I was glad that I could answer the question. I said that I didn't know."

Witticisms Directed Against Selectivity of Memory

Francois Fauvel-Gourand called memory the "library of the mind." Freud's discoveries prove that the librarian is highly selective in his recollections, preferring to split the painful and shameful recollections up and deposit part of them in the unconscious, thus repressing them. "Recollections" are therefore not reports; they are also apt to stray still further from reality when, as is common, fantasy is remembered as fact. There is a third source of falsification in recollections, and this is the masochistic wish to involve oneself in difficulties (see last example in this section).

Memory is the diary that chronicles things that never have happened and couldn't possibly have happened. (Oscar Wilde)

People with good memories seldom remember anything worth remembering. (Anon.)

Memory is the power to gather roses in winter. (Anon.)

After publication of my book, *Conflict in Marriage*, a complete stranger called me on the telephone. As soon as he heard my voice, he introduced himself as follows:

"I am an admirer of Tolstoy."

There was nothing for me to say but "How do you do."

He brushed my amenity aside. "What right have you to misquote Tolstoy? The first sentence of your new book reads, 'All happy families resemble one another; every unhappy family is unhappy in its own fashion,' and you say it was written by Tolstoy. That's fraud! Tolstoy never said that! And I know everything he wrote nearly by heart."

"You are mistaken, sir. If you are such a specialist in Tolstoy's work, please start quoting the beginning of the first chapter of *Anna Karenina*."

The voice on the telephone promptly began quoting—the *second* paragraph of the opening chapter of that work, dealing with the discovery of Oblonsky's affair with the French governess. It is a long paragraph, but the unknown recited it all, and then triumphantly asked, "Correct, eh?"

"I assume the words are correct. But you left out the first paragraph."

"This is the first paragraph!"

"It is not. Your Tolstoy must be handy; you can look up the opening chapter of *Anna Karenina*."

"Will you wait?"

"I will."

"Why?"

"To teach you a lesson."

After an appreciable time the voice returned to the telephone. It was considerably deflated: "Incredible! The sentence really exists. How could I have forgotten it?"

"This, my unknown friend, would take a few years to find out in analysis. Goodby!"

Witticisms Based on Thwarted Expectations

These jokes are the sour-grapes consolation of the disappointed; the other fellow's failure warms their hearts. By being "aggressive" towards the other person, an attempt is made to convince one's own conscience of one's own aggressiveness, thus permitting rejection of the superego's "standing invitation" to feel guilty because of inner passivity.

The young author of a recent best-seller was the hero of an anecdote widely told during the period when his very realistic novel about the war was at the height of its popularity. A famous actress had come up to him at a party: "Oh, Mr. X, I am so glad to meet you! I have been wanting to meet you for some time!" This enthusiastic greeting spelled compliments and the young author swelled with pride, but he coyly asked, "Why?"—"Because you are the only person I know who spells the usual four-letter word incorrectly!"

Another story with a literary background has to do with Alexander Woollcott. Attending a dinner party in London, Woollcott was immediately flattered when the Prince of Wales drew him aside for a private talk. This was what the Prince told him: "Woollcott, you have something to do with that blasted New Yorker magazine, haven't you? Well, why the devil do my copies reach me so irregularly?"

Caruso's car once broke down when he was deep in the hinterland. He walked to the nearest farm and appealed to the farmer for help; the farmer obligingly came to his assistance. Full of gratitude, the renowned tenor rewarded the farmer by singing to him. The farmer then asked his guest's name, and Caruso, all pride and bombast, identified himself. The farmer was in seventh heaven: "You, Caruso! Why, I have read about you for years! What an honor! The great traveler, Robinson Caruso, in my kitchen!"

Publishing a volume of verse is like dropping a rose-petal down the Grand Canyon and waiting for the echo. (Don Marquis)

Witticisms Directed at One's Own Family, Especially One's Mother-In-Law

In *Totem and Taboo,* Freud presented his explanation of the most common of family jokes—that directed against the mother-in-law. He adduced the taboos forbidding contact between mother-in-law and son-in-law so frequently encountered in primitive societies. The common denominator linking these various taboos seems to be an unconscious defense against incest. Freud also mentions the disturbing and interfering effect of the mother-in-law upon the illusion of love; nobody wants to see his wife mirrored in the older and often unattractive woman. This last is a recurring theme in literature; it tends to be used as a final, unanswerable argument:

> Je tache en vain sous mes baisers
> de ranimer l'âme ephemere.
> C'est fini. Le charm est brisé.
> Et tu ressembles à ta mère. (Paul Geraldy)[18]

All this may very well apply, but a deeper reason also exists, and this has a direct bearing on psychic masochism warded off with pseudo-aggression. In addition to all its other meanings, marriage also signifies an unconscious attestation of rebellion against involuntary submission to the image of mother. The newly acquired mother-in-law (especially if she is a busybody) revives this infantile dependence. The defense of pseudo-aggression is directed against the unconscious charge of dependence and passivity. It seems likely that the adult, having escaped the mother's preponderance in the family, objects to perpetuation of this very preponderance now presented in the wife's (husband's) mother. The exaggerated aggression covers masochistic attachment to the original image. The pseudo-aggression is reinforced by the coalitions which often exist between psychically dependent wives and their mothers.

This hostility is exemplified in many jokes. For instance:

> A stingy but witty fellow suggests a money-saving device: instead of sending expensive gifts to newlyweds, why not make a more "valuable" donation—some of one's own allotted time on earth. The idea catches on, and at the wedding rehearsal a prospective donor announces: "I am offering the bride ten minutes of my life." The next donor makes it fifteen minutes, and the stakes continue to increase until it is the turn of the originator of the idea. He proposes to give the bridegroom *ten years* of life. Everybody is horrified, but the donor continues calmly: " . . . ten years of my mother-in-law's life."
>
> A man rushed into his neighbor's apartment yelling for help. "Something terrible

[18] I try in vain, under my kisses,
to reawaken the fleeting soul.
It's over. The enchantment's blown away.
And you look like your mother.

has happened," he gasped. "My mother-in-law just hanged herself!" The horrified neighbor seized a knife to cut her down, and started off at top speed, but the son-in-law pulled him back: "Don't be in such a hurry—she isn't dead yet."

The wide popularity of mother-in-law jokes does not guarantee immunity to wives by any means:

"Does the doctor think your wife is going to die?"
"If I only knew."
"But didn't he tell you at least something about her chances?"
"He said to prepare for the worst, and I'm damned if he hasn't got me guessing!"

Witticisms About Death and the Gruesome

Intellectually, every adult knows perfectly well that he is going to die; unconsciously, this knowledge is meaningless. As one grows older, the once-meaningless concept becomes more real, more frightening. Even then, the fear pertains to misconceptions, but they are misconceptions which awaken terror.

One of the most puzzling of the earlier analytic discoveries was Freud's conclusion that death is not represented in the unconscious. Unconsciously, every person thinks of himself as immortal; death is something which happens to others, not to him. Analytically, fear of death is actually fear of bodily harm; this must be so, because death is not part of the human being's personal experience. Conscious fear of death is merely a concession to the consciously accepted fact that death is inevitable. Unconsciously, death means fear of pain and fear of danger either to the body as a whole or part of the body. It is occasionally represented as intense loneliness. This unconscious translation of the unknown into the known follows a familiar pattern; the unconscious operates according to the same principle used by children or primitive people who must adjust to the unfamiliar. The American Indians, for example, overcame their fear of the inconceivable monster, the steam-engine, by linking it with accepted phenomena and calling it a "fire-breathing horse." Since the elements "fire" and "horse" were part of their daily lives, the engine (thus "translated") could be understood and accepted without terror.

All fear is a warning signal. Conscious and rational fear, which pertains to reality factors, serves to mobilize defensive actions. But conscious manifestation of a fear is not necessarily proof of its conscious origin. Unconscious fears appear consciously also; since their origin cannot be traced, they are secondarily rationalized and explained away.

In my opinion, unconscious fear pertains only and exclusively to a repressed masochistic pattern. Via a series of unconscious detours, the fear is changed into a pseudo-aggressive action involving the violation of educational precepts. The fear is then shifted so that it appears to have a reality basis.

Death possesses a good deal of real estate, namely, the graveyard in every town. (Nathaniel Hawthorne)

Strange, when you come to think of it, that of all the countless folk who have lived before our time on this planet, not one is known in history or legend for having died of laughter. (Max Beerbohm)

Death seems to provide the minds of the Anglo-Saxon race with a greater fund of innocent amusement than any other single subject . . . The tale must be about dead bodies or very wicked people, preferably both, before the Tired Business Man can feel really happy. (Dorothy L. Sayers)

"If one of us dies, I'm moving to New York," said the little man in a small town to his rich wife.

"Boy, will this be a great lament in the *morning*," said the traveling salesman at night, just after receiving a telegram informing him of the death of his wife.

Some writers specialize in "blending humor and horror," as the literary phrase has it. Among them are Ambrose Bierce, John Collier, Max Beerbohm, and others. Collier's calmly macabre tales are extremely effective; one of the best of them is *Another American Tragedy*.

This is the story of a young man who had all of his perfectly sound teeth pulled as the first step in an elaborate plot to dispose of his toothless invalid uncle, who happens to be a millionaire. While the nurse is out of the room, the nephew suffocates the uncle, slips his body under the bed, and disguises himself as the invalid by removing his false teeth and his own clothing, putting on his uncle's nightshirt and slipping into bed. He then sends the nurse for the uncle's lawyer, intending to make a new will in his own favor, sign it, and then replace the uncle's body in the bed, and reappear a little later in his own clothing to weep for his loss and take possession of his fortune. But the doctor appears, not the lawyer, and he promptly proceeds to kill the "uncle" who has mentioned him so generously in his will.

Oliver Herford, the extremely witty painter and illustrator whose best-known mot was his characterization of his wife as having "a whim of iron," had a decided talent for grim witticism. On one occasion, a group of visitors was at the Players' Club viewing a collection of death masks of famous actors. A lady said of a mask of Richard Brinsley Sheridan, "I had no idea he was so frail a man." Herford replied, "When that was taken, Sheridan was not really himself."

In explaining why he always wore gray suits, Herford said: "It saves me a world of trouble. When spring and autumn come around, I merely write to my tailor, send him a small sample of dandruff, and tell him to match it exactly."

When Herford was dying, his wife, his sister, and two other ladies were at his side. Herford looked at the assemblage, beckoned to his doctor, and whispered in his ear: "To think that I should die—the President of a Woman's Club . . ." These were his last words.

Ambrose Bierce had a masterly touch:

> You are not permitted to kill a woman who has injured you, but nothing forbids you to reflect that she is growing older every minute. You are avenged 1440 times a day.

And J. K. Huysmans, who is decidedly not noted for his humor, occasionally carried his treatment of the gruesome to the point where it became a witty comment on life. This is Des Hermies speaking in *La Bas*:

> Speaking of dust, in reference to its origin and its objective, are you aware that after we are dead, our carcasses are disposed of by different species of worms according as they are corpulent or lean? In the corpses of stout people are found one sort of creatures, the rhizophagi, in those of thin people only phoras can be discovered. Evidently these latter are the aristocrats of vermin, ascetic worms that scorn rich repasts and disdain the meat of big, swelling bosoms and the spicy feast of fat, paunchy bellies. To think there is not even perfect equality in the mode in which worms fashion the dust of death in each one of us!

Witticisms Directed at One's Own Profession

The ostensible reason for this type of witticism is self-irony; actually, self-irony here is merely a camouflage, and the unconscious target of attack is the teacher-mentor from whom the one-time child learned the fundamentals of his specialized profession.

On writers:

> The dramatic writer must be as stupid as his audience actually is, so that his audience can believe itself as smart as the author. (Herman Bahr)
>
> You must not suppose, because I am a man of letters, that I never tried to earn an honest living. (G. B. Shaw)
>
> The most "popular," the most "successful" writers among us (for a brief period, at least) are ninety-nine times out of a hundred persons of mere address, perseverance, effrontery—in a word, busy-bodies, toadies, quacks. (E. A. Poe)
>
> An incurable itch for scribbling takes possession of many, and grows inveterate in their insane breasts. (Juvenal, *Satires*)

On critics:

> I never read a book before reviewing it. It prejudices one so! (Sydney Smith)
>
> I look upon reviews as a sort of infant disease to which new-born books are subject. (G. E. Lichtenberg)

On philosophers:

Perhaps the only true dignity of man is the capacity to despise himself. (G. Santayana)

When he to whom one speaks does not understand, and he who speaks himself does not understand, this is metaphysics. (Voltaire)

The art of writing is the art of applying the seat of the pants to the seat of the chair. (Mary Heaton Vorse)

I do my work sitting down; that's where I shine. (Robert Benchley)

Unless one is a genius, it is best to aim to be intelligible. (Anthony Hope)

Most writers regard truth as their most valuable possession, and therefore are most economical in its use. (Mark Twain)

The writer who aims at producing the platitudes which are "not for an age but for all time" has his reward in being unreadable in all ages. (G. B. Shaw)

Someday I hope to write a book where the royalties will pay for the copies I give away. (Clarence Darrow)

Poets are born, not paid. (Addison Mizner)

He writes his plays for the ages—the ages between five and twelve. (George Jean Nathan)

After being turned down by numerous publishers, he decided to write for posterity. (George Ade)

Many books require no thoughts from those who read them, and for a very simple reason—they made no demands upon those who wrote them. (Charles Caleb Colton)

It took me 15 years to discover that I had no talent for writing, but I couldn't give it up because at that time I was too famous. (Robert Benchley)

If you want to get rich from writing, write the sort of thing that's read by persons who move their lips when they're reading to themselves. (Don Marquis)

I'm a Hollywood writer, so I put on a sport jacket and take off my brain. (Ben Hecht)

In Hollywood the woods are full of people that learned to write but evidently can't read; if they could read their stuff, they'd stop writing. (Will Rogers).

Art is collaboration between God and the artist, and the less the artist does, the better. (André Gide)

Manuscript: something submitted in haste and returned at leisure. (O. Herford)

To avoid criticism, do nothing, say nothing, be nothing. (Elbert Hubbard)

The secret source of humor is not joy but sorrow; there is no humor in heaven. (Mark Twain)

A humorist is a man who feels bad but who feels good about it. (Don Herold)

Biography is a region bounded on the north by history, on the south by fiction, on the east by obituary, and on the west by tedium. (Philip Guedalla)

If you read a biography remember that the truth is never fit for publication. (G. B. Shaw)

The artistic temperament is a disease that afflicts amateurs. (G. K. Chesterton)

Obscenity can be found in every book except the telephone directory. (G. B. Shaw)

On surgeons:

Surgeon: "Are you sure this pipe will stand up under the pressure?"
Plumber: "Look, Doc, I'm a specialist . . . "
Surgeon: "I'm a specialist myself; that's why I'm asking."

On theatrical directors of the Second Empire:

"Your theatre—" he began, in dulcet tones. Bordenave interrupted him with a savage phrase, as becomes a man who dotes on frank situations. "Call it my brothel!" (Emile Zola)

Witticisms Demoting Success and Gloating Over Failure—of the Other Fellow

Here the *defensive* aggression is paramount and used as shield against reproaches of conscience pointing to the gloater's own failure.

Ordinarily, he is crazy, but he has lucid moments when he is only stupid. (Heinrich Heine, commenting on the appointment of a minor figure to the post of French Ambassador to Frankfurt in 1848.)

Waterloo is a battle of the first rank won by a captain of the second. (Victor Hugo)

Macaulay is like a book in breeches . . . He has occasional flashes of silence that make his conversation perfectly delightful. (Sydney Smith)

Success depends on three things: *who* says it, *what* he says, *how* he says it; and of these three things, *what* he says is the least important. (John, Viscount Morley)

Fame is a food that dead men eat,—I have no stomach for such meat. (Austin Dobson)

We grow tired of everything but turning others into ridicule, and congratulating ourselves on their defects. (William Hazlitt)

There's many witty men whose brains cannot fill their bellies. (Benjamin Franklin)

All celebrated people lose on close view. (Napoleon)

Training is everything. The peach was once a bitter almond; cauliflower is nothing but cabbage with a college education. (Mark Twain)

Success is counted sweetest
By those who ne'er succeed. (Emily Dickinson)

Fame is the advantage of being known by people of whom you yourself know nothing, and for whom you care as little. (King Stanislaus Leszczynski, 1763)

The final test of fame is to have a crazy person imagine he is you. (Anon.)

Witticisms Directed at "Stupidity"

The most primitive form of wit is that directed at "human stupidity." So far, nobody has been able to explain why stupidity should be accounted laughable; the banal point that such laughter is evidence of "superiority" is readily granted, but it proves nothing. The observation neither explains the *necessity* for showing one's superiority, nor the reason for choosing precisely laughter as a means of manifesting that superiority.

Moreover, the urge to show one's fellows up as "stupid" is carried so far in some people that their prime target is no longer the stupidity itself but its alleged perpetrator. Such wits are addicted to quoting foolish statements, supposedly made by people of note; actually, these statements are more often than not made up out of the whole cloth. Howard Dietz has suggested the term, "donorism" for the tendency to ascribe witty but anonymous sayings to a known wit; the opposite tendency—that of putting some *idiotic* remark into someone else's mouth—is a "negative donorism," and it is equally prevalent. Most if not all of the "Goldwynisms" so popular a few years ago are examples of "negative donorism"—originating, understandably enough, in the movie colony.

The whole frantic search for "stupidity," in fact, characteristically starts off on the wrong foot. *Stupidity per se is not laughable at all. The laugher laughs at his triumph over his own inner conscience, to whom he has successfully presented a substitute scapegoat. The whole process of donorism is of course unconscious.*

"Negative donorisms" prove this conclusively. If A. says of B., "Yesterday B. told me he could never understand why the sun shines in the daytime—there's enough light without it; but he said he does understand why the moon shines at night—it's dark, and so the light is of some use," A. has made a monkey out of B. and therefore feels "superior." He has unconsciously diverted the attention of his inner conscience to an artificial victim. The same holds true of Sydney Smith's well-known statement: "No one minds what Jeffrey says; it is not more than a week ago that I heard him speak disrespectfully of the equator."

One night a policeman notices a drunk walking up and down the street staring at the pavement; he is obviously searching for something, and when questioned, explains that he has lost a dollar bill. "Are you sure you lost it here?"—"No, I lost it on the next block."—"Then why in hell are you looking for it here?"—"The light is better on this corner."

In pre-Hitler Vienna, a man killed a passerby on the street for no apparent reason. When arrested and interrogated, he explained, "Well, the man was a Jew."—"So what?"—"Well, don't you know the Jews killed Jesus Christ?"—"But that was two thousand years ago!"—"That's possible, but I only heard about it yesterday."

"So you're going to Europe! By boat or plane?"
"Boat, of course."
"Why 'of course'? A plane is faster."
"Yes, but in a plane you are *too* much in God's hands."

Witticisms of the "$64 Question" Kind

This teaser is based on submitting a question which is apparently unanswerable, or which can only be solved by cutting a Gordian knot. It is a reversal of the infantile situation in which many adult questions impressed the child as unanswerable. Moreover, the child felt—via projection— that malice was behind the questions.

A stranger once called me on the telephone, introducing himself as "a gambler from Brooklyn."

"I've read some of your stuff on gamblers," he said. "When I'm in the chips, I think that gambling is a reasonable business, and I'm sure that your idea that a gambler has an unconscious wish to lose money is a lot of hooey. But when I hit a losing streak, I think you're right—and I don't have the money to consult you. If you're so smart, tell me: what's the answer to the $64 question?"

"That's simple. The next time you are winning, deposit a substantial sum of money with a friend, telling him that he is under no circumstances to let you use it for gambling. Then call me up, and I will recommend a colleague who will treat you."

There was no reply for some time, and then the indignant answer came: "Cannot be done." The telephone connection was then broken—by him. He did not explain why it could not be done: perhaps because he had no reliable friend, or because this solution would have required him to divert money to an "unproductive" use; the typical gambler is convinced that what he needs is not a psychiatrist, but "more money and more luck."

Sometimes a highly complex problem is pseudo-naively solved: "Love is a transitive verb," mused an anonymous wit.

Witticisms Directed at Eccentricity

Eccentricity reigns in Bedlam, claimed Sydney Smith in *Elementary Sketches of Moral Philosophy*, because eccentrics are not influenced by one another's laughter. The psychology of eccentricity is complex; to the extent that clinical material is available, it seems to indicate that eccentricity involves either an *unconscious* "negative magic gesture" ("I'll show you how badly you treated me"), or a faintly pseudo-aggressive gesture of defiance, covering more deeply repressed masochistic vicissitudes. Since both cornerstones of the eccentric attitude are unconscious, eccentrics cannot be deterred by other people's laughter; such a comment is unconsciously foreseen and welcomed. The heartier and more profuse the laughter is, the stronger the unconscious accusation against the enshrined infantile image of the mother (father) becomes.[19]

> A famous scientist, a Nobel Prize winner, in the habit of making extensive mountain tours, once narrowly escaped being arrested for putting heavy pavement stones into his knapsack. The policeman did not believe him when he explained his reason: to make his mountain climbing more difficult.
>
> Another scientist had two openings made in the bottom panel of his front door. One was for the "mother cat," the other for the "daughter cat." It did not occur to him that the smaller cat could also have used the larger opening.

[19] There are connections with schizoid personalities, and also with reclusoids. For psychology of the latter, see *Money and Emotional Conflicts*.

Many "absent-minded professor" jokes belong in this category. "Why don't you concentrate?" is one of the standard educational reproaches. Later this point can be singled out, and the "pseudo-moral connotation of neurotic symptoms" enters the distorted picture (see pp. 129ff).

Witticisms Directed at Busybodies' "Knowledge" of Specialized Topics

This technique consists in airing one's considered opinion, at the top of one's lungs, on a topic of which one is really ignorant. There are many subdivisions of this general type; a noteworthy one is the logorrhoic, who cannot stop talking even though he is hopelessly confused by his own deductions. A logorrhoic's starting point at a dinner, for example, might be a remark on the origin of the potatoes served. He could then proceed to relate the history of the cultivated potato and arrive at a discussion of the socio-economic value of the vegetable. The finale is inevitably the firm impression that the talker does not know what he is talking about.

The difficult part in argument is not to defend one's own opinion, but rather to know it. (André Maurois)

Human reason is like a drunken man on horseback; set it up on one side, and it tumbles over on the other. (Martin Luther).

Many are destined to reason wrongly; others, not to reason at all; and others, to persecute those who do reason. (Voltaire)

Witticisms Directed at Inability to Think Things Through

The "one-track mind," in pursuit of its half-baked idea regardless of self-damage, is the butt of this form of wit. Such witticisms are an ironic reversal perpetrated by the child in the adult; they show up the enshrined adult as obsessed with one single pet idea.

A young boy consults his uncle, who is a doctor specializing in venereal diseases. "Uncle, I want a good case of syphilis."—"Are you crazy?"—"Not at all. If I have it, then my kid sister's governess will have it, and if she has it, my tutor will get it, and I hate his guts."

A man goes to his dentist; he is suffering from a severe toothache and he wants the tooth pulled. "Which tooth is it?" the dentist inquires. "You tell me—you're the doctor," the patient answers. One particular tooth seems likely to the dentist; he touches it and asks: "Is this the one?" The patient says "yes," and the tooth is pulled. As soon as it is out, the patient laughs triumphantly, "You guessed wrong!" and so on, till all the teeth are out.

Witticisms About Taxes

There are practically no pure witticisms about taxes; all jokes of this type reveal a large admixture of anger or angry resignation. Perhaps cracking a joke about taxes diminishes the tragedy of paying—and the typical taxpayer has no desire to minimize this tragedy. Where would his grievance be?

> Pay the income tax
> And break your heart upon't. (Elizabeth Barrett Browning)
>
> As sure as death and taxes. (Old saying)

By and large, therefore, jokes about taxes are directed at the misfortunes which grow out of them:

> A famous surgeon in Vienna was called to the office of the collector of internal revenue. "Professor," he was asked, "did all the patients you operated on last year die?"—"You must have spoken to my competitors. Dead, all of them? Of course not! What gives you that idea?"—Well, I see that your return lists only receipts from estates—that means the patients died. What about the patients who are still alive?"

Ex-president Hoover's lament over the decimal point is an indirect allusion to taxes:

> When I comb over these accounts of the New Deal, my sympathy arises for the humble decimal point. His is a pathetic and humble life, wandering around among regimented ciphers, trying to find some of the old places he used to know.

We laugh delightedly at the spectacle of the formidable gangsters of the prohibition era, finally brought to book—not for their murders, which could not be proved—but for failure to pay their income taxes.

One of the best examples of humorous treatment of taxes appeared in a recent issue of the New York *Herald Tribune*. This was a column written by Art Buchwald, Paris correspondent for the *Tribune*; it was entitled "A Non-Deductible Friend":

> One of the most exciting things about coming to New York is seeing old friends that you entertained in Paris. As soon as we checked into the Savoy Plaza we called our good friend Al Capp, the cartoonist of Li'l Abner fame. Mr. Capp said he was delighted to hear from us and told us he would be happy to reciprocate in any way for the fine times we showed him in Paris.
>
> We told him that we had only two weeks to spend in New York and we really wanted to see the town the right way. He said he would certainly make an effort to make our stay a memorable one.
>
> But the next day he called up and seemed somewhat distressed.
>
> "Say old man, I've just heard some bad news. I've talked to my tax lawyers and they've just informed me you're not tax deductible. You know I'm a heavily taxed man and I would like to entertain you expensively but that is apt to cost money and money is something we pleasure-mad Americans are not permitted to spend much of on personal pleasure."
>
> We protested. "But entertaining me wouldn't be a pleasure. I can prove it. Ask Henry Morgan, ask Darryl Zanuck, ask Elsa Maxwell. Besides you can list me as a dependent."

Capp said he'd call us back the next day. He was as good as his word.

"Just got the ruling on it from the Internal Revenue Department. They said it's no go. You've already been listed as a total dependent by Faye Emerson, Errol Flynn, Fred Allen, Barry Gray, Milton Berle, Spyros Skouras and Jenny Hecht. You're considered by the tax department as persona non gratis."

* * *

"Entertainment's deductible," we said. "Could I be considered entertainment?"

"Not really," answered Capp. "I couldn't put you down for that after remembering those evenings we spent in Paris."

We didn't answer. We remembered the same evenings.

"What about endowments? Could you make an endowment out of me? You always said I was a square. Maybe you could build a town around me in France."

Capp hung up.

* * *

We will say he did try to find a way. He tried to list us as a capital gain and then as a capital loss. He tried writing us off as a physical culture, a studio rental, an Equity dues, a valet, and an automobile. He even asked the tax people if we could be considered a depreciation. But they were firm. It wasn't anybody's fault but we just weren't tax deductible.

Witticisms About Fashion

Jokes about fashion are nearly exclusively produced as a masculine revenge on women's subservience to the dictates of Paris: a woman is ready to be half-suffocated or at least made highly uncomfortable in pursuit of the noble aim of being "in the fashion." At the core of these jokes lies irony directed at the mother-image, as well as a generous dash of injustice-collecting: "She loves dresses, not me." Another subdivision refers to the child's revenge for all implanted rules of decency—some feminine clothes are proof of the opposite, or so the child thinks.

The real joke in fashion is not even known to the wit: most of the absurdities of fashion correspond to the unconscious revenge taken on fashion-obsessed women by homosexual fashion designers. This is the thesis of my book, *Fashion and the Unconscious* (1953).

Fashion is a form of ugliness, so strong that we have to change it every six months. (Oscar Wilde)

The modern woman's clothes are like barbed wire fence—they protect the property without obstructing the view. (Anon.)

She looks as if clothes were thrown at her with a pitchfork. (Jonathan Swift)

It's an ill wind that shows no pretty knees. (Anon.)

Divorce court records show that women don't wear as well as they used to; but, thank Heavens, they wear a lot less. (Anon.)

A strait-laced and untraveled farmer comes to New York and notices a sign on a shop window: "Ladies' Ready to Wear Clothes."—"It's about time," he comments.

The custom of fashion today will be the awkwardness and outrage of tomorrow. So arbitrary are these transient laws. (Alexandre Dumas)

Women cherish fashion because it rejuvenates them, or at least renews them. (Madame de Preizeux)

Witticisms About Drinking

The psychology of pathological drinking[20] is complex. Such drinking goes through four descriptive phases, popularly designated as: jocose, morose, bellicose, comatose. At bottom, the adult's authority is ridiculed in jokes on drinking.

A man sits at a bar all evening drinking steadily. When he gets his bill, it is over $10, and he tells the bartender that he has no money. At first the bartender thinks this is a drunk's idea of a joke; when he is convinced that the customer really has no money he threatens to call the police. "What's the fine for hitting a man," the customer inquires suddenly. "Twenty bucks or three days, usually," the bartender answers, "but what's that got to do with your bill? You want to hit *me*?"—"No, you hit me and we'll split the change."

What's drinking?
A mere pause from thinking. (Byron)

There are two things that will be believed of any man whatsoever, and one of them is that he has taken to drink. (Booth Tarkington)

I drink when I have occasion and sometimes when I have no occasion. (Miguel de Cervantes)

There are more old drunks than old physicians. (François Rabelais)

"Talking about dry towns, have you ever been in Leavenworth, Kansas?"
"No liquor at all?"
"Only for snakebite. I stood in line for three hours, but when my turn came the snake was too tired to bite."

"Judge, I wasn't drunk."
"The officer says you were trying to climb a lamp post."
"Oh, that, yes. A couple of pink elephants were following me around, and I admit they got under my skin."

Witticisms Directed at Minutiae Detached From a Greater Context

The technique consists of deliberately overlooking the essentials, and concentrating on non-essential minutiae. Once more, irony at the expense of the adult is included. The irony reverses the parental reproach once directed at the child: "You don't understand the matter as a whole." For example:

Some Sights Worth Seeing in New York: A fat woman trying to squeeze through the narrow aisles of the Fifth Avenue buses . . . People trying to get their pennies back from the subway gum vending machines . . . The looks the other fellows give the man who takes his hat off when a woman enters a crowded elevator . . . (Burton Rascoe)

---

[20] For elaboration, see *The Basic Neurosis.*

These three details may be amusing enough to the observer; projected against the background of the largest city in the world, they are so infinitesimal in significance that the choice of them is an obvious attempt on the part of the observer to reduce greatness to nonentity. The aggression is directed against greatness.

Here is another example:

Babies haven't any hair;
Old men's heads are just as bare;
Between the cradle and the grave
Lies a haircut and a shave. (Samuel Hoffenstien)

The same technique, in reverse, forms a subdivision of this type of witticism. In the following examples, William Hazlitt takes minutiae and deduces great context from them:

Do you suppose we owe nothing to Pope's deformity?—He said to himself, "If my person be crooked, my verses shall be straight."

Dr. Johnson thought Shakespeare's comedies better than his tragedies, and gives as a reason, that he was more at home in the one than in the other . . . The labour which the Doctor thought it cost Shakespeare to write his tragedies, only shewed the labour which it cost the critic in reading them, that is, his general indisposition to sympathise heartily and spontaneously with works of high-wrought passion or imagination.

Witticisms—Silently Enjoyed—By People "In The Know" When Confronted With "Great Achievements"

J. M. Barrie's aphorism from *What Every Woman Knows* is paradigmatic:

Every man who is high up loves to think that he has done it all himself, and the wife smiles, and lets it go at that.

The silliest woman can manage a clever man, but it needs a very clever woman to manage a fool. (Rudyard Kipling)

It is most important in this world to be pushing, but it is fatal to seem so. (Benjamin Jowett)

The road to success is filled with women pushing their husbands along. (Lord Dewar)

A well-known writer told me this story in analysis. In his leaner days, he had been hired to write a book for a wealthy man; the book's appearance, of course under the wealthy man's name, was celebrated by a party. The disgruntled and furious writer was accosted by a guest who asked him, "Are you the host?"—"No, the *ghost*," murmured the angry writer, ostensibly to himself.

There is a corollary to this story: detraction seems to be the inevitable by-product of every real achievement. Thus, all successful writers are accused of employing ghosts.

Witticisms Devaluating Gratitude

The human capacity for true and spontaneous gratitude—which must be differentiated from the cultural stereotype expressed in an automatic "thank-you"—is decidedly limited. There are reasons for this; gratitude has a genetic record.

The very young child is not grateful for the food, attention and loving care given him, since his only yardstick is his own megalomania. According to his earliest concept, everything "good" is a gift from himself to himself, and only the "bad"—or the refusal—comes from the outer world. In consequence, everything "good" is taken for granted, and everything "bad" (including refusals necessitated by his own welfare) is viewed as a terrible injustice.

Parents can build up the feeling of gratitude in the child by making gratitude a moral dictum. The comparatively normal child, identifying with precepts communicated by his parents, will learn to translate his original megalomaniacal reaction into a feeling of appreciation. The more easily he does this, the more successful he has been in correcting his early misconceptions, and in adapting to reality.

Restrictions are unavoidable during the educational process, but the neurotic child will interpret educational restrictions as malice, and will retaliate against the "aggressor." Limitations imposed on the child's aggressive and libidinous wishes lead first to frustration, and then to hatred in the child. If the child rejects the normal solution, which is to identify with the educator and internalize the educational precepts, there is only one solution open to him: he pays the price of suffering in exchange for the privilege of continuing the old "slave revolt" in disguised form—a road leading to the "psychic masochistic solution."

The neurotic child, now become an adult, is incapable of gratitude. Clinical experience proves that it is really dangerous to be kind to some neurotics; the kindness arouses them from their previous indifference, and they repay their benefactor with a direct act of aggression. This "illogical" reaction emerges because the benefactor, in performing his kindness, has entered the magic circle of the individual's neurotic repetition tendency. The neurotic then projects upon him the injustices allegedly experienced in the past, and at this late date "evens the account." It is of no importance that the benefactor is not identical with the disappointing educator of childhood, and has not "disappointed" the neurotic. The unconscious identification of the benefactor with the early disappointer is sufficient to start the mechanism going.

Two other factors must be taken into account to explain the inner aggression shown by some neurotics towards their benefactors. The first is the limitlessness of the child's desire for love and exclusive attention. Within the magic circle of the beneficiary's past, the standards of reality do not apply. The benefactor's act of kindness, therefore, is measured against the insufficiency of love, kindness and attention allegedly given the neurotic in his childhood. These arrears are projected upon the benefactor, and his kindness thus becomes merely a small part payment on an old debt. The neurotic thus changes a kind act into a negligible installment on an unpaid billion-dollar obligation.

The second factor has to do with quantitative variations in the unconscious self-damaging tendencies present within the individual neurotic. The psychic masochist is submissive to a "strong" person, aggressive towards a "weak" one. The benefactor is classified as "weak" because of his good deed, and is therefore treated aggressively, even though the attitude towards him, previous to the kindness which stigmatized him as "weak," had been one of respect or indifference.

Some people advance the idea that gratitude is rare because people dislike being reminded of their own beginnings, when they needed help from others. This deduction is faulty. People forget both their early dependence and their bill of gratitude, because they unconsciously live on the basis of their autarchic fantasy, in which worthwhile things coming from the outside are negated. Again, this is a remnant of infantile megalomania.

At the beginning of his political career, Talleyrand was a protege of Mme. de Stael. Through her connections with Barras, Talleyrand was appointed Secretary of State. At a later period, Talleyrand was asked whether Mme. de Stael was a "good friend."—"She certainly is," he replied, "she would throw her friends into the water to have the pleasure of rescuing them."

A man was indebted to a friend for a long series of helpful acts; this did not prevent him from playing a dirty trick on his benefactor. The benefactor was indignant: "Who helped you when you were down? Who put you in business? Who paid your debts? And the hospital bills for your child?"—"You did, sure. But what did you do for me *recently*?"

Witticisms Directed Against Manners and Snobbery

The irony here is directed at the innocent parents who taught the children the necessary rules of culturally proper conduct. These witticisms are also attacks on the ego ideal, which (in later stages of development) enshrines the parental law-tables.

Ghosts, like ladies, never speak till spoke to. (Richard Harris Barham, 1788–1845, *The Ghost*)

His life was formal. His actions seemed ruled with a ruler. (Charles Lamb)

No furniture is so charming as books, even if you never open them or read a single word. (Sydney Smith)

Talk to every woman as if you loved her, and to every man as if he bored you, and at the end of your first season you will have the reputation of possessing the most perfect social tact. (Oscar Wilde)

Manners are the happy way of doing things. Manners have been somewhat cynically defined to be a contrivance of wise men to keep fools at a distance. (Ralph Waldo Emerson)

Snobbery is but a point in time. Let us have patience with our inferiors. They are ourselves of yesterday. (Isaac Goldberg)

Now she is dead she greets Christ with a nod,—(He was a carpenter)—but she knows God. (Virginia Taylor McCormick)

Then here's to the city of Boston,
The town of the cries and the groans,
Where the Cabots can't see the Kabotschniks,
And the Lowells won't speak to the Cohns. (F. P. Adams)

She tried to found a salon, but only succeeded in opening a restaurant. (Oscar Wilde)

The difference between a man and his valet: they both smoke the same cigars, but only one pays for them. (Robert Frost)

The hardest thing is writing a recommendation for someone we know. (Frank McKinney Hubbard)

After Calvin Coolidge was nominated for vice-president, he was invited to many dinner parties. As a guest, he was decidedly unsatisfactory, since he neither spoke himself nor encouraged his partners' conversation. One of his hostesses lost her patience and remarked pointedly, "It must be very boring for you, Mr. Coolidge, to go to so many dinners."—"Well," answered Coolidge, "a man must eat."

Witticisms Directed at Inability to Understand Accepted Pleasures in Life

Swift's exclamation, in *Polite Conversation*, is typical: "Lord! I wonder what fool it was that first invented kissing?"

In a recent moving picture, a depressed soldier cannot be aroused to interest by a discussion of baseball. His pal reproaches him: "What's the matter with you? Are you a foreigner?"

Witticisms Directed at Pedantry

Once more, educational pedantry is attacked. In part, too, these witticisms are attempts to deflate the adult as he appeared in his earliest guise—as possessor of knowledge, manifested in a bombardment of incomprehensible references.

"Doctor Livingstone, I presume?" (Henry M. Stanley, greeting the long-lost explorer in the African jungle in 1871)

And still they gazed, and still the wonder grew,
That one small head could carry all he knew. (Oliver Goldsmith)

The bookful blockhead, ignorantly read,
With loads of learned lumber in his head. (Alexander Pope)

Witticisms Directed at the Sublime, Deflating It to the Ridiculous

"Elevated" language, lofty turns of speech and concepts, all contain—for the hearer—the reproach of not having achieved enough. To counteract the reproach, the child in the adult tries to devaluate the elevated. Nothing escapes:

Only kings, editors, and people with tapeworms have the right to use the editorial "we." (Mark Twain)

Moral indignation: jealousy with a halo. (H. G. Wells)

A cartoon appeared in *The New Yorker* shortly after General MacArthur accepted the position of Chairman of the Board of the Remington-Rand Corp. The cartoon showed an office door, marked *Chairman of the Board:* on the doorknob was hung the usual "out-to-lunch" placard; it read, I SHALL RETURN.

The cruel and unjustified irony is directed at the memorable statement made by the general when he promised that the Philippines would be recaptured from the Japanese.

Witticisms Reversing Accepted Moral Standards

Normally, we expect a hero to "fight to the last ditch," no matter what the battleground; Napoleon, however, said of love:

Success in war means surrounding your enemy, routing him, and driving him from the field. Success in love means—escape.

In Sascha Guitry's *History of a Cheat*, a boy is sent to bed without supper as punishment for a minor misdeed. In the morning, every one else in the family is dead: the supper had included poisonous mushrooms. Morality is thus punished and not rewarded, and the "immoral" boy is the only survivor.

Guitry once rode in a bus, and after a while realized that the lady opposite him was sitting in a position which flagrantly revealed her private parts; evidently, she had recognized the famous author and was endeavoring to attract his attention. As he left the bus, Guitry leaned over her politely and inquired: "But you do not object to my keeping *my* pants on?"

In *The Madwoman of Chaillot*, the brilliant elaboration by Maurice Valency of the Giradoux comedy,[21] a "broker" takes a "little man's" life savings for a silly speculation (after the sucker practically begs him to do so):

LITTLE MAN: But I beg you—It's my only chance—Please don't turn me away.
BROKER: Oh, all right. (He sweeps the money into his pocket.) Well?
LITTLE MAN: I thought—perhaps you'd give me a little receipt . . .

[21] Random House, New York, 1947.

THE PRESIDENT: My dear man, people like us don't give receipts for money. We take them.
LITTLE MAN: Oh, pardon, of course. I was confused. Here it is. (Scribbles a receipt) Thank you—Thank you—Thank you.

All these witticisms are attempts by the child in the adult to reduce educational rules to absurdity.

Witticisms Directed Against Poor Grammar

We make fun of people whose grammar and syntax are faulty, thus pretending that adherence to rules is important. On the other hand, we enjoy jokes about too-strict grammar and too-rigid syntax. A good part of Josh Billings' effectiveness as a humorist derives from this form of wit. How can we reconcile this contradiction?

Grammar and syntax are forced upon the child by his elders. The child's ambivalence causes him to shift from acceptance to rejection, from identification with to rebellion against these educators; thus both jokes upholding correct grammar and those rebelling against it become part and parcel of the "adult" attitude.

Witticisms of Anti-Intellectualism

Numerous witticisms are directed against the technique used by the adult to impress the child with his power. These witticisms are merely an advanced stage of the common childhood sneer, "Ya think ya know so much!" In his helplessness, the child devaluates knowledge (which we are correctly told is power); the adult uses a more effective weapon for exactly the same purpose.

A specific sub-group of anti-intellectualism goes one step further; its originators are intellectuals themselves.[22]

A highbrow is a person educated beyond his intelligence. (Brander Matthews)

A highbrow is the kind of person who looks at a sausage and thinks of Picasso. (A. P. Herbert)

Our intellectual marines,
Landing in Little Magazines,
Capture a trend. (W. H. Auden)

* *

Although wit produces laughter on an intellectualized plane, the basis goes back to the pre-intelligence stage (in the adult sense). Hence, unless we understand the child in the adult, wit—with its constant aim of counteracting the severity of the inner conscience—remains unintelligible.

[22] An amusing though purely descriptive elaboration is found in Russell Lynes' "Highbrow, Lowbrow, Middlebrow" and "The Upper Bohemians" (*Harper's Magazine*, February, 1949, and February, 1953, respectively). Mr. Lynes is so enchanted with his types that he overlooks the essential: the little matter of an explanation.

5. The Four Pillars of that Mysterious "Sense of Humor": Wit, the Comic, Self-Derision, Jokes in Lieu of Sympathy

I have found you an argument; I am not obliged to find you an understanding.
Samuel Johnson, from Boswell's *Life*, Vol. II, p. 536

HUMOROUS PRODUCTIONS, viewed in toto, present a picture of confusion when they are examined without differentiation, simply as units; a great part of this confusion can be ironed out by separating these productions into their categories: wit, the comic, self-derision, grim humor. Most of the disorder and perplexity encountered in scientific literature dealing with humor can be accounted for by the absence of classification; proponents of theories on laughter tend to make their deductions from study of a single subdivision and to apply such theories to the whole of risible matter, while their detractors attack their conclusions with new theories drawn from other subdivisions. As a result, they both observe and theorize at cross pruposes.

The basis of all humor (*and here the word is used in its broadest connotation*) *is an alibi presented to the inner conscience, and a denial of one's fear of one's own psychic masochism. The disclaimer takes various forms: in wit* (see previous chapter) *and the comic, it is defensive pseudo-aggression:*[1] *in self-derision, it becomes a preventive attack upon oneself to forestall others' ridicule;*

[1] The masochistic basis of laughter, warded off with pseudo-aggression, is so difficult to grasp emotionally that even analysts who have tangentially approached the problem shy away from it immediately, or restrict it to a small sector. An example for the first attitude is H. W. Brady's "The Meaning of Laughter" (*Ps. An. Quarterly*, 1950); for the second, Lucille Dooley's "Relation of Humor to Masochism" (*Ps. An. Review*, 1941, pp. 37–46).

Brady starts with the strange statement that laughter is a defense best left undisturbed in analysis. In his opinion, laughter expresses aggression in a roundabout way: "Unable to express the *sadistic* drive more directly, the laugher turns part of the sadism against himself." He concludes: "The more normal person, who has learned to manage his hostilities and is unafraid of his *aggression*, is capable of occasional laughter." According to Brady, "laughter results from a sudden reduction in *sadistic* psychic tensions; it has definite relations to both masochistic and compulsive dynamisms." Although Brady's examples pertain to masochistic patients, he generally gives them credit for—sadism. This is especially evident in compulsives: "the depressed person, involved with his own *hates*, is unable to laugh because its meaning is too evident to him." Here, real and defensive aggression in anal regression (see *The Basic Neurosis*) are confused. By failing to distinguish different forms of huin witnessing or in listening to "grim humor" it becomes *a saving of painful masochistic identification;* in producing a grimly humorous remark, it becomes a *negative hallucination of the tragedy at hand, a defense executed on a narcissistic basis.*

Thus, all attempts to play *hostility jokes* off against *sympathy jokes* are senseless; the two represent separate tributaries to the great stream of humor.

* * *

As pointed out before, the sense of the ludicrous goes through three triads:

Laughter at "the comical" is Triad No. 3 in the child's development of "a sense of humor"; it is the successor to Triad No. 2, that of megalomania, and Triad No. 1, the smile and laugh which is the very young child's *direct* reassurance against terror-like fears. In the child, laughter at the comical denotes *indirect* reassurance; in effect, it says, "I'm starting to turn the tables on the powerful adults." The child's notion of what constitutes "the comic," therefore, differs considerably from that of the adult, but only in the choice of topics. The difference can be explained by the disparity between the child's fears and those of even the most fear-ridden adult.

---

morous productions, Brady arrives at the formulation that "the ostensible gaiety of laughter masks emotions such as fear, hate, sadness, despair, regret, or triumph." Finally, he adduces E. Peto's "Weeping and Laughter (*I. J. Psa.* 1946, pp. 129–133); Peto believes that the "laughing process consists of movements which aim at putting the joy-causing stimulus into the mouth, i.e., when the infant feels joy he tries to receive, to introject, the exciting stimulus." Whereas Freud concluded that the beginning of the infant's smile is the satiated nursling's sign of "enough" Brady sees in it "the *satisfaction of its own activity*, possibly of having devoured the breast or having introjected mother." Without seeing the contradiction, Brady says, "It is the most psychopathological and the healthiest people who can laugh easily" (my italics).

Lucille Dooley limits application of masochistic tendencies to witticism directed against oneself or grim humor (see p. 166, footnote).

Recently, attempts have been made to work out a "mirth response test" using cartoons. Since both psychic masochism and defensive pseudo-aggression are neglected by these authors, the avenue they propose to take is not promising. The same objection applies to half-hearted "acceptances" of psychic masochism as a determinant in some segments of humorous production; in these pseudo-acceptances the meaning of the pleasure-in-displeasure pattern is changed. E.g., M. Brenman in "On Teasing and Being Teased", the *Ps. An. Study of the Child*, VII, 264ff., rejects both theories on masochism, that of instinctual expression and that of defense mechanism, subscribing instead to a theory of her own which, in its present stage of fragmentary elaboration and general haziness, is not productive: "They are a rather highly complex set of configurations which issue from special varieties of infantile need and rage pitted against a variety of mediating defense mechanism and in interplay with the available creative or adaptive ego functions . . . " (pp. 272–3).

Considerable controvery has been evoked by Freud's not too cautious statement, "The child lacks all feeling for the comic." This thesis, stated without qualification in 1905, is today untenable. Freud may very well, of course, have meant "the comic" in the adult sense. There is no doubt that children have an excellent perception of the comic—as they understand it. Freud was obviously trapped by his interpretation of the comic; if comic laughter results from "a difference of expenditure produced in the effort to understand the other person" (Freud, *Basic Writings*, p. 767), obviously the very young child cannot be capable of such laughter, for he has not had time to build up his individual standard of comparisons. Freud thus assumed the existence of some sort of "lost infantile laughter," to which the adult tries to return via the different techniques of humorous production. The thesis that we originally possess the capacity for "original infantile laughter"—no reason asked and no reason given—is not borne out by facts; if our assumption that there are three triads in the development of laughter is correct, the concept of a mystical and "original" infantile laughter can be shelved as an interesting, though faulty, hypothesis.

Moreover, Freud's explanation of the comic entirely disregards the child's fundamental primum movens: *infantile megalomania*. The constant blows sustained by this cherished fantasy constitute the greatest tragedy of infancy, babyhood, childhood. Numerous defenses are intrapsychically installed to counteract these defeats;[2] one of these counter-measures is the demotion of the fear-inspiring adult. Numerous cartoons and "funnies" (Mickey Mouse, Popeye the Sailor, Bugs Bunny, etc.) depict the victory of the weak over the strong, the stronger always being the butt of the joke. Devotees of these productions are not enshrining the "lost laughter" of infancy, but the *irrational megalomania* of infancy, defects of which are attenuated to the point of becoming merely comic by reversing the real state of affairs.

On the other hand, Freud states that "the comic difference would be found either, a) through a comparison between the other and one's self, or b) through a comparison altogether with the other, or c) *through a comparison altogether within one's self*."

Enlarging on this definition, Freud explains that in the case of a), the "other" would be viewed as a child; in the case of b) he would be viewed as putting himself on a child's level; and in c), the child would be found in the viewer and not the viewed. Comic effects flowing from movements, shapes, psychic activity and character belong in category a), so that the "other", if acting foolishly, would be seen as a lazy child or, if acting "badly," would be seen as a naughty child. The only pleasure here which

[2] Summarized in *The Basic Neurosis* and *The Superego*.

might exclude adults would be that of the pleasure derived from one's own physical motions.

When the "other" is found to be comical because he has dropped to a child's level, perception of the comic depends on empathy; laughter of this type grows out of the comic situation, or out of caricature, imitation, debunking, or showing up a masquerade. The comic situation is based on embarrassment, which is the emotion accompanying the child's realization of his helplessness, and of his imperfect control of the physical functions. A situation can also become comic through repetition. Here the pleasure is reminiscent, since it echoes the child's desire for repetition of favorite stories, rhymes, games. The response to caricature and exaggeration corresponds to the child's lack of moderation, and his ignorance both of limits themselves and of reasons for limits. Moderation comes only after inhibitions have been developed; when inhibition is weakened, as in dreams and in psycho-neuroses, immoderation again appears.

Comic imitation is the direct descendant of the imitation which characterizes most children's games. The child is not concerned with making his mark among his fellows; he is interested in doing what the adult does. The child's relation to the adult is also at the core of the comic effect of degrading or debunking; it is the adult who loses caste. Showing up a masquerade is pleasurable for the same reason; it reveals the adult as merely a child behind his mask.

The whole problem of child's play, as discussed in the non-analytic literature on humor, lacks the decisive element: the "unconscious repetition compulsion" (Freud)—active repetition of passively endured experiences in order to restore one's narcissism (see p. 273).

As for the third category, that of a comic difference ". . . found . . . through a comparison altogether within one's self," Freud admits that it is difficult to discover the infantile determinant here. The ability to appreciate this form of the comic develops at a late stage, and it is likely that the child sees only disappointment in situations of the type which are considered comical by adults. But finding one's self comical "as a child" can be related to the child's characteristic attitude of expectation and gullibility.

It is clear, therefore, that Freud's view of the child's inner needs is by no means as "naive" as his anti-analytically oriented detractors in the literature on laughter have claimed. It is equally clear, however, that his assumptions need further clarification.

This elaboration is best begun with an analysis of a feeling which is diametrically opposed to the comic—*the feeling of uncanniness.* I believe that the comic cannot be understood without adducing the uncanny; farfetched as the detour may seem, it is unavoidable.

In 1919, Freud defined the uncanny as a separate subdivision of the fearful, and subdivided the uncanny, again, into two sections. The first type grows out of a revival of repressed infantile complexes, the second from a revival and seeming confirmation of primitive beliefs once held but since discarded.

Practically speaking, these two subdivisions tend to merge, for primitive beliefs are closely intertwined with infantile complexes and, in fact, develop from them. Freud calls the uncanny a concealed but familiar emotion that has been driven into repression and then "escaped." Such superstitions as the omnipotence of thoughts, instantaneous wish-fulfillments, secret power to do harm, and the return of the dead, though they are laughed at, still remain rooted within us and tend to emerge in a feeling of uncanniness and semi-belief when events arise which seem to confirm them as realities. This type of uncanny feeling, however, is impossible when one has "completely and finally dispelled animistic beliefs."

In 1934,[3] I began the work of correlating newer analytic findings with Freud's study of the uncanny; my earlier opinions were later modified to accord with my theory of anxiety.[4] Today I believe that the feeling of uncanniness encompasses, in a singularly condensed form, the entire *history* of infantile megalomania and its end result, psychic masochism. It is a lightning-fast review of megalomania, fury, the crushing of megalomania through the varieties of the septet of dangers which is subsequently subsumed under the "septet of baby fears," the turning of aggression against oneself, and the final step, libidinization of fear. The feeling of uncanniness is probably the most powerful of human fears; its intensity accounts for the frequency with which it is encountered in game form. To meet with the uncanny in the form of a movie, a book, or even at a spiritualistic seance means that two needs have been satisfied: the need for masochistic pleasure and the need for reassurance, "It's only a game."

The *condensation* inherent in uncanniness differentiates it from any other type of fear. The powerful emotions involved in infantile megalomania, including its after-phase of dreary defeat and masochistic elaboration, are concentrated in one split-second of uncanny feeling; the impact must be both shocking and terrifying.

The initial step in uncanniness is the *reaffirmation of the aggressive contents of infantile megalomania*; superficially, this step seems to recapitulate the heyday of the omnipotence fantasy. This explains the megalomaniacal (through repressed) pleasure felt in uncanniness. The first step is followed by a recapitulation of the *masochistic end* of megalomania. Psychic masochism (as pointed out) is a state in which "I create, unconsciously, a situation in which *my* wishes are refused, denied, inhibited"; it is therefore the

[3] "The Psychoanalysis of the Uncanny, "*Int. Journal of Psycho-Analysis* London, 1934.

[4] *The Basic Neurosis*, pp. 38ff.

act of choosing, creating or perpetuating one's own self-approved defeats. Remnants of megalomania are thus seen to be enshrined in psychic masochism, and in its clinical picture.[5]

The feeling of uncanniness reaffirms both the *aggressive* content of the fantasy of omnipotence, and the *masochistic elaboration* of this fantasy which is the successor of the aggressive period. The unconscious pleasure in uncanniness derives from bòth affirmations; it is this double pleasure which makes uncanniness so alluring.

As in all cases involving fear phenomena, the aggressive connotation is unconsciously admitted and used as an alibi in an attempt to prove innocence of the more deeply rooted, more serious offense: psychic masochism. As usual, aggression is put forward as a defense against psychic masochism.

Curiously enough, uncanniness prevents prolonged anxiety and psychic work, since the brief lightning-stroke of strong emotion substitutes for the protracted recollection of that infantile tragedy, the destruction of the fantasy of omnipotence.

The intensity of an adult's emotion is only a pale copy of the emotional capacity of the child. In my opinion, the *intense terror* experienced in uncanniness represents only an attenuated remnant of the child's original feelings when he was confronted with obstacles to his fantasy of megalomania. The most profound terror of uncanniness, multiplied by one thousand, would still be only a faint approximation of the child's feelings during the period of "the septet of baby fears."

The element of condensation in uncanniness, coupled with its brevity, has a paradoxical effect: the shock is cushioned. The unconscious intent is to make uncanniness into "a fear to end all fears"; the fact that this aim can at best be achieved for a short time only can be explained by the connections with "pleasure in fear."

Like any other fear, the fear inherent in uncanniness is also a warning signal. The human being's unending capacity for suffering accounts for the tendency to traverse the whole scale of terror in uncanniness, until it is cut short by the saving grace of "pleasure in pain." The inner lawyer (the unconscious ego) reduces the masochistic fiesta to a short moment, warning of even greater damage.

In my opinion, the uncanny is a specific elaboration of psychic masochism; it enshrines the whole dreadful end of infantile megalomania.[6] *The "comic feeling," I believe, is another elaboration of the identical emotion which appears in the uncanny. In both feelings, the starting point is the graveyard of infantile megalomania; in the comic, this historical fact is elaborated on*

[5] For differentiation between clinical and genetic pictures see *The Superego*, pp. 47ff.

[6] For elaboration, see *Neurotic Counterfeit-Sex.*

victoriously; in the uncanny, the elaboration is fearful and defeatist. At bottom, it is a fearful regret for one's lost infantile megalomania.

Formulated slightly paradoxically, one can say that adult perception of the comic corresponds to the artificial flowers we "plant" at the graveyard of our lost infantile megalomania.

In seeing or hearing something which strikes us as comical, *we do indeed make the comparison postulated by Freud, but the comparison pertains to an illusion which we have given up, while the other fellow has not.* Our laughter is the external expression of the inner conviction: "He will find out."

There is no more convincing evidence of the effectiveness of the unconscious ego's protective efforts than the ability to "get a laugh" out of our own defeats in the sphere of megalomania.

One of Freud's examples of comic situations is that of the bowler who has released his ball but who continues to make motions with his arm "as though he were still able to control it." He is still controlling it—with imaginary weapons drawn from the arsenal of infantile megalomania. Freud also brings up the familiar example of the child, just learning to write, who faithfully follows with his outthrust tongue the unaccustomed movement of his pen. The child thus cancels an offense against his megalomania (inability to write) by simulating a victory for megalomania: his tongue "obeys" though the pen may be resistant.

As a general rule, the child uses the comic as an instrument for the demotion of adults, a fact which Freud has correctly stated. His deduction, however, fails to explain the child's constant need to do so. The situation becomes understandable only if one adduces offenses to megalomania. This is by no means an argument against Freud's early discoveries; quite the contrary. Freud himself has applied this principle in two other instances: in the creation of the ego ideal in postulating the unconscious repitition compulsion. In *The Superego,*[7] I have tried to enlarge on this point by explaining the general principle of "accepting defeats under narcissistic safeguards," taking five mechanisms as examples. This was the gist of my deduction:

In creating the ego ideal, the child's purpose is to restore self-esteem and eradicate a narcissistic wound. The ego ideal, according to Freud's formulation, is established to save the child the repeated blows to his narcissism which are a consequence of being forced to accept educational commands. In introjecting the commands of his educators, he is no longer yielding passively to force, but acting of his own "volition."

Again, in Freud's conception of the "unconscious repetition compulsion," which is beyond the pleasure principle, the child *actively* repeats experiences which he has been forced to bear *passively,* thus wiping out the narcissistic

[7] See pp. 47ff.

humiliation of enforced passivity. This latter principle (as Eidelberg and I showed in "The Breast Complex"[8] in 1933) is unconsciously applied by the boy in overcoming the trauma of weaning. He negates the loss of the breast by identifying breast and penis, milk and urine. Later in life the now grown-up child is actively pushing an oblong organ into an opening (the vagina and his own baby mouth are unconsciously identified and milk, urine and sperm are unconsciously equated). He acts the giving mother, reducing the woman to an image of his own infantile self. This activity atones for the passivity of the past.

The same mechanism is applied in the psychology of tender love, as Jekels and I described it in "Transference and Love," 1934. The formula seems to be: "There is no deflating discrepancy between my ego (achievement) and ego ideal (enshrined promises of achievement); by projecting my ego ideal on the beloved, I am credited in advance (without needing to offer proof) with having fulfilled all the promises made as a child."

The clinical picture in psychic masochism, the fifth mechanism, is a very telling illustration of the tendency to accept pain, as long as protection is afforded to one's narcissism. In psychic masochism, the unconscious story is: "It is not the bad mother, or her representatives, who is punishing me; I started the whole thing by my provocation, and *made* her punish me."

The various forms of comic productions—caricature, parody, travesty, unmasking, imitation, the funnies, etc.—are all derived from one unconscious aim, and are all offshoots of one internal technique: that of debunking the superego.

The comic situation, however, needs to be more fully explained.

Freud declared that the pleasure which we obtain from the "*comic situation*" is based on our realization that we would have done the same thing in the same situation. The protagonists are the all-too-powerful external setting, and our helplessness in the face of it. "Thus every person is really defenseless against being made comical." The comic situation is frequently used to deflate the pompous.

I fully subscribe to this deduction; I believe, however, that it needs further elaboration.

1) No matter how careful the adult is in his relationship with a child, he cannot entirely strip himself of his pseudo-superiority. Somehow, somewhere, sometime, the child is bound to feel that he is not being taken quite seriously. In after life, the comic situation reverses this process via Freud's "unconscious repetition compulsion," and the powerful adult is thrust into an "impossible" situation which suddenly reveals him to be just as silly as the child once appeared to the parent.

2) In the course of the educational process, infantile megalomania was

[8] *Int. Zeitschrift fuer Psychoanalyse*, 1933.

crushed by the adults. In the comic situation, the child in the adult gloats over the helplessness of the one-time Juggernaut; he who was once an irresistible force is now confronted with something stronger than himself.

3) It is not by chance that (as Freud has already hinted) the comic situation often refers to bodily needs (excremental, urinary, sexual). This is due to the presence of another element: the desire to show up the hypocrisy of adults. The child finds "proof" of adult hypocrisy in such matters as the changing attitude towards feces in the course of the educational process. To begin with, feces are over-valued; as indications of the baby's health and well-being, the Giants of the nursery are intently interested in their color, frequency, consistency, etc. Later on, it becomes bad manners even to mention these products without "decent" circumlocution. In cases of ambivalence, the conviction of parental hypocrisy is especially marked.[9] This explains reactions like the following:

> Let an ambassador speak the best sense in the world, and deport himself in the most graceful manner before a prince, yet if the tail of his shirt happen, as I have known it happen to a very wise man, to hang out behind, more people will laugh at that than attend to the other. (Alexander Pope)

4) Situations which are "objectively comic" in their nature are the most difficult to understand. An example is the well-known story of Hemingway's manuscript, *Death in The Afternoon.* According to the contract Hemingway had signed with Scribner's, the publishers had no right to make any change whatever in the manuscript, not even in a single word. Scribner's brilliant editor, Maxwell Perkins, was reading the manuscript when to his horror he came upon a four-letter word from the Anglo-Saxon beginning with the letter "f." He rushed into the office of the elderly Charles Scribner, read him the passage, and anxiously pointed out that the contract forbade the publishers to change a single word in the book. Mr. Scribner sighed, told him that they would have to discuss the matter at greater length when he returned from lunch, and then absent-mindedly jotted the word down on a pad headed "What To Do Today." One sometimes hears a postscript to the story, dealing with Mr. Scribner's secretary. While Mr. Scribner was out to lunch, she looked at his pad, saw the notation, and gasped: "Is a secretary supposed to remind her boss about *everything*?"

The situation is undeniably comic, but who is the butt? Perkins, Scribner, Hemingway, the secretary? The slight admixture of irony directed against the hypocrisy which forbids "frank" language accounts for some of the listener's amusement, but only a small part. I believe the story (whether it is true, padded, or "donated") is an example of the "impersonal comic."

[9] For elaboration, see *Neurotic Counterfeit-Sex*, pp. 149ff.

It seems that the child in the adult still nurses his grievance against being held personally responsible for impersonal factors beyond his control. If a chain-reaction is set off "by chance," the child in the adult triumphantly proves his point: "I'm not responsible." This triumph is shifted to the "*impersonally* comic."

In unequivocally neurotic reactions, a specific type of comic situation becomes markedly present. This is the incessant search for "feet of clay." In a previous study, "Anxiety, Feet of Clay and Comedy,"[10] I pointed out that this "demotion of the 'potential enemy' is, at bottom, an unconscious attempt to demonstrate that the alleged adversary is too weak to be dangerous."

There is a clear-cut difference between the unavoidable *observation* of the relatively healthy person to the effect that everyone has his peculiarities and ridiculous attitudes, and the *compulsive necessity* of neurotics to find the "weak spot." The healthy person uses his observations for the purpose of making fun; the neurotic, under the disguise of making fun, uses them for the *diminution of latent anxiety*.

From the common sense point of view, there is something puerile and immature in this constant search for "feet of clay." The whole search is based on the erroneous assumption that people without weaknesses do exist. The actual state of affairs is reflected in La Rochefoucauld's maxim: "If in some people the ridiculous part of their nature has not become apparent, obviously one has not yet searched thoroughly enough."

To prove that a person you have put on a pedestal has "feet of clay" is as simple as to prove that everyone has a nose; nevertheless the demotion of "god" to "half-god" is a favorite sport of the neurotic. Experience teaches that the easiest path to disappointment is to expect too much.

In a previous paper on writers ("Further Studies on Psychoanalysis of Writers," the *Psychoan. Review*, 34, 468–499; 1948) I have described a specific aspect of this technique.

> The problem of "ocular malice" is closely connected with it. A series of writers whom I analyzed showed a remarkable ability for ocular malice. It was a selective ability of seeing exclusively the dark and petty-ridiculous side of human behavior. I got the impression that an inner defense mechanism was involved: *the first observation pertained to the person himself; basically to the person's own masochism.*
>
> *To counteract the resulting feeling of guilt, voyeurism was used as a proof that everybody else was malicious and silly.* It was remarkable how malicious and, at the same time, petty and insignificant these observations were. This *malice of insignificant details*—in very precise contradistinction to significant details—is in itself the result of feelings of guilt. It is precisely this guilt which makes these observations worthless. In the analytic transference this type uses a specific technique: these patients often refuse to use the couch since they constantly wish to observe the analyst.

---

[10] From *The American Imago*, 6, 2; 1949.

They *have* to find some insignificant and at the same time ridiculous detail—then they feel safe. The conversation of these writers has the same topic as their books: a compilation of petty malice. Once such writer told me triumphantly that he observed human nature so perfectly that not *one* decent person was described in his books. The man did not even grasp the severity of this self-indictment; he did not see that he was just running frantically after his favorite inner defense mechanism: not that I am masochistic, but the outer world is mean. One could ask why these writers who make malice their business do not make significant observations. The material is, surely, not lacking. The clinical fact is that these writers are either blind to the important facts, or, even if they see them, they present their observations with a twist which makes the tendentious approach too obvious and defeats their own aim. The reason seems to be inner feeling of guilt.

A more important "reassuring," fear-diminishing tendency is also involved.

Frequently the compulsive tendency to demote everybody is connected with cynicism. The conscious intention, in cynicism, is to prove one's own "smartness" and the fact that one "knows the ropes." (see p. 121f.)

It is worth noting that the unconscious affective basis for the widespread interest in biographies of "great men" is to a minor extent identification with the hero, and to a much greater extent desire to ferret out the reassuring "weak spot." A female patient, for example, worked through the nine hundred pages of Robert Sherwood's *Roosevelt and Hopkins*, and retained only the facts that the late president was served poor food in the White House, disliked salad, and never did anything to improve the quality of the cuisine. The patient immediately made a case for her own mother's "neglect" and father's "weak attitude."

The French wit, Madame Cornuel, uttered the statement, later attributed to various "great men": "No man is a hero to his valet." Since that is the case, it is senseless to acquire the knowledge of a valet. A man must be judged by his ideas and achievements, not by his inherent silliness.

One could object that this deduction unjustifiably disposes of comedy and satire. On the contrary; it clarifies the difference between *enjoying* ridicule of others' foolishness, and being *forced* to find the ridiculous for oneself.

Satire and comedy, as literary products, serve a specific purpose in the psychic economy. They are denials of inner dependence on the upbringers in childhood, a dependence later projected upon the "great" and not so great. Compulsive irony, wit, satire, are the weapons of the weak, and who is weaker than the child in his relation to the "people with the halo" in the nursery? Hence irony—"biting" irony—develops early in the child. Its later development depends on how the narcissistic wounds of babyhood were healed, on whether they were compensated for, or remained open. The state of that early narcissistic wound—its healing or failing to heal—

determines, among other things, the extent of the need for irony and scorn in later life.

If the wound unavoidably inflicted upon the child's narcissism does not heal, the inevitable result is fixation "on the rejection level." This psychic masochism is counteracted, as we have said, by superego reproaches. Again there is an unavoidable result: secondary inner defenses must be instituted. *One* of the possible results is the "proof" that *one is not frightened of one's own psychic masochism, simply because the punishing person, who is now externalized, is weak and ridiculous.*

In Ludwig Jekels' highly and justifiably esteemed study on comedy ("Zur Psychologie der Komoedie," *Imago*, XII: 328–335; 1926), he presents the deduction that comedy is at bottom an aggressive attack on the Oedipal father. Jekels saw in comedy a reversal of the roles of father and son, with the father demoted to the role of the son. Jekels subscribed to Bergson's "le monde reversé" formula, first espoused in *Le Rire* (1901), and he supported Bergson's argument with analytic deductions and evidence.

There is a good deal of truth in Jekels' thesis, although a series of qualifications are necessary.

First: The unconscious ego's attack is not a direct onslaught against the pater familias; it is aimed, rather, at the internal ego ideal, the enshrined intrapsychic images of the giants of the nursery, *plus* the child's own narcissism. Thus the attack is directed against the Daimonion, the antilibidinous section of the superego, which typically misuses the ego ideal for its torture purposes. That correction became necessary after Jekels and I published our theory on the development and structure of the superego in the already-mentioned "Transference and Love."

Second: The unconscious ego's attack is directed not only against the image of the Oedipal father, but also against the image of the pre-Oedipal mother. "Authority" comprises *all* the restrictions binding the child; the Oedipal father is but the successor to the pre-Oedipal mother.

Third: The aggression against the ridiculed representative of authority in comedy is not real aggression; it is compensatory *pseudo-aggression*, covering more deeply repressed psychic masochism.

Fourth: The real problem facing anyone in a situation of dependence is this: Is he confronted with a *nuisance*—at worst a painful nuisance—or does this psychic situation provoke the *severe reproach of conscience* pertaining to undigested and bygone *psychic masochistic allure*? The first alternative is that of the more or less healthy person; the second is the neurotic reaction. The normal reaction to comedy thus differs from the neurotic reaction; comedy and satire are the normal person's spice and he can take them or leave them, while they are staples in the psychic diet of the neurotic.

It is interesting to observe that real satiric comedy on stage or screen is an extreme rarity. The reason can be found in the specific psychic make-up of the writer of satiric comedy. He is a writer who has at his disposal a *stronger* defensive aggression than that of the typical literary man. In my opinion, the writer's many-faceted conflict basically comprises his more or less *successful* alibi: "It is not true that I want to be masochistically *refused* by mother! Mother does not even exist! I am autarchic, and I act the good, *giving* mother with *myself*, on *myself*. *I give* to *myself*, out of *myself* beautiful words and ideas!" With this unconscious magic gesture, and unconscious negative hallucination which negates the mother's very existence, the writer pulls himself up by his autarchic bootstraps and produces his *unconscious alibi*—literary work. There are other mechanisms involved as well, it goes without saying; the "scopophiliac exchange" is one of them. The writer changes imagination (voyeurism) into exhibitionism (publishing) in this mechanism. (See *The Writer and Psychoanalysis*).

The writer's bogey is the frantic fear that his inner conscience will not accept the alibi—his literary work—at face value, and will persist in saying, "All your disguises, camouflages and alibis are fake; you are still a masochistic glutton for punishment and want to be *refused*." From the study of literary sterility ("writer's block"), one can learn that in this emergency the writer resorts to a still stronger alibi: "I don't want to be refused, *I* refuse." Thus, the giving of ideas and words to oneself is inhibited, and the neurotic and *unsuccessful* alibi achieved. Unfortunately, the "cure" is worse than the disease; the inhibited writer's alibi automatically inhibits productivity.

This desperate neurotic alibi also shows that the moment the writer descends from his self-created alleged autarchic "unity" to the mother-child duality, his productivity ceases.

The writer of comedy is somewhere between the two extremes. He must use his *strongest* defensive aggression without falling into the neurotic alibi-trap of the "refusing" role. Successful negotiation of this tight-rope pathway, it seems, is very rare.

Another complication is also present. It is an old observation, and it has been confirmed by a series of analytic authors, that satirists are "melancholy" people. Even satiric writers are sometimes aware of this fact; Wilhelm Raabe, for example, said, "Laughter is one of the most serious things in this world."

An anecdote appearing in the preface to *The Man of Genius* by Cesare Lombroso, also supports this observation: "A patient one day presented himself to Abernethy; after careful examination the celebrated practitioner said: 'Go and hear Grimaldi; he will make you laugh, and that will be better for you than any drugs.'—'My God,' exclaimed the invalid, 'but I *am* Grimaldi.' "

Satirists seem to be on the borderline of psychotic depression; their saving grace is an occasional manic defense. How *not* to be a psychotic of the manic-depressive type and *still* produce is their problem. It is exactly that "temporary health in the shadow of psychosis" which explains why the necessary psychic ingredients are so seldom met with, and these ingredients are indispensable for the writer of satiric comedy.

I have observed in clinical analysis that the writer of satiric comedy often cannot muster the necessary defensive aggression. This case seems paradigmatic: A writer always asked himself, when working out the plots of his malicious comedies, "Who will suffer?" For a long time, he could not comprehend that in a real comedy the full impact of aggression is always and exclusively directed at the butt of the joke, *without allowing the spectator to identify with the victim.* In this case, the patient's masochism led him to confuse comedy with tragedy.

I once had the opportunity to observe the spontaneous emergence of a satiric "talent" in a non-writer. This patient, who was employed in a bank, suffered from deep depression. He was a very shy, inhibited, frightened young man, but one day he handed me "something he had written," adding that it was his first attempt. It turned out to be the most witty satire on analysis that I had ever read.

In a short dramatized sketch the patient described his situation forty years hence. He is still in treatment, still poor, whereas I live in luxury, have achieved fame, and work only "for fun" with a few selected millionaires. Then followed an elaborate description of an appointment on Christmas Eve. Because of the exorbitant fees I charge, the poor patient, now an old and decrepit wreck, can afford *only one appointment a year*, and that of *only five minutes duration.* He rings my doorbell, but the butler refuses to admit him, thinking he is a beggar. He finally convinces the butler that he, the patient, is a relic of my past, and is allowed to wait. After a long time, a lady comes out of the consultation room, recognizes him, and asks with surprise, "Is it really a year, already, since I saw you last?" The lady, too, has been in treatment for a very long while, and measures time only according to how often she sees the relic. Finally, I come out and take a look at the patient. I size him up leisurely, although I know I have only five minutes to put at his disposal, and that he starves himself throughout the year to scrape up the fee for these five minutes. As I am finishing my ocular inspection, the patient collapses and dies of starvation. I state coldly and with some surprise: "I didn't know you had that symptom, too!"

Flashes of satiric writing like these are not rare; it is the sustained effort which makes the difference between the writer of satiric comedies and the person who can, in an exceptional situation, produce a satire. In a case described in a previous study ("A Clinical Approach to the Psychoanalysis of Writers," the *Psychoan. Review*, 31, 1; 1944), I outlined the history of a woman writer who had written one satire some years before she entered analysis. The satire was directed at her husband, an executive manager, made jobless by the crash of 1929. It was a success, and the critics encouraged her to persist, but after this one tour de force she wrote only silly and sentimental short stories. In studying situations in which this "flash" appeared, the prerequisite appeared to have been for the person to be at the lowest ebb in his defensive efforts against reproaches of the superego accusing him of psychic masochistic pleasure. The frantic pseudo-aggressive defense in these people takes the form of satire. In the case of the bank clerk's satire on analysis, the unique, never repeated impetus appeared at the high point of the patient's transference in repetition of the masochistic attachment to the pre-Oedipal mother. In the case of the woman writer mentioned above, the impetus appeared during the months of her husband's unemployment in 1929. The loss of "social face," as she called it, made her very unhappy consciously, but on the other hand it fulfilled her unconscious craving for the badly needed proof that her mother (projected upon her husband) was really "refusing." Her conscience caught up with her alibi, accusing her of masochistic enjoyment, and as a defense she produced the devastating satire directed at that "unemployed big shot," her husband.

In analyzing the bank clerk's satire, one can detect the mechanism pathognomic for a "joke against himself." I am indebted to Henry Adams for the phrase, and use it to describe jokes for which no audience is necessary, since the joker is making his effort for the benefit of the forum internum. Self-flagellation is easily visible in the satire on analysis; the pseudo-aggressive disguise is extremely thin. If hatred had been the driving motive of the satire, the author would have described a case of poetic justice, in which he would have been triumphant and I would have been humiliated. The aggression displayed in this tour de force was needed only for the purpose of contrast, in order to "prove" how unjustly he was treated. The whole satire was unconsciously imbued with masochistic "suffering"—gladly accepted.

Freud's theory on humor (see pp. 39 and 201) has one weak point: the humorist's superego is described as lenient; indeed, as occasionally joking with the humorist. This is in direct contradiction to Freud's own statements on the cruelty and severity of the superego. One can compare the "joking" superego of the humorist with the hangman who jokes with the man he is about to execute. *Humor appears only in desperate situations—*

situations brought about by the superego. Not much leniency is discernible.[11]

The mechanism underlying the joke quoted above has the following features: Self-derision is a technique used exclusively by psychic masochists. One can go so far as to state that a normally aggressive person seldom makes such remarks at all, and is sometimes even disgusted with the pronounced self-humiliation implicit in self-derision. If the self-derisive technique is not overdone, he enjoys "as a joke" the humiliation of the victim, when it is administered in small doses. He relishes the joke in spite of his instinctive suspicion of the victim. He understands the Charlie Chaplin technique, and that of his modern successors—after all, they get paid for it. But constantly to offer oneself as the butt of a joke; more, to produce it oneself, passes the typical person's understanding.

Every expression of self-derision and "grim humor" presupposes an unhappy situation. The condemned prisoner who remarks, on his way to the electric chair, "I hope I don't catch cold," negates for a split second the bodily destruction in store for him, and rises above the situation in a sort of negative hallucination, but he can only make that face-saving remark after he has accepted the condition of death.

Specifically, the technique rests on a quadrangular basis, as elaborated in my study in 1937, quoted above:

Act 1: The humorist's superego has brought about aggressively, or helped to bring about, a desperate situation for the ego by tolerating a masochistic dilemma, being "bribed" by the unhappiness and self-damage involved in the act.

Act 2: The masochistic ego turns to the superego in a sort of prayer for help and love, begging at least to be loved by the superego after punishment, and at the price of it.

Act 3: The superego's answer is to scorn the ego and undertake aggression against it.

Act 4: Driven to desperation, the disappointed ego now undertakes aggressions itself, against the superego (more precisely, against the ego ideal sector of the superego), lapses into primary narcissism, deceives itself as to the reality for a few seconds in a kind of negative hallucination, and enjoys itself in a sort of intoxication.

---

[11] The analytic literature on the topic (summarized in my study, "A Clinical Contribution to the Psychogenesis of Humor," the *Psychoan. Review*, 1937; reprinted in *The Battle of the Conscience*, pp. 172–189) is of a confirming nature, making desperate efforts to find a reason for the superego's exceptional leniency in the humorist. In this study, the *masochistic* basis of humor directed against oneself is elaborated. The only exception is Lucille Dooley. Dooley takes masochism into consideration, although she adheres to the theory of the leniency of the superego in humor. (See "A Note on Humor," *Psychoan. Review*, 1934, and also "The Relation of Humor to Masochism," *Psychoan. Review*, 1941).

Applying these assumptions to the bank clerk's satire:

Act 1: The analyst is unjust; he is exploiting, not curing him.
Act 2: Instead of spurning the malefactor (the analyst), he holds on to him, and even starves, to afford five minutes a year with him (!), and woos him for love.
Act 3: The kick, expected and wanted, is promptly administered with coldness and determination; first the analyst cheats him of his precious seconds, and then even his pitiful death elicits only scientific curiosity and even an incorrect diagnosis.
Act 4: Narcissistic megalomania is triumphant; he even knows what's going to happen after his death. Added is a slight admixture of spurious aggression, comparable to the masochistic Oriental technique of hanging oneself before the malefactor's doorstep. What is overlooked in this technique is that it pre-supposes the victim's death.

The writer of satiric comedies is handicapped in his productivity by the constant duality of deep, masochistically tinged, depression *and* the tendency to direct unproductive irony against himself. Only in exceptional cases does he—the self-rescued defendant living under the shadow of manic-depressive psychosis, having outrun and outwitted the shadow—muster enough aggression to "hit back." That rarely encountered half-miracle makes him a writer of satiric comedies. Thus he answers Ibsen's question: "Is the great really great?"

* * *

The *involuntarily comic* is a specific sub-group which is popularly assumed to comprise both the "comic situation" *and* making oneself appear ridiculous or even idiotic *without* the ameliorating properties of the "comic situation." Strictly speaking, this term should apply only when the person being ridiculed participates—either half-consciously or unconsciously—in the performance. An example is the statement made by Charles X of France: "I shall never abdicate, at least not till I've spoken to my wife, the Queen."

The involuntarily comic is by no means a simple phenomenon. This form of comic situation, in which there is active participation of the person who *unconsciously* offers himself as the butt of the joke, is determined by one of the following factors:

1. There may be unconscious irony on the part of the ego; the irony is directed against enshrined educators.
2. There may be a masochistic trick played on oneself.
3. There may be a counter-action on the part of the superego; this is directed against the elated ego.
4. There may be an unsuccessful attempt at irony on the part of the ego; the method is by paying exaggerated lip-service to external taboos.

5. The participation may be an example of "over-doing" to diminish inner fear.
6. The participation may be an attack on "officialese" and pompousness.

Examples are easily found. When an English female gynecologist, Dr. Jean Mallison, writes in the Foreword of her book, *Any Wife or Any Husband*: "I might add that I hold a part-time hospital appointment; that I have been long enough in practice to hear the problems often of two generations of the same family, and that I am myself a grandmother," the grandmother theme is an example of the involuntarily comic, though it is seemingly directed against the English hypocrisy of seeing "immorality" in any discussion of sex. But if the same author states, in discussing impotence and frigidity, "A common and fortunate adaptation is where a woman with vaginal anasthesia marries a husband with precipitancy; then both may be spared efforts which could only end in frustration" (p. 112), it is obvious that another motive must be adduced.

If Kinsey in his by now notorious *Report* states that premature ejaculation proves hyper-manliness—

> Far from being abnormal, the human male who is quick in his sexual response is quite normal among the mammals, and usual in his own species. It is curious that the term "impotence" should have ever been applied to such rapid response. It would be difficult to find another situation in which an individual who was quick and intense in his responses was labeled anything but superior, and that, in most instances, is exactly what the rapidly ejaculating male probably is. (p. 580)

—the deduction illustrates the involuntarily comic, though Kinsey is unaware of the fact.

The satirist Stephen Leacock wrote:

> There at least *Punch* stands high. It keeps clean away from that terrible obsession of sex which is creeping like a green slime all over our imaginative literature . . . In a later chapter of this book I discuss the obsession over sex as one of the worst hindrances to the continuation and cultivation of real humor. It may very likely be that this outbreak of sex-obsession came as one of the unforeseen byproducts of the emancipation of women . . . Someone may object—that this sex-stuff is no new thing, and that in the domain of humor dirty jokes are as old as the history of laughter. But that is quite another thing. Dirty jokes are all right when the humor is strong enough and clear enough to wash away the dirt.

Again the deduction is involuntarily comic, though Leacock's moralizing is seriously meant. The same applies to the statement, in seeming opposition to Leacock's, made by the British poet George Barker in his recent book, *The Dead Seagull*: "Without the inherent and inherited magnification of original sin, we live in a world where a sneeze and an orgasm hold meaningless candles to each other, and illuminate nothing."

An example of the "over-doing" variety of the involuntary comic is contained in *Against Dicing*, by John Northbrooke, published in 1577:

> Dice playing is a door and window into all theft, whoredom, swearing, blasphemy, banqueting, dancing, rioting, drunkenness, pride, covetousness, craft, deceit, lying, brawling, fighting, prodigality, night-watching, idleness, beggary, poverty, bankrupting, misery, prisonment, hanging, etc.

A similar case of absurdity via over-zealousness is found in Emerson's dictum: "To live without duties is obscene."

If a cookbook states, in a recipe for preparing trout, that "fishes love to be broiled in butter"; if a winebook proclaims "Nothing equals the joy of the drinker except the joy of the wine in being drunk" (Anon., quoted by Maurice des Ombieux in *Nouveau Manuel de L'Amateur de Bourgogne, 1921*) —all this is involuntarily comic.

Officialdom tends to be a rich source of the involuntarily comic. A military order issued to the Neapolitan army in 1848 enjoined the soldiers to "make their faces fierce" ("Faccia feroce"). Our own official instructions almost always call for "the illumination" to be "extinguished"; hardly ever for "the light" to be "put out."

The involuntarily comic is present in Emerson's statement in *Poetry and Imagination* (1876): "God himself does not speak prose, but communicates with us by hints, omens, inferences and dark resemblances in objects lying all around us." The purpose is reverence, the hidden accessory is irony. The definition reminds one of an illiterate who "does not speak" a foreign language.

For good measure, here is Goethe's lapse into the involuntarily comic: "The assassination of Julius Caesar was in bad taste."

I do not put much trust in the theory of "the inherent silliness of people." Clinically examined, most cases of the involuntarily comic prove to be masochism in disguise.

A sophisticated, well-read, and very successful man in his early forties entered analysis because of marital and characterological conflicts. For a time, he was a model patient. His transference situation—repetition of a passive-submissive attitude towards the mother, warded off with pseudo-aggression—was explained, and he half-accepted it with good humor, and good-sized disbelief. His dreams were indicative. During this period, the man's tenseness in business eased off considerably, and he repeatedly expressed gratitude and surprise that "an interpretation" should have made life "so much easier." It was interesting that he failed to grasp the mechanism of transference and resistance. He intellectualized a great deal; inwardly, it was clear, he viewed analysis as in a way a course of learning. He was warned again and again of the pitfalls which might accompany his attitude. He always humorously disagreed, without changing his opinion.

One day, in the fourth month of his analysis, he began the appointment by reporting how well and how smoothly, without the "usual tension," he had handled a specific business situation. He even gave due credit to analysis for this improvement. His next sentence was, "Who is a good analyst in New York?"

The ironic question called for an ironic answer. "You are already in the hands of a bad one; why do you need a good one?"

"I am serious. Who is a good analyst?"

I handed him the roster of the American Psychoanalytic Association. "Here are the names of three hundred competent analysts. Every one is excellent."

"You are joking."

"Not at all. I am just expressing my confidence in well-trained and experienced colleagues. By the way, what do you need the name of a good analyst for?"

"I want to check on you."

"Do you mean, check on my professional reputation? You've already done that. You were recommended to me by a well-known neurologist. You checked with a friend of yours, a well-known analyst. You read, you told me, one of my books on marriage and divorce, in order to form your own opinion. All of this happened before you consulted me."

"You misunderstand. I am satisfied with that part. I want to check on the actual progress of my analysis."

"That is technically impossible. Your actual analysis is interwoven with transference and resistance—a highly personalized repetition, once it is established. Didn't you tell me that you were highly satisfied with the results of your four months of analysis?"

"That's true. But I always check on my physicians. I am never satisfied with only one opinion. When I was told that my blood pressure had increased, for instance, I checked with four specialists."

"You cannot compare taking blood pressure with analytic treatment. The one is a mechanical process, depending on an apparatus; the other is a personalized affair."

The patient shouted, "If you are scared of being checked on, I have no confidence in you."

"Nobody is scared. You retain all rights—you can leave analysis, if you want to. You can change your analyst. You also can check on your analyst, but if you do that you must check out, too. Why don't you continue your analysis with the physician you want to consult?"

With mounting excitement, the patient continued to shout: "If that's analysis, the whole thing is witchcraft and I don't want to have anything to do with it. I will complain to my friend (he named one of the highest judicial dignitaries in the country), to the Secretary of the State of New York, and to the Medical Society. Your attitude constitutes an abridgement of constitutional rights and privileges!"

"You can do all that. For your information, no personal attitude is involved; every Freudian analyst will tell you the same. In any case, as long as you are here your resistance will be analyzed. Isn't it strange that you started this conflict precisely at the time when you had just complimented me on the specific results achieved thus far? Isn't it more likely that your psychic masochism cannot tolerate even preliminary success? And isn't it also more likely that, since you achieved remarkable therapeutic progress through me, you feel passively overwhelmed—an infantile repetition—and *therefore* use pseudo-aggression as a defense?"

"That's a trick. The American Constitution is built on check and countercheck, balance and counter-balance of powers."

"I suggest that you invoke that venerable document second, and work out your resistance first. Unfortunately, you never grasped the meaning of resistance and transference. This puts you at a disadvantage, even in comparison with my most stupid patient."

"Nonsense. My mistake was that I told you my intention."

"Once more, proof positive that you don't understand the analytic ABC."

"That's the reward for telling the truth."

"I suggest that you think over your resistance. If you cannot see your way clear, as you call it, continue analysis with somebody else. Don't forget the other side of the story: There is no law forcing a physician to treat a patient, except in emergencies."

"No law, my eye. There is one—a surgeon has no right to interrupt an operation he started."

"An operation protracted over two years, the probable duration of your analysis? Your comparison is—let's say—slightly amusing. Where is the emergency in your case? Sophism is a friendly word for your deduction. Well, think it over."

The next day the patient was rather apprehensive. When his statements were quoted to him, he denied having made most of them. He claimed that his remarks were distorted.

I asked him: "What would you say if somebody, during one of your deals, threatened you with the District Attorney?"

"I did not threaten you with the District Attorney."

"You did. You wanted to complain to the Grievance Committee of the Medical Society. The latter is prosecutor and judge at the same time."

"Nonsense."

"Assuming that it *is* so, please answer my question. What would you say if someone threatened you with the D.A.?"

"I would say, 'Go ahead, you fool.' "

"Well, we are more polite in analysis. We say, 'Let's analyze your resistance.' "

The episode was concluded and the patient continued treatment. However, for some time he was resentful of what he sarcastically called the "analytic untouchability."

The illogicality of this and all similar behavior patterns is based on infantile magalomania ("I can afford it"); the spectator's pleasure is derived from the previously described comparison of dual psychical expenditure.

The analysis of another patient began with his recital of his childhood difficulties with his mother. Whenever he got into a temper with her, he would run away from home, usually finding refuge in the home of an aunt. He was always brought home by force, and severely punished; he would retaliate by "*taking an oath not to talk to my mother*; once I stuck it out for *six days*." This information was given at the end of an appointment. When the patient arrived for his next appointment, he gave me a friendly greeting, proceeded to the couch and then lapsed into utter silence. None of my openings elicited a single word from him. At the end of the appointment, there was again a friendly (and not at all ironical) greeting. The next appointment followed this precise pattern.

I began to suspect that his silence had some connection with the infantile "oath" he had mentioned, which was now being repeated in the transference situation. He had "stuck it out," he said, for six days; the question was, how long had he intended to keep his oath of silence? Six weeks, I hoped, but months passed, monthly bills were paid, autumn gave way to winter—and still the patient remained silent. During all this time, I "interrupted" his silence at ten-minute intervals, explaining what he was repeating in the transference neurosis: "Sorry to intrude on your private life, but you are paying me for that." No response. As time progressed, it became more and more clear that the patient would "stick it out" for six months (I optimistically excluded the possibility that it would be six years), and that this time limit probably corresponded to his original "oath."

Once during this period, the patient did open his mouth; at the end of one appointment, he said in a completely matter of fact tone, "Things are getting more and more complicated." There was not even a response to my laughter; he just looked blankly surprised.

It is difficult to reproduce the tragi-comedy of the situation; I thought that remark was the funniest I had ever heard.

The patient broke his silence exactly at the end of six months. He had remained completely blank during his silent appointments; "like in a daze," as he expressed it. My beautiful interpretations of his "oath," and his system of showing his mother how "helpless" she was, had been completely wasted; he had heard nothing. The quantitative factor (and the desire to show his "mother" that he was powerful enough to win the battle of silence) was stronger than his appreciation of reality and my analysis of his resistance.

I became personally convinced of the correctness of my formula, "*the comic feeling is located at the graveyard of infantile megalomania*," after this experience. It should be mentioned that this patient suffered from personality difficulties of a banal masochistic nature. With monotonous regularity, he maneuvered himself into situations where he was "mistreated" by a woman, fully oblivious both to his attraction to, and his choice of, shrews. When, after months of absolute silence, the patient casually remarked, "Things are getting more and more complicated," my laughter was uproarious, but it was obvious that a person not intimately involved with the entire situation would find this sentence considerably less laughable. My subjective reaction should therefore be explained.

The protracted stalemate preceding this comment was, I admit, some kind of narcissistic defeat for myself. It was mitigated only by the fact that I understood the reasons for the patient's silence. Still, his complete inflexibility in the face of the correct[12] interpretation, his resistance to every technical device (I tried everything, from talking to silence, from interpretation to cajolery) was decidedly irritating. Aside from everything else, there was a touch of the uncanny in these silent meetings. Trying to analyze my own irritation, I first discarded the obvious answer that it was due to furor therapeuticus, and finally came to the conclusion that at bottom I envied the patient for his display of unbridled megalomania. I remember thinking: "Who on earth can afford to live out his infantile 'oath' of megalomania so completely?" Now, the patient's remark, and especially the facial expression of blank surprise which greeted my laughter, forcefully demonstrated the absence of any reason for envy: he was not an "omnipotent" wielder of forces, but a victim of forces beyond his control, forces which damaged *him*. My laughter, therefore, was gloating laughter; the partial sacrifice of my own infantile megalomania—sacrificed in adaptation to a stronger reality—was shown to have been purposeful and worthwhile. My laughter was consolation for an inevitable bereavement, and even an attempt to extract pleasure from it. Thus I compared two expenditures within myself, and the outward manifestation was hilarious laughter.

* * *

Boners are "authentic errors of children compiled from classrooms and examinations." The esteem in which they are held by the reading public

[12] At that time, the interpretation was of course still an assumption. Later events —the patient was cured—confirmed the suspicion.

is interesting; in the introduction to a recently re-issued boner book it is claimed that four of the author's books on boners achieved a total sale of a million and a half copies.[13]

Why do people laugh at boners?

1) The superficial explanation, which is the usual one, is that the boner affords one the "harmless enjoyment of stupidity"—in the other fellow. Since the butt of the laughter is a child, it is not reasonable to assume that the target is sufficiently substantial to provide much satisfaction for the big lug of a man who is doing the laughing. It is not likely that any adult, even one not noted for intelligence or erudition, will remember with pride the occasion when he corrected the statement that "the Crusades were a movement to drive the turkey out of Europe."

2) The boner allegedly supplies a "feeling of superiority." What "superiority" does an adult feel when he hears that "the French Revolution was caused by over-charging taxis"? Or that "many of the Indian heroes were killed, which proved very fatal to them"? "Superiority" is the result of competition on approximately one's own level.

3) Some authors claim that one's emjoyment of the boner is not at the child's expense, but at the teacher's. The supposed target of ridicule is the mechanical-acoustic system of learning by rote, a deduction which appears to be borne out by such boners as:

Mexico was conquered by Kotex.
A bamboo is an Italian baby.
Posthumous—a child born after the death of its parents.
The equator is a menagerie lion running around the earth.

4) Another explanation could adduce the problem of naivete (see Chapter One). For example:

Acrimony, sometimes called holy, is another name for marriage.
Celibacy is the crime a priest commits when he marries.
Discretion is the difference of sex between animals.

It is of course doubtful whether all the naivetes of children (including the story of the theatrical performance that Freud witnessed—see p. 35) are genuine, or contain a subtle admixture of irony directed at adults.

5) In some cases, boners appear to be evidence of acuteness and not stupidity in the child. Confronted with a problem he cannot solve, the child uses all his available cunning to get out of the noose. If in an examination he is asked to define an extrovert, he figures out that it must be "an animal with its spinal column on the outside." Similarly, a grass

[13] Alexander Abingdon, *Bigger and Better Boners*, Viking Press, 1952.

widow is deduced to be "the wife of a vegetarian," and a palimpsest "a sect that spread its religious views by pamphlets."

6) Other boners are explained as unconscious ironies aimed at adult precepts:

A paradox is a four-sided triangle.

Trigonometry is when a lady married three men at the same time.

Queen Elizabeth was the "Virgin Queen." As a queen she was a success.

Matrimony is a place where souls suffer for a time on account of their sins.

All these and similar explanations seem insufficient to me. I believe that people laugh because of the difference between the psychic expenditure of their adult selves and that of their lost but remembered infantile megalomania. How easy it is for the child to disregard—and inwardly scoff at—all adult rules and definitions! We admire an irretrievably lost province!

* * *

Malapropism by no means originated with Sheridan's Mrs. Malaprop, but the playwright's brilliant characterization, in *The Rivals*, of an adult addicted to linguistic boners has supplied an apt name for this familiar failing. Sometimes the malapropist has gone through a period of apprenticeship, producing boners; whether the final stage should then be defined as arrested development or a form of rejuvenation is debatable.

From the auditor's point of view, malapropism has one decided advantage: it is comparatively timeless. Mrs. Malaprop's howlers are as fresh today as they were in 1775:

Few gentlemen, nowadays, know how to value the ineffectual qualities in a woman!

I would by no means wish a daughter of mine to be a progeny of learning; . . . for instance, I would never let her meddle with Greek, or Hebrew, or algebra, or simony, or fluxions, or paradoxes, or such inflammatory branches of learning—neither would it be necessary for her to handle any of your mathematical, astronomical, diabolical instruments . . . I would send her, at nine years old, to a boarding-school, in order to learn a little ingenuity and artifice. Then, sir, she should have a supercilious knowledge in accounts. . . .

A modern Mrs. Malaprop, the wife of a nouveau riche, was asked whether she had attended the first performance of a new play, and whether she had noticed the new fashions displayed by the ladies.

"Of course, isn't this what plays are for? The whole *haute sottise* was present."

"And how was the play?"

"It wasn't bad, but not good enough for a first night."

The upstart confuses *haute société* (high society) with *haute sottise* (high stupidity), and a theatrical performance with a fashion show. To top it, she fails to understand that "first night" means only the night when a play opens; she is so obsessed with high society and the glamour of an opening that she obviously considers a "first night" to be a special honor granted only to certain plays.

There seems to be a universal tendency, in all countries, to single out a certain more or less well-known personality as the malapropist. In Imperial Vienna, the newly ennobled Baroness von Pollak held this enviable position for decades without being challenged by the opposition. (A remarkable feat—politicians envied her.) In this country, a movie magnate was the standard bearer for several years. This magnate is reported to have said, when asked for a decision on whether he would or would not join in a business venture, "Gentlemen, the best I can give you is a definite maybe." Later, having made up his mind, he declared: "Gentlemen, I've reconsidered my decision; you may include me out."

Another Hollywood malapropism is attributed to a studio bigwig who decreed the purchase of movie rights to a play which had been enormously successful in France. His horrified assistant exclaimed: "But the play is about Lesbians "—"So what," answered the great man, "we'll make them Americans."

It is probable that these and similar stories are all examples of what Howard Dietz calls "donorism" (see p. 139). To quote Dietz' argument in favor of his phrase: "Plagiarism is taking something from someone else. Where is the word for giving something away? How about 'donorism'?[14]

* * *

As previously stated, confusing various forms of humor—the comic, wit, self-derision, grim humor—or failing to make the necessary differentiations between them frequently leads to faulty evaluation of the over-all problem. In *The Enjoyment of Laughter*, Max Eastman attempted to prove his own theory of humor (see pp. 197f.) by conducting some kind of running interview with a number of contemporary humorists. Here is Eastman's "most provocative" question:

> The question I found most provocative, when a mere raising of the general problem was not enough, was this: "What do you think of the idea that there is hostility, or a feeling of superiority, in all laughter—or, to put it another way, that all jokes are 'on' somebody, and that all laughter is at bottom ridicule?" In one or two cases I quoted a sentence from Bergson as illustrating an eminent authority who takes this view. (p. 329)

There are two major drawbacks to this question. The whole matter of

[14] From Howard Dietz' introduction to the Goodman-Rice anthology, *I Wish I'd Said That*.

grim humor is bypassed, and it is in grim humor, according to Freud, that enjoyment is derived from economizing on expenditure of pity. It also misrepresents Bergson to some extent; Bergson laid stress on the social function of laughter, and otherwise based his theory on "mechanization of the living" (Chapter One, p. 21).

Because Eastman skirted the entire area of grim humor, many of the answers referred to grim humor without differentiating it from wit, and used these references as the basis for statements that some laughter is *not* hostile. This, in turn, was taken by Eastman as positive proof of his theory's correctness. Neither interviewer nor interviewed were conscious of the irony of the situation. This is not surprising; what is surprising is that none of the humorists interviewed was familiar with this part of Freud's theory. Dorothy Parker did not agree that a feeling of superiority made jokes successful; in her opinion, the most successful humorists are those you "laugh with." In Robert Benchley's writings, she points out, the reader identifies with Benchley's troubles, which explains his pleasure in the recounting of them. A humorist, she believes, is always on the verge of "the dumps."

Miss Parker clearly refers to "grim humor," where the listener "saves" pity. On the other hand, Miss Parker's own forte, the devastating witticism, is entirely overlooked in her statement. Even Miss Parker would not claim that she was overflowing with the milk of human kindness when she cracked this one (of an actress): "She ran the gamut of emotions from A to B." Or this one: Female playwright, motioning to Miss Parker to precede her through a doorway: "Age before beauty." Miss Parker, proceeding through the doorway: "Pearls before swine."

Eddie Cantor frankly admits perplexity in his reply to Mr. Eastman's questionnaire. He, too, denies that there is truth in the theory that superiority or hostility explain a successful joke, and that laughter is at bottom ridicule. It may *sometimes* be ridicule, he believes, when humor is in the form of satire. Satire is malicious and likely to hurt, whereas the "genuine quality of humor" is tender and gentle. On the basis of his twenty-five years of experience. Mr. Cantor asserts that the most pleasant kind of laughter is not often prompted by comments on human "follies or deformities."

Here, at least, some differentiation is made between laughing at somebody else's expense (wit) and the other types of humor. What this other kind of humor consists of is not explained.

* * *

The great popularity of the "funnies" has never been satisfactorily explained. It could not be, because unconscious factors were not taken into consideration.

To start with the problem of form. The combination of pictorial representation *plus* verbalization is in itself a mysterious taste. The *imaginative* person, reading a novel, provides for himself the contours of the people depicted. This is *his* contribution; we know how frequently a person is "disappointed" with a stage or screen dramatization of a novel he has read. Many rationalizations have been offered to explain this; at bottom the "disappointment" measures the discrepancy between the self-made and the ready-made image.

On the other hand, the *unimaginative* person does not seek this play of fantasy; he *wants* a ready-made image served to him on a platter.

Deeper analysis proves that the terms, "imaginative" and "unimaginative" represent less and more inhibition in the sphere of voyeurism. The preliminary conclusion therefore reads: Inhibition of voyeurism seems universal—as universal as love for funnies.

Another infantilism is included as well. The child sees and understands ("recognizes") pictures earlier than he understands the written word. The technique of combining "picture plus words" seems to attest to the child in the adult that he can comprehend both media. In the funnies, he can revert to the pre-reading stage, and flatter himself that he can read, too.

The problem of "mastery" of the material from both spheres in the funnies has been suspected by astute observers. Eastman says:

> My own explanation of the popularity of the comic strip and the funny pages is that, the dialogue being scrawled into the picture in a rather messy manner, it requires a little brain work to decipher it and see how it applies, and to people who use their brains as little as the average American newspaper reader does, this intellectual effort is an exciting adventure—especially on Sunday mornings when he has had a good long sleep and feels up to it.

There happens to be a comic strip named "Pogo" which seems made to order for Mr. Eastman's argument; each character in this strip speaks in a different and complicated dialect, and their remarks are spelled out in different type-faces, some of them extremely elaborate and therefore difficult to decipher. Reading "Pogo" is real "work."

As is well known, the funnies have changed considerably in the last few years. The once-simple comic strip has become "the comic": the pictorial story of adventure and fantasy. This evolution has gone hand in hand with the ascendency of "science fiction," a euphemism for utopian megalomaniacal-sadistic-masochistic adventure. A murder is no longer enough; the detective story has become tame. Now whole continents and galaxies are marked for uncanny "destruction" and "domination." In short, the defense against masochism is enlarged and intensified.

Certainly there are comic strips on different levels; they range from the primitive to the "sophisticated." It is probably not by chance that Li'l Abner's marriage, in Al Capp's cartoon, was a national event. The funnies are that important. It is also not by chance that John Steinbeck recently declared that the best writer in America is—Al Capp. He calls him "the greatest collector and inspector of entrenched nonsense":

> It is one thing to criticize and quite another to make the criticized not only admit but accept and enjoy criticism. I can think only of Cervantes and Rabelais who have succeeded in doing this before Capp. He makes savage forays into other fields but his standard everyday target is the American family. The hero Li'l Abner, big, strong, beautiful, innocent and illiterate, the very archetype of the football players our daughters fall in love with every autumn. Daisy Mae, innocent, stupid, beautiful, constant, virginal and naked and built like you know what—in a word, every adolescent's dream girl. Li'l Abner's mother, small, tough, the best fighter in Dogpatch, the ruler of the family and the community, the real matriarch and yet capable of going into a tight spin and passing as a miracle. The father of the family, stupid, ineffectual, lovable and bumbling. . . .

Let us invoke two other authorities on Li'l Abner; Charlie Chaplin and Al Capp himself:

> Li'l Abner makes a play for the attention of all who love violence and superhuman strength. (Charles Chaplin)

> Publishers having discovered that worrying the hell out of people paid off a lot more in circulation than simply amusing them, publishers declared a New Order for the comic page. Out went the simple fun, the pratfalls, the gentle satire, and in came the "suspense continuity" . . . But with the coming of the New Order, the comedians had been banished from the comic page—and in came the detectives, the apemen, the big, lovable prize-fighters who sobbed as they slaughtered their opponents because they didn't really want to hurt anybody and were doing it only because their mothers needed expensive treatment for leprosy, and the little orphan girls with no daddy but the N.A.M. to guide them. . . Out went the laugh, the guffaw, and the chuckle that were the purpose of the old-time comic strips—and in came the gasp, the shudder, the cold sweat on the brow, the sick feeling in the pit of the stomach that were the new purpose of the "suspense continuity" comic strips . . . Therefore, while "Li'l Abner" characters themselves are broad burlesques in the traditions of my ideals, the immortal Goldberg, Opper, Milt Gross, Maurice Ketten—the situations in which I plunge 'em are macabre, horrible, thrilling and chilling in the new "suspense continuity" fashion . . . My formula is to throw comedy characters into melodramatic situations and to show them solving their monstrous tribulations in a simple-minded way.[15]

Thus, combining the appeal of the simpleton's feeling superior to the "innocent" with the simpleton's masochistic needs ("worrying the hell out of people"), the publishers sell papers.

The question arises: Is this appeal—in its possible identifications with the monstrous and anti-social—not of some danger for adolescents? The

[15] All quotes from *The World of Li'l Abner*, by Al Capp. Ballantine Books, 1953.

problem is identical with the problem of gangster films, mystery stories, the "penny dreadfuls" in general. It is of course senseless to believe that the "bad example" per se makes a person antisocial. Dostojewski's Raskolnikov, in the murder of the old woman who was a pawnbroker, wanted to check on whether he could act "like Napoleon." It is not quite correct to blame Napoleon for the murder committed by Raskolnikov . . . The whole problem of criminosis has to be reviewed,[16] to prove that "bad example" cannot account for crime. It is true that a person with specific inner conflicts can make a self-consoling alibi out of the glorification of violence he can find in any type of literature—highbrow, lowbrow, or whatever. But this explains nothing.

The idea that unconscious attraction to masochism and its pseudo-aggressive defenses can be counteracted by laws is, to say the least, exaggerated. What could be done is to propagandize the idea that crime is *not* heroic. But de-glamorizing crime would not be very effective either, for *unconscious* defenses are not accessible to *conscious* knowledge.

* * *

The problem of *tickling* has been greatly exaggerated in the literature on laughter. One gathers the impression that investigators, utterly unable to come to grips with the essentials, have turned with relief to the only sure source of laughter, tickling, and concentrated on that. The emphasis seems unjustified to me—as unjustified as it would be to investigate the problem of crying by concentrating on onions, a sure source of tears.

J. C. Gregory (see Chapter One) is the only author to question the "imperative of tickling" as postulated in the literature. Gregory quotes a series of authors who have observed specific conditions under which tickling does not arouse laughter. According to Bacon, "in tickling, if you tickle the sides, and give warning . . . it doth not move laughter so much." Darwin noticed that tickling is more effective when the precise point of touch is not known. Gregory adds that fear, or any strong suggestion of hostility, "completes the divorce between tickling and laughter." Gregory builds tickling into his theory of relief.

It is probably that (as some of the authors quoted in Chapter One assumed) the infant views tickling partly as a threat, partly as sexual excitement. In my opinion, the laughing face of the adult reassures the infant, according to the formula: "smile = satiation = no danger of being eaten." One can also say that tickling means being passively-masochistically

[16] The problem is discussed at length in *The Battle of the Conscience* ("The Neurotic Who Bargains for the Electric Chair," Chapter XV, p. 261ff.) For further elaboration, see "Mystery Fans and the Problem of Potential Murderers," *Am. Journal of Orthopsychiatry*, 15, 309–317; 1945.

overwhelmed, with the saving grace of being marked with a "No Danger" sign, since the threat is not serious. *Tickling, in my opinion, is one of the few ways in which masochistic feelings of being overwhelmed can be enjoyed by the child without guilt.* But we say, ironically, "I'm tickled to death," intuitively sensing the masochistic danger which lurks beneath the playful surface.

* * *

What is the basis on which one decides that a joke is "good" or "poor?" What rates a half-smile, and what a real belly-laugh?

Freud came to the conclusion that a poor joke results when a "shortcut" between two words is achieved by a double meaning or a slight modification in the pronunciation of a word, and this shortcut is *not* accompanied by a meaningful association between the two ideas. The only existing link between the two widely disparate ideas then consists of one word. But if the word, besides being similar in sound, uncovers a similarity in meaning at the same time, the infantile expectation is satisfied and the joke is "good." As examples, Freud cites "traduttore—traditore (translator—traitor)" and "amantes—amentes (lovers—lunatics)."

According to Freud, therefore, two conditions are required for a "good" joke: similarity of sound and similarity of meaning. It is interesting that Freud specifically notes that even "poor" witticisms "are by no means poor as witticisms, i.e., they are by no means unsuited for the production of pleasure."

This, of course, opens the floor to another question: what is the value of the distinction in the first place? *Practically* speaking, a joke can be rated only in accordance with the amount of laughter it produces. *Theoretically*, one can say that some people laugh at "high-class" and some at "low-class" jokes, and that the former group seems identical with "good" jokes, and the latter with "poor" jokes.

The majority of nonsense-jokes are certainly "poor" jokes according to the above definition, so "poor" in fact, that Freud refused to classify them as jokes at all. Still, they are greeted with uproarious laughter.

I believe that another yardstick should be used. The true yardstick distinguishing the good from the poor joke is not the amount of intellectual refinement in its construction, but *the listener's unconscious ability to use the specific witticism as a weapon against the reproaches of his inner conscience. The most "primitive" nonsense-jokes, therefore, can be extremely effective.*

Moreover, the *belly-laugh* is distinguished from the *smile* (as far as reactions to jokes are concerned) by the *domicile of the material*: fully repressed in the case of the belly-laugh, preconscious in the case of the smile.

6. Irony, Sarcasm, "Life's Little Ironies," Repartee

General Alexander Smith, a tedious speaker in Congress, observed, "You, sir, speak for the present generation, but I speak for posterity."

"Yes," said Mr. Clay, "and you seem resolved to speak until the arrival of your audience."

From *The Life of Henry Clay*, by Epes Sargent

WIT AND THE COMIC can be combined; one of the specific subforms of this combination is irony. The technique of irony is verbal expression of one's meaning in terms of its opposite. Nothing is more easily misunderstood than irony; the ironic sentence, therefore, is characteristically delivered in a tone of voice or with an inflection that will identify it as a pronouncement that is not to be taken verbatim. Gestures, innuendos in style, facial expression, etc., are also used for the same purpose. In print, these interpretive aids of course do not appear, and the reader is even more apt than the listener to take the ironic remark literally. An exasperated wit once proposed that it be made obligatory for everyone using irony to announce the fact before making the remark. Obligatory or not, many people protect themselves with the preventive phrase: "I'm only kidding."

Webster's *International Dictionary* defines irony and sarcasm thus:

> *Irony* (Greek ironeia—dissimulation): a sort of humor, ridicule or light sarcasm, which adopts a mode of speech the intended implication of which is the opposite of the literal sense of the words, as when expressions of praise are used when blame is meant . . . Irony may be gentle or cutting . . . The essential quality of *sarcasm* is bitterness and taunting reproachfulness; it may or may not be ironical, but is always cutting or ill-natured (as irony need not be).

The history of the term can be looked up in J. A. K. Thomson's *Irony, An Historical Introduction*. The 235 pages of the book shed no light on modern irony, since they deal exclusively with the different forms of irony used by the writers and philosophers of ancient Greece (a special type of irony is attributed to each). The text also labors under the burden of the author's over-enthusiastic appraisal of his heroes. His uncritical evaluations bring to mind Thomas de Quincey's observation:

> Readers not sufficiently masters of a language to bring the true pretensions of a work to any test of feeling are forever mistaking for some pleasure conferred by

the writer what is in fact the pleasure naturally attached to the sense of a difficulty overcome . . . There can be no doubt that this particular mistake has been a chief cause of the vastly exaggerated appreciation of much that is mediocre in Greek literature. (*Collected Writings*, A. & C. Black, London, Vol. I, p. 25)

This particular passage is adduced, in A. M. Ludovici's *The Secret of Laughter*, as an explanation of our reasons for laughing "more heartily and loudly at a joke in a foreign language, which we happen to understand, than at a joke of equal merit in our own language."

The purpose of irony is always the aggressive reduction of an opponent to absurdity. Three techniques are possible:

1. Exaggeration;
2. A derogatory remark presented as a pseudo-compliment (representation through the opposite);
3. Taking the opponent's remark verbatim and exaggerating it.

An example of the first technique may be found in the typical family quarrel, where the wife complains that her husband was not sufficiently cordial to the elderly female guest, and the husband ironically inquires: "What did you expect me to do—kiss her feet?"

An excellent example of the second technique is found in *Julius Caesar*, in Mark Antony's meaningful repetition of "For Brutus is an honorable man." The ironic use of "honorable man" elicits the intended response: "They were traitors—honorable men!"

Some understatements also belong in this category, although there is no reason to limit the meaning of the word "irony" to understatement alone, as Max Eastman does (*The Enjoyment of Laughter*, p. 197).

Talleyrand once used technique #3 in pantomime with telling effect. At a gala party in Warsaw, Napoleon asked his previous Secretary of State to fetch him a glass of lemonade. With measured steps, supporting himself with his cane and balancing the glass of lemonade on an enameled plate, Talleyrand proceeded through the enormous, crowded room, a napkin on his arm, to present the requested drink to the sovereign. (According to Countess Potocka, who alludes to this incident in her memoirs, Talleyrand always treated Napoleon as a parvenu. See Blei, *Talleyrand*.) Talleyrand thus turned what might have been an indignity into an effective counter-insult; his use of the waiter's napkin clearly indicated that the emperor had made a fool of himself, and his solemn progress through the room, leaning on his cane, made it certain that no one would miss the incident.

The same technique of irony without words is found in the story told by Bergson: a wife gives her husband, each morning, a list of his domestic duties for the day; when she falls into the well, one day, the husband consults his list, finds no mention of this chore—and does nothing.

In sarcasm, the identical mechanisms apply, though a few drops of bitterness are added.

Fred Schwed, Jr. tried, without success, to buy a few copies of his own books from his publisher. He received no books, and was not even honored with a reply to his request. Finally, one year after his first attempt, he wrote to the sales manager of the firm, making a "revolutionary proposal":

> It was one year ago today that I began my efforts to purchase from your organization 12 copies of *Wacky The Small Boy*. Since that distant time, this project has taken on more the nature of a campaign than that of a mere whim to buy something. I would now like to make a bold suggestion, indeed a revolutionary proposal. I propose that hereafter when people order books from your house, you send them those books. Believe me, I am not insensible to the perils inherent in such a policy. There would be the not negligible costs of postage, wrapping, and boxing, not to mention the loss of the books themselves . . .

"Irony," claimed E. A. Whipple in *Literature and Life* (1849), "is an insult conveyed in the form of a compliment." The "compliment" reduces itself to the use of one of the three techniques enumerated—pseudo-approval, so magnified that it becomes patently absurd. The accompanying "insult" consists of verbal aggression directed against the butt of the irony.

The child learns irony very early in the educational process. Invariably, adults apply irony in their social intercourse with each other; frequently, they apply it to the child himself. Recently I overheard a conversation between a mother and her three year old boy. They were at a street corner, waiting for the traffic light to change:

"Why do we have to wait?"

"We're waiting for the light to change."

"But I *did* change it just this second!" (Actually the light was just changing.)

Ironically, the mother replied, "You are pretty good, aren't you? By the way, what color is the light?"

The boy began to sing, "Red, green, green, red . . . " Obviously he could not yet distinguish colors verbally. . . .

The boy's megalomaniacal braggadocio was countered by the mother's deflating irony. Incidents of this type, whether admitted or not, are typical. A more important factor, however, is the child's gradual use of irony in his "battle of the conscience." Here its purpose is to reduce the impact of the superego's cruelty. I have come to the conclusion that this technique—for example, in neurotic symptoms—is invariably applied. As explained in *The Superego*, and previously pointed out on p. 127:

> Educational precepts, actually communicated to the child in the course of the educational process, are twisted in a manner which hits the enshrined images of educators with their own stick. *This ironic pseudo-acceptance of ego ideal precepts* (by taking actual commands verbatim and applying them at the wrong time and place) has the advantage of temporarily wresting the most powerful weapon from Daimonion, which typically executes its torture by showing up the discrepancy between ego ideal and ego. The defensive-ironic technique of the unconscious ego is also a pseudo-aggressive retort on the part of the otherwise masochistically beaten-down sector of the personality. (p. 109)

And again:

> Every secondary defense (of the unconscious ego against the superego) is chosen in such a way that it coincides, if only tangentially, with some precept enshrined in the ego ideal. Without exception, this secondary defense will contain a mocking irony directed at the educators. The moral precepts communicated to the child are reproduced verbatim—a deadpan approach which results in distorting their meaning and reducing them to absurdity. Verbatim parroting of enshrined precepts strengthens the unconscious ego's ability to defend neurotic symptoms by claiming pseudo-moral connotations for them. This pseudo-moral connotation, it now seems clear, is a powerful unconscious weapon of resistance: its strength has so far been underestimated. (p. 259)

It amounts to a lip-service conformity with ego ideal precepts.

* * *

"Life's little ironies" include a large group of phenomena. The term (used by Thomas Hardy as the title of a novel) commonly denotes either a situation in which "the best-laid plans of mice and men" are thrown out of gear by *unexpected and unforeseen external events*, or one of *repetition in reverse* ("the biter bit").

An example of the former is the defeat of the British at Saratoga in the American Revolution when the armies of Burgoyne and Howe failed to meet because Lord Germaine had forgotten to forward the necessary orders. One can imagine Burgoyne's reaction; as Shaw has him say in *The Devil's Disciple*: "the British soldier can stand up to anything except the British War Office."

A banal example of repetition in reverse is pictured in a recent Bette Davis picture. Wanting to do away with her accomplice in a murder, the heroine offers him a poisoned drink. The accomplice is suspicious, and refuses, taking instead a drink from a container which he had previously filled himself. The container is also poisoned, and the accomplice dies. The heroine faints, and a solicitous neighbor revives her—with a drink from the poisoned flask. She regains consciousness, realizes the situation, bursts into ironical-hysterical laughter—and dies.

These accounts come from *The Story of the Confederacy*, by Robert S.

Henry, (Bobbs-Merrill, New York, 1931):

> Major Anderson (the commanding officer at Fort Sumter on April 13, 1861) had no hope of successful resistance. He knew the caliber of Beauregard (Confederate commander at Charleston). By one of those ironies so common in the Civil war, it was Anderson who had taught artillery to Cadet Beauregard at West Point. So apt a pupil had he been that, on his graduation, Anderson retained him as assistant instructor in the same subject. For more than a month now, the Major had been noting in his diary the evidences of military competence and skill shown by the beleaguering force under his old pupil and associate. Only one day or so before the demand for surrender he had noted, with misgiving, a battery of forty-two- and thirty-two-pounders which had been secretly erected on the upper end of Sullivan's Island in such a position as to render untenable the barbette guns on the parapet of Sumter . . . (p. 31)
>
> Unconditional Surrender (U. S. Grant)—a bit of luck for which he could thank not his parents who had christened him Hiram Ulysses, but the registrar at West Point who had mistakenly entered his name as Ulysses Simpson. (pp. 85–86) ["Unconditional surrender" was Grant's answer to Buckner at Fort Donelson.]
>
> The meeting at Fort Donelson was for Grant and Buckner a strange sort of reunion. They had been cadets together at West Point, and friends. Eight years before the war, learning that Grant was stranded in New York after his resignation from the Army, Buckner had hunted him out and advanced funds to take him home. (p. 86)

The commander of the Confederate forces at Vicksburg was General Pemberton, a Pennsylvanian who sided with the South. He surrendered Vicksburg on July 4th after strong and hopeless resistance, and was accused of treason for having surrendered on that date and thus given the Union an emotional lift. This was his defense:

> "I am a Northern man; I know my people; I know their peculiar weakness and their national vanity; I know we can get better terms from them on the fourth of July than on any other day of the year. We must sacrifice our pride to these considerations." *The Story of the Confederacy.* (p. 263)

To clear himself of blame, General Pemberton later exposed himself recklessly at Petersburg. To enter the Southern service, he had broken with his wealthy family and thrown away his inheritance. After the war he established himself with his family on a rented farm in the South.

* * *

Why do "life's little ironies" produce laughter in the victim?

The victim has the feeling that he is being teased and tantalized—by Fate. External fate is unconsciously seen as a projection of an inner "department"—the superego, with its enshrined images of the educators. Even when the external circumstances are a matter of pure coincidence, the child in the adult unconsciously perceives them as a plot deliberately devised by parental malice. The collapse of the individual's own plan is thus interpreted as parental punishment and lack of love.

This being the case, fury and despair should be the appropriate reactions. Nevertheless, fury and despair are frequently preceded by uncontrollable laughter.

This uncontrollable, *bitter* laughter pertains to the pseudo-aggressive preamble, manifested either directly or via identification in the execution of the original plan. Merely by having megalomaniacally foreseen events and by having acted upon them (and such action is in the majority of cases directed *against* moral rules implanted by the parents), the individual has released *fictitious* aggression aimed at the enshrined educator and his precepts. Although the plan has collapsed—and the bitter laughter acknowledges that defeat was foreseen—the child in the adult ignores the outcome for a split second, and fixes his attention on the pseudo-aggressive *concept* in the plan. In short, the child in the adult acts as though it had outsmarted the adult by performing a forbidden act. (It has previously been pointed out that this peudo-aggression is merely the cover for more deeply buried masochistic tendencies.)

Overlapping and mingling with the stage of bitter laughter is the stage of masochistic despair; laughter of this type changes into crying and self-pity.

There are connecting links with neurotic pessimism. All neurotic pessimists are injustice collectors; they, too, bend all their efforts to constructing, in one way or another, a situation which ostensibly confirms their image of the mother as mean, cruel, forbidding. But in the injustice collector self-pity follows such "confirmation"; in neurotic pessimists there is instead a rather ironic-sarcastic complacency which seems to say, "I knew all along that I'd be on the receiving end."

These people behave as if their purpose were prediction, not psychic masochism. Although they end up behind the eight-ball, they are not disturbed; they "knew it all the time." *They apparently accept defeat, but only on condition that they predicted the defeat.*[1]

These neurotic pessimists derive a peculiar satisfaction from *not* having been fooled; it is their means of reasserting infantile megalomania. The typical psychic masochist is content with his unconscious creation of defeat, humiliation and self-damage. The neurotic pessimist goes him one better; he wants to be a good crystal-gazer as well. In the clinical picture of ordinary psychic masochism, infantile megalomania has an important place;[2] the defeat is accepted only on condition that it is inwardly self-created. In neurotic pessimists, the emphasis on infantile megalomania is even more pronounced; on one level, defeat is unconsciously self-created, and on another, it is omnisciently foreseen.

[1] First stated in "The Psychology of Oral Pessimism," *Imago*, 20, 330–376; 1934.
[2] For elaboration see *The Basic Neurosis* and *Neurotic Counterfeit-Sex*.

* * *

Self-irony is a preventive mechanism; it is designed to ward off an anticipated attack. Obviously, self-derision includes masochistic elements. There is a superficial resemblance between self-irony and what in scientific German is called "Humor," for which the nearest (but still not exact) English equivalent is "grim humor," or "humor of the gallows." One salient difference between the two forms is the fact that self-irony requires an audience, while "Humor" is exclusively directed at the forum internum. There is another difference: self-consoling humor appears only in situations where an irrevocable defeat is accepted and is then used to squeeze out some degree of narcissistic elevation.

* * *

Repartee is a clever, ready and witty retort; it generally appears in answer to an opponent's witty statement, or when another person's remark leaves an opening for reducing to absurdity. Webster informs us that the term is seldom used; going into semantics, Grabb (*English Synonyms*) adds that "repartee" is a misspelling of "repartie," feminine past participle of the French "repartir" (from the Latin "re," meaning again, and "partire," to divide) and thus means to lunge, to answer thrust by thrust, cut with cut; repartee, Grabb says, "is commonly an answer to the wit of another where one returns wit with wit."

The technique of repartee is that of double irony. Sometimes the center of the problem is reduced to absurdity; sometimes the attack only reaches the periphery. The external purpose of the procedure is invariably to secure the laughter of the audience at the expense of the opponent.

A typical peripheral retort is that made by Clay to General Smyth (quoted at the head of this chapter). The General's invocation of posterity is countered by an attack on his tediousness and long-windedness.

On the other hand, when Oscar Wilde admiringly declared, after hearing one of Whistler's epigrams, "I wish I'd said that," Whistler hit the exact center with his "You will, Oscar, you will"; Wilde's tendency to plagiarism, and the fact that many of his paradoxes had been originated by Whistler, were well known.

The winner in an exchange of repartee is not always entitled to full credit for the final, killing retort; frequently the opening is obligingly—and masochistically—provided by the opponent. ("Hoist by his own petard" is the classical comment.) Sometimes the masochistic tendency is betrayed by the choice of words; sometimes in the fact that a mediocre fencer has challenged a notorious one.

Most punning retorts seem so obvious—after the event—that one cannot help suspecting some unconscious collusion. A case in point is the courtroom exchange between two famous New York lawyers at the turn of the century; when one lawyer sarcastically referred to the other's "Chesterfieldian urbanity," he provoked a description of himself as an example of "Westchesterfieldian suburbanity"—an epithet much harder to live down.

When Napoleon Buonaparte rashly remarked, "Gli Italiani *tutti* ladroni" (The Italians are all thieves), he was corrected by a woman who said, "Non tutti, ma *buona parte*" (Not all, but a good part of them)—a pun on both his name and his Italian descent. He had left himself wide open for that one.

A patient, disgusted with analysis, called it "bunk"; it reminded him, he said, of David's fight with Goliath. "What can the David of analysis do against the Goliath of neurosis?" he asked. He invited my reply: "How masochistically you are arguing—if we are to trust tradition, David killed Goliath. Couldn't you have chosen a giant who was victorious in the end?"

In order to be "licked before you start," it is merely necessary to choose an adversary whose gift for sarcasm is known. Freud's famous retort belongs in this category. In a private discussion, an opponent attacked Freud with malicious personal arguments, finally quoting the familiar tag, "Even a dwarf on the shoulders of a giant sees farther than the giant himself." Freud replied dryly, "Quite true, but the louse on the philosopher's head does not see farther than the philosopher himself."

People who "ask for it" are not merely tinged with masochism. Boswell's *Life of Samuel Johnson* abounds with examples of this type. Johnson's deadly wit was notorious, and prudent members of his circle stayed out of its way. Yet Oliver Goldsmith, who had written, "There is no arguing with Johnson; for when his pistol misses fire, he knocks you down with the butt end of it," frequently allowed himself to be dragged into the unequal fight. Johnson summarized his opinion of Goldsmith in these words: "No man was more foolish when he had not a pen in his hand, or more wise when he had."

But even a passive-masochistic person like Goldsmith, who "asks for it" again and again, is capable of a brilliant stroke when he is pressed too hard. The defensive pseudo-aggression then produces an answer like this:

> . . . Goldsmith said, that he thought he could write a good fable, mentioning the simplicity which that kind of composition requires, and observed that in most fables the animals introduced seldom talk in character. "For instance," said he, "the fable of the little fishes who saw birds fly over their heads, and envying them, petitioned Jupiter to be changed into birds. The skill (continued he) consists of making them talk like little fishes." While he indulged himself in this fanciful reverie, he observed Johnson shaking his sides and laughing. Upon which he smartly proceeded, "Why, Dr. Johnson, this is not so easy as you seem to think; for if you were to make little fishes talk, they would talk like *Whales*."

Here are some other examples of repartee, which Molière called "precisely the touchstone of the man of wit."

When Alexandre Dumas, père, was asked, "Who was your father?" he replied: "My father was a Creole, his father a Negro, and his father a monkey; my family, it seems, begins where yours left off."

A snobbish Englishman was taken to see Mt. Vernon. He approved of only one thing —the hedge. "Quite good," he said of it condescendingly, "obviously Washington got it from dear old England."—Quite true," answered the guide, "he got the whole blooming country from dear old England."

British marines remained on guard at the White House during Churchill's first wartime visit to President Roosevelt. When Harry Hopkins saw them, he grumbled: "Don't know what these fellows are doing here; the last time they were here they burnt the place down."

"I'd rather be right than president!" roared a self-important member of the House of Representatives during a discussion. "Don't worry, you'll never be either," answered his opponent.

Rabbi Levi and Father Kelly were at a banquet. The waiters brought roast ham, and Father Kelly leaned over to the rabbi and asked mischievously, "Rabbi Levi, when are you going to become reasonable enough to eat ham?"—"At your wedding, Father Kelly," retorted the rabbi.

A professional humorist was hired to entertain a dinner party. When he finished his act, one of the guests—a lawyer who prided himself on his wit—stood up, nonchalantly thrusting his hands into his pockets. and inquired: "Doesn't it strike the company as unusual that a professional humorist should be funny?" The professional retorted: "And doesn't it strike the company as even more unusual that a lawyer should have his hands in his own pockets?"

Isadora Duncan once said provocatively to Shaw, "Think of the child we could have—my body and your brain!"—"I know," replied Shaw, "but suppose the child was so unlucky as to have my body and your brain?"

"I wouldn't be a fool if I were you," said a pompous advice-giver to a friend. "If you were me, you wouldn't be," was the reply.

Mark Twain's neighbors were very well aware of his habit of "borrowing" all sorts of objects. Once he asked a neighbor if he might borrow a book, and was told: "With pleasure, but you must read it in my library."—Some time later, the same neighbor wanted to borrow Twain's lawnmower. "Certainly, but you must use it on my lawn."

A toastmaster once introduced the humorist Irvin S. Cobb at a dinner party, saying: "All you have to do is put a dinner in his mouth, and out comes a speech." Cobb thanked the toastmaster for his gracious introduction, acknowledged the compliment, and added. "Your toastmaster is far more remarkable. All you have to do is put a speech in his mouth, and out comes your dinner."

Repartee at its best is produced under pressure. Having been pushed by one's opponent into the masochistic corner, the inner conscience misuses the situation and attacks in its turn; the effective retort then constitutes both an inner and outer defense. I was once present at a scene in which a famous writer (a former patient) was ironically attacked by his wife for his alleged tendency to exaggerate. He countered with a brilliant aphorism: "Exaggeration is the pigmentation which makes truth discernible."

On the other hand, some effective retorts which are ostensibly "off the cuff" are actually prepared beforehand. "He's winding up the watch of his wit, *by and by* it will strike" (*The Tempest*). Samuel Johnson's judgment on Lord Chesterfield: "This man I thought has been a lord among wits; but I find he is only a wit among lords" and Oscar Wilde's reply to a customs officer's question upon landing in New York in 1882: "I have nothing to declare but my genius," are examples of rehearsed repartee.

The cynicism which permits a wit to practice and polish a supposedly spontaneous retort grows out of a problem of unconscious ambivalence. All cynics, whether pronounced or moderate, are under constant pressure from the superego on this score. The cynic's defense against the superego's charges is to make the outer world into his ally by forcing his audience to applaud his iconoclastic utterances. The laughter of his audience is proof that he is no exception, "everybody else feels the same way."

The cynic's target of attack always is authority, or the opinions accepted by the majority. Intrapsychically, his target is still—as it was in childhood—the enshrined image of the educator, to which he remains masochistically and ambivalently attached. His projection of the attack upon outer authority and majority opinions is a double attempt to appease the superego; his aggression is a defense against the accusation of masochism, and his production of allies who agree with his "forbidden views" is a defense against the superego's reproach that he ambivalently loves and hates the same person at the same time.

A specific cynicism is often applauded, but the cynical attitude is never approved by general opinion. The habitual cynic pays his "conscience money" to the superego in the form of his rejection by the outer world, which laughs at his jokes but at the same time dismisses him as a clown who is not to be taken seriously.

* * *

All the subdivisions of irony have a common defensive structure. It is interesting that in John Ray's *English Proverbs* (1670) one can read, "Weak men had need to be witty." That is quite true of people with a *compulsion* to display irony at *all* times, even on the most inappropriate occasions. Such people should not be confused with those who *sometimes* utilize the mechanism of irony to ward off the idiocies of daily life, and to defend themselves against unwarranted attacks. The difference is that between "I have to" and "I can"; nevertheless, both types are prodded into irony by the inner conscience.

7. Two Fascinating Theories on Laughter, Regretfully Disputed

There is always a well-known solution for every problem—neat, plausible and wrong.

H. L. Mencken

THE INNUMERABLE non-analytic interpretations of laughter include two theories of outstanding interest: that of Bergson, and that of Max Eastman. The two theories contradict each other at almost every important point; nevertheless, each theory, when published, exercised considerable influence over contemporary thinking, and both theories have a magnetic appeal for many people because of their seeming probability.

Bergson's theory is based on an amazing observation. Everything in human actions that is reminiscent of a machine provokes laughter, he points out. "*Something mechanical encrusted on the living*" is the guiding pattern of the French philosopher's explanation of laughter, which was first stated in *Le Rire* (1901). He views all forms of the comic from this bastion; it is also the base from which he proceeds to assign to laughter a purely social function, calling it a method of forceful adaptation to the customs of a specific group, or of society in general.

Laughter is always the laughter of a group, he claims, asking his readers to think back to an occasion when, seated as individuals in a restuarant or other public place, they could hear the laughter of a group of people nearby, and also hear the stories which prompted their amusement. If the spectator had been a member of the group, he too would have laughed; as an outsider, he felt no impulse to do so. A man, who remained dry-eyed when everyone else who heard a certain sermon shed tears, explained that he did not cry because he was not a member of the parish. The need to "belong" implied in the man's excuse is more inherent in laughter than in tears. Even when laughter appears to be spontaneous, a kind of companionship or even complicity with other laughers is required; this complicity may be real or imaginary. It is a truism in the theater that laughter is heartier in a full house than in a sparsely filled one. On the other hand, it is also well known that humor is often untranslatable because it rests on knowledge of the mores and ideas of a specific social group.

The process of living, in itself, Bergson continues, and the requirements of society, in addition, call for the ability to grasp the immediate situation and to adapt oneself to it. Thus two complementary forces are involved: alertness and tension so that an event can be evaluated promptly; elasticity of mind and body so that adaptation can take place. If the body does not possess a sufficiency of these forces, illness, infirmity and accidents are inevitable. If the mind does not possess them, every variety of mental deficiency and of insanity develops from the lack. And finally, if they are missing from the character, there will be serious inability to adapt to social life . . . Society distrusts inelasticity—of character, mind, and even of body—because it may be a sign of activity unused, or of an activity with "separatist tendencies" which would tend to detach the individual from society's common center. And yet society cannot act at this point, since it has not been confronted with an act, but merely with a symptom which makes it uneasy. The symptom is hardly a threat; at the most it is a gesture. Society replies, therefore, with a gesture. Laughter must be "a sort of social gesture."

In searching for the basis of laughter, Bergson reluctantly refers to laughter's origin in human aggression, and sweetens the pill with the consoling thought that "the bad is put to work for the good." Apologizing for comparing an important matter with a trivial one, he cites as an example the experience of a young man entering a military academy. The new student successfully weathers the ordeal of the entering examination, only to find a series of additional ordeals in the offing. This is a system that has been devised by his seniors as a means of "breaking him in" to his new life. This device is common to all small societies formed within the larger group of society as a whole; a vague instinct impels the small society to proceed in this way in order to overcome the rigidity of alien habits. Society as a whole proceeds in the same way. The individual must always be aware of his social surroundings and key himself to his environment. He must not retreat, on his own terms, to his ivory tower. If he does, he knows that society may at any time retaliate, if not with "correction," at least with a snubbing—a small punishment, but dreaded none the less. This must be the function of laughter. Laugher is a kind of "ragging" on the part of society; the object of laughter is always humiliated by it.

Towards the end of his dissection of laughter, Bergson vaguely hints that some comic effects can perhaps be traced back to blurred memories of children's toys and early childhood. He does not enlarge on the idea; he merely suggests that it might be rewarding to carry simplification back even more, and try to trace, from recollections of earliest laughter, the combinations that still remain mirth-provoking to the adult. And he warns against the tendency to ignore the child-like element which lies hidden in the majority of our joyful emotions.

Freud commented on Bergson's formula in *Wit*, pointing out that Bergson believed a comic impression always resulted when a human being performed the motions of an inanimate machine. Bergson connected the comic of imitation with a problem posed by Pascal in his *Thoughts:* why do we laugh when comparing two similar faces when we would not laugh at either face, seen separately? Exact repetitions or complete similarities in life ring false, he declared, and arouse the suspicion that some mechanism is at work in the background. If two faces are too much alike, the impression one receives is of two heads cast in the same mold, two impressions of the same soul, two positives from the same negative—in other words, of a manufacturing process of one kind or another. This turning of life into a mechanical process is the real cause of laughter here; it might be called degrading humanity by making it mechanical or inanimate.

If these persuasive arguments are accepted, it is not difficult to fit Bergson's view into his (Freud's) formula, Freud continues. We are taught by experience that no human being is the same as another; that no human being can be understood without an expenditure from our understanding. If we are confronted by a perfect copy or a convincing imitation, we are disappointed, (in the sense of being relieved) because no new expenditure is required. This disappointment renders superfluous the expected expenditure, and it is discharged in laughter. The same formula also explains the examples of comic rigidity cited by Bergson, such as professional habits, fixed ideas, and ways of expressing oneself which are used on every occasion. In all these cases the expenditure of expectation is less than is commonly required for understanding, since the common requirement calls for observation of individual variety and human variability.

The Bergsonian formula which specifies that life is overlaid with a patina of the mechanical contains, in my opinion, a kernel of truth, despite its misplaced emphasis. At first the child is not amused by machine-like actions, but frightened; such movements are not seen as comic, but as terrifying or even uncanny. For the imperturbability and invariability of a machine is proof of something the child is not willing to accept: the fact that he is not the center of the universe. More, it drives home to him another unpalatable truth: the realization that something outside of himself exists at all. In evaluating the infant's reaction to any phenomenon, one cannot lose sight of *infantile megalomania* without losing one's first important contact with the entire thread of understanding.

Bergson's deduction lacks a vital genetic substructure: consideration of the fact that the very small child lives for quite a long period of time on the basis of fictitious omnipotence. Subsequently, a slight concession to reality is made and other people are acknowledged to exist, although they are still assumed to exist only for the purpose of executing the child's commands. The child still believes himself an omnipotent sorcerer; other people are merely his instruments, his *machines.* When the child stretches his miniature hand out for an object, and his mother gives it to him, the *ob-*

jective fact is that the mother's kindness has prompted her to fulfill the child's wish. *Subjectively*, this is not the story at all. The child believes the mother has performed as the executive organ of the child's sorcerer-like omnipotence. It is probable that machines, observed at a much later period, remind the child of this inner fantasy. The *comic aspect of machine-like actions and gestures is thus derived from aggression against the more powerful (though in fantasy subservient) adult.* On the other hand, *machines are uncanny and frightening*, and *therefore revive the old fears of babyhood*, for the fiction of omnipotence originated as a defense against complete submersion in a feeling of helplessness and frightening dependence (Ferenczi). Thus, once more, our formula—pseudo-aggressive defense against masochistic fear—is confirmed.

Moreover, a machine seems to "move by itself." This, applied to the child's organs, spells observation of an organ that "moves by itself"—mother's breast, and later, the male organ. Fear of erection is by no means uncommon in small children.

A specific group of neurotic symptoms can be characterized by the peculiar dramatization of a "tertium comparationis." The term is used in ars poetica to denote the comparison between two widely different objects which have only one element in common. This point of similarity is called the "tertium comparationis." When Homer compares the Greek soldiers storming Troy to a swarm of bees, the similarity of the Greek soldiers in movement (clinking their armor) to bees seems far-fetched. The common denominator for the poet, however, is that both produce noise. That noise is the "tertium comparationis." As in poetry, we find in neurosis that certain symptoms seem to be built upon this formula. Here is a clinical example.

An obsessional patient produced the symptom of fear of acquiring a tic. Every time he saw a person who had a facial tic, especially one involving the neck muscles, he was terrified and disturbed lest he himself should acquire that symptom. The patient was an actor and every night faced an audience in the theatre. Automatically he would "choose" among these people a person afflicted with a tic—not too difficult a task among fifteen hundred spectators—and begin to worry. His conflict increased when he discovered that one of the other leading actors in the show suffered from a facial tic. He could offer no explanation for the development of this fear, which at times dominated his neurosis, except to say that after the annulment of his marriage because of his impotence (twenty years before he started analysis) he "became more conscious of human suffering." This fear of a tic was at times so pronounced that all of his other abundant neurotic ideas, compulsions and obsessions became secondary.

The analytic interest was automatically centered on the fact that the interest in tics and the disturbance of potency became apparent at the same time. It was clear that in the superficial layer the patient identified his penis with the heads of the various sufferers and consoled himself, so to speak, with the facts that his symptom was not as conspicuous as a tic and that other people suffered, too. Furthermore, his fear was related to exhibitionism; "everyone will see that you are impotent" was the unconscious masochistic wish which was being warded off. Still, the two explanations did not suffice and did not affect his deep-rooted fear. The next question was: what attracted the patient's attention to a tic? This he explained by saying that the automatic nature of the tic, the inability to control it, was the most conspicuous and fascinating part of it. Projecting this idea upon the penis, he seemed to be saying unconsciously: "I am not responsible for my erections; they come without volition."

Here we seem to have reached an impasse. Why should he be afraid of erections, the very erections whose absence he deplored so much? The answer was that his reaction was that of the child in him. His disturbance of potency was based on his obsessional misunderstanding of sex; the idea of anal soiling predominated for him. The fact that his potency was disturbed and his marriage annulled served to activate his old masturbation fear. He behaved as if his sexual disaster in marriage was a direct punishment for masturbation: "You played with your (anally perceived) penis too much; the result is impotence." The defense against that superego reproach was furnished by the alibi: "I did not play with my penis; the erections came of themselves." In other words, the automatism of an erection and movement of the penis were used by the patient as an excuse. The tic then became for him the symbol of this idea that certain things are automatic, independent of our wilful actions.

This patient produced his fear of tics not only as a symbolic demonstration of his phallic and masochistic exhibitionistic wishes, but also—and this is the decisive fact—to demonstrate his main alibi, automatism. This automatism was the "tertium comparationis" between an erect penis and a tic-movement of the head. It was as if he were using an example from another field, stressing the "tertium comparationis," to prove his innocence.

The infantile fear of the machine tends to persist in the adult. When Heinrich Heine visited England early in the last century, and there saw mechanization for the first time, he pointed out that these machines had an uncanny, frightening effect:

> The perfection of machinery, which is applied to everything there, and has superseded so many human functions, seems to me like something uncanny; this artificial life on wheels, bars, cylinders and a thousand little hooks, pins and teeth which move almost passionately, fills me with horror. I was frightened no less by the definiteness, the precision, the strictness, in the life of the English; for just as the

> machines in England seem to have the perfection of men, so the men seemed like machines. Yes, wood, iron and brass seem to have usurped the human mind there, and to have gone almost mad from fullness of mind, while the mindless man, like a hollow ghost, exercises his ordinary business in a machine-like fashion. ("Second Night," *Florentine Nights*, Bong Edition, Vol. 6, p. 150.)

This observation can be tested time and again; in this mechanical age we are of course accustomed to machines, but that is a secondary development.

Bergson is in error, again, when he specifically stipulates that *absence of feeling* usually accompanies laughter. The disturbing effects of the comic, he believes, must be registered on a thoroughly calm and unruffled surface. The comic flourishes in an atmosphere of indifference, because emotion is the natural enemy of laughter.

Exactly the opposite is observable and its genesis can be deduced: laughter is an antidote to *inner* emotions, most notably to such emotions as fear of masochism and accusations stemming from the inner conscience.

And Bergson's basic formula—that of mechanization—even when strengthened by the addition of genetic structure, holds true only for a limited sector. To give an example: It is reliably reported that Saint Just, Robespierre's henchman, used gestures resembling the falling knife of the guillotine in delivering speeches denouncing Robespierre's political adversaries to the Convention of the French Revolution. Such denunciations were automatic sentence of execution though the detour of trial before the revolutionary tribunal was taken. One cannot deny that the element of monotonous-repetitive mechanization was present; whether even foreign and therefore detached spectators could have found this "mechanical" gesture comical is extremely doubtful.

Finally, Bergson's example of the failure to be amused at jokes when they are merely overheard, as in a railway station (see above), does not at at all prove that there is a "social" element in laughter. Bergson disregards two facts here. The first is the feeling of being excluded, which activates the infantile grievance of not being part of the adult circle. As for the second, it should be remembered that the laughter of the group has a guilt-diminishing effect, since guilt is distributed among all the members of the group (Reik); consequently an audience is necessary.

Despite all these objections, and despite the development of modern psychiatric-psychoanalytic research which has outdistanced as well as outdated Bergson's findings, his theory remains an interesting pioneer work.

* * *

Max Eastman's theory of "*instinctive enjoyment of laughter*," (as expounded in *The Enjoyment of Laughter*), is based on a truly fascinating premise: "All jokes are mere foolishness; all jokes are, in their comic essence, offenses and frustrations." Thus "*unpleasant experiences playfully enjoyed*" form the substratum; how the human being is enabled to perform this rewarding tour de force and transform the "unpleasant" into the "playfully enjoyed" remains enigmatic. The author bypasses this problem with the help of two assumptions. The first of these is that laughter is an instinct, hence biology is the sponsor. As to the second, the "how" of the transformation, the question is declared to be unsolved or unsolvable: "The mechanism of comic laughter may never be explained." The author thus simplifies the problem by denying its existence. The balance of Eastman's theory is a shrewd combination of the assumptions of Aristotle and Kant:

> The next time you are called upon to entertain a baby, I will tell you what to do. Laugh, and then make a perfectly terrible face. If the baby is old enough to perceive faces, and properly equipped for the calamities of the life that lies before him, he will laugh too. But if you make a perfectly terrible face all of a sudden, without laughing, he is more likely to scream with fright. In order to laugh at a frightful thing he has to be in a mood of play.
>
> If that perceptual effort is beyond him, try a practical joke. Offer him something that he wants a little and will reach out to get, and when he is about to grasp it, jerk it smilingly away. Again he may let out a yell of indignation, or he may emit a rollicking and extreme cackle, a kind of kicking scream, as though at the most ingenious joke ever perpetrated since Adam lost a rib.
>
> Those are the two orthodox ways of entertaining a baby. And they correspond to two of the most famous definitions of the comic ever given. Aristotle defined the comic as "some defect or ugliness which is not painful or destructive," and added: "For example, the comic mask is ugly and distorted, but does not cause pain." In other words, it is making terrible faces playfully.
>
> Another famous philosopher, Immanuel Kant, defined the cause of laughter as "The sudden transformation of a strained expectation into nothing"—or in other words, as reaching after something and finding it is not there. (p. 9)

Eastman concludes that the identical technique applies in adult jokes; the anticipated meaning has been snatched away (like the baby's toy), and "a trick has been played upon us," resulting in resuscitation of baby laughter; in unpleasantness made jocular the other mechanism of "terrible faces" made funny is revived.

On the basis of this theory, Eastman wittily and energetically attacks everyone who disagrees with him, frequently using arguments to the effect that he doubts whether the attacked author has ever seen a baby, or been one. As for Freud's theory, he rejects it with scorn. He accuses Freud of having committed "a great sin against humor and against the art of enjoying it" by "making it all furtive."

Aside from its wholesale simplification, and its casual rejection of nearly the whole theory of the unconscious, Eastman's formulation is significant, for it brings up one serious and important problem: the necessity of explaining the laughter of children. Admittedly, Freud's early assumption that children lack humorous perception is untenable, and the problem needs further elaboration. Although I believe that Eastman does Freud an injustice in ignoring the obvious fact that Freud concentrated on the study of *adult* laughter, I also believe that Eastman put his finger on the weakest point in Freud's deduction: appreciation of "pure nonsense" jokes and the meaning of children's laughter. To this extent, the merit of Eastman's exposition is undeniable, even though his deduction and his conclusions are more than doubtful.

The problem of *pure and unadulterated nonsense* has been neglected in the psychoanalytic study of wit. Freud acknowledges as humorous only nonsense which makes sense. Eastman's strongest arguments are forged from Freud's underestimations of nonsense, and these arguments remain telling even though his explanation of "nonsense" is far off the target:

> The trouble with Freud . . . is that he does not distinguish between nonsense in the abstract, or mere gibberish, and nonsense as the failure of some specific claim to sense. The latter alone is comical, and is comical in the same essential way to grown-ups and to children.
>
> "Didn't I meet you in Buffalo?"
>
> "No, I never was in Buffalo."
>
> "Neither was I. It must have been two other fellows."
>
> It may not be so in Vienna, but in the Anglo-Saxon world that kind of joke—formerly known by the name of "Irish Bull"—is always greeted with laughter. It is the kind of joke which is sure-fire as a witty insult or a risque quip. And it does not matter whether it comes in the form of a jesting remark, or is dressed up with the attributes of a "funny story." Here is a funny story that traveled about New York in the winter of 1934:
>
> Two of our most eminent intellects were leaning against the bar at the Players' Club. One of them, emerging from a momentary coma, remarked:
>
> "When I was born I weighed only 2½ pounds."
>
> "Is that so? Did you live?"
>
> "You ought to see me now."
>
> . . . Thus even when jests have no point, they still have two distinguishable elements: the plausibility, or suggestion of some approaching sense, and the frustration or failure of the sense to arrive . . . Perhaps a good way to convince the Freudians that pure nonsense can be funny would be to assert that it can be funnier, when delicately engineered, than nonsense which makes sense.

Yes, Eastman is correct in stating that "pure nonsense" can be funny. The reason, however, is by no means "the logically perfect want of meaning" and "the compelling swing, both logical and emotional, of the pretense or claim to meaning." The reason is simply this: *In "nonsense," the educational authorities are unconsciously attacked; the weapon of irony sub-*

dues those who tried to imbue the child with respect for logic. The joke, therefore, is at their expense; the level of intellectuality is of no importance.

The technique which Eastman uses in presenting his vehement polemic against Freud contains in itself an unconscious joke which, it is quite clear, the polemicist does not even guess at. Freud based his theory of neurosis on repressed remnants of unconscious infantilism in the adult; Eastman goes back to an even earlier period when he stresses the *conscious* attitude of the baby as an element in the acquisition of "enjoyment of laughter." He thus appears to *out-Freud* Freud, though in reality the additional steps he has retraced are nullified in significance by his complete omission of the dynamic unconscious.

Eastman's hatred for Freud goes so far that he accuses Freud of deriving his theory from Spencer and Lipps; a simple comparison shows where the differences are. Moreover, in the course of a polemical discussion of an example of Freud's concerning "sceptical" jokes, he suggests that Freud may not really "mean" his theories:

> It is characteristic of that tendency toward amateur and irresponsible generalization which can be detected elsewhere in Freud's writing, that he should erect an entirely distinct class and kind of wit called "sceptical," for no better reason than that he has thought of a good story which awakens in him a pleasurable speculation. If he had thought a little longer he could have erected many other classes of tendency wit besides the hostile and the sexual—as many as there are impulses unsatisfied in man. Let us hear the story, however. It is about two Jews who meet in a railway-station:
>
> "Where are you going?" said one.
>
> "To Cracow," said the other.
>
> "What a liar you are!" said the first. "You want me to believe you're going to Lemberg, and that's why you say you're going to Cracow. But I know very well you're going to Cracow!"
>
> The remoteness of our pleasure in this story from a mood of hostile or obscene aggression against the existence of truth may justify us in taking the rest of Freud's classification somewhat lightly. We may indulge a little scepticism of our own at his expense. When he boldly asserts—as he quite often does—that all of a large number of things may be "united under the viewpoint" of sex, he may be employing a little Jewish bravado not unlike that of the man who was going to Cracow. He knows very well that we will not believe they can all be united under the viewpoint of sex, but he is wilful enough to say that they all can, in order to get us to believe that most of them can. (*The Sense of Humor*, pp. 195–196)

But hatred is sometimes half-clairvoyant, and Eastman's violent anti-Freudianism does succeed in ferreting out some weak spots in his opponent's deductions. A number of contradictions in Freud's early formulations are cited, and this is a meritorious contribution. Unfortunately, the solutions Eastman proposes are fully as untenable as some of the early Freudian formulations he condemns.

Furthermore, the tacit formula of the *baby* and not the child as "father of the man" has been an analytic commonplace in the last several decades, a fact which Eastman gratuitously ignores, both in *The Sense of Humor* (1922) and *The Enjoyment of Laughter* (1936). If Eastman had said: "Freud's formulations on laughter and wit stem from 1905; since then analysis has changed, but Freud failed to correlate his newer experiences and his original theory," he would have been one hundred per cent right. Instead, he "catches Freud out" on the basis of a book which blazed a trail in 1905 and has not been revised since.

To complicate matters, Eastman seems unfamiliar with the differentiation between the purely psycho-oeconomical and metapsychological viewpoints in analysis. The formulations presented by Freud in the early years of the century belong exclusively to the former category, as is indicated by the term, "saving of psychic expenditure." The metapsychological view —the division of the unconscious into its three great "provinces" (id, superego, unconscious ego) and the tracing of their interconnections—is necessarily missing from *Wit*, since Freud did not formulate this thesis until eighteen years later, when he wrote *The Ego and the Id*. Freud's only attempt to incorporate the metapsychological viewpoint into his theory of wit and humor was undertaken in 1927, in his short paper, *Der Humor* (*Ges. Schriften* XI, pp. 402–408). In my opinion, this is the weakest paper Freud ever wrote; his conclusions, unfortunately, are more than questionable.

The basis for my doubts is Freud's statement that in humor the superego is consoling the ego. Freud characterizes the relationship between the ego and the superego of the humorist as follows: The humorist displaces large quantities of cathexis from his ego to his superego; the result is a hypercathexis of the latter. The superego, otherwise the "stern master," allows the ego a limited but intense gain in pleasure in accordance with the motto: "Look here! This is all that this seemingly dangerous world amounts to. Child's play, the very thing to jest about!" The superego, in humor, "speaks kindly words of comfort to the intimidated ego," and tries to "comfort the ego, and protect it from suffering." What is overlooked in Freud's deduction is the fact that this "consolation" is bestowed only after the superego has allowed a miserable and hopeless situation to arise for the victim, a fact elaborated on in my study on humor in 1937.[1]

[1] In his justifiably acclaimed paper on "Ferdinand the Bull" (*The American Imago*, 1940), Martin Grotjahn confirms a good many of my assumptions on the psychology of "humor" (especially the "negative hallucination" in negating reality); he makes the interesting statement: "the contrast of laughter is shock." Still, he reverts partially to the conclusion that the superego is benevolent: "The superego may relax and may assume a kind attitude because it faces a harmless joke."

As if these misunderstandings were not confusing enough, Eastman involves himself in a problem of semantics and terminology. Eastman is not familiar with the fact that the German scientific meaning of the term "Humor" is completely dissimilar to the popular English connotation of the word "humor." This has been pointed out previously: Freud meant by "Humor" what we sometimes call 'grim humor" in English. To cite Freud's example: "The condemned man, on his way to the gallows early Monday morning, says, 'The week is starting nicely.' " This "gallows humor" negates personal tragedy for a second, substituting for the reality of the ordeal to be faced an assumption of continuing life. At the same time, the listener enjoys a "saving of expenditure of pity." Misunderstanding the term, Eastman simply subsumes Freud's explanation under the heading of a misguided attempt "to have tried to think up some way of making the enjoyment of an unpleasant thing seem *reasonable*"; Eastman's solution of the same problem is to assume an "innate response."

Despite these regretfully presented objections, Eastman's theory (even though it is questionable) has advanced scientific research on laughter. Eastman's emotional rejection of Freud's theory, I believe, blinded him to its undoubted usefulness within a restricted area, and to the possibilities for enlarging and building on Freud's theory which have been suggested in this book. Eastman's polemic against Freud, on the other hand, has obscured for him the banal fact that aggression is plentifully represented in witticism and that analytic "pansexualism" is a mirage of the critics.

Summarizing, one can say that Eastman's achievement is as good as we can expect from a theorist working within the framework of *purely conscious mechanisms*. But even the best, with this limitation, is not enough.

It should also be mentioned, with respect, that Eastman's contributions to the topic of American humor (discussed in Chapter Eight) are perhaps the best part of his book; in my opinion, they are of lasting value.

An interesting side issue is to be found in Eastman's insistence on the benevolence of all laughter, and his violent denunciation of all "scoffing" theories. Originally, his negation of the aggressive element in laughter provoked many objections; it was frequently declared to be in opposition to observable facts:

> A modern writer like Eastman is amusing in his perplexity over Hobbes and his followers. He cannot understand unsympathetic or anti-sympathetic theories. (J. C. Gregory, *The Nature of Laughter*, p. 18)

> But first of all, let us thoroughly clear up the fact that laughter can be, and often is, felt as offense. This is one of the stumbling-blocks for those writers like Max Eastman, whose one anxiety is to purge laughter of every trace of unpleasantness. No one, indeed, has made a more valiant effort than Max Eastman to champion laughter as an innocent, charming and delightful pastime . . . (A. M. Ludovici, *The Secret of Laughter*, p. 65)

These objections, like Eastman's insistence, take only conscious manifestations into account. But if my assumptions are correct, the enormous amount of aggression in witty-comical productions is *not* real aggression; the aggression displayed is but an inner defense against the inner conscience's accusation of psychic masochism.

Thus, in a sense quite different from that intended (Eastman, who negates the dynamic unconscious, could not possibly accept any conclusions derived from it), Eastman hit on a part of the inner truth.

8. The American Sense of Humor, Based on Anti-Pompousness

The American people never carry an umbrella. They prepare to walk in eternal sunshine.

Alfred E. Smith

MAX EASTMAN has correctly stated, in *The Enjoyment of Laughter*, that this country has made a definite contribution to both the production and the enjoyment of humor. It is not by chance that many languages use the term "American sense of humor." For the record, it should perhaps be mentioned that this term (notably in Europe) has often carried with it a derogatory connotation, but this is immaterial. It proves only that this is a specific and individual type of humor which tends to puzzle the neophyte.

Intelligent foreigners, if they are able to forget the prejudices which inevitably arise from the fact that the United States is the most powerful country in the world, are surprised to find, when first visiting these shores, that the ordinary way of expressing oneself is with jocular and good-natured irony. Everything seems tuned to the basic formula: "Don't take yourself so seriously; don't take yourself so tragically; cut out the airs and get down to earth!"

This attitude is so deeply ingrained that native authors, writing books on the American character, do not mention the trait at all. They take it for granted as a natural thing, while actually it is a unique attribute, found in this country and in this country alone.

Once the visitor has recovered, to some extent, from his first shock—and it is quite a shock to see European pompousness rudely dispossessed—he is apt to take stock of his initial impressions. Typically, he will pay his respects to American industrial genius, and then list six ingredients which, he will claim, comprise the American mentality. These are over-optimism, over-buoyancy, over-sentimentality, over-cynicism, anti-intellectualism and "low humor." If his stock of intellectual knowledge permits, the visitor may even quote "competent domestic authorities" to bolster his point of view; George Santayana, for instance, said: "American life is a powerful solvent. It seems to neutralize every intellectual element, however tough and alien it may be, in native good will, complacency, thoughtlessness and optimism."

But if the same visitor lives in this country for a few years, he is bound to eat his words—unless he is so incapable of adapting himself to changed conditions that he holds on for dear life to the superciliousness of his first impressions as the only compensation for his failure to "fit in." The less inflexible European, if he keeps his eyes and ears open (and if his own pompousness has not permanently impaired sight and hearing), will sooner or later acknowledge: "These people are amazing in their objection to any type of pompousness; they are capable of debunking even themselves; they are always ready for a good laugh. They force even their politicians to have a sense of humor, or borrow one to use in addressing their constituents. When I called their jokes 'low humor,' I simply didn't understand what they were talking and joking about."

The sheer quantity of "kidding," "teasing," and "being funny" is so over-dimensional, so unexpected to a European (and this cannot be stressed often enough), that he must unlearn a good deal of his "seriousness." And precisely because there is such a preponderance of "kidding" in our humor, any attempt to unravel the problems of distinctly American humor must of necessity start with an explanation of this trait.

A typical example may be found in a factual article called *Night Fighters Over New York*, by the brilliant magazine writer, Phil Gustafson, published in the *Saturday Evening Post* on February 2, 1952. This is the caption for the article:

> While you sleep, interceptors roar into the dark after every suspicious plane to approach our shores. Their guns are loaded, and they're not fooling—for if enemy A-bombers ever do come, men like Bull Mileski and Killer Kane will have the big job: Stop 'em!

"Bull" Mileski is a "big, good-natured" radar operator, and "Killer" Kane is a pilot:

> Around their squadron, Kane and Mileski are regarded as something of a pair of characters. The Killer, whose real name is Capt. John K. Kane, is a scanty five-feet-seven, with the face of a dead-pan cherub and a *sense of humor that keeps popping off like a whistle on a peanut roaster*. He weighs a bare 158 pounds; Mileski strains the scales at 200. Mileski—Lt. William E., to the mailman—stands six-feet-two in his socks, not counting his bushy crew haircut, and when his nose isn't glued to his radar set, *everything strikes him as funny*. He looks down on Kane with the benevolent grin of a man about to pick up a three-year-old and toss him toward the ceiling.
>
> "They have to have a big radar observer along with these little pilots to keep them out of trouble," he explains with a patronizing smile at Kane.
>
> "Trouble with Bull is he weighs too much to fly," Kane comes back. "If I ever get in a scrape, I'll have to jettison him."
>
> Actually, Bull is first to admit that he is too big to fly—at least in the crowded after cockpit of the present F-94. Bull practically has to be put in with a shoehorn, and he sits with his knees drawn up under his chin, mourning the days when he flew in P-61 night fighters during World War II and had a cockpit big enough to dress in.

> Kane and Mileski *subject each other to merciless ribbing on the ground*, and *the same thing seems to go for other all-weather pilots and observers*. Listen to the pilot tell it and you'll come away with the notion that all radar observers are fools. Take it from the observers, and all pilots are nincompoops. Both Kane and Mileski pretend that the other is about as useful as a good-sized hole in the head.
>
> "When I go out on an intercept, it's just like taking a taxi," says Mileski. "I merely tell the driver where I want to go."
>
> "I always think of myself as driving in strange country," Kane comes back, "and picking up some local yokel who happens to know the territory."
>
> In reality, pilot and observer are so dependent on each other's skill in the air that they develop a respect for each other which amounts almost to affection. To offset this touching faith, they generate a compensatory toughness toward each other that *takes the form of endless razzing on the ground*. [My italics.]

The identical situation—a deadly-serious situation—could not be described in this way in any but an American publication. Every-day American humor is clearly characterized here; witty teasing takes the place of seriousness, boredom, and pompousness. The teasing is so pronounced that it seems the verbal equivalent of the "practical joke."

What foreign observers erroneously call "the typical American low humor" pertains exactly to this constant "teasing," "ribbing" and "razzing." Unfamiliar with this approach, the neophyte—accustomed to more gravity and fewer witticisms in daily life—deprecates the unfamiliar tone.

The psychological substratum of teasing is always the same: a revulsion against pompousness expressed in simulated aggression. The anti-pompousness is the landmark; it can be historically explained as a heritage of the colonial period. Most British colonies tend to become more British than the mother country; the available evidence tends to indicate that this was true of the Tories in the American Revolution, and that they differed from the Revolutionists in attitude as well as politics. One can only speculate on the reasons for this, and such speculation is outside the province of this study, but even unsupported by explanations the fact is unquestionable: unlike all other offshoots of the British Empire, the post-revolutionary United States is a country in which anti-pompousness dominates.

Strangely enough, Americans themselves are often self-conscious about their possession of one of the greatest assets in humor. Josh Billings claimed: "Americans haven't had time yet to bile down their humor and git the wit out ov it."

Thus a distinction is made between "humor" and "wit," aristocratic privilege being ascribed to the latter. This also corresponds to the effects of these two types of humor—on the one hand the amused smile, and on the other the explosive belly-laugh.

In *The Enjoyment of Laughter*, Eastman makes some shrewd observations on the topic of American humor. He declares:

It is in the humorists rather than the poets that imagination in its full vigor has flourished among us. That is what has made these humorists something of a sensation in the world. They did of course exaggerate. Imaginative humor runs out automatically into exaggeration. How could you play laughing havoc with the qualities of things, and not pile them up into quantities that also overwhelm the mind? The two things go together like size and shape—the inordinate quantity and the preposterous image. Ring Lardner said that "if the penalty for selling honest old beer to minors was $100 fine why 2 to 14 years in a meat grinder would be mild for a guy that sells white pop on the theory that it is a drink." As a modification of the penal code that is indeed extreme, but it is also—is it not—fantastic? And the fantasy, not the extremeness, is what makes Ring Lardner's hand unmistakable in the writing of it.

After citing similar images from the works of Ring Lardner and citing Mark Twain's "Twenty-four years ago, I was strangely handsome . . . In San Francisco, in the rainy season I was often mistaken for fair weather," Eastman goes on to say:

You can find all the exaggerations you want in Baron Munchausen, but you cannot find a phrase to match those in any writer of English before Mark Twain . . . American humorists, casual and unsustained as their flights are, belong to the tribe of Shakespeare . . . More even than in individual writers this fact is evident in the humorous antics of our slang . . . [The creation of slang terms] is to employ, with a humorous twist, the very language of Shakespeare. And the language of Shakespeare with a humorous twist is, in all essentials, the language of Rabelais. There is nothing else in the world, that I ever saw, so like a page of Rabelais as a page from a dictionary of American slang. A man who put that much imaginative vigor, and vigor of the tongue muscles, into serious speech would be one of the great poets of the world.

. . . It is the blending of . . . two strains—the primitive vigor of imagination and the mature enjoyment of nonsense—that gives its distinct flavor to American humor.

. . . the great American art of laughing at oneself . . . was not original with us, nor with anyone in history. But with us, I think, it first became a humorous convention . . . We hold ourselves up to laughter because we believe in laughter.

Discussing the understatement that is so characteristic of American humor (as in Lincoln's comment on the dog who swallowed a bomb with the fuse attached: "Rover was a good dog, but as a dog I'm afraid his days of usefulness are over"), Eastman says:

It is our hard, rapid, unliterary way of slapping it down, rather than our leaning toward exaggeration, that makes American humor seem a little crude.

Discussing irony, Eastman traces the word back to the original Greek:

The *eiron* was the soft-spoken, poker-faced boy, canny and restrained, who always had something more in mind than he was telling you. On the comic stage he was set off against another character called *alazon*, a loud-mouthed, blustering, swanking, cock-and-bull-story-telling lad . . . It is characteristic of the Greek view of life that the triumph of the *eiron* over the *alazon* became almost a settled convention of their comic theatre.

. . . the Greeks were keenly sensitive to these two qualities of humor, . . . the humor of big talk and of understatement. Comedy, you might say, was born into the world as a playing off of the one against the other. And the word *irony* arose out of this crude clash. It described the "taking down" of the big talker by the man who says less than he means.

American humor also arose in history with this contrast plainly to be seen. The New England Yankee with his "dry" humor—we call it dry as we do a dry wine, I judge, because its geniality is not sweetened by smiling—is the American *eiron*. And the loud-mouthed backwoodsman, "gamecock of the wilderness," with his tall tales and preposterous asseverations of prowess, is the *alazon*.

Constance Rourke, writing in *American Humor*, also has made significant observations:

Though the American scene had been drawn, an American literature was hardly definable in 1834. Twittering poetasters and essayists, pretty story-tellers, and studious novelists were springing up by the dozens as if to refute the classic charge that the Americans were coarse. There was a great effervescence of what may be called the false-feminine . . . English literature was accepted as the single great American heritage; and American literature was counted one of its provinces. . . .

Scant, fitful, sporadic as American literature has proved to be, it has had roots in a common soil. Through the interweaving of the popular strain with that of a new expression on other levels a literature has been produced which, like other literatures, is related to an anterior popular lore that must for lack of a better word be called a folklore. No literal sequence followed from the comic mythologies, no simple, orderly completion. Extravagantly and wilfully, as though it were possessed by the very essence of the comic spirit, American literature turned aside from these materials for the most part, and discovered others of its own. The wealth of a native mythology was left behind, except as Melville used this, and a few other writers. Yet the Yankee, the backwoodsman in minstrelsy—though the influence there was less direct—the strollers of the theater and of the cults and revivals, the innumerable comic story-tellers and myth makers, had made a groundwork for this literature. (pp. 160–62)

The difference between wit and the "humorous story" has been defined by Mark Twain:

The humorous story is American, the comic story is English, the witty story is French. The humorous story depends for its effect upon the *manner* of telling; the comic story and the witty story upon the *matter* . . . The humorous story is told gravely; the teller does his best to conceal the fact that he even dimly suspects that there is anything funny about it . . . The humorous story is strictly a work of art, and only an artist can tell it; but no art is necessary in telling the comic and witty story, anybody can do it. (*How to Tell a Story*)

* * *

There may be people who find it objectionable to hear that there is infantilism in laughter, and that the infantile produces laughter, but this cannot be helped: *all* laughter *is* infantile. But the word "infantile" has two connotations: it may refer to the historical vistas of childhood, or allude to immaturity, in which case the vistas are those of adult censorship. When one scorns some peoples' laughter because it is "infantile," the allusion is of course to "adult censorship"—the implication is that "an adult should be above such nonsense." Nevertheless, and despite all the highfalutin rules of intellectualism which call for laughter to progress to more rarefied strata as the I.Q. progresses to more rarefied heights—an adult just isn't above nonsense. To prove the point, one need only note the frequency with which "intelligent" people laugh "in spite of themselves" at infantile jokes. The secondary distinction which divides "naive" people, who laugh exclusively at "nonsense," from the intelligentsia, which allegedly finds only *intellectualized* nonsense humorous, is entirely unjustified.

The American type of humor, uniquely, finds shrewd people who are "in the know" failing to take refuge behind the typical hypocrisy of intellectual gourmanderie in laughter. Even the "elite" admits to "infantilism" and honors it with a belly laugh. This may, as some people claim, be a proof that American humor is "low" humor; in my opinion, the proof points in exactly the opposite direction.

The how and why of the typical Eurpoean accusation that ours is "low" humor can be stated very simply. Generally speaking, the serious-minded and educated western European has a fixed ambition: to make his place in the social class which is *above* the average. Automatically, therefore, he will reject "natural" manners, just as he will reject practical jokes, "primitive" kidding, word jokes, nonsense jokes; they all belong to a social level below the one he identifies with. Humor of a "higher" type is for him a proof of higher social and intellectual status, for only the "plebs" do it differently. "Simple humor" thus acquires the connotation of naivete and unsophistication; it is "peasant" humor.

Visiting the United States, the educated Western European discovers that people of *all* social classes are addicted to "simple humor." The erroneous conclusion follows almost logically: humor is "simple," therefore it is "rude," uncultured, low. And usually the newcomer does not even suspect that his standards are meaningless in the new situation which confronts him, for here even shrewd people frankly and openly indulge in simple humor. Since the situation is unheard of, the misunderstanding is almost inevitable.

9. Fun-Deficiency—The Bores and the Bored

Society is now one polished horde,
Formed of two mighty tribes, the
Bores and Bored.
Byron, *Don Juan*, Canto XIII

Boredom, declared Casanova bitterly in his old age, is that part of hell that Dante forgot to describe in *The Divine Comedy*. Boredom is not simply a disagreeable mood; it is an emotional experience which tends to threaten the psychic balance of the individual. It is a universal phenomenon, despite the comparatively few complaints about it. Most people suffer boredom silently; it is by their hectic and almost always futile search for "fun" that they betray its presence. This constant search for "fun" characteristic of many people is the inner protective device against the constant danger of boredom.

There are people who pride themselves on the fact that they are "never bored." The statement is pure bravado, and easily punctured. It can be stated as clinical fact that a person who is "never bored" doesn't exist. It is of course true that the period of recovery from boredom varies from individual to individual, and some people are quick in attaching their psychic energy to a new interest after a spell of ennui. Boredom may then be forgotten, but it should still be recorded.

The after-effects and by-products of boredom are dissatisfaction, emptiness, inability to concentrate on either work or pleasure, restlessness, or its converse, impassivity. These manifestations are comparatively superficial; a deeper danger is also present. Boredom may result in the feeling that all one's endeavors, attachments and aims are senseless, and this feeling that all is meaningless merges with an intense and terrified loneliness. In not too severe cases, the promptness of the automatic though temporary recovery is in direct ratio to the intensity of one's inner loneliness.

Generally speaking, boredom is an interim feeling, disagreeable enough, but harmless and transitory. But a quantitative increase may render it unmanageable, and it then becomes a disease-entity. I have a very personalized relationship with that disease; I was the first to describe it genetically and to name it.[1] I chose the name "alysosis" in acknowledgement of the very human attitude of familiar irreverence for the allegedly known; I assumed that nobody would be content to admit that he suffered from so "banal" and "simple" a disease as boredom. But what if one used

[1] "On the Disease-Entity Boredom ('Alysosis') and its Psychopathology," *The Psychiatric Quarterly*, 19, 38–51; 1945.

the Greek equivalent—*alys*? The mantle of scientific terminology was bound to make a difference, I concluded, and alysosis it was.

Boredom consists, at bottom, of absence of pleasure, but what people understand by "pleasure" is of course as variable as their specific wishes, defense mechanisms, and neurotic reactions. Everyone must find some specific remedy for the potential danger of boredom. The danger, it should be noted, varies quantitatively from individual to individual. No one can argue about the advisability or efficacy of a chosen antidote. There are no connecting links of understanding between the stamp collector, the baseball fan and the inveterate gossip—to mention three "hobbies" at random. These hobbies fulfill specific unconscious wishes and defense mechanisms; at the same time they are also preventives of boredom. The process, of course, is not conscious.

The opposite of boredom is the concentration of interest upon a specific field. The intensity of this interest will of course lessen at certain times, but even the layman realizes that the surgeon feels a continuing interest in his surgery, the historian in his research into the mediaeval period, the ship captain in navigation. In general, however, people make a very precise distinction between work and "fun." The ideal situation, it goes without saying, is one in which work is also "fun." Expressed scientifically, the more completely one's work serves for the sublimation of unconscious defense mechanisms, the more pleasurable one's life is. But for the majority of people, unhappily, work is only some kind of hardship, essential in order to provide a livelihood, but good for no other purpose.

There are two types of sufferers from boredom: the complainers and the disguisers. The *complainers* are wistful and hungry-eyed; they seem to be appealing to all comers to lift them up out of the Slough of Despond. After a short time, they give up hope; your remarks have been of no use, and they sink back into disgusted silence. Nothing appeals to the complainer or distracts him; he is helplessly sulky and permanently unresponsive.

The *disguisers* are the fun-hunters previously mentioned.

The openly bored are an infinitesimal minority in the huge army of the dull. The huge majority are not recognizable in their true colors without the key. Phenomenologically, they seem to suffer from an utterly dissimilar disease. They are restless and constantly on the go; they behave as if they would be penalized for sitting down and relaxing for more than a minute. They seem to be driven by some inner whip. Their slogan is, "Let's have fun," but every variety of fun which they propose is found wanting, and quickly dropped for a substitute brand. None of their chosen antidotes to boredom works; the only result is agitated funlessness. The pitiful fun-hunter wants something very badly, but he does not know what he wants.

All bored people—whether they disguise their sickness or not—suffer from "fun-deficiency." The term denotes lack of balance in the inner department of pleasure. (If the term itself needs some justification, I point to the precedents: vitamin-deficiency, calcium-deficiency, iron-deficiency. The analogy ends here; vitamins, calcium and iron can be administered to restore a balance, but there are no injections of "fun" available. To cure "fun-deficiency," the inner obstacles in the way of perception of pleasure must first be removed. The ability to experience fun may be inhibited, but the basis is always present.)

What is "fun"?

Fun is an extremely personalized feeling of well-being produced by concentrating psychic energy on a freely-chosen, usually extra-curricular endeavor. Fun is the classical antidote against the constant danger-signal of boredom. A well-balanced, *fun-loving and fun-experiencing* person, therefore, is one who has found his specific and temporarily effective palliative against boredom. Under normal conditions, the connection between boredom and fun is parallel to that between being hungry and eating one's favorite dish.

The choice of one's specific brand of fun is dictated by unconscious motives; the individual is of course unaware of these reasons. This factor, also, is visible only indirectly, in the universally supercilious attitude towards somebody else's notion of fun:

This world is a difficult world, indeed,
And people are hard to suit,
And the man who plays on the violin
Is a bore to the man with the flute. (Walter Learned, *Consolation*)

Common sense does not explain why the other fellow's fun should be considered silly, "idiotic," infantile, and one's own brand intelligent, clever and adult. Following the rule, "where logic ends, the unconscious takes over," we can guess that the intolerant rejection of all brands of fun except one's own is in some way linked to the inner battle which preceded establishment of the temporary boredom-antidote. The first impression is that the ironic rejection of the other fellow's antidote reflects that ironic rejection pronounced by one's own superego against one's own fun. That inner rejection is subsequently projected outward.

What do people use as antidotes to boredom? *Fantasy, hobbies, entertainment, work.* The first two are self-created; the others make use of external factors, pressing them into service as sources of "fun." Of these four, fantasy and hobbies are the most important.

Fantasy has first priority because people are limited in the time they can devote to their hobbies. Since most people find work a disagreeable duty, they sugarcoat their working hours with fantasies. A hobby is a self-created diversion which, for unconscious reasons, becomes the rallying point for many unconscious defense mechanisms.

Among remedies for boredom, reading of novels, adventure and mystery stories, etc., looking at movies and television, are important. A double identification takes place here: consciously with the hero, unconsciously with the victim. (For elaboration, see *The Writer and Psychoanalysis*.)

* * *

In my opinion, boredom is always associated with three inner disturbances ("triad of boredom"). It is based on a triad consisting of weak or frangible sublimations, inner inhibition of voyeurism, and defense against the accusation of masochistic pleasure.

1. *Weak sublimations*. In all cases of inability to create sublimation, or where sublimation is weak, the individual's store of aggression is out of the ego's reach, and is taken over by the superego for use against the ego. Psychic masochism—the unconscious ego's counteraction—is the result.

Where sublimation is merely weak or unstable, boredom represents the unconscious ego's defense against the intermediary phase of the superego's attack. That attack is always the aftermath of conscious defeat, and it shakes the very foundation of sublimation. The superego seizes on external defeats as torture material, and then attacks. The attack is not powerful enough to destroy the sublimation, but it does succeed in making the sublimation temporarily unworkable. This interim period has a surface manifestation: the conscious boredom which is the unconscious ego's defense.

2. *Voyeurism*. Fantasy, which is imagination in free flight, is a product of the scopophiliac instinct. It is therefore logical to expect boredom in persons having a neurotic inhibition of fantasy (and consequently of voyeurism). Observation proves that such neurotics are the most frequent sufferers from boredom. The reason for the inhibition of voyeurism is to be found in its unconscious connection with pre-Oedipal and Oedipal fantasies.

3. *Defense against superego reproaches of psychic masochism. Boredom is a desperate preventive measure on the part of the frightened ego; it anticipates a superego raid*. Zoology reports a comparable phenomenon, called autotomy. If an animal's leg is caught in a trap, the animal will sacrifice that part in order to save its life. The psychic dilemma of boredom implies that the ego is weak and the superego strong. When there is successfully maintained sublimation, on the other hand, we know that the unconscious ego has been strong enough to best the superego, for the superego is the enemy of sublimation. Aggression in that particular personality, therefore, is not concentrated exclusively on the torture chambers of the inner conscience.[2]

[2] The problem of sublimation is highly complex, and only the defense against the defense comes to the fore. For further elaboration, see *The Battle of the Conscience*.

This fact can be clinically observed: the psychic health or illness of a person can *also* be measured in the stability or instability of his sublimations. The more stable the sublimation, the better the chances of health in a specific individual. This is by no means the only yardstick; the others are the individual's adaptation to reality, his sex life,[3] and his general contentment. One cannot separate that quadrangular sequence of events, and single out sublimation as the *only* measuring rod, simply because sublimation is often the last effective barrier to neurotic collapse. There are many reasons for the fact that work is frequently "the last bastion engulfed in neurosis."[4]

Aside from all its other attributes, neurosis is a notable consumer of psychic energy, drawing energy away from normal depositories. Hobbies which had once been enjoyed become meaningless and tiresome. The mood in general deteriorates, and depression, dissatisfaction and inner insecurity become patent. The individual's emotional life is centered on his neurotic unrest, and the symptoms, which include diminution or lack of sexual interest, become widespread. The mechanical ability to work, however, is usually preserved. Only rarely is this ability affected at the beginning of an acute stage of neurosis; at its high point, of course, the individual's enjoyment of his work and the originality of his ideas are decidedly impaired. Nevertheless, the neurotic continues to be capable of work for a considerable time.

Why is work the last fortress to be taken over by neurosis, and how can one explain the exceptions to this typical sequence?

In discussing the problem of work one must distinguish between *enforced* and *self-chosen* occupations or professions. There is a difference between the man who lackadaisically went into his father's business, because it "made sense," and the man who "always" wanted to be a mechanical engineer and worked his way doggedly through school in order to become one. The unconscious reasons behind the man who makes sacrifices to achieve his goal, or who at least knows it and cannot be swerved from it, are analytically clear: although the man is not aware of it, his self-chosen profession satisfies, in sublimated form, unconscious defense mechanisms covering deep inner wishes.

The advantage is obvious. Work which does not reflect a deep inner wish is mere drudgery, as inescapable and unpleasant as taxes. Work which is a sublimation is both satisfying and pleasurable.

[3] The wording, "sex life," is not meant to describe only the functioning ability of the sexual apparatus; it also means the ability to love *tenderly*. For further elaboration, see *Neurotic Counterfeit-Sex*.

[4] See the writer's "Why is Work the Last Bastion Engulfed in Neurosis?," *Diseases of the Nervous System*, VIII; 10; 1947.

Work plays a decisive role in the psychic economy. It is the normal repository of unconscious guilt. By paying ranson in the form of work, the typical person pays his debt to his inner conscience. Since no person is free of inner guilt, the punitive connotation of work is immensely valuable. The connotation of work as punishment is a well-known phenomenon analytically (Jekels, Reik), and it has been intuitively known to mankind since time immemorial. In Genesis we are told that Adam and Eve, expelled from Eden, were compelled to work as punishment.

There is a strange paradox in the effect of neurosis upon one's working ability: *the more pleasurable work has been in "normality," the more promptly it is absorbed in the neurotic process.* The ability to work at a job to which one is indifferent is maintained for a longer period, because of its greater admixture of the punitive quality.

There may be an additional reason for the preservation of working ability in neurosis. Curious as this may sound, the unconscious is well aware of the "game" quality of neurotic pleasures, and all games have strictly specified limits. A comparison of two cases may help to clarify these points.

Mr. A., a writer of distinction, developed a writing block at the age of 39. He had published many books, and his last one—which he himself did not like—had made the best-seller lists. After the initial elation of this success, he became moody. He no longer enjoyed transitory affairs with women of his acquaintance. Everything seemed boring. He started a new novel, but could not get on with it. He took a long trip, and to his dismay discovered that he could not write any more. In his despondency, he thought seriously of drowning himself. Finally he entered analysis.

Mr. B., a lawyer of 45, entered analysis because of a marital conflict. He was not interested in his wife, and his girl friend was pressing him, quite urgently, to marry her. In his indecision, he figured out what he thought was a good excuse for doing nothing. By entering analysis, he would "immobilize" his girl friend; he would tell her that analysis required suspension of vital decisions until the unconscious reasons were clarified. At the same time, he had another—a real—reason for entering treatment.

Mr. B. had become a lawyer at the urging of his family, and not because of his own interest in the profession. He entered his uncle's law office and did his work mechanically, neither badly nor well, as he put it. His main interest in life was gambling; for years he had lived in a state of strange excitement, with his "life for the day" starting at the card table after work. This excitement had not affected his professional duties until shortly before he entered analysis. During these last weeks, he had been feeling depressed, and had attributed his state of mind to his "conflicts" with his wife and girl friend, and to his steady losses at poker. He did not think his addiction to gambling was pathological; like all gamblers, he believed that he needed more money and more luck, not a psychiatrist. One day, in court, he was about to make a motion on behalf of his client. At the last second, he caught himself, realizing that the move was too dangerous. "At that moment," he explained, "I really got frightened. I discovered that I was transplanting my gambling instincts to my profession."

Case A is an example of a freely-chosen, Case B of an enforced, profession. Working ability collapsed very quickly in the case of the writer, but continued for a much longer period in the case of the lawyer. This is in line with the statement previously made: the more pleasurable work is in "normality," the more promptly it is absorbed in the neurotic process. In his vocation, the writer used unconscious defense mechanisms corresponding to unconscious pleasures, while the lawyer used his work only for making a living. It was only at a late stage that the lawyer projected his neurotic conflict into his profession.

The writer fought an intrapsychic battle against a deep passive-masochistic wish to be mistreated, rejected, humiliated. That tendency, corresponding to the end result of his specific infantile conflict, was passed off as a defense by being transformed to its opposite: pseudo-aggression. In his novels, Mr. A. used strong he-men as heroes. He overdid his defensive efforts, and his characters were called "lifeless" and "unreal" by the reviewers. In the novel which reached the best-seller lists, he had made his hero more human. He paid for this relaxation of his defensive efforts with a severe inner reproach. One step further, and his defensive cover would approximate the real unconscious situation! This inner danger was so great that his external success was inacceptable as an alibi. Previously he had used his he-man heroes as "proof" that he was neither "weak" nor masochistic; now this defense collapsed and his inner conscience rejected the old excuse. The result was—writing block. In his best-seller, the man had nearly failed to represent his unconscious defenses.

The sequence of events in the writer's working process was: first, fight against inner conflicts; second, rational aim of making money.

The lawyer-gambler had a completely different approach to his work. He did not work to solve inner conflicts, but merely to earn a living. His inner conflicts were deposited in his gambling; gambling was his real "profession." At the card table, he fought a never-ending battle to maintain his infantile megalomania with masochistic means. He behaved as if he could control the winning cards.

The gambler uses a specific technique for the preservation of his fantasy of omnipotence. He "acts" omnipotence, accepts the punishment in the form of an unconscious wish to lose (every gambler loses in the long run), and libidinizes his defeats by unconsciously "enjoying" psychic masochism. He unconsciously identifies his opponent (or the roulette wheel or other gambling instrument) with the authorities of his childhood, thus aggressively reducing them to absurdity as "giving" persons. This in turn reinforces his unconscious wish to lose.[5]

This sort of gratification reminds one of the tale of the farmer's wife who disputed her husband's ukase on the best method of cutting garden flowers. He specified a knife, while she insisted on shears. The end of their quarrel was that the man shoved his wife into a nearby stream, and she, in the very act of drowning, made a triumphant scissors-like gesture with her fingers.

The sequence of events in the case of the gambler-lawyer, as far as the disposition of his inner conflicts was concerned, was as follows: To begin with, work was a rational means of making money; it was more or less free of neurotic admixtures. All his inner conflicts were deposited in his gambling. Late in life, when his neurosis spread (every neurosis increases with age), the previously untouched area—his working ability—was drawn into the sphere of inner conflict.

Work satisfies not merely rational factors but also—unconsciously—reverberations of the triad of aggressive, libidinous and narcissistic tendencies (Freud). In freely-chosen professions the admixture of emotional elements is dominant; in enforced professions the emotional admixture remains negligible for a long time. Punitive unconscious elements are present in both types. Under neurotic stress, work in freely-chosen occupations collapses early because of the inherent emotional involvement, whereas in indifferent professions work is the last "fortress" to give way. The punitive element embedded in work makes it more resistant to attacks stemming from the punitive inner conscience.

A deeply depressed patient, who had occasional witty moments, once asked me ironically:

"How do you cook boredom?"

"It doesn't need artificial preparation," I replied, "it is presented to the sufferer on a platter."

"I know that from my own experience. But suppose there were a collection of psychic recipes. What would the eager reader find?"

"Well, you need three ingredients for the 'triad of boredom': inhibition of peeping, a good dose of psychic masochism, and weak sublimations."

"You know my predilection for short and concise formulas. Could you offer one for boredom?"

"At your service. Boredom is the alibi of the emptied head."

"That's too short for me."

"You should have realized that complicated psychic phenomena cannot be boiled down into eight-word slogans. . . . Boredom represents an un-

[5] For further elaboration see *Money and Emotional Conflicts*.

conscious defense mechanism created by the unconscious ego under pressure of a frantic superego attack. *It is a preventive method of proving 'I'm a good boy.' The method consists of clearing all dangerous and incriminating material out of the psychic chambers, leaving them empty.* It is like the familiar mystery story ruse—the corpse is removed before the police arrive."

"But in a detective story the room is not stripped of all its furniture. In boredom, there is complete inner emptiness. How do you account for that?"

"In constructing his alibi, the bored person goes one step further than the character in the mystery. He doesn't merely remove all incriminating material and toys in the second before he is caught red-handed by the inner conscience. He denies, so to speak, that the premises could be furnished at all, even at some future date. He is the good boy on a promissory note. . . "

* * *

The bored person unconsciously furnishes his alibi of innocence, and once he has done his duty, becomes obstinate in a peculiar way: he refuses every substitute for the pleasures he has renounced. His behavior, in this layer, is like that of the child who has been forbidden a specific activity. Substitutes are suggested, but are sulkily ignored; nothing can amuse him now.

If one were to believe bored people their difficulty is that nothing appeals to them; all they ask is that something be found that will amuse, distract or entertain them.

In *inner* reality, they do not want to be amused at all. After having submitted fully to the tyranny of the superego, they stage an ironic comeback in the form of a miniature slave revolt. Self-assertion becomes essential, and it is accomplished by reverting to infantile megalomania, where the ego's place is in the center of the universe, and the outer world plays the role of court fool, providing amusement. Reality having been demoted, all the substitute pleasures that reality could provide are rejected. It is as if the educational authorities of the past were being reduced to absurdity. "Let's see what you have to offer," is the scornful question, and all offerings are "tried out," only to be abandoned as "dull."

* * *

It is worth while to listen to the rationalizations presented as "reasons" for habitual boredom. One widely accepted explanation is that certain individuals have certain "predilections"; if these predilections are frustrated, boredom results. Another is that boredom is the aftermath of monotony and routine.

Neither of these popular attempts to clarify the phenomenon casts any light on the problem. To begin with, "predilections" cannot be taken for granted; they must be genetically explained. They, too, have reasons for being. But even if we make the nonsensical assumption that a specific predilection is fashioned for a specific person without a specific reason, it still remains necessary to explain why that particular predilection, once pleasurable, has become stale and boring.

As for the second "explanation," it is not true that monotony and boredom are identical. This is especially clear in self-chosen occupations. The surgeon who cares about his profession can operate every day for forty years without becoming bored with surgery; the sailor who loves the sea does not become bored with his ship; the driver goes on finding his car a pleasurable possession—except when he has to pay for repairs. To repeat: in self-chosen professions or occupations, where a large number of unconscious wishes and defenses find expression, there is little danger of boredom.

* * *

The confusion surrounding boredom is so extensive that the first step towards clarification must be to define what boredom (alysosis) is *not.* Here are ten misunderstandings of alysosis:

1. *Every* tension—irrespective of source—is unjustifiedly called boredom, provided it does not progress to fear. The whole waste-land of "dissatisfaction," caused by inner tension, is thus included.

2, 3, 4. Of the neurotic moods incorrectly subsumed under the heading of "general tension," three are of major importance. These are the "tensions" connected with gambling, alcoholic addiction and neurotic sex. None of these "tensions," which appear when the neurotic refuses to "give in" to his particular solution, or when extremely inhibited, has any connection with boredom. All three neurotic manifestations are unconscious defense mechanisms, and *the tension experienced corresponds to an anticipatory helplessness against the reproaches which will be leveled by the inner conscience* if the neurotic is caught without a defense. In contra-distinction, *alysosis is in itself a specific defense mechanism, and consequently an inner alibi.*

5. Amusingly enough, people tend to equate intellectual achievement with the "ability" to experience boredom. H. G. Wells, for one, stated that it is a "higher phenomenon" to lose interest in a stimulus which is both repetitive and meaningless. As proof he adduced the case of the dog without cerebral hemispheres, who is thus incapable of inhibitory processes originating in the cortex, and never becomes inured or indifferent to persisting stimuli, but actively evinces curiosity whenever the meaningless stimulus is repeated.

Putting it another way, he declares, the boredom resulting from a tiresomely repeated stimulus testifies to activity in the highest part of the brain. This boredom is a means of self-protection. If it were not for this ability to render oneself indifferent to certain stimuli, the organism would be incessantly occupied in reacting to events of no significance. Merely noting essentials is not enough; at the same time one must be able to ignore the unimportant (*The Science of Life*, Chapter IV). Here the confusion lies in the misuse of the word "boredom." What Wells calls "selective indifference" is a *healthy* defense; it is entirely unconnected with alysosis, which is a *neurotic* defense. Rejection of meaningless distractions (whether the rejection be conscious or pre-conscious) is *not* identical with boredom.

6. Another loose use of the term "boredom" adds to the mass of confusion. People say, "That bores me" to indicate rejection of a movie, a person, a social gathering, a particular activity. Boredom as a *pathological* entity is the inability to attach one's interest to an activity that is self-chosen and thus possesses unconscious reverberations. The inability to feel interest in a specific form of "amusement"—even if it is generally accepted as "amusing"—is not boredom.

7. Contrary to general opinion, intellectual limitations do not make a bore. In *Vivian Grey* (1826), Disraeli claims that "the true bore is that man who thinks the world is only interested in one subject because he himself can only comprehend one." A person can, of course, be a "monomaniac," and therefore a nuisance and a bore to his environment. This does not make him clinically "alysotic"; he is not boring to himself.

8. Alysosis is also confused with the face-saving device which some neurotics resort to. In order to minimize their various fears, some neurotics claim that they are "bored" with them.

9. Boredom is sometimes mistaken for the need to return to healthy activity after a period of rest. Paradigmatic are the moods which tend to arise in the end-stages of vacations. If a man, accustomed to a specific type of work which represents his specific outlet for sublimation, takes a vacation, he will enjoy his leisure for a time but gradually yearn for his return to work. This transitional period between full enjoyment of leisure and reawakened interest in work will be described as "boring."

On the other hand, the person who is awkward and uncomfortable whenever he is away from his desk is a slave to his inner alibi. In his case, the pre-stage of pseudo-boredom is a disease; pseudo-boredom of the type first described may have a salutary effect. A witty man once said that "vacation provides all the boredom required for a full year, and permits you to find the work you damn in July pleasurable in September. The griping starts around Christman again—Blessed July!"

The neurotic element in the inability to take vacations is well expressed in an ironic letter I received from such a person during a vacation:

> I hope you feel fine and that the food is excellent. The other pleasures of a vacation are easier to accept. I am fine and bothered only by reproaches of conscience: to leave the city and travel somewhere. Under this disturbing influence, I am making a few futile gestures: I went to the American Express Company to "discuss" my vacation plans. After finishing this alibi-ing motion, I am appeased. . . . In spite of all that, I shall leave in a week, though I don't know where to. In masochistic orgies, I imagine the terrors of vacationing: fresh air (that alone is suffocating), quiet and solitude (this, too, is deadening), nice scenery and similar traps. Well, one has to do penance . . .

10. Boredom is confused with other neuroticisms, such as neurotic depersonalization, neurotic and schizoid depressions, etc., which can only be distinguished by the psychiatrist.

It is clear that not every "dead" feeling, to use a patient's description, clinically constitutes boredom. There are many other completely unrelated reasons for "lack of feelings." The diagnosis of boredom, its therapy, and its differential diagnosis are jobs for the psychiatrist.

* * *

There are two types of reaction in boredom, as O. Fenichel observed (without explaining).[6] These are the motoric or fidgety reaction, and the immobile. The existence of these varied reactions becomes understandable when one remembers that every neurotic libidinal drive is inwardly warded off with pseudo-aggressive tendencies, and every neurotic pseudo-aggressive tendency, by libidinal ones. A passive-masochistic inner conflict, which is warded off by pseudo-aggression, results in surface activity; surface immobility and passivity results from an inner aggressive conflict.

The type of boredom is therefore a direct clue to the underlying forces which are being warded off.

* * *

As stated before, voyeurism plays an important role in combatting dullness and ennui. The scopophiliac instinct, comprising inner voyeurism and inner exhibitionism, seems to be of major importance in preventing boredom. Everyone indulges in fantasy at certain times; if these fantasies do not interfere with action, they are good antidotes to boredom.

Heine was once asked how he had spent a few days. "I gave audience to my fantasies," he replied. It is interesting to note that the role of fantasy (voyeurism) was intuitively known to Voltaire. In his *Discours* we find the following statement: "Le secret d'ennuyer est celui de tout dire."

[6] The analytic literature on boredom is sparse and explains nothing. For elaboration see my original paper, "On the Disease-Entity Boredom."

("The secret of being a bore is to tell all.") What is unspoken arouses curiosity, stimulates fantasy and imagination (psychic voyeurism), and thus prevents boredom.

It is only when fantasy takes so predominant a place, quantitatively, that it becomes a substitute for normal action that one can speak of it as a neurotic sign, like the fantasies observable in neurotics. Imagining action, in fantasy, is a prerequisite for normal action. "Thinking is rehearsal of action" (Freud).

One is therefore prepared to expect that in persons having a neurotic inhibition of fantasy (genetically, of voyeurism), boredom will appear more frequently than in others. This expectation is borne out by observable facts. The reason for the inhibition of voyeurism is to be found in its unconscious connection with pre-Oedipal and Oedipal fantasies.

* * *

The normal person unconsciously counteracts the latent danger of boredom with work, hobby, fantasy, amusement and entertainment; the neurotic's most frequent antidote for boredom is—worry. Neurotic worry is primarily the result of an inner conflict; its *secondary* use is as a remedy for boredom. And the remedy, as one would expect, is often worse than the disease. There is no rationality in these symptoms and pseudo-remedies, and the victims can neither choose nor dismiss them arbitrarily and consciously.

There are three groups of neurotics in particular who are largely immune to boredom. These are obsessional neurotics, hypochondriacs and depersonalized persons. Consciously, these sick people are always worried; they concentrate all their attention on their obsessions (compulsions), imaginary diseases, and disturbances of perception, respectively. They are so seldom troubled with boredom, because in all these neuroses *voyeurism remains undisturbed.* A good dose of unrestricted imagination is the prerequisite for the worrier; it is familiar to hear the worried person enumerate a list of possible dangers that would never occur to an unworried person in the same situation.

When these three types of neurotics become bored, it is only after prolonged torture, and even then boredom is infrequent. This type of boredom represents an unconscious defense against the reproach of the inner conscience, which claims that the fantasies and defense mechanisms are masochistically enjoyed. To ward off that reproach, reactive boredom appears in consciousness.

Abortive reactions of the same sort are observable when a person ponders a problem for a long time and is unable to find a solution. After a while the unsuccessful thinker gets "bored." The inner conscience has seized on the vain concentration of psychic energy for purposes of torture, and the ego's defense is, "I don't enjoy failure, I am bored with it." At the same time, the narcissistic ego is *denying* the defeat by means of the very same defense.[7]

* * *

Infantile megalomania plays an interesting role in boredom, especially in extremely narcissistic people. Every duty, every activity which is in any way forced upon one, is perceived as an offense against infantile delusions of omnipotence and therefore rejected. Worse, the superego takes advantage of this exaggerated narcissism, and levels an accusation of passivity and psychic masochism. The very activity, therefore, which when voluntarily performed is seen as "pleasurable" and "diverting," is rejected at any hint of pressure and scorned first as "intolerable" and later as "boring."

Schopenhauer had a very faint inkling of that fact, or one could benevolently conclude that he did. He wrote:

> And the extremes meet; for the lowest state of civilization, a nomad or wandering life, finds its counterpart in the highest, where everyone is at times a tourist. The earliest stage was a case of necessity; the latter is a remedy for boredom.

* * *

---

[7] To show the difficulties of the differential diagnosis, I am adducing an example. A hysterical girl, full of buoyancy and "pep," active in her self-chosen profession and "never bored," had this to say about a week-end visit to a married girl friend in Philadelphia:

"This was the most boring week-end of my life. That middle-class milieu, that routine of child care, that harmless husband—brr, I shudder at the idea that *that* is marriage. But my friend seems to be quite contented."

My patient's psychic conflict centered on an unsolved attachment to her father. Her inner conscience accused her—and quite justifiably—of being unable to find the "right" man to marry because of her unconscious reluctance to leave her father. Analytic interpretations activated the latent conflict. In her friend's house, she was confronted with a typical and evidently rather pleasant marriage. To ward off the superego's reproach, pointing out that she was unable to achieve even such a marriage, she identified with her friend's fancied boredom. She had to distort the facts to construct her alibi, since she admitted that her friend seemed content. First she created her mirage, "My friend *cannot* like her home, her husband, and child; she must be *inwardly* bored, even if she doesn't show it," and then she identified with it in order to prove, "It isn't my attachment to father that keeps me from marrying; I stay single because marriage itself is a boring, antiquated institution."

The young lady's alibi was not too successful. After returning to her own home, she felt depressed. She explained this depression as the aftermath of her dull week-end; actually it was the punitive effect of the inner conscience's reproach.

The example shows that boredom can be used to bolster up other neurotic defenses. The case is not typical; it is reported as a warning against simplification.

Mr. X. is an example of a bored person who is also a bore. He is of Dutch extraction and aristocratic descent. His wealthy father was a hobby-scholar who specialized in Roman history; although a tense person, he was fond of preaching to his family. His mother was a hysterical, easily excitable person, irrational in her educational methods. She would at times be over-solicitous about her only child's welfare, giving him minute instructions about what to do and what not to do; at other times she was totally preoccupied with herself, and forgot him entirely.

The child was left a good deal alone. At an early age he had developed a detached and taciturn attitude. He felt "empty," unhappy; he resented any interference from his parents and disliked their "preaching." He objected to any affectionate contact with them, and especially detested the family custom which required him to kiss both parents before going to bed. "I never could understand the pleasure people get out of kissing," he commented. Although his attitude towards his parents' mode of life was one of revulsion, he accepted—and even exaggerated—their code of mediaeval honor. One of his ancestors had participated in the sixteenth century war against the Spanish occupation of Philip II while another had been a governor of Java. The family fortune stemmed from these two forbears; with the fortune came the concept of "honor" as the greatest of all virtues and cowardice as "the most detestable of vices."

Precisely why this man should have accepted his family's archaic code of honor, while rejecting virtually all of their other ideological dogmas, remained at first unclear. Consciously his attitude towards the Roman virtues cherished by his father was one of scepticism.

During his rather checkered school career, the patient had been a poor and inattentive pupil on the whole, except for a short period during adolescence when he became interested in history. At that time he wrote a short pamphlet attacking all historic writing, quoting such authorities for his stand as Napoleon ("History is a fable agreed upon"), Carlyle ("History, a distillation of rumor"), and Henry Ford ("History is bunk"). In this foray against his father's life work, he was following in the footsteps of a cousin, an unsuccessful writer who was given to ironic comments on his "successful" relative.

When the patient's brief stage of interest in history passed, it had left some marks on the father-son relationship, for the father had resented the boy's scorn of his hobby. The father was rather startled, too, when his son suddenly shifted from "intellectualism" to single-minded devotion to "sport and nothing." The boy's sport was swimming, and he became a champion. The "nothing" department, as the father called it, referred to the boy's boredom and boresomeness, both of which became so pronounced that they could no longer be overlooked. "Nobody in our family, not even our dead ancestors in their graves, is as dead as that boy is," complained the indignant old man.

The patient himself finally became aware of being "inwardly dead". His long and unbroken silences, when he realized them, appalled him, and he consoled himself with the biographies of strong and silent heroes like Lord Kitchener.

His life was empty; he found even swimming competitions "boring." He lost his championship in a strange way. Weeks before the date of the contest in which he would defend his title, he had become convinced that he would lose. He had "tossed it out" in his own head, a procedure which he described as follows: "I emptied my head of all thoughts, which was not difficult anyhow because all I had in my head was worry and emptiness. Then I tossed a coin in my imagination. I lost. All that happened weeks before the race—I was beaten before I started. In the first few seconds of the race I was convinced that something would happen, but to my surprise nothing did; all went well. I was so surprised that I was preoccupied with my own thoughts, and lost the title in the last few seconds. My competitor didn't beat me, my surprise did."[8]

After a few years spent aimlessly wandering from country to country, he enlisted in the Netherlands army and received a commission as a reserve officer. The Netherlands resistance collapsed quickly, and he was captured by the Nazis. He spent four years in a prison camp. This tragic interlude, surprisingly enough, made very little subjective impression on him. He had hardly any specific recollections of these years; his recollections had not been repressed, they were merely non-existent. Day followed day monotonously in prison—but this was no change from his previous life. On the contrary, he found camp life actually less boring, for he was occupied with an anxiety: did his fellow officers consider him a "coward," or had he behaved "properly" during the short campaign against the Nazis? He dwelt upon his combat fears, and asked himself why he was personally so inadequate—was he a coward?

That thought overshadowed everything else—personal danger (for S.S. guards frequently killed prisoners, allegedly for "attempting to flee," for "rebelliousness," for "disobeying orders"), personal misery, the fate of his country. Reality hardly touched him, and his fellow prisoners were deceived by this into thinking him a tower of strength, a person they could look up to. This reputation was furthered by his historic name, and his former prominence in the world of sports.

After the war, the old boredom and boresomeness continued. He came

[8] As far as the problem of "bores and bored" is concerned, this case is complicated by its undeniable schizoid elements.

to the United States to "amass new impressions." What he meant was that travel was one of his ways of hunting for an antidote for boredom.

In his analysis, it became obvious that he was completely aware of being a bore. In a detached way, he complained about his inability to hold a person's interest. He seldom mentioned his own boredom, even though he knew only two mental processes: worry about being a "coward," and "deadly boredom." He could not even depend on his anxiety to counteract boredom: "When I worry for some time, I get bored."

The man had virtually no day dreams with pleasurable contents. "I have no imagination for anything unreal. On the other hand, my imagination plays havoc with me when it takes up my disagreeable past. I don't just relive situations in which I acted like a coward. I make the crime worse by building in stories that never happened, mostly to the effect that people noticed every small detail that showed me up as a coward."

In Mr. X.'s "fits of boredom"—which meant all the hours of the day when he wasn't worrying—he was very "jumpy." He would try to read a book, lose interest or fail to understand the author's meaning, smoke one cigarette after another—or rather, light a cigarette, take a few puffs, throw it away and light another—drop in at a movie and leave after a short time, etc. "I often ask myself: does it make sense? Is life worth the trouble it takes?"

His conscious sex life was practically non-existent. Early in life, he had discovered that he suffered from premature ejaculation; connecting this manifestation in some way with his "cowardice," he gave up the "senseless effort." Twice he had been "in love," each time with a girl who did not care for him. He had not even told one of these girls about his feelings. Girls who showed him that he "was welcome" bored him. He claimed that he did not remember the fantasies connected with the "remnants of my sex life" after waking from a sex dream.

One fact was undeniable, though Mr. X. never formulated it in this way: the only boredom-antidote he ever discovered in his round-the-world travels (which left only the most superficial and uninteresting impressions) was *worry*. As long as he was busy worrying about his cowardice, he was not bored, merely tense and full of reproaches. Gradually, however, that avenue of escape became blocked as well. His observation has already been noted: "When I worry for a long time, I get bored." It goes without saying that X. did not consider worry to be an antidote to boredom, simply because it was consciously so disagreeable.

Descriptively, X. completely lacked a sense of humor. He never made a joke, or appreciated one. He never smiled. He knew laughter only from observing it in others. He spoke in a monotonous way, with only minute vocal modulations. Even his complaints were recited in a matter of fact tone. He never felt any emotions towards people: "Sometimes a little pity for their silly illusions."

His very person emanated boredom. Mr. Logan Pearsall Smith (see p. 235) would have said of him that his presence could make the stickiest room feel air-cooled—cooled with the aroma of death.

For a considerable time his analysis made little headway. His inner cuirass of coldness made the emotional experience of the analytic situation a mere exercise in intellectualism. His high I.Q. made for speedy understanding of the masochistic components of his personality, but there the matter rested. His own complaints bored him, his life history was quickly exhausted, his dreams never remembered. He began to ask me when I would lose patience with him, saying—not without reason—that no fee could compensate for enduring his atmosphere of boredom. I explained that we were not closeted together to amuse each other, and that he was repeating, in his transference situation, the resistance he felt when his parents had tried to change his attitude.

The patient then asked, with a tinge of irony:

"Don't you want to change me?"

"Not in the infantile sense you assume. You're not hurting me by being obstinate, as you did hurt your parents. Analysis is an attempt to give you ammunition to use against your neurosis. Whether or not you accept and use this ammunition is your business."

One day Mr. X. remarked—still in his usual matter-of-fact tone— "You seem to have a much better time with other patients. I've often observed you laughing with another patient as you both left the appointment room. That never happens with us."

"Don't you see that your complaint is an echo of your childhood? True, you now make the complaint unemotionally, but in your childhood the missing emotion must have been present. It is not visible now, so it must be repressed."

"You are wrong there. I suffered from too much, not too little attention. I resented their constant interference."

"That's what you consciously remember. You resented all the preaching, teaching, scolding and exhortation you got from both parents, because you felt—obviously without justification—that their only interest in you was to mold you according to their principles."

"What's wrong with that?"

"The point is what you felt about it. You constructed the fantasy of being unloved and became masochistically attached to it."

"How can you prove my resentment? I accepted their standards on honor and cowardice. Didn't you say so?

"I didn't. What I claimed was that your inner conscience took up their mediaeval tradition because it could be used for purposes of torture. Just look what you did with it. Instead of living according to your quixotic code, you took these unattainable precepts and tortured yourself with them for forty years. And it isn't even true that you accepted your parents' slightly antiquated ideas. You exaggerated these ideas and made them into a caricature just so you could reduce the code to absurdity. 'Your silly precepts are good for only one thing—you can torture yourself with them,' you said. And you do."

"I still don't see any connection with my deadly boredom."

"You seem to think that analysis is a *fault*-finding expedition. No. We are on a *fact*-finding expedition. These facts point conclusively to the direct connection between your resentment and your boresomeness. In being a bore, you are perpetuating the irony directed at your parents' preaching and teaching attitude. You take over the role of bore that they played by preaching to excess."

"If I could laugh, I would do it now. Unfortunately, that's a gift I didn't get from nature. You are making the fantastic claim that I—the greatest bore in the world—am playing a diabolical joke on my parents."

"You are. But the joke is on you. You are damaging yourself. Just imagine the extent of the self-damaging tendencies required to act out the boring attitude of an educator in reverse."

'That's strange."

"It is. There is another argument proving my point. I am speaking of your pamphlet on the fallacies of history. Was that resentment against your father, or wasn't it?"

"It was irony against history."

"History is an abstract concept, personified for you by your father."

"I am sorry, but I see only contradictions in this. On the one hand, you claim that only a psychic masochist of the first order is capable of damaging himself the way I do—by being a monumental bore in order to reflect my parents' attitude. On the other hand, you are saying that I was aggressive to my father. Make up your analytic mind—is it one thing or the other?"

"The contradiction exists only in your fantasy. I have explained, again and again, that you are basically fixated on the rejection level. That means that you are a lover of disappointment, refusal and rejection, and you settle for punishment in general. Your inner conscience objects to this form of enjoyment, and so you are forced to create an unconscious defense mechanism, or in other words an alibi. Your weak alibi was your short adolescent period of fake aggression. Doubly fake, because the aggression directed at your father must have been shifted from your mother—why else would you have fallen in love only with women who would reject you?"

A few days later the patient came to his appointment and asked, slightly ironically, "You pigeon-holed the question of my being a bore. What about my boredom?[9] Don't forget that."

"Are you aware that you just used a dash of that precious commodity, irony? Be careful; next time you are liable to laugh and disturb nature's pre-determined course."

A faint innuendo of a mirthless smile appeared on the patient's face. He looked like a man who had found vinegar in his ice-cream, but who somehow knew that he had put the vinegar there himself to play a practical joke on someone else. "That doesn't answer my question," he said.

"It was not intended to. Speaking seriously, your boredom comes from a combination of three ingredients. First is your superabundant masochism. Is there agreement on that score, or shall I go through the rigmarole again?"

"I know enough about that."

"Thanks. The second ingredient is equally important: your lack of imagination. You must have been a Peeping Tom as a child—all children are. Your conscience is incessantly accusing you of sexual peeping, and therefore you don't dare use your imagination for pleasant fantasies. Your imagination is productive only when you torture yourself with pictures pertaining to what you call cowardice."

"I have no recollection of being a peeper at all."

"That proves nothing. Don't forget that recollections conveniently preserve the inner alibis. Let's take, for example, your aversion to kissing. Don't you think it possible that your aversion was preceded by—the opposite?"

"I doubt that. I cannot imagine finding any pleasure in that occupation. I consider the Eskimo nose-rubbing no more senseless. I cannot imagine getting any pleasure from either. For me, the two are identical."

"You forget that you had no experience with nose-rubbing in your childhood, though you had some experience with kissing. Didn't you say that your mother alternated between too much affection and complete coldness?"

"Are you going to tell me, again, that I am acting out her attitude—her coldness?"

"Perhaps. To return to your peeping. There is another proof at hand—indirect but very impressive. It ties up with the third prerequisite for boredom—shaky sublimation. Did it ever occur to you that the only sublimation you ever approached was swimming? Otherwise, you weren't interested

[9] Mr. X. was "jumpy" in his "spells of boredom." According to the findings reported earlier in this chapter, he must have been fighting a libidinous aim. He was; he was battling against his masochistic wish. That was warded off with pseudo-aggression, turned against himself because of inner guilt. This explains his "jumpiness."

in anything. And don't you exhibit when swimming? With your body, your skill, your movements? We know that exhibitionism is but an inner defense against peeping."

"But then why didn't I shift my exhibitionism to something else when I got too old—and, as you claim, too masochistic—for swimming competition?"

"That's exactly the point. As your neurosis progressed, the defensive alibi of exhibitionism was rejected more and more."

"A good point—if true. How can you prove it?"

"Very simply. After you lost the championship you traveled through many countries and visited famous places all over the globe. Look at your meager exploits. What did you observe? And mark that observing has some connection with peeping. Well, what did you observe? To quote your own words, you noticed that street cars are green in one city and red in another. How remarkable! All the beauties of a tour around the world were lost on you—because of your peeping-inhibition!"

* * *

In his specific inner tour de force, the bored person exorcises his internal Frankenstein, the unconscious conscience, by compromising with his inner inhibitions. In a situation of acute danger, this may seem a good solution; on a long-term basis, the solution itself becomes dangerous. As James Russell Lowell said, "Compromise makes a good umbrella, but a poor roof."

The alibi of boredom is dangerous from the standpoint of the internal economy; nobody can thrive on a diet exclusively composed of "being a good boy." That is the expedient of the bored person, but he soon finds that libidinous admixtures are necessary, even for his meager meals.

It is true that his life is not so completely stripped of pleasure as it seems at first glance. Since he is a psychic masochist, he derives unconscious pleasure from his conscious displeasure. Consciously, he is unaware of this; consciously, he is entirely miserable.[10]

* * *

[10] Bored people are prone to the use of satisfactions provided by the mouth zone as minor antidotes. They are chain-smokers, or chain-lighters-of-cigarettes; they chew, drink, nibble, gnaw pencil-ends and cigarette holders. Some observers have concluded from this phenomenonologic evidence that bored persons are orally regressed (by "orality" these observers understood simply "greed"). Nothing of the kind is clinically visible. In a dangerous situation, all people—regardless of the stage of regression—revert to familiar channels of reassurances. The oral reassurance is one of the first experiences in life. In their helplessness, bored people revert to the first of all remedies, only to discover that not even that panacea helps.

Here are a few descriptive statements from bored people:

Mr. C.: "Boredom is rather tragi-comic, and still I consider it one of the most painful experiences. At first I feel ashamed of being bored—as if it were some personal deficiency. Here I am—a person who considers himself intelligent—and still I can't feel any interest in anything. I've tried everything to counteract an attack of boredom: reading, listening to the radio, eating, drinking, even sex. All in vain. The only thing that helps, stupid as it may be, is running to a movie. In general, when I'm not in one of my bored periods, I'm rather choosy about my intellectual diet. In my spells of boredom I flee to the nearest movie. It doesn't matter if I like or dislike that particular type of movie; it doesn't matter if I've seen the movie before. And when I'm in the movie, I sit there in some sort of a daze. I don't concentrate on the action on the screen, and I don't care. But looking, just stupidly staring, helps a little, at least."

Mr. D.: "People always ask me why I look so bored and disgusted. That's the fault of my long head; people with long heads often give the erroneous impression of being depressed and bored. Amusingly enough, when people tell me that I look bored I'm not bored; I'm just thinking. But if people ask me whether I'm in pain, then I'm really bored. When I first noticed my facial expression in the mirror during an attack of boredom, I was really amazed. It was the face of an unhappy person, acutely in pain. It's difficult to describe the feeling I have in such situations. It is as if my skin were not large enough, as if I would 'jump out of my skin.' I remind myself of a fish out of water, stranded on the beach, making all kinds of helpless and convulsive movements. What it amounts to is a complete emptiness in my head, combined with excessive jumpiness, dissatisfaction and discomfort. I think it's interesting that my facial expression doesn't correspond to my feelings; I'm not aware of suffering any pain. *Extreme jumpiness—that describes it best. . . .* There was one time, a few months ago, when I suffered real mental pain during such a seizure. I was with some people, not too interested in them, and they were talking about Joe Louis. Suddenly I got my attack of boredom. They noticed that something was wrong, and I had to assure them that I wasn't having gall-bladder pains, or appendicitis. Then somebody said, 'Of course you, the great artist, aren't interested in so profane a topic as boxing.' I left the room and —believe it or not—I cried like a little child. I *am* interested in boxing."

Mr. E.: "I get the creeps when I think about an attack of boredom. I classify them—big and small attacks. The first kind takes a whole day; the mild ones last from half an hour to two hours. My big attacks are really something. *I am not exactly paralyzed, but in effect I am.* For all practical intents and purposes, I am—dead. I cannot move. I have no energy at all. My head is empty. I am always reminded, afterwards, of the mediaeval Spanish king who, because of his religious fanaticism, spent one hour every day in his future grave. I cannot describe the feeling precisely. I feel helplessly alone, like I was propelled into some strange planet, cut off from every living soul. It is like a full-dress rehearsal of death: utter desolation, utter loneliness, utter nothingness."

Mr. F.: "Boredom is more than a disease with me, it's a curse. In general, I'm a jolly fellow, good company, and even witty. But when the curse of boredom comes over me, I'm a wreck—good for nothing, either for myself or for others. My wife knows that and she leaves me alone; she tells people that I have a 'splitting headache.' What irony! My disease has to be hidden from strangers. My wife claims that boredom is not a presentable excuse; people wouldn't understand—they'd think I was bored with them in particular. So, to avoid offending people, I officially suffer from headaches. Somebody should rehabilitate boredom! The strange thing about boredom is that everything I find amusing in quiet times—meaning un-bored periods—becomes drab and unattractive. I lie on my couch without moving; I'm too disgusted even to change from an uncomfortable position. . . . In quiet times, I like to eat, and every evening meal is a pleasure. I collected a great many quotations about eating. Byron supplied several:

'All human history attests
That happiness for man—the hungry sinner!—
Since Eve ate apples, much depends on dinner.'

And:

'That all-softening, overpowering knell,
The tocsin of the soul—the dinner bell.'

Samuel Johnson said this: 'For a man seldom thinks with more earnestness of anything than he does of his dinner.' My wife and I often tease each other with quotations about our gourmanderie. In my quiet times, the dinner gong is really the 'tocsin of the soul'; when I'm bored, the word changes its spelling and becomes 'toxin'—I can't even get up enough energy to eat. If boredom left me the vitality to talk, which it doesn't, I would then quote a rather tragic statement by Byron:

'Indigestion is that inward fate
Which makes all Styx through one small liver flow.'

I don't know whether Byron meant psychic indigestion as well. Boredom is more than one Styx—it's a dozen of them . . . "

Mr. G.: "I cannot concentrate my energy on any one topic for any length of time—I get bored too easily. For me, boredom means depression, emptiness and the inability to find something worthwhile to do or think. At these times, I have a gloomy outlook on life. I often think that we are spending our time in an idiotic attempt to fill our hours with some trash. The *trash*—whatever we happen to be doing—*is debunked at times, and these times are technically called boredom.* I remind myself of my childhood; I was always inclined to boredom. My mother used to be my entertainer and the master of ceremonies for my routine; she was always directing my attention to some fun or what she called fun. Most of the time I was sulky. Now, I try to be my own master of ceremonies—I am no more successful than she was. What a life!"

Mrs. H.: "I am two people in one: an efficient publicity director and a *bored idiot.* The 'bored idiot' part of me comes on me unexpectedly, like fever. When it hits me I'm no good for anything: dull, incapable of thinking or listening—even to jokes. I leave the office, go on a buying spree—and then return the clothes and hats I buy, because *even my taste deteriorates.* Finally I give that up, too—go home, mope and suffer. Would you believe that even three Martinis don't pep me up?"

* * *

This question now arises: Is the problem of weak object-relationships not involved in boredom to an appreciable degree? Theoretically, one could assume that the alysotic's feeling of emptiness is an outgrowth of his poorly developed ability to love. After many comparative studies, I have come to the conclusion that this factor does not contribute anything to the genesis of boredom.

My reasons are as follows. First of all, we find that alysotics are composed of all types. Some alysotics have excellent attachments to wives or husbands; some have neurotic attachments; some are emotionally dead. If the ability to develop normal human relations constituted an antidote to boredom, spells of alysosis would be impossible for happily-married people. That assumption simply does not conform to clinical facts. On the other hand, if poorly developed object-relations were a boredom-promoting factor, every neurotic would be bored. Again, the assumption does not correspond to clinical facts. Some neurotics are bored; some are not. It has already been stressed that three large groups of neurotics seem to be virtually immune to boredom: hypochondriacs, obsessionals, depersonalized people (see pp. 222ff.). These groups owe their immunity from boredom to the fact that their voyeurism is not impaired.

The second reason flows naturally from the nature of neurotic attachments. *Neurotics are incapable of tender love.* That statement is unequivocal; it pertains to all neurotics, and leaves no room for exceptions. The neurotic's approach to the object of his attachment is not love but "transference." Transference denotes the continuance of attachment to infantile images. This ' unfinished business" is projected on outsiders, who are used—like a movie screen—as background for re-enactment of the old, though unconscious, conflict.

The decisive argument against the theory that weak object-relationships contribute to the genesis of boredom is the clinical observation that boredom is basically a scopophiliac disease.[11] The outstanding ingredient in the "triad of boredom"—inhibition of voyeurism, psychic masochism, shaky sublimation—seems to be the element of neurotic peeping. *A person with unimpaired imagination just isn't bored.* The antidote is too powerful.[12]

* * *

The best of all possible worlds is full of injustices, and both bores and bored have reason to complain about it. The bore is generally viewed as an inferior, rather stupid person. The opposite qualities are conceded to the bored; the popular notion is that the bored person is mentally so superior that conventional pleasures leave him cold.

Why this stereotype? Objectively, the bored person may be a half-moron; his sickness still gives him the cachet of "superiority." The bore, on the other hand, may have a high I.Q.; he will still not be spared the misfortune of being considered a half-moron.

The only excuse for the popular idea that a bore is inferior is the fact that he frequently seems to be unaware that he *is* a bore. His apparent obliviousness to an obvious fact leads the unperceptive to the notion that he is "dumb" and dull.

Neither the demotion of the bore nor the elevation of the bored would be possible if people realized that both disabilities are the result of intrapsychic conflicts, and have nothing whatever to do with intellectual activity.

Sometimes a bore is defined as a pompous person who "lacks humor." This accusation complicates matters and adds another burden to those already carried by the unfortunate bore, but it is not an accurate description.

A bore, descriptively speaking, is a person who habitually bores others. Some bores are aware of their unhappy attribute, some are not. In any case, the yardstick is the reaction of the environment.

[11] In my original publication, I suggested that alysosis be subsumed under "scopophiliac diseases," with depersonalization and erythrophobia, two diseases previously described as based on other scopophiliac difficulties.

[12] There exists a different type of "something like boredom," for which I suggested the term "*pseudo*-boredom." It consists of an anticipatory tendency of imagining future events and being "bored" when they really happen. The real reason is ego's fear of the superego's "reopening the case." For elaboration see *The Superego*, pp. 228ff.

The bore has a bad press and no defenders. Here are some examples:

> But there are certain people I simply can't put up with. A dreariness and sense of death comes over me when I meet them—I really find it difficult to breathe when they are in the room, as if they had pumped all the air out of it. Wouldn't it be dreadful to produce that effect on people! But they never seem to be aware of it. (Logan Pearsall Smith, *All Trivia*)
>
> Sherry [Thomas Brinsley Sheridan] is dull, naturally dull, but it must have taken him a great deal of pains to become what we now see him. Such an excess of stupidity, Sir, is not in Nature. (Samuel Johnson)
>
> Always the dullness of the fool is the whetstone of the wits. (Shakespeare, *The Merchant of Venice*, V. II. 59)
>
> "L'ennui me tue."
> "Je le crois; il n'engraisse que les sots."[13]
> (Beaumarchais; Rosine's complaint and Figaro's reply, from *The Barber of Seville*)[14]
>
> The man who lets himself be bored is even more contemptible than the bore. (Samuel Butler, *The Fair Haven*, Chapter 3)

"Dreariness and sense of death"—"difficult to breathe when they are in the room"—"excess of stupidity"—"dulness of the fool"—"contemptible"—the poor bore is buried in epithets.

The best literary description of a bore in modern literature is to be found in Aldous Huxley's *Two or Three Graces*. The bore, the heroine's husband, is always discussing Finnish finances, and is quite unaware of his audiences' reactions.

Clinical analysis of bores shows conclusively that the superciliousness and scorn which are the general approach to the problem (see the above quotations) are meaningless.

I have analyzed a long series of bores, and I am convinced that the chronic bore is unconsciously acting out a very complicated game. Unconsciously he is making use of a mechanism which is a subdivision of the negative magic gesture.[15] He is demonstrating, via caricature, a masochistic complaint directed at the main educator of his childhood. In effect, he is saying to

[13] "Boredom is killing me." "I believe you; only fools fatten on it."

[14] The first appearance in English literature of the familiar phrase, "bored to death" was, as far as I could discover, in Dickens' *Bleak House*, 1853. It is a reference to Lady Dedlock: "My Lady Dedlock says she has been 'bored to death.' "

[15] In general, a negative magic gesture denotes an unconscious demonstration of how one did *not* want to be treated in childhood. It is a dramatized caricature of the upbringers. The bore uses this frozen caricature, demonstrating the end results of his resentment at the way he was treated as a child, in combination with the objectionable attitude of his upbringers. For elaboration, see *The Superego*, pp. 123ff. Infantile megalomania is no less visible in the bored than in bores. The construction of the negative magic gesture is one of the slave revolts of the masochistic elaboration of megalomania.

that educator: "*My behavior will show you how you bored me.*" And he proceeds to dramatize the boring actions and attitudes of the authority in his past (see previously reproduced case history).

The aggravating obtuseness of the bore, his obliviousness to the "deadening" reaction others get from his presence, is also an *unconsciously dramatized irony*: "You, boring educator, had no idea of how you bored me!" The same holds true for the monotony of the topics chosen by the bore, and even for the deadly sameness of his tone and delivery. The same theme and the same manner are repeated ad infinitum. The unconscious irony here, again directed at the educator, is: "You are always pounding away at the same thing!"

Of course, only an over-dimensional psychic masochist can go to such length of self-damage in order to exact revenge for the wrongs done him in the past. The bore's demonstration—"See what you did to me!"—is too little and too late for revenge, but not for self-damage.

I also get the impression that the boring attitude is maintained because the superficial—though unconscious—aggression against the main educator (in my cases, originally always the mother) can subsequently be used to provide an intrapsychic alibi of aggression. That alibi becomes increasingly necessary as the inner conscience continues to reproach the psychic masochist for enjoying self-torture. Here the defense, "I'm aggressive," becomes useful.

The old rule warning us never to underestimate people is confirmed again in the case of the bore. Here is a person who seems to lack any trace of a sense of humor, yet *his attitude is a dramatization of an unconscious irony*! Consciously, of course, this makes him no more amusing.

Why is the reaction to a bore frequently one of antipathy, sometimes bordering on fury? Clearly, this can only be answered by studying the furious reaction itself.

Again the key to the problem is the inner conscience. The person so easily provoked to fury prides himself on not being a bore, and can even prove his contention by means of witnesses who esteem him precisely because he is "good company" and "has a sense of humor." But his own superego is not among these applauding listeners. On the contrary, it points ironically at the bore who is so intolerantly rejected and says, "That's you—at times." To counteract that accusation, the bore is regarded with antipathy and indignation.

La Rochefoucauld's aphorism is to the point here; he said, "We forgive people who bored us, but never those whom we bored."

* * *

Another characteristic of both the bore and the bored person is that of a faulty sense of humor, as expressed in ability to make or appreciate jokes. The reason for this impairment is found in the disposition of inner aggression in each case.

The bored person is under concentrated attack from his inner conscience, which has usurped all the aggressiveness in that particular personality. The bored person's defense is the intrapsychic proof of inner emptiness and dissatisfaction. But compensatory aggression is required for both producing and enjoying jokes. The bored person's inner depository possesses neither; he is busy fighting for his life in Frankenstein's battle of annihilation.

This state of affairs explains the typical statements of bored people to the effect that they "dry up" during a spell of boredom. This applies to all bored people, to those whose sense of humor is good in "quiet times" and to those whose sense of humor is always poor. To quote from the descriptive statements reproduced earlier in this chapter:

> *Mr. F.:* In general, I'm a jolly fellow, good company, and even witty. But when the curse of boredom comes over me, I'm a wreck—good for nothing, either for myself, or for others.
>
> *Mrs. H.:* When it hits me I'm no good for anything: dull, incapable of thinking or listening—even to jokes.

The old saying: "Even the most beautiful Parisian cannot give more than she has," applies here with some modifications.

There is an even more important element involved in the bored person's "drying up" attitude. He wants to prove to his inner conscience that he does *not* enjoy himself, as the indictment claims. That attitude of pronounced suffering also contributes to his inability to make or take a joke.

What about the *bore*'s sense of humor? He shows it only unconsciously, as has been pointed out. His whole attitude represents frozen irony directed against the boring educator; that attitude is his personality. The bore's pompousness and his conscious imperviousness to wit are one of the prerequisites and part of the paraphernalia of his unconscious role.[16]

* * *

Another constituent of the "sense of humor" is the ability to be "a good sport." That implies that you must be the opposite of a killjoy; if a joke is directed against you, you must take it gracefully and "in your stride." Most people are more or less wanting in this respect; even long training often produces no better than a sour smile combined with inner anger.

[16] A specific subdivision of the bore's lack of humor is his tendency to tell a stupid joke in a monotonous voice, and to laugh idiotically at his own "joke." This, too, is unconscious irony at the expense of his upbringers.

If either a bored person or a bore is put to this test, it will be found that the bored person does not see the joke at all, but knows that he should. This realization increases his feeling of inadequacy, and he consequently flees company. Sometimes he feels unjustly treated; the wits have "kicked a man when he is down."

The bore, on the other hand, does not understand the joke at all. Often he takes the joke as a serious statement, and argues about it. The outer world, again, takes this attitude as proof that the bore is a dull and impossible person. The bore's intrapsychic situation is more complex. His failure to understand jokes directed against himself is a complicated revenge on the boring educator with whom he fights an anachronistic and never-ending inner battle. The bore will not take the chance of easing the situation; his formula seems to be: "I have you now where I want you, and you will not escape with a few jokes."

It may seem contradictory that bores and bored persons, both of whom possess such substantial stores of psychic masochism, should never take themselves as butts of a joke. The explanation lies in the nature of the self-punitive joke; it represents an attempt at narcissistic consolation, and such consolation would counteract the inner aims of either the bore or the bored person.

In his autotomy, the bored person attempts to prove to his inner conscience that he is a good boy, a sober boy who never smiles. He accentuates his depression, therefore, to serve as alibi.

The inner irony of the bore, as has been said, consists of playing the role of the boring educator; his attitude represents the latter's boring behavior. Even a trace of irony, therefore, would diminish the effectiveness of his "proof."

The cheerless result in both cases is identical, though it stems from different sources. It is the total absence of that type of humor in both the bore and the bored person.

In general, one can state that people "without a sense of humor" are neurotics of the "bores and bored" variety. And there are no spontaneous "self-cures" among these neurotics. This automatically disposes of the aristocratic pride of people who boast of possessing a "good sense of humor" and look askance at the less fortunate. It would be equally logical to feel superior to someone who suffers from cancer, for neurosis is *the* psychic cancer.

* * *

Two basic convictions are required for the maintenance of the individual's psychic equilibrium. First, he must convince himself that his current aims are worth striving for and have meaning. Making allowances for the ability to delude oneself (the most remarkable and best-developed quality in the entire psychic apparatus), all will then go well—until the inner conscience intervenes. If there is such intervention, it is proof that the individual has failed to fulfil the second prerequisite: that of convincing his inner conscience that he is a "serious" person with adult aims. *Not to be taken seriously by one's own inner conscience is the greatest psychic tragedy that can befall mortal man.*

It should never be forgotten that the inner Frankenstein, unconscious conscience, is the creation of the individual but not his friend. The inner conscience is always ready to scoff ironically at the individual's current aims and ambitions, frighten him by showing them up as senseless, and to say, "This is all rubbish; you are still playing with childrens' toys." In defense, the victim hides his "toys," empties his head—and is bored.

Viewed from this unexpected angle, boredom is still a bargain. A transitory spell of boredom is easier to bear than fear. In general—though it is never a matter of choice—people prefer being bored to being frightened. This is proven by their intrapsychic actions. An unknown author of the late 19th century wrote a stanza called "The Solitary Way," which is illustrative:

> There is a mystery in human hearts,
> And though we be circled by a host
> Of those who love us well and are beloved,
> To every one of us, from time to time,
> There comes a sense of utter loneliness.

Translating from poetic into psychological language, this means that from time to time the superego tells you that all your attachments are valueless, that you are basically alone, as you will be in your *lonely grave*.[17] This last innuendo is one of the cruelest weapons in the superego's armory.

When the inner conscience launches these attacks, it devaluates the individual's aims, attachments, hopes, illusions, and nods in the direction of the grave. This may, perhaps, explain why so many expressions in all languages associate bores and bored people with death. "Bored to death" and "bored stiff" are perhaps the commonest of many familiar cliches. Logan Pearsall Smith has already been quoted: "A dreariness and sense of death comes over me when I meet bores—I really find it difficult to breathe. . . ." Bores and bored people cast a shadow of the inevitable, and the reaction is to "hate it like death."

[17] The Pantheon in Paris awards to only one woman the high honor of resting beside her husband, who was an astronomer and geographer. The woman's merit consisted of the fact that she died on the same day as her husband—out of love. The majority of loving wives do not go this far; the grave, even if they do, remains a lonely place. Here is one time when the superego deals with cold, hard fact.

The other half of this reproach of the inner conscience is an echo of childhood, when one of the most frequent admonitions the individual heard was: "Stop playing; do your homework." The dichotomy between play on the one hand, and serious work—meaning duty—on the other, was much stressed. The inner conscience uses this archaic reproach for purposes of torture. The reproach scores the neglect of work for play, and not vice versa, only because work is more torturing than "play".

Under normal conditions, the adult preserves a limited "right to play." He has wrested this right from his anti-libidinous inner conscience. In the case of the more neurotic person, the inner conscience is in full control, and makes no such concession.

That differentiation explains why neither bores nor bored people are found in the ranks of the not-too-neurotic. Even so-called normal people, however, may have transitory spells of boredom. These are unavoidable, and are especially apt to occur after external defeats, which automatically increase the power of the inner conscience. External defeat makes it possible for the superego to say, ironically, "I told you so." And the senselessness of all aims is then outlined in vigorous and convincing terms.

* * *

When boredom is both recurrent and quantitatively pronounced, it represents a neurotic disease. The general public is largely unaware that this disease exists, and that it can be psychoanalytically cured. There is no reason to assume that dissemination of this knowledge can be achieved either easily or with celerity, nor is it likely that such dissemination would induce many bores, or bored persons, to undertake treatment. Both types have in their psychic make-up a good dose of psychic masochism, and psychic masochists unconsciously want to suffer. Why interrupt the "natural" cycle?

To venture a guess, I would say that the much maligned, "stupid" bore will consult the psychiatrists of the future more frequently than the "highbrow" bored person. Regardless of whether the bore admits the fact, or camouflages it successfully, he feels that he is "inwardly dead." Moreover, the bore is a nuisance to his environment, while the bored is a nuisance only to himself. Public opinion, which unjustifiably favors the bored person, can be a propelling factor.

The bored are to be counted among the most misunderstood of all people; the bores among the most maligned. Popular opinions regarding both are based on simplifications and misunderstandings, fostered by the typical attitude of the "highbrow" who adds his contribution of superciliousness and derogation to current misconceptions. As Samuel Butler said in another connection:

> The public buys its opinions as it buys its meat, or takes its milk, on the principle that it is cheaper to do this than to keep a cow. So it is, but the milk is more likely to be watered.

* * *

Disillusion tends to lead to bitterness and cynicism, and bored people tend to excel in both qualities. There is no advantage to be found in whistling their neurotic tune, popular as it may seem to be at times. Hawthorne once pointed out that "life consists of marble and mud." One should also bear in mind the quantitative distribution: a great deal of mud and a small marble niche.

Nobody needs to be told that life is no picnic, that hopes do not always materialize. But it is absurd to say, as a bored and depressed patient once said, that Samuel Hoffenstein's "between the cradle and the grave lies a haircut and a shave" should be "enlarged with a few shattered illusions, and you will have the entire contents of life." It cannot be denied that people live, emotionally, on the basis of fantasies. And as long as these fantasies are harmless and pleasurable, nobody cares:

> When I could not sleep for cold,
> I had fire enough in my brain,
> And builded with roofs of gold
> My beautiful castles in Spain! (James Russell Lowell, "Aladdin.")

10. Corrupted Laughter—Anti-New, "Directed," and Prostituted

I told him Mr. Johnson's bon mot upon the innovators: that truth is a cow that will yield them no more milk, and so they are gone to milk the bull. Rousseau said, "He would detest me. He would say, 'Here is a corrupter, a man who comes here to milk the bull.' "

James Boswell, *Dialogue With Rousseau*

THE DIGNITY of man is also upheld by the incorruptibility of laughter. Man can "sink as low" as his psychopathic trends or even his criminosis will allow him; he can sell his opinions, his principles, his freedom of expression. But he cannot prevent his *involuntary* laughter from coming to the surface; he has no control over that. Even in an absolute dictatorship, jokes against the regime are created, circulated, and relished.

Laughter is a private matter; an "inside arrangement" between the unconscious ego and the superego. Since even psychopaths and criminotics possess accusing inner consciences,[1] there is no exception to the rule that the ego counterattacks and deflates by means of laughter.

This eulogy of laughter does not blind us to the observable fact that laughter can also be used for unsavory purposes. Three situations, in the main, lend themselves to the corruption of laughter.

I. LAUGHTER AT ANYTHING NEW

Without exception, the initial greeting extended to an innovation is indignation mixed with laughter, or its variant, laughter mixed with indignation. The stand-pat bore uses the first, and the stand-pat would-be wit the second technique. Johnson's ironic stab at men who "milk the bull" is paradigmatic.

Now, the new is as likely to be reasonable as to be foolish, but novelty per se guarantees neither merit nor the lack of it. The objection here is to the automatism of the initial reaction of laughter. This laughter is not selective. It is impartially bestowed upon both reasonable and foolish innovations; both are new, ergo both are laughable.

[1] Unfortunately, the conscience of the psychopath or the criminotic, because it works differently from that of either the "normal" or merely neurotic person, does not prevent impossible actions at their outset. The penalties, none the less, are very much in evidence. For elaboration see *The Superego* and *The Battle of the Conscience*.

Innovators have always been emphatically indignant at this "unexpected" reaction. They have pointed out that the universal risibility excited by the new, merely because it is new, is a decided impediment to progress. This attitude has at times been so pronounced that Percy Williams Bridgeman once exclaimed, "There is no adequate defense, except stupidity, against the impact of a new idea." But their indignation, while highly vociferous, has also been highly unrealistic and therefore meaningless. The new cannot be accepted with immediate enthusiasm, for everything new is *inwardly frightening, and for this reason is automatically rejected—at first.* An innovator who does not take this attitude into account beforehand is naive or masochistic—or both.[2]

The history of every invention, of every new idea, attests to the universality of this initial rejection. As already stated, the Frenchman, Leban, was mocked and ridiculed for his invention of gas light; the first test of gas light was made by the city of Manchester years after Leban's death. Before that, nobody would believe that there could be artificial lighting without the use of a wick. When railroads were first built in Europe in the early 19th century, the authorities took the precaution of asking the medical faculty of the University of Munich to assess this innovation's probable results "on the mind." The learned body concluded that the passengers would be endangered; more, mere onlookers would suffer from serious vertigo. They prescribed the building of high fences on both sides of the tracks. When Edison's "talking machine" was first exhibited in Paris, a high technical authority "exposed" it as a typical American hoax; he explained that a ventriloquist was concealed in the audience. Even after the invention of the telegraph, the British were unconvinced of its utility until a telegraphed message from a provincial town to London enabled the police to capture a murderer before he got off his train in the London station. This feat gave the people "food for thought." And the ridicule heaped on Freud is only recent history.

II. "DIRECTED" LAUGHTER

"Laughter kills," claims a French proverb. That is an exaggeration, of course, but it is true that laughter is an effective weapon. Unfortunately, this weapon can be used in two ways—to promote or to demote a good cause.

In political campaigns, for example, laughter is used as a weapon by *all* parties, and to further both worthy and unworthy causes.

An interesting sidelight is the by now half-forgotten story of how the famous caricaturist, Thomas Nast, helped considerably to overthrow

[2] For a discussion with an innovator who reacted neurotically to the initial rejection of his ideas, see pp. 342ff. of *The Superego.*

William Tweed, then political boss of New York. The effectiveness of Nast's cartoon attacks on Tweed can be gauged by an anecdote recounted in Denis Tilden Lynch's "*Boss*" *Tweed* (Boni & Liveright, New York, 1927).

Nast was visited at his home by an officer of the Broadway Bank, the chief depository of the Tweed Ring. He had heard, he said, that someone had offered to send Nast abroad to study art. Was he going? Nast was not going; he did not have the time. But he would be paid, the official persisted; one hundred thousand dollars would be given him. Could he get two hundred thousand, Nast inquired. Possibly, said the bank official, adding that Nast needed a rest, needed to study, and in addition might be getting into trouble with the Ring. Nast then asked if he could perhaps get five hundred thousand for the trip. The official agreed that he could get half a million dollars in gold for dropping his campaign against Tweed and leaving the country. Nast laughingly refused, saying that he had made up his mind to put some of the members of the Ring behind bars, and intended to do it. The banker then left, warning the cartoonist that he might get himself into a coffin before he got the members of the Ring behind bars (p. 364).

In democracies, the use and misuse of laughter for political purposes is relatively harmless; some principles may be temporarily distorted, but the basis remains intact.

In dictatorships—meaning countries under the heel of a megalomaniacal or shrewd criminotic—laughter is one of the important propaganda arms of the regime. One should not underestimate the power of irony, distortion and caricature, as used by Goebbels and his Russian imitators, in attacking external and internal political enemies.

III. PROSTITUTED LAUGHTER

This type of laughter is created by people who would sell their souls for the honor of arousing a laugh. They are not exactly interested in hurting the object of their attack; their choice is incidental rather than spiteful, and their main interest is in "getting a laugh." A famous poet and columnist once reviewed a production of *King Lear* for a midwestern newspaper. He wrote: "Last night a visiting actor, who shall be nameless, played King Lear. He played the king as though he expected someone to play the ace." I have no data on whether this devastating comparison was justified or not, and I know no more of the critic's ability as a critic than that he was reputed to have had "a nice personality." This example, therefore, is used only as a hypothetical possibility. Assuming that the performance in question was *good*, the type of person who prostitutes laughter would have used the derogatory joke *anyhow*.

In a different connection, Frank Norris alluded to this type in *The Pit*:

He's the kind of man that gets up a reputation for being clever and artistic by running down the very one particular thing that everyone likes, and cracking up some book or picture or play that no one has ever heard of.

This neurotic is under constant pressure, because of the reproaches of his superego, hence his pseudo-aggressive defense is an inner necessity. If these people have power, they misuse it.

This anecdote from *The Goncourt Journals* (Doubleday, Doran, 1937) is illustrative:

> If people only knew the kind of thing it is that induces Sainte-Beuve to write a book! We found him today all in a dither over a plan to do a book on Mme. de Stael and her circle, to serve as a pendant to his famous work on Chateaubriand, with the same viper's nests as footnotes; and this, not out of interest in Mme. de Stael, not because he had been fascinated by certain new materials, but simply in order to annoy the De Broglies [relatives by marriage], whom he detests. At bottom, there is a malicious monkey in Sainte-Beuve. (p. 256–257)

11. Ego's Dread Lest the Internal Wit-Tables be Turned

The superego is a brutal teaser.
From the author's *The Superego*

IF OUR MAIN THESIS—that laughter is an internal debunking process, plus, directed at the superego through the creation of a substitute victim to be thrown to the inner lions—corresponds to clinical facts, it necessarily follows that the unconscious ego must live in constant dread of the possibility that the superego will take over the weapon and use it against the ego. This seems to be the actual case; we can deduce this fact from the ego's frantic effort to nullify the superego's cruel irony by making it *unintelligible*. In its end effects, this tactic on the part of the ego results in a diminution of astuteness or intellectuality, or in the presence of peculiar blind spots in an otherwise keen intelligence.

In *The Superego*, I expressed the suspicion that the use of symbols in the unconscious, (for which Freud stipulated two reasons—archaic language and circumventing the "censor"), serves a third purpose as well. The symbolism of the unconscious saves the conscious ego pain and humiliation, because of its very unintelligibility.

One can adduce a number of phenomena in support of this deduction: the "rules of torture"[1] stemming from the superego; dreams; certain facets in hypnagogic hallucinations; "senseless" repetitive words, tunes, pictures "creeping into one's mind."

I. THE SUPEREGO'S "RULES OF TORTURE"

In *The Superego*, I elaborated on the twelve rules of torture, according to which the inner conscience conducts its "business" of torturing the ego. These are:

Rule 1: The anti-hedonistic principle is paramount.

Rule 2: Although all-powerful, the superego pronounces its judgments in accordance with specific mock-rules of procedure.

Rule 3: The peculiar formalism of the superego is one of the few direct loopholes in an otherwise impervious system.

Rule 4: The superego adheres to the rules of procedure in still another point: there must be "proof" that the forbidden wish or defense is really harbored by the culprit.

Rule 5: Wish and deed are equated.

---

[1] For further elaboration, see *The Superego*, pp. 19ff.

Rule 6: No excuses, justifiable or otherwise, are accepted.

Rule 7: The superego camouflages its cruelty by accepting the cultural standards of the specific environment.

Rules 8 and 9: Both failure and success can be converted into material for torture.

Rules 10 and 11: Immediacy of torture and irony in delayed, though over-severe punishment are rules invoked at different times by the superego.

Rule 12: The superego understands but one language: that of force.

Of these rules, numbers 7 and 11 are especially tinged with irony.

The camouflage which the superego assumes in accepting the environment's cultural standards (rule 7) leads naive observers to the faulty deduction that the individual is the product and mirror of his surroundings. If we assume, for the sake of argument, that the superego's exclusive interest is in torturing the ego, the nature of the particular prohibition used as pretext for torture certainly cannot matter. The common denominator is still a series of 'don'ts.' On the other hand, the acceptance of the specific taboo (which will of course be one of a group which varies in each cultural orbit) imposes an odd restriction on the superego. Anti-libidinous as the inner conscience is, it is helpless in the face of actions approved by the specific environment.

As for rule 11, which deals with irony in delayed rather than immediate torture, this delayed-ironic cat and mouse play in which the superego sometimes indulges is in seeming contradiction to the rule of immediacy of torture. This play goes so far that the torturer even allows some kind of elation (or at least optimism) in the period between the setting of the trap and the denouement—punishment.

To cite a banal example. A woman patient who neurotically hates housework (this trait is just being analyzed) "forgot" an analytic appointment by confusing the day of the week. . . . During the whole forenoon, she did her housework merrily, to her great surprise, only to drop into a deep depression *after* realizing (hours later) that she had been fooled.

II. DREAMS

It is impossible to reproduce the long deduction, elaborated on in *The Battle of the Conscience* and *The Superego*, based on the Jekels-Bergler formula:[2] every dream represents unconscious wishes *and* refutation of superego reproaches. The attack of the superego which the dreamer tries to refute is frequently couched in malicious irony.

[2] First presented in "Instinct Dualism in Dreams," paper read at the XIII International Psychoanalytical Convention, Lucerne, 1934. Published in *Imago*, 20, 383–392; 1934. Translated: *Psychoanalytic Quarterly*, 18, 325–350; 1949.

Here is an example of an anti-fallacy dream, a type commonly encountered during analysis as a result of the analyst's effort to debunk the patient's "basic fallacy"—his erroneous picture of his real childhood situation, or misuse of that situation for unconscious purposes—for the purpose of revealing his true conflict. The superego maliciously misuses the analytic clue for its own anti-libidinous purposes.

A patient who was being treated for premature ejaculation had as his basic fallacy the fantasy that he was an innocent victim of his mother's cruelty. Actually, he was masochistically attached to her. After his fantasy had been repeatedly exposed as false, he dreamed that his mother was in the hospital, asking to see his sister-in-law. Associations dealt with two separate facts: his mother's actual illness, and the early days of his own marriage. His mother was dying of cancer; this had not changed the family's habitual quarrelsomeness, nor lessened the enmity between the patient's wife and his mother. This enmity had begun when the patient abruptly announced to his mother—the day before his marriage—that he would be married "tomorrow." Infuriated, his mother refused to attend the ceremony. There were endless quarrels between the two women subsequently, though the lion's share of provocation came from the patient's wife.

As usual, analysis could prove that the patient's mother was in no way the direct cause of his neurosis. The mischiefmaker was the patient's own unconscious masochistic attachment, which he kept alive by constant provocation. His "inability" to keep the peace between his two warring women was typical, as had been the "invitation" to attend his wedding. His masochistic attachment also explained why he had chosen to marry a second edition of his nagging and disagreeable mother. Officially, he had married to escape his mother; unconsciously, he had selected a wife who duplicated his mother's unpleasant traits. His marriage, therefore, was not the "escape" he believed it to be, but a continuation of unresolved infantile trends. His whole life reflected this technique of masochistic provocation, warded off with pseudo-aggression. His refusal of sex based on oral regression confirmed this: he "gave," but mockingly, in a way unconsciously calculated to deny the woman pleasure.

In this dream, which occurred after this material had been worked through for a few months in analysis, the superego proved to the victim that his comforting "basic fallacy" was pure nonsense: "Mother gives, even when you provoke her; she still wants to see your wife (represented as her sister in the dream). And besides, she is dying of cancer, and you won't give up your fake grudges!"

An especially malicious note is struck by the identification of the patient's wife with her sister. The patient had always thought his mother "half-crazy." At this particular time, the family was much worried about his sister-in-law, a highly neurotic person who had recently developed paranoiac ideas. In the dream, therefore, the inner conscience asks: "What right do you have to accuse your mother of craziness? What about your wife's family?" The identification of wife with sister-in-law strengthens this reproach, since it hints at their inner similarity. The ironic theme of the dreams seems to be: "Look who's finding fault." Only one weak attempt at a counterattack comes from the unconscious ego. In an attempt to take the blame for the lesser crime, there are hints of the patient's identification with the sick sister. This is a double admission: of unconscious feminine identification and of psychic illness. This latter admission includes a pseudo-aggressive implication: "If I am sick, it's my mother's fault—isn't she half-crazy?"

A more vigorous example of defense on the part of the unconscious ego is found in the "neurotic vindication dream," though the superego's malice maintains its usual high level.

A woman of forty-four, an orally regressed neurotic, dreamed: "My mother-in-law sends me a present for my second wedding anniversary. It is a neatly wrapped package containing horse-manure. An accompanying note explains that the manure 'blossoms' only once in a hundred years. My husband asks me seriously to thank his mother for her present, and objects to my use of the word "manure' in my letter. He wants me to use a more refined word."

The patient's mother-in-law was wealthy, aggressive, rather crude, cynical and purse-proud. The patient neurotically misused the older woman's aggression; she was unable to resign herself to the mother-in-law's tactlessness. She also accused her husband of taking sides with his mother against her. The husband was a pedantic person who constantly corrected his wife's "inelegant" language. The "blossoming" of manure (anal conception of sex) related to the patient's guilt about her age and myoma, and therefore her inability to have children.

The dream begins with the ego's counter-aggression to the superego's reproach: "It is not true that I'm masochistic. My mother-in-law is really aggressive, and my husband backs her up." There are ironic thrusts at the mother-in-law's stinginess and the husband's pedantry.

But the inner conscience persists in its accusation of psychic masochism—the accusation which prompted this type of dream to begin with. "You couldn't get pregnant if you tried for a hundred years. You are old (a hundred years old). And even if your mother-in-law is impossible, she has a right to be disappointed in you because you can't have a child." The ironic defense comes forward again at this accusation: "That old horse of a woman [the mother-in-law actually had what is called a "horse-face"] can't produce anything but sterile sons." The blame is thus shifted, and "vindication" achieved.

Another patient, who in the process of being cured of writer's block had already resumed creative productivity, dreamed: "I was at a party, quite the center of attention, holding the floor. Suddenly someone (or was it I?) said condescendingly: 'Not bad for a journalist'."

The superego's irony is directed at the patient's ability as raconteur, which had not been affected at all by his writing block. Delivering a telling blow, the inner conscience points out: "You are—at best—a story teller; as a story writer you're merely—a journalist."

III. HYPNAGOGIC HALLUCINATIONS

The "hypnagogic hallucination," described but not explained[3] by Silberer, is a phenomenon which may be observed in situations of drowsiness upon awakening, or before going to sleep. The initial thought is rational; it is followed by the flash of a dream-like picture, which is then dismissed with a slight feeling of surprise. The original train of thought is then resumed.

A patient reported a "dream-like" picture, and asked whether it should be described as a dream. Before going to sleep the previous evening, he had been making fun of the methods of analytic interpretation, dwelling particularly on the constant emphasis placed on "so-called unconscious connections." This pleasant diversion had lulled him into a half-sleep; suddenly he saw the picture of "an uncanny being, who gripped me under the arm and hovered with me over a deep abyss." When the patient awakened—and he stressed the fact that only a few seconds could have elapsed—he was astonished at the "picture" he had seen, and rather surprised that it had caused him no feeling of anxiety. He was perfectly calm. He then thought of Mephistopheles, and—forgetting Faust—went on to draw some more ironic parallels between psychoanalysis and the subtleties of the Talmud. He continued in the trend of thought he had pursued before the "picture-experience."

When I asked the patient for associations, there was a short pause and then he exclaimed: "Now I know where I got the scene. In a series of reproductions of details of Luca Signorelli's frescoes of 'The Damned' in the cathedral of Orvieto, there is a scene in which the devil is carrying a man to hell. The whole picture I reproduced is simply a satire on psychoanalysis."

I happened to be familiar with the Signorelli frescoes, and with the book of reproductions to which the patient alluded. By taking the book down from my bookcase, and confronting the patient with the very fresco in question, I was able to convince him that he had altered two details. The figure of the "damned" is not a man at all, but a woman, and the devil is not gripping her under the arm but carrying her astride his shoulder and

[3] Elaborated in the author's "An Inquiry Into The 'Material Phenomenon'," *Intern. Journal of Psycho-Analysis* (London), 16, 203–218; 1935.

forcing her arms down. The evidence could not be disputed, and the patient did not attempt to do so. He even volunteered the connection himself, interpreting the "pictures" as his unconscious, passive feminine wishes. All the anger of the patient was based on exactly that interpretation.

To reconstruct the situation which preceded this "flash": The man is ridiculing analysis—which had confronted him with the contention that he harbored feminine identification. His defense is counteracted by a superego reproach confirming the interpretation. The unconscious ego changes the impact into a "senseless picture" which the patient shakes off—investing it with a slight feeling of surprise. He then reverts to his previous line of defense. Without that strange and successful unconscious expedient, the patient might very well have been sleepless and depressed for hours.

IV. SENSELESS WORDS

The insistent echo of a word that has no apparent relevance, or of a scrap of a tune, or the repeated mental picture of a locality that cannot be placed, is a phenomenon which sometimes intrudes into an ordinary, rational activity such as working, "logical" thinking, reading, writing, talking. The typical reaction is surprise combined with a minor degree of irritation; even that reaction appears only when the repetitions persist for any length of time. The phenomenon never becomes really torturing.

I have come to the conclusion[4] that this manifestation embodies a severe inner reproach leveled by the superego. The element of "senselessness" and the absence of conscious understanding are the work of the unconscious ego, which thus frees the conscious ego from the need to pay penance. The conscious feeling, which would otherwise be guilt, is transmuted into mild surprise, or at the worst mild annoyance.

A patient complained: "I woke up at four in the morning and couldn't get to sleep again. Nothing was really bothering me, except a vision of—a protruding eye. I know how foolish it sounds, but there was this protruding eye, and it kept me faithful company until I got up to keep my appointment with you. The eye is hard to describe. I don't even know if it belonged to me or to someone else. My own body was like a sham, or a jellyfish."

"How about a few associations?"

"I know that trick. I've tried it. No results."

"How do you know you will still get no results when you try it now?"

"I just know."

"You shouldn't predict. Let's have it: what about protruding eyes?"

"The only thing that comes to mind is a girl friend of my wife's. The girl

[4] In "A Senseless Word is Persecuting Me," *Bulletin Tohoku University* (Japan) 6, 33–49; 1937. Enlarged in "Small Change Of Guilt Feeling," the *Psychiatric Quart. Suppl.*, 23, 54–62; 1949.

really has somewhat protruding eyes, perhaps because of a slight case of Graves' disease. My wife raves about her; she claims that this girl is the only nice person we know."

"What do you mean by 'nice'?"

"A friendly, kind person. Not one of those bitches."

"Your distaste for associations is quite unjustified. You have just solved the riddle."

"I don't get you."

"Let's connect a few loose ends. After long inner conflicts, you divorced your first wife—a kind, friendly person—because you were not sexually attracted to her. You attached yourself to your present wife, not in spite of her aggressive nature, but because of it. She satisfied your wish—your unconscious wish, to be sure—to be kicked around. We have discussed these connections again and again. You yourself have admitted that your recent divorce made you jumpy, although you shifted the blame very plausibly to guilt at having made your first wife unhappy. Yesterday you reported that your ex-wife had called you up. Your conscience picks up the thread, and in an innuendo tells you: 'You are a weakling (jelly-fish). You cannot stand real love and kindness, which were provided by your first wife'."

Here the unconscious ego is at its work of neutralizing severe reproaches. Only an image—highly symbolic and therefore highly unintelligible—becomes conscious. The unintelligibility of the superego's reproach has an attenuating effect; it is only mildly disturbing.

The disadvantage of the technique, of course, lies in its tendency to diminish the radius of intelligence. This is a quality which it shares with all other internal techniques of defense which require a large expenditure of psychic energy.

A person's intelligence can be defined as a credit balance. The ego's ability to evaluate objective reality correctly and quickly is its original capital; deductions are made from this capital in order to pay psychic debts; the residue is the ego's working intelligence. Just as an owner who sells a mortgaged house receives only the difference between selling price and mortgage, the individual intelligence must be viewed as a *net* figure; it is what remains after the priority payment to the unconscious has been made.

This "inner mortgage" weighs heavily on the individual who must expend much psychic energy in order to keep painful, shameful and guilt-laden infantile material in repression, or who must always be on the alert to elude conscious pain by camouflaging superego attacks. When a disproportionate portion of psychic energy goes for this purpose, comparatively little remains at the service of objective reality, and intellectual deficiencies and restrictions become visible on a neurotic basis. Neurotic "stupidity" is a sure indication that the inner "mortgage" has been too high.

The single items comprising that "inner mortgage" which affects intellectuality are as follows:

1) Furnishing of suitable defenses when the internal situation becomes so precarious that defense is more important than objective understanding. Inner defenses are built for the purpose of proving "innocence" to the accusing inner conscience. *When objective facts conflict with inner defenses, the inevitable loser is mental keenness.* To quote Juvenal, "There is nothing a man would not believe in his own favor." The neurotic who is under attack from his superego will readily believe distortion of facts or even the most bare-faced prevarication. The inevitable result is neurotic restriction of intelligence.

2) From a purely quantitative viewpoint, there is an automatic ceiling to human working intelligence, since every human being has only a specific amount of psychic energy at his disposal. When psychic energy is diverted in quantity to the unproductive field of neurotic defense, the residue cannot be imposing.

3) The limitation increases with the automatic progress of the neurosis. Every neurosis is a progressive and not self-limiting disease. For example, a person who is fighting off his specific repressed masochistic tendency will, as his basic defensive tactic, attempt to avoid this one isolated danger spot. He will fail. Elaborating on his fundamental tactic, he will attempt to avoid *all* feelings, not merely masochistic ones. As a result, he will become blank to an increasing number of areas of understanding.

4) There is still another restriction of intelligence in the form of an instinctive "horror of self-knowledge," which can be observed as a generalized phenomenon. Unfortunately, intuitive knowledge of others presupposes the ability to achieve a split-second identification with the object of observation. What, however, happens if this identification brings the individual into the dangerous vicinity of a topic tabooed in himself? Complete avoidance is the answer, and the result is the complete inability to comprehend the other fellow and the facts surrounding his situation.

* * *

Why don't we laugh in dreams? The question has seldom been posed, and never been answered.

Freud proved that many of the mechanisms utilized in dreams are also part of the "wit-work," notably the triad: "condensation, displacement, and indirect expression." This would seem to indicate an affinity between the two products, but their differences are as salient as their similarities. According to Freud, the main difference between the dream and the witticism is a matter of "social behavior": the dream is a totally asocial psychic product, and its function is to "guard against pain"; wit is "the most social of all those psychic functions whose aim is to gain pleasure."

This last is a rather doubtful statement; primarily, wit is an inner alibi directed against the unconscious conscience. When dreams are deciphered, they frequently contain explosively witty material, and we can therefore conclude that wit is an inner alibi expressed symbolically in dreams as well as consciously during our waking lives. Why do we not, therefore, react with laughter in dreams?

One point can easily be understood: The savagely ironic superego attack, delivered in a dream, is neutralized to incomprehensibility by the unconscious ego *in order to save itself pain*. After all, the producer of the dream *is* the unconscious ego.

The reasons behind the ego's *neutralization* of its own defenses and attacks, on the occasions when the superego's rebuttal takes the form of irony and wit, are less easy to understand. But this is the case; the ego does supinely retreat. Why?

I would suspect that these six reasons account for the retreat:

1) The enormous condensation of any dream surpasses the condensation of any witticism. If "brevity is the soul of wit," hyper-brevity is the heart of the dream.

2) The ego is directly confronted with the monster, the superego; there is "nobody around" to be pressed into service as an ally. Freud's formulation must not be forgotten: wit requires three people—narrator, butt, and listener. It is possible that this solitary confinement with the dreaded enemy deters the frightened ego.

3) The ego's technique of "playing dumb"—as visible in the successful effort to deflate the superego's ironic attacks by rendering them unintelligible consciously; hence the hidden irony in defensive dreams is used only indirectly.

4) The use of symbolic language in dreams counteracts laughter in the first place; the innuendo in witticism must be translated. Since the dream language is not translated in the dream proper, laughter cannot occur.

5) It is also possible that lack of bodily mobility in dreams (the dreamer is motionless) prevents explosive laughter. We know that the "happy convulsions" called laughter have a connection with physical movement. The quite reasonable objection that the same point applies to crying (which does occur in dreams) can be refuted. Less motility is required, to begin with, and in addition crying can be used as a technique for influencing the superego: "See how I'm suffering!"[5]

[5] In an interesting paper ("Laughter in Dreams," the *Psychoan. Quarterly*, 14, 2; 1945) Martin Grotjahn, whose valuable contribution to the psychology of wit (in a series of eight papers) has already been mentioned, explains the rarity of laughter in dreams "by the highly asocial, individualistic nature of the dream, and the sociable nature of laughter." He concludes, "laughter in dreams constitutes partial awakening." Sensu strictiori, as pointed out in my text, laughter does not occur in dreams proper.

6) The decisive point seems to be the weakness of the ego. The ego does not dare to attack the superego openly. The most it can do is neutralize the steady stream of reproaches issuing from the superego. The ego's motto is still: ninety per cent scaring, ten per cent daring. This is so faithfully adhered to that the witticisms contained in a dream, though immediately evident to the analyst, are at first reported quite seriously by the patient, who shows no signs of understanding these witticisms until they have been interpreted.

12. Nothing New in the Wit-World

Quixotic is his enterprise and hopeless his adventure is,
Who seeks for jocularities that haven't yet been said.
The world has joked incessantly for over fifty centuries,
And every joke that's possible has long ago been made.

W. S. Gilbert

"OUR NEW THOUGHTS have thrilled dead bosoms," said George Meredith. "A new thinker, when studied closely, is merely a man who does not know what other people have thought," said Frank Moore Colby. "There is nothing new, except what is forgotten," is the contribution of Mlle. Bertin. And Lord Dewar quipped: "If Adam came back on earth again the only thing he would recognize would be the old jokes." If this is true of thoughts, how much more pointed it becomes when applied to wit, where the scope is much more limited!

Freud took cognizance of the limitations of originality in a little-known essay written in 1923 (*Josef Popper Lynkeus and the Theory of Dreams*, *Ges. Schriften*, XI, p. 295):

> Many interesting comments may be made about what appears to be scientific originality. When, for instance, a new idea appears in science, that is, an idea which is at first considered new and, as a rule, attacked as such, an objective research soon proves that it is not really so novel. Usually, the discovery has already been made, repeatedly, often at periods far apart, and has fallen into oblivion. Or at least it has had forerunners, has been vaguely anticipated or incompletely uttered. That this is so is only too well known and needs no further discussion.
>
> But the subjective side of originality is also worth considering. A scientist may ask himself whence have come the original ideas which he applies to his material. He can find, without great difficulty, the suggestions on which part of it is based, the data he has procured elsewhere and modified and further developed. The source of another portion of his ideas he cannot find so easily. He is forced to assume that some of his thoughts are created through his own mental capacity—though he does not know how; upon these thoughts he bases his claim of originality. But careful psychological examination limits his claim still further. It reveals hidden sources, long forgotten, from which his apparently original ideas have sprung. Thus, what has been forgotten he revives and applies to a new subject; replacing the presumably new creation. No regrets are necessary: we had no right to expect that "originality" could be derived from thin air and represent something incapable of more precise determination.

As Eddie Cantor wrote in his preface to *World's Book of Best Jokes* (The

World Pub. Co., 1943), "It's a little silly to write an introduction to *World's Book of Best Jokes*. You just don't introduce people to old friends."

Nothing new under the sun—not even in the joke department. And especially not in the core of the joke; the time, the place, the wrapping, the local color and the names all change, but the essence remains unvarying. The reason seems to be the uniformity of the repressed material used.

Robert O. Foote has written a delightful satire on this theme, centering about Joe Miller, the compiler of the jokebook so much admired by Lincoln. "Who was Joe Miller?" is included in Untermeyer's excellent anthology, *A Treasury of Laughter*, and it traces many familiar jokes back, not to their first, but to their first printed versions:

Humor, say philosophers, is the index of an era's sophistication. Because the present day laughs at broad jokes, it is inclined to fancy itself as tolerant; "modern" is the popular word. The stories we tell in mixed company would only have been whispered by grandfather to his barroom cronies. Ipso facto, we're pretty darn sophisticated. But are we?

Examine a case example: You see a cartoon—or will shortly when the gag men realize what they've been overlooking—which shows a young man getting out of bed in which still reposes a lovely dame. The caption says: "I think I'll get up and rest."

Now, except for the manner of its telling through the aid of a drawing reproduction process unknown to our ancestors, instead of completely by words as was necessary with them, that is the identical joke at which our forbears of two hundred years ago were snickering. Here is its exact wording, No. 164 in the now priceless first edition of *Joe Miller's Jests*:

"A Young Lady who has been Married but a Short Time, seeing her Husband going to Rise pretty early in the Morning, said 'What, my Dear, are you getting up already? Pray lie a little longer and rest yourself.' 'No, my Dear' replied the husband, 'I'll get up and rest myself.' "

Even then it was an old joke, like all of Joe Miller's . . .

While there is no record of any joke book having been compiled in English prior to the invention of printing, that innovation was applied to the service of laughter even before it came to the aid of piety. The first complete Bible in our language was that issued by Miles Coverdale in 1535; almost ten years before that, in 1526, there was issued the first jest book, called *C Mery Tayls*.

. . . Examination of copies of that earliest jest book . . . reveals that its conviction that marriage is an essentially comic matter to all but the victims, would easily pass current as keen wit in this day. Here is a specimen:

"A man asked his neighbor which was but late married to a widow how he agreed with his wife, for he said that her first husband and she could never agree. 'By God,' quoth the other, 'we agree marvelous well.' 'I pray thee how so?' 'I shall tell thee,' quoth the other, 'when I am merry she is merry and when I am sad she is sad, for when I go out of my doors I am merry to go from her and so is she and when I come in again I am sad and so is she.' "

. . . There were Farmer's Daughters in humor nearly four hundred years ago. Indeed, it is possible to trace with almost exactitude the time that she stepped into folklore. In that first jest book of 1526 is a story of a bridegroom who was forced to allow his bride to wait at the church, while at the instigation of the irate father of another sweetheart he made a pecuniary settlement upon the previous object of his affections. The point of the tale is that the bride, upon later wheedling the facts out of her new husband, proved herself above small reproaches. She was content to comment that the girl had been foolish to betray the affair to her father. She, the bride, had been carrying on, she said, in like fashion with a man-servant for a year but her husband was now the first person to whom she had ever made it known.

When the tale reappears a century later in *Archie's Jests* of 1639 (and much better told) the deceived sweetheart has become not simply the "mayd" she was in the earlier version, but a "Farmer's Daughter"—her first appearance as a stock character of ribald wit.

. . . The Elizabethans recognized the essentials of lasting humor exactly as we do. To every age its own language; to all the ages the same fundamental risibility.

[The Elizabethans'] primary conviction was that the fact of there being two sexes was quite a joke upon humanity; exactly the same imperishable joke to be found in the last issue of any smart magazine. Many of the jests of those gusty early Englishmen were sadly naive. Their practical jokes, their execrable puns, their witty retorts, their puncturing of ostentation, take a decided sharpening up for modern taste, though it is being done daily, in print and on the air. But when they wanted a belly laugh they went to the relationship of the sexes, just as we do.

Whether or not we do it any better is a matter of opinion. . .

To trace the development of such tales, which now appear again as the "very latest—stop me if you've heard it before," is a rare delight. Many such yarns, particularly the bawdy ones, have been printed over and over, down the centuries. . .

The Emperor Augustus, being shown a young Grecian who very much resembled him, asked the Young Man if his Mother had not been at Rome. "No, sir," answered the Grecian, "but my Father has."—*Joe Miller*, 1739.

A young Gentleman playing at Questions and Commands with some very pretty young Ladies, was commanded to take off the Garter from one of them; but she, as soon as he had laid hold of her Petticoats, ran away into the next Room. "Now, Madam," said he, tripping up her heels, "I bar squealing." "Bar the door, you fool," cry'd she.—*Joe Miller*, 1739.

A handsome Wench, for some suspicious business, being brought before a Justice somewhat late in the evening and he taking compassion of her because she was fair and seemed modest, wished the man that brought her before him, to take her home and lodge her that night and he would hear the case at length in the morning: "With all my heart," saith the man, "Master Justice, so you will commit my wife, which is now at home, to the jail till the morning."—*Archie's Jests*, 1639.

Upon a time Tarlton and his wife, as passengers, came sailing towards London a mighty storm arose and endangered the ship, whereupon the captain charged every man to throw into the seas the heaviest thing he could best spare to the end to lighten somewhat the ship. Tarlton, that had his wife there, offered to throw her overboard; but the company rescued her and being asked wherefore he meant so to do, he answered "She is the heaviest thing I have and I can best spare her."—*Tarlton's Jests*, 1570.

This sort of stuff demonstrates that humor has changed less the last four hundred years than in a thousand previous years. Joe Miller, despite the popular assumption of the contrary opinion, was not the first man to collect ancient wheezes. The very first of whom there is record was one Hierocles of the Fifth Century, about whose exact identity scholars still quarrel but about whose list of twenty-one alleged jokes there can be little dispute—they are the foundations of the most ghastly wit in all creation. Suffer through a few of the least intolerable; you probably have heard their revision within the last month on the air:

A scholar wishing to teach his horse to eat little, gave him no food at all; and the horse dying, "How unlucky," said he, "as soon as I had taught him to live without food, he died."

A scholar meeting a person, said to him, "I heard you were dead." To which the other answered, "You see I am alive." The scholar replied, "Perhaps so, but he who told me was a man of much more credit than you."

Hearing that one of two twins was dead, when he met the other, a scholar asked, "Which of you was it that died? You or your brother?"

A scholar in Greece receiving a letter from a friend who desired him to buy some books there, neglected the business. But the friend arriving some time after, the scholar said, "I am sorry I did not receive your letter about the books."

This latter is one of the standard jokes of the world, in every age and every language. Joe Miller's version of it is hung upon an Irish lawyer who left this note for his servant: "I am gone to the Elephant and Castle where you shall find me and if you can't read this Note, carry it down to the Stationer's and he will read it for you."

Which brings us back to the most famous of all humorists and the least deserving of the title. Almost exactly two hundred years ago an enterprising publisher gave to the English reading world its most universally accepted designation for an old joke—a "Joe Miller."

Too dead to resist, Joe Miller had immortality thrust upon him. He was a fairly popular actor who had died the previous year. Following the custom of the times, his name was hung upon the next London collection of supposedly funny stories, most of which he probably never had heard. The book, *Joe Miller's Jests*, became upon its publication in 1739 the first best seller on record and it has had the longest run in history. It is still being reissued, in modern guise. Joe Miller's chestnuts are never so stale but a re-roasting will revive their flavor.

Untermeyer comments: "It is impossible to decide which are *the* most famous jokes of all time. Every comedian has his own private (or public) stock, a collection which experience has assured him will always rouse the responsive laugh. But Eddie Cantor's edition of the *World's Best Jokes* differs considerably from Powers Moulton's *2,500 Jokes for All Occasions* and Bennett Cerf's not-too-strictly-contemporaneous *Try and Stop Me*. Josh Billings wrote ungrammatically but accurately 'There is very few good judges of humor, and they don't agree'."

Max Eastman sums it all up: "What are most jokes about, and what have they been about through the ages? Mother-in-laws, unpaid bills, drunks, taxes, tramps, corpses, excretory functions, politicians, vermin, bad taste, bad breaks, sexual ineptitudes, pomp, egotism, stinginess and stupidity" (*The Enjoyment of Laughter*, p. 25).

The list—while by no means complete—demonstrates the uniformity of human experiences and of the human fears which must be elaborated inwardly. Since the superego uses external reality as a hitching post for internal torture, the battered ego must defend itself by deflating and deriding this reality.

All jokes are "old"; only unsuccessful jokes die young, and are forgotten. But a good joke remains "fresh" even though it is "old," for it is perpetually transformed with new "make-up" to suit new circumstances and occasions. This is not so much a matter of conscious plagiarism as of a need to make use of the restricted number of situations which lead to the production of jokes.

Compare, for example, these statements made by people of different eras, backgrounds, and standards of culture:

> If you steal thoughts from the moderns, it will be cried down as plagiarism; if from the ancients, it will be cried up as erudition. (C. C. Colton, 1780–1852.)
>
> If you steal from one author, it's plagiarism; if you steal from many, it's research. (Wilson Mizner, 1876–1933.)
>
> They voted dry, and lived wet. (Popular American saying in the '20s.)

In all these, and similar utterances, one sees the child looking for contradictions in "adult" evaluations.

It is an accepted fact that witticisms are mostly permutations and adaptations, locally colored, of already established bon mots. Here is an example:

Daniel Spitzer, once-famous feuilletonist of the *Neue Freie Presse*, prefaced the second collection of his witty pieces published between 1871 and 1875 as follows: "I hope that my previous readers will approve of this collection—though not all of them. At an elaborate dinner party a very funny story was told which amused all of the guests. Only one young girl remained unmoved, or so it seemed to the gentleman sitting beside her. He asked: "Don't *you* laugh" —"Thank you," answered the well-bred lady, "I have laughed already."

Henri Bergson, in *Le Rire* (1901): "A man who was once asked why he did not weep at a sermon when everybody else was shedding tears, replied: "I don't belong to the parish." (p. 6)

Bennett Cerf used the same plot in *Try and Stop Me* (1944). In this version the setting is a women's club in New Jersey, and the occasion is a talk by a feminine book reviewer. When the speaker recited the plot of a tear-jerking novel, she was rewarded by sobs from every member of the audience except one, who sat calmly and collectedly through the recital. When the talk was over, the lecturer approached the lady and asked her why she had not wept. The answer was prompt. The dry-eyed lady was not a member of the club. (p. 115)

Similarly, some of my previous readers to whom primarily I am offering this collection, will modestly reject it and answer, "Thank you, I have laughed already."

These three examples are put side by side as testimony to the spontaneous regeneration of "old" jokes. Although no one can doubt that Mr. Cerf has heard of Bergson, the chances are against his having encountered Spitzer's satires, and the clubwoman of New Jersey was most likely innocent of contact with either Bergson or Spitzer. Moreover, the example illustrates the simplest way of "adapting" a joke; the difference between case two and case three is a mere alteration of local color. Spitzer's joke (and he died in 1893, eight years before the publication of Bergson's book and almost half a century before Cerf's) uses the same wit-technique, slightly modified.

Here are other examples:

Sir Thomas Browne (1605–1682) in *Religio Medici*: "The man without a navel (Adam) yet lives in me."

Bennett Cerf in *Try and Stop Me*: "A famous detective arrives in Heaven, and is asked to solve 'a little problem.' Heaven has by now become so overcrowded that Adam and Eve cannot be located. The detective immediately singles out a couple; they are Adam and Eve. 'How did you recognize them?'—'Elementary, my dear God,' answered the detective, 'they have no navels.' "

Napoleon: "Success in war means surrounding your enemy, routing him, driving him from the field. Success in love means—escape."

John Barrymore: "The only way to fight a woman is with your hat. Grab it and run."

The time lapse is shorter in this example, but still sufficient to establish seniority:

Oliver Herford: "A gentleman is one who never hurts anyone's feelings unintentionally."

Lillian Day: "A lady is one who never shows her underwear unintentionally."

To compare two other stories:

A bunch of village loafers were standing on the banks of the Hudson. They were throwing stones into the river to see who could make the longest throw. A tall, raw-boned, slab-sided Yankee, and no

An Indian Maharajah offers a prize of one hundred thousand rupees to anyone who can teach his favorite white elephant the English language. While instruction is going on, the candidate for mistake, came up and looked on. For awhile he said nothing, till a Yorker in a tight jacket began to try his wit on Jonathan.

"You can't beat that," said the Yorker, as he hurled a stone way out into the river.

"Maybe not," said Jonathan, "but up in Vermont in the Green Mountains we have a pretty big river, considering, and t'other day I hove a man clear across it and he came down fair and square on the other side."

His auditors yelled in derision. "Well, now, you may laugh," said Jonathan, "but I can do it again."

"Do what?" demanded the tight-jacketed Yorker quickly.

"I can take and heave you across that river yonder, just open and shut."

"Bet you ten dollars on it!"

"Done!" said the Yankee. Drawing forth a ten note, he covered the Yorker's shinplaster. "Can you swim, feller?" he asked.

"Like a duck," said the tight jacket.

Without further parley, the Vermonter seized the knowing Yorker stoutly by the nape of the neck and the basement of his pants, jerked him from his foothold, and dashed him heels over head into the Hudson. A shout ran through the crowd as he floundered in the cold water. He put back to the shore and scrambled up the bank.

"I'll take that ten-spot, if you please," said the shivering loafer, advancing to the stake-holder. "You took us for greenhorns, eh? We'll show you how to do things down here in York."

"Well," said Jonathan, "I reckon you won't take no ten-spot just yet, captain."

"Why? You lost the bet!"

"Not exactly. I didn't wager to do it the first time. Just said I could do it, and I tell you I can." And in spite of the loafer's utmost effort to escape him, he seized him by the scruff and seat and pitched him farther into the river than upon the first trial.

the prize will be splendidly lodged in the royal palace. The offer is magnificent, but there is a catch. If the linguist fails, he will be beheaded. No contestant offers himself. Finally, a wise old man accepts the challenge. His friends try to dissuade him, telling him he is committing suicide. "By no means," the wise man answers. "I did not say that I can do it at once. I asked, and was granted, a teaching period of ten years. In ten years many things can happen. The Maharajah can die; I can die, perhaps even the white elephant can learn English."

Again the Yorker floundered back through the icy water.

"Third time never fails," said the Yankee, stripping off his coat. "I can do it, I tell you!"

"Hold on!" said the victim.

"And I *will* do it, if I try till tomorrow morning," said Jonathan.

"I give up!" shouted the sufferer between his teeth, which now chattered like a mad badger's. "T-take the m-m-money!"

"Oh, well, if that's the way it's done in York State," said the Vermonter, pocketing the money, and coolly turning away.

The Yankee story dates from about 1820. It is from an anonymous book, *Green Mountain Boy*, excerpts from which are included in *Native American Humor* (collected by James R. Aswell, Garden City Publishing Co., 1949). The Maharajah story, as far as I have been able to discover, is not an Indian story at all. It derives from a Jewish joke, though further scouting might turn up an even earlier origin, perhaps Chinese.

One definite advantage stems from the fact that all jokes are composed of a universal theme adorned by a contemporary mutation. There are no plagiarism suits in the field of humor. Authors frequently claim that their "ideas" are stolen, but nobody seriously claims that a joke is exclusive property. All professional humorists know that some jokes are Joe Millers, but all jokes are Methuselahs.

One of the reasons for the constant "plagiarism" of jokes and witticisms is the *method of their dissemination—oral*. This "mouth-to-mouth" technique inevitably makes for confusion. A case in point concerns Somerset Maugham's *The Verger*, one of the three short movies presented a few years ago under the title of *Trio*. The plot of this piece is an ancient Jewish joke. The shammes (doorman) of a synagogue is dismissed from his position when it is discovered that he is illiterate. He emigrates, goes into business, and becomes a millionaire. On his seventieth birthday, an admiring journalist exclaims: "Imagine what you would have been if only you had been able to read and write!"—"I would have been the shammes in my little home town!" the millionaire replies.

This plot had also been used by an American writer, now deceased. His daughter saw the Maugham film, and wrote indignantly to the New York *Times* that Maugham had used her father's plot. Maugham counterattacked, stating that he had heard the story from an English surgeon, had never read the American writer's story, and had learned that this and similar jokes were to be found in the Talmud in any case . . . He then promised to study the Talmud.

A less excusable example is an error made by F. P. Adams in his book of quotations. He quotes Hegel's famous dictum: "If the facts are against me, so much the worse for the facts," and calls it "an old American saying."

The examples could be multiplied.

* * *

One can prove the contention that there is nothing new in the world of wit from another angle: by adducing jokes about one of the world's newest sciences, psychoanalysis.

Witticisms taking analysis as target are comparatively few in number; they are limited both by the complexity of the topic, and the obvious necessity of possessing specialized information before one can be witty at the expense of a specialized subject. Those witticisms which are in circulation are both poor in quality and narrow in scope; the almost invariable theme is the alleged naivete of the analyst. Most of them are either collateral or direct descendants of the following story:

> A woman consults an analyst. She explains tearfully, "My family thinks I'm crazy. And why? Because I like pancakes. Tell me, what's wrong with liking pancakes?" The analyst reassures her: "Of course there's nothing wrong with liking pancakes. I like them myself."—"You do!" cries the delighted patient. "I'll give you some of mine—I have a whole bureau full of them!"

Among the earliest jokes about analysis were an army of puns on "anal" and "anal-ysis." The Oedipus complex was also considered good material for witticism. This joke dates from about 1910:

> A hysterical girl consulted a famous physician; her complaint was that she was terrified of the man who hid under her bed every night. "Cut down the legs of the bed," was his advice, "there will be no room for him to hide." She did so, but consulted the physician again shortly afterwards. She was now troubled with the fantasy that a man was making a hole in the ceiling of her bedroom. Would the doctor advise analysis? "What for?" was the prompt reply. "An analyst will take three years to tell you that you wanted to sleep with your father; I can do it in one sentence."

The same line of thought produced the anonymous witticism:

> What's the difference between a weather-prognosis and an analytic prognosis? The former can be proved false the next day: the latter only a few years after it is authoritatively pronounced.

These examples betray the extent of the misunderstanding which surrounded the ABC of the analytic procedure.

Other jokes center about the money problem; in a not-too-bright comedy, for example, an analyst is made to say: "We must exploit all avenues, especially Park Avenue."

A more elaborate version of this theme produces a better joke:

Analyst (to patient): "What are you thinking about? What are your free associations?"
Patient: "*Free* associations? Nothing free here."

The more acute witticisms about analysis are the product of analytic patients, or of potential patients. Not that their products are particularly impressive, either—the bias behind the joke is too pronounced for that. Here are two examples of witticisms emanating from "insiders":

A patient once asked, ironically: "What's the difference between an analyst and a prisoner? That's easy—a prisoner changes his jailer every eight hours, an analyst every forty-five or fifty minutes."

A young man married an inexperienced girl just as he was emerging from analysis. His wife was alarmed and upset on their wedding night when he retired to the bathroom before going to bed, and remained there for an interminable time. Finally she got up enough courage to approach the bathroom and listen at the door. The bridegroom was monotonously reciting: "I should not forget that she isn't my mother."

Another joke is of particular interest because its ancestry can be so easily traced. The newest version of this theme is a thrust at analysis; the identical catch-line in a sexual setting was widely circulated about a decade ago, and this in turn is a lineal descendant of a Jewish joke dating from the eighteen-eighties. Here are the three jokes:

1950: A man saw a friend running desperately along the street. "What's wrong?" he cried. "Why are you running?"—"I'm due at my analyst's," the friend called. "If I'm late he'll start without me."

1940: A glamorous actress had been refusing an admirer's invitations for a long time, but he was not discouraged. He followed her about, interminably asking for her favors. He finally cornered her at a party, and she could not get rid of him. "All right," she agreed at last. "Here's my key. I'll stay on at the party for a while, but you go on to my apartment. And if you get tired of waiting, start without me."

1880: Two Jewish recruits of the Czar's army quarrelled. Since they were now soldiers, they decided to settle their argument in a soldierly way—by a duel. The challenge was issued, the seconds chosen, and time and place set for the duel. The challenger and his second arrived at the duelling place in good time, but the opponent did not show up. The hour had long passed when the second appeared in the distance, running at top speed. "Shmuel is coming, but he will be late," shouted the second. "He sent me with a message—if you're tired of waiting, start without him."

The following example deserves to be plagiarized, but I have encountered no variations on it as yet. A patient of mine, a well-known writer, was repeatedly "insulted" by confreres during his pre-analytic days: the "insult" consisted of their advice that he "do something analytic" about his protracted writer's block. His answer to this advice was invariably: "Why, I did—this year I consulted three analysts—and cured two of them." Bragging did not help.

Sometimes analysts are responsible for analytic jokes; what it really amounts to is the use of irony to reduce the specific resistance of the patient to absurdity.[1]

I once treated a professor of English literature whose difficulties included a linguistic purity complex: he saw red at every incorrectly used word, thus easily achieving his daily quota of self-torture. I told him: "When you start with the modest capital of one and one half million words in the English language, you can hardly go bankrupt. Why, you can even achieve the status of an 'injustice collector'."—"Don't use that word—it's simply impossible!"—"But why? Doesn't the language include the words tax collector, stamp collector, and garbage collector?"

A patient slipped on the carpet in my waiting room. Since he was in a phase of violent negative transference, he promptly though only half-seriously accused me of having placed that particular carpet that particular way so he would "break his neck." To make his projection clear to him, I

[1] Dr. Martin Grotjahn, who contributed a series of important papers to the psychology of wit, took up the problem of "the joke as technical means of giving interpretation" in his study, "Laughter in Psychoanalysis" (*Yearbook of Psychoanalysis*, VI, 1950). He finds that the method is "dangerous, like everything else in psychoanalysis, if abused." However, he points out that "by using the disguise of witticism an otherwise unacceptable truth can be made conscious." I fully agree with Grotjahn, and refer to my remarks concerning hypersensitivity of analytic patients towards irony, summarized in *The Superego*, pp. 265ff:

"The weak ego is an ironic ego, which explains why our patients are hypersensitive to irony directed at them. For a long time after I first made this observation, I interpreted it to mean that the infantile ego wants to be taken seriously; these patients complain that one is 'making fun' of them, and cannot understand that the irony is aimed, not at them, but at the infantile 'conflict solution.' Nor do they understand that this irony includes an invitation to an alliance and an identification, whereby they, too, can be inwardly above the situation, and even ironic at the expense of the neurosis.

"I see now that their protests arise from a much deeper source. Since irony is typically a part of the neurotic symptom or personality structure, neurotics are unconsciously wary of the danger of 'wising up' the superego. From their point of view, therefore, irony should be taboo—to the analyst. Moreover, in analysis the superego seems to be attacking on two fronts, for patients project parts of the superego on to the analyst. Thus, an ironic remark from the analyst means that they 'are being seen through' by the superego!

"Irony, therefore, is a powerful weapon in the hands of the analyst. This does not mean that one should 'make fun' of the patient—quite the contrary. It does mean that *irony can be included* with profit in one's formulations and explanations."

said: "You are worth more to me alive than dead. Just figure out the complications if you really injured yourself in a collison with the carpet. I would have to get you to the hospital, notify the insurance company, remove the carpet, lose a good patient, and so on. Convinced?"

A girl with a gold-digger complex consulted me for "advice" on whether she should marry for "love or money." I replied that the problem did not exist, because her neurosis made her incapable of loving. After some detours, she expressed the wish to go into analysis. "For what purpose? To become a better gold-digger?" "I resent the word 'gold-digger'."—"Very well, what would you suggest as a synonym?"

A patient was disturbed when he finally understood how extensively he had been damaging himself with his over-developed psychic masochism. At his next appointment, he referred to the problem as "the masochistic theory of analysis." I answered: "I suspect you are alluding to the analytic theory of masochism."

The "smart aleck" has a hard time when confronted with the analytic procedure: his main defense—that of playing "the wise guy"—does not work in this situation, and (which is more tragic) does not alter his problem. Nevertheless, he tries hard, as in this example:

"Why did you publish your monographs on frigidity and impotence as separate volumes? Why not combine both under the title, *The Ideal Marriage?*" I replied: "I am just about to follow your suggestion, with a slight modification, in the title of my new book, *Neurotic Counterfeit-Sex*."

Reluctantly, in response to his wife's urging, a man appeared at my office one day. His wife had reported him as "half-crazy with worries," but his attitude was one of indignation. First he called me Mr. Buttinski; then he made a crack about my name, saying ironically: "I've come in contact with a lot of crooks who pretended to be honest, and I must say that a man who *admits* right in his name that he's a burglar at least deserves credit for originality. Maybe he's even honest, who knows? Or is it a trick to divert suspicion in just that way?"

"First," I said, "you cannot spell. Second, I permit only patients who are outraged by the fee to call me a burglar. Third, by making this pun you freely admit to being a neurotic. I treat only neurotics, and in order to argue about the fee one must be a patient. Are you a patient?"

"Did you think up that answer on the spur of the moment?"

"Instead of investigating my personality and my quickness at repartee, you'd better tell me whether your wife's reports about you are true."

The bubble of good humor collapsed, and the curtain rolled up on his own tragicomedy—that of looking for security. Having saved some money, this man had decided that one couldn't get rich on being a C.P.A. (his own profession), and had fallen into the hands of promoters who sold him on the idea of riches through wonder cinder blocks. It turned out that the business had to be reorganized, a specialist hired; competition, it further developed, was tough. He had to put up more and more money; his life became one great big hell lined with cinder blocks.

I asked the usual question: "How could you, a specialist at figures and account sheets, fall for these crooks you allowed to become your partners?"

"You know the human weakness for getting rich," he answered.

Sometimes the shoe is on the other foot, and the patient scores. One patient had an especially pompous manner, which contrasted oddly with his habitually jerky physical movements. To reduce him to absurdity, I asked at the beginning of one appointment, "How is Your Majesty today?"—"Why, is that the way you feel about me?"

A few years ago, the elevator in the building in which my office is located was rebuilt for self-service; during this period my patients had to use the service elevator, and even after the work was completed, the new elevator tended to break down frequently. One day I became furious when I was told that the elevator was out of order again. The patient who had brought me the news listened patiently, and then summed up the situation: "It could be worse."—"You mean the building could collapse?"—"No, it could happen to me." His thrust was quite justified; one must be on the alert and refrain from taking oneself too seriously, even when it hurts.

Sometimes humorous incidents arise from simple misunderstandings, from the patient's specific traits when applied to inapplicable situations, or from the mere fact of the patient's pompousness. I once made notes on the opening interchange of remarks with a lawyer-patient during his first interview:

This taciturn and bitter-looking man consulted me because of general depression. His depression was, as he said, accentuated by the fact that he had not taken a vacation for years.

"Why?" I asked.

"Business."

"Don't the courts close for the summer months?"

"I said, business."

"Isn't being a lawyer your business?"

"Partly."

"Do you always speak in monosyllables?"

"Mostly."

"Why?"

"Depression."

"Will it irritate you if I phrase my sentences in the accepted rather lengthy and conventional manner?"

"Suit yourself."

"Thanks. What is the nature of your additional business?"

"Plastics."

"Do you know something about plastics?"

"The troubles."

"How did you, a criminal lawyer, happen to hit on plastics?"

"Clients."

"Whom you defended in criminal court?"

"Some."

"Some of them, or you defended them only a little?"

For the first time a mirthless smile appeared on the man's face; the smile fitted into none of his facial wrinkles and obviously was not much used. After rearranging his face into its more customary expression of gloom, he allowed a single word to escape his lips:

"Acquittal."

"Whose acquittal?"

"Clients."

"The same clients who persuaded you to enter the plastics adventure?"

"Mistake."

"Meaning you made a mistake in trusting them?"

"Ingratitude."

"Meaning that instead of showing gratitude, your clients dragged you into this venture, which you financed?"

"Talk too much."

"Who? The clients or I?"

"Both."

"Have you perhaps taken a vow of silence? Become a Trappist?"

"Through with talking."

"In court, too?"

"Substitute."

"Meaning you don't go into court any more?"

"Depressed."

"Maybe you have seen too many movies caricaturing strong silent cowboys and Indians."

"Never movies."

"Stop that comedy and start talking. How did it happen that you, a criminal lawyer, were taken in by a bunch of crooks and chiselers?"

"Security."

"Why aren't you consistent enough to use sign-language instead of one-word sentences?"

"Depressed."

"I heard you before. You will have to give information or I cannot help you."

Whereupon the man dropped his pose of taciturnity, started to cry, and came out with his pitiful tale. He had defended some chiselers who, through the use of some brilliant legal tricks on his part, had got off. These people then suggested that he accept, in lieu of a fee, partnership in a scheme involving plastics. The money was provided, in ever larger sums, by the lawyer (the patient), who found himself becoming more and more involved. In telling his story he stressed specifically the fact that plastics actually were being manufactured and that there was no swindle connected with their production. The crookedness existed in his partners and their relations with him, and this, with the worry and excitement it caused him, had begun to be more than he could bear.

Another instance, though based on different reasons, pertained to a manufacturer:

A successful manufacturer in the middle forties came to psychoanalytic treatment by a rather peculiar detour. Wishing to consult his diagnostician because of varicose veins, he found that the physician was on vacation and was examined by a substitute, a younger man. The latter asked some questions about the patient's life. It came out that the patient was completely impotent, and his wife—after fourteen years of marriage—still a virgin, having married him to support her family and being frigid and rather puritanical. Conscious of his impotence, he was in the habit of solving his sexual problem by pressing himself against young girls in his office, ejaculating without erection. This idyllic situation was disturbed by the accidental encounter with the younger physician, who recommended him to me.

The patient proved rather shy and embarrassed. He did not really want treatment but did not know how to get out of the quandary he found himself in. However, when the question of fee came up for discussion, he came to life quickly, and energetically declared (for he felt himself, now, on familiar territory) that it was entirely too much. Obviously he expected me to bargain with him; when he realized that I had no intention of doing so, he behaved as though my refusal were an immoral action and complained repeatedly about hard times, high taxes, etc. During this tirade he kept looking at the analytical couch, avoiding my glance. At last he said in a tone of some disgust, "All right, I'll pay."

I wondered what had caused him to change his mind. Nothing could be elicited from the patient. However, at the beginning of every appointment, as I placed a small paper towel at the head of the couch, he made a curious joke, always with the same laugh: "You have terrible expenses." At first I ignored the joke; then one day I answered: "You're right; every three appointments, from now on, I'm going to put an extra penny on your bill." At last I pressed the point—and discovered that this man, who was totally ignorant of all details concerning psychiatry and had never heard of the institution of the analytic couch, believed that the latter was a part of the medical instrumentarium for curing his potency disturbance. In other words, he assumed that I would provide a prostitute for the purpose of teaching him sex and, this being so, my fee was not unreasonable after all—since it must cover the cost of providing the prostitute. Disabused of this idea, the patient was very much disappointed and expressed the opinion that there was nothing more to discuss. The situation looked hopeless; the man wanted only to be left alone. He was not interested in changing, nor did he have the slightest understanding of the analytical procedure; every attempt to analyze his conflict produced obvious surprise and revulsion, and it was plain that he kept asking himself, "How can I take my leave gracefully?"

Having written him off as unanalyzable, I still thought I would try an experiment. There must be, I told myself, a point at which even this man could be made to become interested in treatment, if one could find it. I started by asking about his hobbies, and learned that he played pinochle. "Are you a good pinochle player?" I inquired. "On the contrary, a very poor one," he replied. "Imagine—here I am a big manufacturer, and not only do I make a lot of mistakes at pinochle but I can't even remember the rules." "Do you lose money?" was my next question. "Of course, but that doesn't matter. What gets me is the way my partners kid me about it."—"If I could make a good pinochle player out of you, would you believe in analysis?" At this the man became very animated. "Could you really do that? By playing with me?"—"No, by analyzing your self-damaging tendencies."

Once more he was disappointed. First no prostitute, and now no pinochle. "I hope it is the last disappointment you will experience with me," I said. Having recovered from this second blow, he agreed to treatment on the terms I had outlined. Before very long he became an excellent pinochle player, as evidenced by the fact that his former opponents, recognizing that they had lost a sucker, refused to play with him any longer. Thus having established, in his own words, the superiority and effectiveness of psychiatry, he even consented to treatment for his potency disturbance . . .

* * *

This entire section is well summed up with a formula supplied by a former patient. At the end of his analysis, this patient arranged to see me once a month, on the fifteenth of the month. After keeping a few of these appointments, he wrote a letter informing me that he had no new complaints, and wished to discontinue the arrangement. "I have figured out a new schedule," his letter continued. "The way to end an analysis should be a modification of the old toothpaste slogan: 'Brush up your masochism twice a day; see you analyst twice a year'."

13. Creation of the Artificial Victim in Laughter

"But what good came of it at last?"
Quoth little Peterkin.
"Why, that I cannot tell," said he;
"But 'twas a famous victory."
Robert Southey

ONE SPECIFIC THEME inevitably recurs in all discussions on wit and humor: the human being's alleged need to show his "superiority." From this, the argument runs, stems the constant use of ridicule as a weapon.

The argument is age-old, as can be seen from the theories quoted in the first chapter of this book. It is age-old—and futile. Its proponents are dealing with *conscious* reverberations of *internal* processes, and their conclusions, at best, can only be amalgams of irreconcilable elements.

This also accounts for the rather comical futility of non-analytic theories on laughter. The gentlemen of limited vision who are responsible for these theories cannot even agree on externals. Hobbes claimed that laughter is identical with hostility. McDougall called laughter a technique of avoiding pain which would otherwise be experienced via identification with the other person's misery. Eastman denied that aggression plays any part in laughter at all. Ludovici wrote a book to vindicate Hobbes's theory of "sudden glory." There are endless other examples.

Obviously, external appearances are deceptive. Unless one penetrates to the real workshop of laughter, and studies the interplay of the different provinces of the *unconscious*, one might as well adhere to the dignified resignation of Darwin's "We don't know" theory on laughter.

Freud once said that there is no means through which an adherent to the theory of exclusive dominance of consciousness can communicate with a proponent of the unconscious. Communication is equally hopeless when one protagonist stresses the theme of "superiority" in laughter and the other sees as the key to the problem the battle for survival waged by the unconscious ego against the superego.

The perennial argument that "one feels superior to the butt of the joke" is entirely meaningless as an explanation of laughter. These points remain in outer darkness: Why the constant need to "feel superior"? Why should "superiority" express itself exactly in laughter, and not simply in triumph? And, most important, since clinical-psychiatric experience conclusively proves that the unconscious plays a decisive part in the vast majority of all human actions and reactions, how can one accept an explanation which works exclusively with the psychology of consciousness, as the theory of "superiority" does? Is it likely that laughter should be excluded from the unconscious's sphere of influence?

As soon as psychiatric-clinical experience is adduced, an important factor enters the picture and must be considered. Even under the most favorable conditions, at least fifty per cent of the individual's psychic energy is consumed in warding off the constant reproaches of the superego. What else is meant by "peace of mind"? What other purpose can be served by the fantastic prevarications and self-delusions universally produced on the conveyor belt to prove oneself right, and one's adversary wrong?

The laughter which deflates the adversary is one of the few semi-successful methods of attack available to the poor ego in its unceasing effort to counteract the reproaches of conscience. *Laugh-ready* means *guilt-laden*—plus. The "plus" is the little private attack which the unconscious ego executes in debunking the external representatives of its chronic internal accuser. And since this weapon involves the use of spurious aggression, the process of debunking with laughter serves as "proof" that the ego is innocent of the accusation of psychic masochism. The star argument here is that the *butt* of the joke is the psychic masochist, not the joker or laugher.

Laughter can be defined as *a series of split-second Pyrrhic victories scored by the unconscious ego over the inner monster, the superego.* After each "famous victory," the victor goes right on suffering. He cannot be blamed for trying again; a new version of his weapon—another joke—is always at hand. No scarcity of those.

* * *

In every witticism, in every perception of the comic, five parallel processes are at work:

1) *An artificial victim* is created to provide a target for pseudo-aggression.

2) Having created this external artificial victim, *one's own masochism is outdistanced*: the "other fellow" is portrayed as ridiculous and masochistic.

3) The artificial victim is presented to one's own inner conscience *as hostage and whipping-boy* (the lash being ridicule).

4) Psychic masochism has thus been warded off with *pseudo-aggression*, but it is partially enjoyed at the same time through *semi-identification* with the butt of the joke. If the enjoyment of masochism through identification is over-done, it leads to counter-reactions, as in the failure of satire when presented at length, e.g. in book form.[1]

5) Meanwhile, the "unconscious repetition compulsion"—*active* repe-

[1] For further elaboration, see "The Dislike for Satire at Length," *The Psychiatric Quarterly*, 1952.

tition of *passively* endured experiences for the purpose of eradicating a narcissistic lesion—is at work. No matter how earnestly the adult endeavors to treat the child as his equal, the child still perceives, and masochistically magnifies, the adult's "superior" attitude. Creation of the artificial victim in witticisms and the comic is a means of restoring one's own "superiority" and wiping out the humiliations of the past.

Thus, by mobilizing pseudo-aggression, many purposes are achieved. The feeling of guilt because of one's own masochism is shifted; the *alibi* of pseudo-aggression created; narcissism is restored; a substitute victim provided as target for the anti-libidinous superego: "If you are thirsty for blood, drink his!"

This simile, already used in the foreword, bears repetition: The internal technique in wit and the comic is a refinement on the familiar tactic used by the schoolboy who brings home a poor report. "Johnny's card is just as bad!" the schoolboy shouts. The ego's strategy elaborates on this simple argument, shifting attention so completely to "Johnny's card" and "Johnny's" misery that its own is quite forgotten. Forgotten, too, is the fact that "Johnny's card" is often not Johnny's at all, but the gloater's own, smuggled into Johnny's books after the name has been erased.

Of this quintet of inner processes described above, *the hostage technique seems to me of greatest importance*. The unconscious ego seems to be certain that the inner "gods are athirst," and is therefore assiduous in providing substitute nourishment.

It may seem strange that the unconscious ego should be capable of manipulating real people, as if they were marionettes or chess-men. For millennia, people have complained of being putty in the hands of destiny:

> 'Tis all a Chequer board of Nights and Days
> Where Destiny with Men for Pieces Plays:
> Hither and thither moves, and mates, and slays,
> And one by one back in the Closet lays.
>
> (Edward Fitzgerald, *The Rubaiyat of Omar Khayyam*)

On a reduced scale, or, more accurately, in miniature because of their helplessness, people "move and mate and slay" their fellow-men, at least intrapsychically. The "artificial victim" technique is but one of many examples of man's misuse and manipulation of *real* people for the sake of *unreal* inner aims.

* * *

Many theorists have been baffled by the attempt to determine whether laughter is a sign of pleasure, or of warded-off displeasure. To name but two divergencies: Hobbes makes the former claim; McDougall the latter.

External appearances favor Hobbes, but the word "pleasure" is elastic: it expresses the satisfaction of a wish, and—psychologically—the successful manipulation of an inner defense. The surface-confusion here arises from the "happy convulsions" called laughter. But laughter is not an original pleasure; it is a defense successfully executed or hoarded for future use.

"Sense of humor" is not the sixth sense, as some authors have suspected. It represents only a specific, individually acquired *attitude*; this acquisition is accomplished unconsciously as the end result of individual inner conflicts. It can be defined as an anti-pompous and anti-solemn[2] approach, combined with a "triad of laughter":

1. Ability to detect and enjoy, via debunking ridicule, the pompous pretenses of others (wit), and remnants of pompousness in oneself (self-derision).
2. The ability to demote one's own tragedies to bearable nuisances, to demote nuisances to incidents which can be shrugged away, always seeing (as well) the irony of the situation.
3. The ability to take a joke (directed against oneself and made by somebody else) in good grace, and to join in the laughter, the motto being, "Live and let live."

* * *

All of this explains a series of facts frequently stressed, though not clarified, in the literature:

Why do people accept any stigma more easily than that of "lacking a sense of humor"? Why is lack of humor so offensive a trait?

The obvious reasons are automatically the superficial ones. It is a social advantage today and perhaps even a social requirement to possess a sense of humor. In the contemporary mores, admitting that one has no sense of humor is equivalent to admitting that one commits a social solecism, or faux pas.

The unconscious situation is far more complex. There are three types of individuals who externally display lack of humor. These are *the bored, the bores,* and *"the psychic masochist with a vengeance,"* a specific sub-order of *homo masochisticus.*

As stated in Chapter Nine, the *bored* views himself as a member of a special, higher, hyper-refined order ("The Queen is not amused"), and does not suspect his fun-deficiency.

The *bore* sometimes realizes his fun-deficiency, and upbraids himself for it; more characteristically, he is oblivious to it.

The third type, *the masochist with a vengeance,* will admit—when under severe pressure—that he or she "takes things too seriously." These in-

[2] "A formal Puritan, a solemn and unsexual man" (P. B. Shelley, *Peter Bell the Third, VI*).

frequent admissions usually follow after quarrels centering around an ironic remark which had been taken at face value.

The propelling factor in this type, aside from the ever-present chip upon the shoulder, is not difficult to find, providing that one is familiar with the pleasure-in-displeasure pattern in general. These children in adult clothing interpret any harmlessly witty remark literally. The consequent misunderstanding is exactly their unconscious intention. By taking offense where consciously no offense was meant, the alleged injustice is magnified and perpetuated. I remember a woman of this type whose reply to a harmless ironic remark was an indignant-exasperated "What on earth are you talking about?" To console her, I answered: "That was irony. To avoid such misunderstandings, I will install an electric sign in front of you reading THIS IS IRONY, and pull the switch every time I misbehave." Result: new offense.

There is still another reason—an unconscious one—for the universal condemnation of "lack of a sense of humor." ("Sense of humor," it should be mentioned, is a misnomer, since nobody is born with it.) Since the "sense of humor" is a weapon effectively used against the inner tormenter, the superego, the accusation that one does not possess the weapon means, in the unconscious vocabulary, that one is a hyper-masochist. And who wants to be called *that*?

What accounts for the magic appeal of anti-logic in wit?

A good many jokes have as targets "lack of logic." The term is not used in its scientific meaning; in this application it refers to an absence of common sense coupled with a failure to accept everyday experience. The laughter thus produced is ostensibly directed at the "stupidity" shown by the butt of the joke.

Behind this superficial facade is hidden our unconscious infantile admiration for, and magical attraction to, any rebellion against the rules forced on the child by *all* educators. All "nonsense" jokes also contain a *reaffirmation of infantile megalomania*, that fantasy of omnipotence for which one of the recognized cures is confrontation with "real facts." The anti-logic of some witticisms activates the old rebellion. The joke therefore persists on two levels of aggression. It is, first, directed against the external butt, and second, against the enshrined educator, who is partially incorporated in the ego ideal portion of the superego. Behind and beneath both layers of aggression is, once more, the masochistic structure, warded off with pseudo-aggression.

In these "nonsense-jokes," the child in the adult unconsciously achieves the otherwise unachievable: he eats his cake and has it, too. On the one hand, a double alibi is presented: "I'm aggressive towards transgressors of accepted rules of common sense," and "I'm also being aggressive towards all enforced rules of conduct by reaffirming my old conviction of omnipotence." It is of no importance that in this peculiar proof of "aggression" one conclusion cancels out the other—for one cannot argue that one is simultaneously a "good" boy and a "bad" boy—the cornered child does not defend himself in accordance with adult rules. In dreams, too, one often meets with two opposing conclusions, when the accusations of the inner conscience are countered with a multitude of contradictory alibis. Freud alluded to this mechanism, citing the old gag of the man who borrowed a pot from his neighbor. When he returned the pot, it was broken, and the neighbor reproached him vigorously. This was his answer: "First, I never borrowed the pot; second, I returned it whole; third of all, the pot was already broken when you handed it over to me."

The reaffirmation of infantile megalomania—Emperor Sigismund's "Caesar supra grammaticos" is a direct expression of every child's feeling about adult rules, and pertains to logic no less than to spelling—explains why even intelligent people are hilariously amused by nonsense. They do not dismiss it as "beneath their level," for it is very much on their "level"—unconsciously.

In his *Reisebilder*, Heinrich Heine said: "The Romans would never have found time to conquer the world if they had been obliged first to learn Latin." This complaint about the complexities of Latin grammar and vocabulary is presented in the form of a nonsense-joke. Viewing Latin, the mother-tongue of the Romans, as a foreign language, and combining this nonsensical outlook with the reproach that it is a waste of time for moderns to study a dead language, adds up to an aggression against the educators who force children to study the unusable dead language. Even an excuse for failure to learn the language is included in the joke: "If I had not been forced to waste time on Latin, I would have used my abundant energies more successfully." The modest allusion to "conquering the world" belongs in the orbit of infantile megalomania.

Why should the child believe that one plus one equals two? Because adults say so? Why believe their silly notions? Isn't infantile megalomania an equally reliable yardstick? Doesn't mother, tired of the child's unending *Why*, frequently cut the discussion short with the proverbial "Because I say so?" The "I" as final arbiter works both ways; for the child, his own "I" takes precedence of any and all adult statements; his "I" has seniority, and therefore carries more conviction. Though, under pressure, he may be forced to accept adult yardsticks, he never fully relinquishes remnants of "private" beliefs. Result: repressed sentimental adherence to—alogic.

Another result of this attitude is ironic belittlement of logic and common sense, leading to specific jokes. Ambrose Bierce's "syllogism mathematical" is typical. He defines logic as the technique of thinking and reasoning in obedience to the insufficiencies and disabilities of the human misunderstanding. Logic is based on the syllogism, which consists of a major premise, a minor premise, and a conclusion. As an example, Bierce submits a major premise stating that sixty men can accomplish a piece of work sixty times as fast as one man, and a minor premise stating that one man can dig a posthole in sixty seconds. The "logical" conclusion, therefore, is that sixty men can dig a posthole in one second. This conclusion he calls the "syllogism mathematical," which combines logic with mathematics to achieve a "double certainty" (*The Devil's Dictionary*).

Other ironic jabs at logic single out the alogical thinking of legalistic, stubborn, sticklers for detail. Ambrose Bierce includes one such irony in his *Fantastic Fables*; it is called "A Defective Petition":

> An Associate Justice of the Supreme Court was sitting by a river when a Traveler approached and said:
>
> "I wish to cross. Will it be lawful to use this boat?"
>
> "It will," was the reply; "it is my boat."
>
> The Traveler thanked him, and pushing the boat into the water embarked and rowed away. But the boat sank and he was drowned.
>
> "Heartless man!" said an Indignant Spectator. "Why did you not tell him that your boat had a hole in it?"
>
> "The matter of the boat's condition," said the great jurist, "was not brought before me."

Similar attacks are leveled against every profession. Medicine is a favorite hunting ground:

> A famous physician had given up a patient, predicting to the family that he would die within ten days. A few months later, the patient met the doctor on the street. "I'm still alive," remarked the patient ironically. The authority remained undisturbed. "My dear man," he said, "scientifically speaking, you are dead."

Nor are writers and poets excluded. *The Goncourt Journals* for 1868 quote Theophile Gautier as saying that one great regret was poisoning Gustave Flaubert's life, and would sooner or later kill him. That great regret was that, in *Madame Bovary*, he had been forced to make one genitive follow directly upon another: *Une couronne de fleurs d'oranger*. It had made him miserable, but he could find no way out.

Why is "concentrated malice" so typically observable in wit?

Sir William Osler is quoted as having said: "The desire to take medicine is perhaps the greatest feature which distinguishes man from animal" (*Life Of Sir William Osler*, Vol. 1, Chapter 14). The great medical clinician omitted to mention the fact that taking medicine presupposes the objective feeling of being sick. He also overlooked another observable fact: before *taking* the medicine of external reality, homo not-so-sapiens *makes* his internal medicine, which consists of a series of unconscious "adaptive" mechanisms (inner defenses). Among these, the most important is psychic masochism.

Every human being is the victim of the "hoax of the two M's": *in his superficial aspects, he is Malice Concentrated, by which he hopes to conceal (from himself) the nature of his deeper layers, which are Masochism Concentrated.*

The confusion between the two M's is consoling and ego-strengthening. Inwardly (and this is only half-admitted), everyone would rather take the blame for being a villain than admit to being a glutton for punishment. Ironically, an accusation of malice is always accepted as a compliment (underneath the indignant protests) when malice is a covering cloak for more deeply repressed psychic masochism.

On the other hand, all people also aspire to the ranks of "decent fellows." In society, malice has a negative moral connotation. To avoid this stigma, a compromise is unconsciously sought, and found (in cultured people) in limiting the expression of malice to witticism. Here, one is "only fooling"—one *has* his cake of defensive pseudo-aggression (covering masochism), and *eats* the moral cake, too.

This defensive core within manifestations of wit and humor accounts for the fact that these phenomena are by no means "pastimes," but are inner necessities.

What is a "wit?"

A "wit" is *not* a person who seizes every opening for the manufacture of a feeble pseudo-joke, but one who can *discriminate.* Le Rochefoucauld knew that: "The distinction between *wit* and *would-be wit* is seldom made," he said. "Witticism," therefore, is a catch-all phrase; it includes both the genuine and the imitation article.

In a discussion with an acquaintance, we touched upon the title of this book.

"Better be careful," he warned. "If you call it *Laughter and the Pleasure-In-Displeasure Pattern,* [my original title] you'll be leaving yourself wide open for a variation on that old gag: 'Good morning.'—'It *was* a good morning until you came along.' The critics will be saying, 'The only displeasure in the pleasure of laughter is this author's pat explanation of the pattern of laughter.' "

"Quite possible," I admitted. "But how can anyone protect himself against pseudo-witty ignorance? Remember Voltaire's 'Joking is frequently a sign of lack of understanding.' I had thought of calling the book *Laughter—An Unconscious Debunking Process.* That's just as 'dangerous.' The critics can twist that one around by saying, 'The only thing that has to be debunked is the author; do that, and you'll get your laugh.' "

"Why not avoid this danger, too, and call it simply *Laughter*?"

"Then you will hear that I plagiarized Bergson's title. And what about the possibility that they will say I involuntarily gave the reader a cue to laugh at the contents?"

"But if you call it *Laughter and the Artificial Victim*, as you say you've nearly decided to do, the same critics might say that the only artificial victim is the one created by you—the reader!"

"Quite possible," I agreed again. "At least, though, that title has one advantage: it puts the main idea of the book right in the center. It directly alludes to the fact that laughter is directed at the superego which accuses the ego of psychic masochism; to disprove the accusation, a hostage is provided."

"You don't seem to think it possible to avoid malice in reviewers."

"I believe that man's masochism is so over-dimensional that he will do *anything* for a defense—and witticism is one of the available defenses. The half-smart defendant will produce a half-smart defense. Regrettable, but true. Critics who misunderstand out of principle, ignorance and inner fear remind me of another old gag. 'Are you the defendant?' asks the judge. 'No,' replies the accused, 'I am the gentleman who stole the chickens.' "

Why is "bitter laughter" so mysterious?

"Bitter laughter" has puzzled the scientific observer so much that not even theories have been constructed in an effort to explain it. Defeat was admitted, and the problem was left at that.

The problem *is* incomprehensible without the clarifying evidence of the existence of psychic masochism. And so far nobody, except for myself, has adduced this "ingredient" in attempting to explain laughter in general.

Bitter laughter is one of the by-products of injustice-collecting; injustice-collecting, as pointed out previously, is the identifying mark of the psychic masochist. Its raw material can be a trifle, hardly worth the trouble of dismissing from one's mind; the injustice collector habitually magnifies trifles because they fit into the constant inner need to prove to the superego that one is the innocent victim of another's malice. Even inanimate objects are utilized for this purpose.

A patient lived on Fifth avenue; before coming to his appointment in my office, he would habitually take a short stroll in the Park, finishing his walk at the corner directly opposite my office. The benefit his digestion received from the walk, he told me ironically, was the "tangible" advantage derived from his visits to me; the efficacy of the treatment itself he viewed as "uncertain." In spite of his "refreshing" walk, he would almost always arrive at my office in a depressed mood. One day he told me why. It seemed that the traffic light had an exasperating way of changing to red just as he reached the curb, thus forcing him to wait a full minute before he could cross.

"Do you assume that there is a conspiracy of traffic lights against you?"

"I wouldn't go so far," the patient also ironically answered. "I just take it as a sign of how everything works out against me."

"A bad omen?"

"Don't be flippant. I would say, rather, a confirmation of my pessimism."

"Isn't it interesting that you are overlooking, changing, even distorting facts to suit your purpose?"

"Prove it."

"That's simple enough. First, you overlooked the fact that the light at the corner is timed for a half minute on green, and a full minute on red. There is a good reason for this: automobile traffic is heavy, pedestrian crossings are light. What you believe to be a bad omen now reduces itself to the greater probability of arriving at the corner while there is a red light."

The patient exclaimed with some excitement: "You are mistaken, it is a fifty-fifty proposition! How do you know that it isn't?"

"Because I observed the same phenomenon, and looked at my watch."

"Don't believe it."

"Just use your watch. That was a fact you overlooked; here is one that you changed to suit your a priori deduction. If you remember, there is a little hill at exactly this corner of the park. To get to the street level you must go downhill. Approximately fifty feet before reaching the pavement, the traffic light comes into view. By regulating one's own speed, therefore, one can 'regulate' the arrival at the light. Is this also my fantasy?"

"Never noticed it. It's true that you go downhill. The light should be visible."

"Now for point three: you distorted facts by omitting the first and second observations only so that you could prove what you were out to prove, that 'everything is against you.' Not to mention the fact that pedestrians in New York pay little attention to lights, and are always crossing when the light is against them. But you stand at the corner like Lot's wife—a statue. To sum up: do you call all these omissions the objective evaluation of facts?"

"I have to check on your facts."

This he did, after which he acknowledged his errors and omissions in this instance. But he shifted to some other "proof," approximately on the same level. A psychic masochist always loses, since losing is his inner aim.

Once the injustice collector has, in his more or less devious way, constructed his essential assurance that the bad mother of his infancy, projected on some contemporary figure, is unkind and malicious, the typical mood is self-pity. It can also, however, be mingled with ironic-sarcastic complacency; the bitter laughter characteristic of this state of mind means, "I knew all along that I'd be on the receiving end."

One such patient compared himself with the hero of an old but good joke. An old man is on his deathbed after a disappointing life; he tells his sons, "I would laugh if things are no better in the other world."

The person addicted to bitter laughter disguises his psychic masochism with pride in his own power of prediction. He will end up behind the eight-ball, yes; but he knew it before the game began. He apparently accepts defeat with a gallant smile; he can do this only when he has predicted the defeat beforehand.

Why is it impossible to "force" a real witticism, or make it to order?

There is no substitute for spontaneity, not even ambition. The "spontaneity" is the end result of an unconscious process, and the process can never be faked. Here are two examples:

A patient informed me, at the beginning of our first interview, that he was suffering from a disease which had been "wrongly" diagnosed as hypochondria, and was at the same time "the victim of the second Shakespearean milk period." (The man was a scholar, specializing in Shakespeare.) As it happens, he was alluding to one of my favorite quotations: "Adversity's sweet milk-philosophy," from *Romeo and Juliet.* I was able, therefore, to understand his quip: the baby is fed on milk, the unhappy adult on milk-surrogate in the form of consolation. As an introduction to psychotherapy, the remark had its uses; as a witticism, it was lame indeed.

Another patient, a neurotic bore, had been reading some anthologies of wit and humor. As a result, he constructed the following "omnibus" joke:

> A literate Scotchman and an over-literate American meet in Paris. They dine together, and become engrossed in a conversation about national characteristics. Politely, they prove that all generalizations are wrong. The American brings up the legend that tips were invented by the proverbially stingy Scotch—the word having been compounded from the initials of the phrase "To Insure Prompt Service." The Scotchman goes a step further, quoting Mark Twain's answer to Paul Bourget, when the Frenchman was witty at the expense of America's proverbial lack of tradition. "When an American has nothing else to do, he can always spend some time trying to trace his family tree to his grandfather," Bourget had said. "Yes," was Twain's answer, "and when a Frenchman has nothing better to do, he can always try to find out who his father was." They are fast friends by the time dinner is over, and when the bill is presented, the Scotchman reaches for it promptly, saying, "This is mine." The next day the newspapers carry a headline: *"Death of an American Ventriloquist."*

This is an unholy marriage of three separate jokes. Each of them, standing alone, is a good joke. Ascribing the invention of the tip to the traditionally stingy Scotch, Mark Twain's repartee, and the ventriloquist headline are all funny—by themselves. The combination strips all three jokes of effectiveness, because their individual points are lost in the over-all plot—and the over-all plot is a total failure.

Why is the interpretation of a successful joke so often silly, and even fantastic? Why are people unable to explain why they laughed?

The psychologically obvious explanation can be noted and passed over: Since perception of a witticism is unconscious, the conscious ego can only produce rationalizations to account for the appreciative laughter which greeted the joke. Obviously, the I.Q. of the unconscious is higher than that of the conscious; this is true of every human being.

Why the conscious rationalizations should be "not bright," and frequently quite the opposite of "bright," is a more complicated question. Three tentative answers can be offered.

1) By "playing dumb"—unconsciously on purpose—the ego assumes the role of the innocent child, thus preventively guarding against putative punishment from the enshrined image of the stern educator, the superego.

2) Having won a split-second victory over the inner torturer, the latter retaliates with the standard accusation of psychic masochism, externally visible in the "dumb" explanation.

3) The ego's victory is so obscure, and so tentative, that the unconscious ego *itself* prevents the conscious ego from understanding what has been going on behind the scenes.

I have tested this phenomenon by submitting two witticisms to a number of intelligent people, asking them to explain their laughter in each case.

Example I. A Jew brings a problem to his rabbi. He had come home unexpectedly to find his wife having intercourse with his clerk on the couch in the living room. What is he to do? "Throw out your wife," the rabbi suggests. "Impossible," the man replies, "my business is running on her money. If she takes her money out, I will be bankrupt."—"Well, then, fire the clerk."—"I can't do that either; he would be sure to start a new business in competition with mine. That would ruin me, too."—"I cannot help you," concludes the disgusted rabbi.—A few weeks later, the rabbi meets the man again, this time in a buoyant mood. "Well, did you solve your problem?" asks the rabbi.—"I certainly did!"—"Did you throw out your wife?"—"I'm not a fool!"—"Did you fire the clerk?"—"I'm not crazy either!"—"What *did* you do?"—"I sold the couch."

The "interpretations" went far beyond my expectations. Here are some of the answers:

"Wish for novelty: *she* has a new lover, *he* a new couch."

"Joke on the attitude which measures everything in terms of money."

"Joke on optimism and resiliency."

"Joke on the thesis: 'life goes on.' "

"Joke on the devaluation of sex."

None of the "interpreters" mentioned the obvious: the ironic comment on the human capacity for unlimited self-deception.

My second test was with Benjamin Stolberg's excellent witticism:

Example II: Yiddish is a form of Desperanto.

The crop of misunderstandings gathered in this test included the following:

"Jews take over—desperate attempt at making Yiddish the world language."

"Jews being a minority, they try to compensate with a universal language."

"Joke on concealed Jewish megalomania."

"Joke on nationalism in general: impossible to unite with the help of Esperanto or any other language."

"A silly play on words—Esperanto and desperado."

"Joke on assimilation; though Jews may speak different languages, they all half-understand Yiddish."

"Joke on attempt to introduce Hebrew as state language in Israel; Jews already have a universal language—the Yiddish jargon."

Not one of those interrogated mentioned the obvious: Just as Esperanto was a failure, the Jews' attempt to stick to their universal language, Yiddish, is a failure—an act of desperado-bravado; Stolberg's joke seems to be on the frequently observed inability or unwillingness to assimilate.

My impression has been that many of those interrogated displayed, not low I.Q., but high M.Q. (masochism quotient).

Why is "humanization of laughter" an important theme in every book on wit?

The treatment given this theme in Gregory's *The Nature of Laughter* is typical. He begins by pointing out that "deformity" and "infirmity" were at one time the outstanding reasons for men's laughter; that the dwarf, for example, was a universal object of ridicule, and only of ridicule. In today's civilization, though laughter at physical misfortune continues, deformity is no longer "a legitimate object of laughter." Laughter "has been humanized," to some extent. Hostile laughter is an older form than sympathic laughter, but laughter has steadily become, "though with many a fluctuation, more gracious, genial, and kindly."

Gregory then contrasts two theories of laughter in order to prove his point: that of Hobbes, and that of McDougall. Hobbes, he says, identifies laughter with "self-congratulatory superiority"; its origin, therefore, is unkindness, for the feeling of superiority arises from "comparison with the infirmities of others" (the quotations are from Hobbes).

Modern theories, Gregory goes on to say, concentrate on the function of laughter rather than its structure. There is another distinction between

McDougall, representing contemporary thought, and Hobbes, representing the ideas of the past: Hobbes declared that men laugh because they lack sympathy, while McDougall believes they laugh in order to avoid becoming too much involved, emotionally, in other people's troubles. Laughter may be the correct reaction to a minor mishap; for example, Gregory declares, "When wit exposes folly laughter may be a better medicine than condolence." In McDougall's theory, the "biological function" of laughter is to defend the organism against the plethora of minor pains to which man is subject because of his highly sensitive sympathetic tendencies.

The highest type of laughter is humor, which represents the least contemptuous and most sympathetic form, and laughter is steadily evolving in that direction, Gregory believes.

In another chapter, Gregory discusses "Laughter and Civilization," enlarging on his theory that laughter is a revealing index to human character, and therefore to the quality of the society in which we live. Alterations in habits of laughter, therefore, reflect cultural changes. *The Arabian Nights*, for example, is replete with practical jokes which are "rough, unfeeling." Do these jokes represent unmixed pleasure at the misfortune of another, or do they include "purely comic perception?" Such laughter "suggests a coarse echo of triumph in battle more than a nicer sense of the comic."

A higher form of humor is represented by satire, which "substitutes mental discomfiture for physical." Gregory cites Aristotle as authority for the theory that a process of humanization is visible in Greek comedy; Homer rejected "personal satirical attack" and removed the element of offensiveness from the laughter his writing aroused by "avoiding personalities." Other Greek authors followed Homer's lead.

Personal invective is the successor to the practical joke, and this refinement, too, tends to be displaced from its pre-eminence in laughter as civilization marches on. Laughter is no more stable a phenomenon than language or thought. Society has multiplied laughter by extending the occasions for laughter from the early limitation of rough buffoonery; the varieties of laughter have been similarly multiplied by the increased perception which comes from civilization.[3]

Gregory then cites a number of authors who described social conditions favoring more "humane" aspects of laughter. George Meredith called for a cultivated and perceptive society, emotionally stable and well-balanced, and with a reasonable equality between the sexes. Sydney Smith's requirement was simpler: he specified only "idleness." Gregory agrees that idleness —if it is relaxation from activity, and not prolonged inactivity—can be

[3] In my opinion, the increased tendency to laughter derives from increased masochism, not greater mentality.

productive of humane laughter; it is probable that the "fullest flavour of humor" is attained during periods of relief from important efforts.

Civilization seems to have spread sympathetic laughter, and to have sharpened the sense of the ludicrous. Laughter must have been less frequent in the "earliest human age"; it may reach an apex and then disappear, but its development in the direction of sympathy indicates that it is in some way fostered by our civilization. When a culture (Gregory here quotes Professor Flinders Petrie) "lives justly, securely, tolerantly, and with knowledge," the opportunities for hostile laughter decrease and "more genial laughter" results: " . . . laughter distinctly seems to be more kindly, as it also seems to be more distinctly sensitive to the ludicrous, in the amusement of the new world than in the amusement of the old."

The same theme can be found in Stephen Leacock's *Humor, Its Theory and Technique* (1935):

> . . . humor, in its highest form, no longer excites our laughter, no longer appeals to our comic sense, no longer depends upon the aid of wit.
>
> We have recalled the picture of little Huckleberry Finn floating down the Mississippi in his raft and discussing with his Nigger Jim the mysteries of the universe. We have seen the poor debtors of Dickens' debtors' prison, with their broken lives, their pots of porter, their tawdry merriment, their pitiable dignity and their unutterable despair. Such pictures as these call forth a saddened smile of compassion for our human lot; it all seems so long past, so far in retrospect, that the pain is gone.
>
> Such is the highest humor. It represents our outlook upon life, a retrospect as it were, in which the fever and fret of our earthly lot is contrasted with its shortcomings, its last illusions and its inevitable end. The fiercest anger cools, the bitterest of hate sleeps in the churchyard . . . (p. 261)

These and similar statements introduce a moral scale according to which crude aggression is shameful. The conclusions drawn are highly moralistic and optimistic: less aggression—more refinement (both in general, and in particular, in wit). These authors' hopes live up to the implications of Lichtenberg's irony, "As nations improve, so do their gods." Unfortunately, their optimism depends on a false premise, for the aggression displayed in laughter is not real aggression, but compensatory pseudo-aggression.

The "humanization of laughter" is a thesis based on purely conscious evidence. It no longer seems plausible when the *unconscious* basis of laughter is taken into account. This unconscious basis, as has already been stated, is the unconscious ego's fight against the accusation of psychic masochism leveled by the anti-libidinous superego. The future of laughter depends on the future progress of masochism in human beings.

One point cannot be sufficiently emphasized: The "childishness" in laughter is not a shameful but an unavoidable quality. Laughter originates in the infant's fears, in the infant's self-created reassurances, and in the child's deflation of adults. If one rejects this origin, consistency calls for rejection of the product as well. Impossible? Of course, because the adult is not as adult as he believes.

The fact that laughter owes both its origin and its perpetuation in part to the individual's masochism (an indictment presented for purposes of torture by the superego and secondarily made pleasurable by the unconscious ego) is indirectly proven, with excellent intuitive reasons, in Bernard Wolfe's ironic novel, *Limbo*. The author satirically describes a future society in which amputation is the highest honor; the more limbs the individual sacrifices, the higher his social status. The purpose of the procedure is achievement of pacifism. As long as people have limbs to fight with, or push buttons with, war will continue. The joke is that cybernetics provides limbs even more effective than those supplied by nature, and so the program fails. In this particular society, the author mentions, laughter is not known. In my opinion, this is a logically consistent point. When masochism (what else could inwardly induce a person to sacrifice his limbs voluntarily?) becomes a state religion, and consequently is officially approved, even the superego must be satisfied. Thus it is no longer necessary to deflate the superego's accusation by means of laughter.

Since my forte is neither satire nor prediction, I will not even venture to guess future possibilities. It is just as possible that some day masochism will be recognized as an illness and psychiatrically treated as that it will remain unknown, as it is today, leading to more and more defensive pseudo-aggression. In the meantime, masochistic suffering continues, as does the production of inner defenses. John Dryden's dictum in *All For Love* proved sadly prophetic: "Men are but children of a larger growth."

* * *

At bottom, laughter is a defense against a defense. Both maneuvers are instituted by the battered unconscious ego itself. The inexhaustible cruelty of the inner conscience, the superego, is counteracted by shortchanging punishment into inner pleasure; thus psychic masochism is "born." The superego, aware of the trick, now reproaches the ego for precisely this inner pleasure. The new menace must be counteracted as well, and the unconscious ego then institutes *two new defenses*: the "triad of the mechanism of orality," and laughter. The former defense consists of proving that one is the innocent victim of other people's meanness (one's own initial provocation is overlooked). The defense of laughter creates an artificial victim to serve as scapegoat ("Kick him instead of kicking me"), and *at the same time*, in wit and in the comic,[4] attacks the ego ideal, thus attempting

[4] In humor (see Chapter Five) the accusation is identical, but the method used to outdistance the accusation is different.

to wrest the instrument of torture from Daimonion. Ironically, one could say that both main defenses against psychic masochism—the triad of the mechanism of orality, and laughter—serve one single purpose: one presented with *deep indignation*, the other with *half-scared laughter*.

* * *

All this is admittedly very complicated. A critic reviewing one of my books made rather a point of stating that an author who wants to be understood must come down to the level of his readers. Agreed, but scientific facts cannot be changed, nor their important and complex ramifications eliminated, to suit popular requirements. One could of course object to simplification on other grounds, for it cannot be denied that scientific books are written primarily for scientists, and the layman's understanding, acceptance, or lack of either, is therefore immaterial. This objection, while accurate, is wholly unrealistic. We live in the age of journalism, and—whether we find the fact desirable or not—scientific books are included within the journalistic sphere of interest, especially if the topic lends itself to journalistic simplification. There is nothing wrong with this procedure, if the facts are correctly presented. Why shouldn't the lay public be informed of scientific findings?

The theory of laughter presented in this book is admittedly not popular, nor is it likely to become popular. The whole concept of the superego, psychic masochism, double inner defenses, belongs in the higher psychic mathematics. The inner facts should be blamed, not the translator—and especially not in this case, when he has described (for a change) a limited victory of the unconscious ego over the superego; in the last few years his energy has been directed to the description of the opposite process, as visible in his book, *The Superego*.

To sum up: "But what good came of it at last?" is the unanswerable question for us as well as for little Peterkin; all we are told is that " 'twas a famous victory." Our victories over the superego are Pyrrhic victories; we score against the superego but cannot disarm it. The meager pleasure we derive from witty and comical productions adds up to no more than a feeble attempt. And if this attitude sounds unduly pessimistic, the reader can be served with an alternative: Lessing's "Not all are free who mock their chains."

Index